I CANNOT, YET I MUST

WADE WILLIAMS DIST.

I CANNOT, YET I MUST

THE TRUE STORY OF THE BEST BAD MONSTER MOVIE OF ALL TIME

ROBOT MONSTER

ANDERS RUNESTAD

RADIOSONDE

Radiosonde Books
www.runestadwrites.com

Cover design by Anders Runestad. Cover fonts are Edo, IM FELL Double Pica PRO, and Voltaire; available at www.fontsquirrel.com.

I Cannot, Yet I Must/ Anders Runestad. -- 1st ed.
ISBN 978-0-6925766-2-5

Contents

For CARRIE, EMMA, NICHOLAS, IAN, and MIA—
who put up with me,

For CHRISTOPHER D. BENNETT—
who shared the dream,

For HARRY MEDVED, PHIL TUCKER JR., and
TOM WEAVER—
who made it happen,

And for
PHIL TUCKER—
who made the monster.

WADE WILLIAMS DIST.

"... if a thing is worth doing, it is worth doing badly."[1]

—G.K. Chesterton

Acknowledgments

This book would not exist without the generosity and enthusiasm of Harry Medved. I had long hoped in vain that someone would write a book about Phil Tucker and his most famous film; later I believed I could scrape together as much as a short article on the subject. But I was pleasantly shocked to learn that Harry's interview with Tucker was far longer than I could have guessed from reading his books, and was boosted by his enthusiasm for this project. Harry graciously supplied me with a transcript of that interview, kept up an occasional correspondence, helped me contact others, and eventually gave me original interview tapes and other material. I would have never written this book without his help, and I hope he finds it satisfying to see his earlier work come full circle here.

Phil Tucker Jr. has been equally friendly and helpful in providing many memories and insights about his father. His steady, patient enthusiasm for the project has been the other major factor in my completing it.

Anyone who researches this era of film history owes much to the hundreds of interviews that Tom Weaver has conducted with those who were there. In addition, he went far out of his way to recommend sources, provide personal connections, and proofread and comment on a completed draft of the book. My debt to him is truly enormous, and I am forever grateful for his kind help to a complete newcomer to this field.

Bill Warren is another person whose writing I frequently relied on. He also made excellent recommendations, participated in interesting e-mail discussions, and was kind enough to reference me in his revised edition of *Keep Watching the Skies!* in 2010. I am also grateful to Rudolph Grey for clarifying some points about Tucker in relation to Ed Wood.

I deeply appreciate the generosity of Wade Williams, who owns the rights to *Robot Monster* and its accompanying publicity material, in granting permission to reproduce pictures, the script, and other material relating to the film. I also extend a special thanks to Bob Burns for providing photos from his collection.

For sharing their memories, many thanks to Forrest J Ackerman, Conrad Brooks, Ewing Miles "Lucky" Brown, Joe Dante, Paul Dunlap, Bert I. Gordon, Michael Hoey, Trustin Howard, Mark Thomas McGee, Gregory Moffett, Bill Phipps, and Vilmos Zsigmond. For help in finding contacts and other information, thanks to George Chastain, Rob Cochran, Dr. John Hagge, Jeff Joseph, Lukas Kendall, Joseph McBride, Ray Nielsen, David Schecter, Mike Schlesinger, and Stephen D. Youngkin. Bill Littman has my deepest gratitude for providing a copy of the *Robot Monster* script. Thanks to Shannon Bowen of the University of Wyoming's American Heritage Center for providing copies of material from the Selena Royle Papers. Thanks to Ned Comstock of the University of Southern California's Cinematic Arts Library for providing copies of Elmer Bernstein's score.

I owe everything to my wife, Carrie: love, understanding, support, and encouragement. I owe much to our children's patience, and I know that they now understand the microfilm reader that once occupied the dining room table, and the old paper box that once burst over with photocopies.

My mother and father, Judith and Jay Runestad, long ago gave up wondering why I would be fascinated by movies like *Robot Monster* and, as with everything else in life, their support has seen me through in ways I can never repay. Both of my parents helped me to understand Phil Tucker at a very essential level. My mom's tremendous ability for genealogical research dredged up all manner of stuff about Tucker's early life. My dad, just by being himself, made me familiar with the personality of the natural-born engineer; thanks to that, I understood Tucker well enough to see through accumulated layers of misinformation and urban legend. Many thanks also to my sister, Julie Fay, for her expert editing and proofreading of some sections of my longwinded writing. Thanks to an encouraging high school teacher, Jane Dupuis, for checking out those many film books for me in twelfth grade English, and thanks to Dr. Leland A. Poague for teaching that summer film class on Dorothy Arzner and Howard Hawks. Thanks also to Dr. Richard R. Ness for the great talks about movies and film music at a long gone classical record shop.

A few longtime friends deserve special thanks. Christopher D. Bennett has been as crazy about *Robot Monster* as I have for just as long a time, and once suggested that this book needed to be written. I hope that he enjoys the book, and knows that in a sense it is also his. Jay C. Janson is an unbelievably talented actor and all-around kind person, and I've always appreciated his appreciation for discussing weird and bad movies. Bill Wentworth was with me when I first saw *Robot Monster* after purchasing Rhino's pseudo-3-D VHS edition. I saw it after years of building it up in my mind and, while Bill did not have that kind of anticipation, I know that it hit him with as much force as it did me. Chris, Jay, and Bill also deserve thanks alongside a lot of friends who with us wasted much time watching far too many truly terrible movies. So, take a bow: Dan Dill, Jeff Doran, Corey Faust, Paul B. Golden, Eric Hiatt, Jesse Howard, Scott Kendall, William McAlpine, and Ted Shannon.

A sincere thanks to some of my co-workers, who also happen to be the past or present local interlibrary loan staff, without whom I could not have done research: Susan Congdon, Wayne Pedersen, Sue Rappenwolf, and Kathy Thorson.

A few notes on the text: for basic filmography information, I often relied on the Internet Movie Database (IMDb), and sometimes the Turner Classic Movies website. The ease of getting information from these extremely comprehensive sources far outweighs some occasional inaccuracies (and noticing a mistake is just another spur toward finding the truth). I have included exact page numbers in print source citations, although it was impossible in a few cases. Finally please note that, in a book of this kind, plot spoilers are unavoidable when discussing many of the movies that crop up.

Introduction

Robot Monster, filmed and released in 1953, is the greatest bad monster movie of all time. It was never declared Worst Movie of All Time as was *Plan 9 from Outer Space* (1959), nor is it as amateurish or senseless as many others, but it contains an image that seared itself into the minds of its countless viewers, and beyond. It is a startling, aggressively surreal icon, impossible to forget, that summarizes an entire era of filmmaking: a gorilla wearing a diving helmet.

Never mind that the diving helmet of urban legend is a cheaply constructed, old-style spaceman helmet. Whatever the head cover, it does not belong on simian shoulders. The stunning irrationality of that image is the touchstone of the stunning irrationality of all such films. Night and day collide in the same shot, narrators drone on nonsensically without connection to the action onscreen, sophisticated aliens can be defeated by a sock on the jaw, ludicrous monsters attack victims who pretend to be terrified, and—yes—a robot-gorilla named Ro-Man talks to itself about its feelings for an Earth-woman.

Robot Monster's iconic status has been recognized repeatedly over the years. Discussed in Monster Kid publications such as *Famous Monsters of Filmland,* the film was given its greatest exposure when the late seventies bad movie cult took off. With impetus from the books of Harry and Michael Medved, the movement would enthusiastically agree with this Medved appraisal of the film:

> What made *Robot Monster* ineffably worse than any other low-budget sci-fi epic was its bizarre artistic pretension. The robot-gorilla, for instance, delivers a long, introspective soliloquy while speaking directly into the camera. "To be like the hu-man!" he passionately declares. "To laugh! Feel! Want! Why are these things not in the plan? . . . I cannot, yet I must. How do you calculate that? At what point on the graph do 'must' and 'cannot' meet? Yet I must—but I cannot!"[2]

But *Robot Monster*'s influence struck early and struck deep, into even more influential terrain than the bad movie cult. Stephen King remembers it as the first thing he saw on television in the late fifties, at the age of eight or nine; "I felt this was art of quite a high nature."[3] Young King was so impressed that his first, childhood story submission to Forrest J Ackerman's *Spacemen* was inspired by the film, but as an adult he unfortunately indulged in recreational drug use before a viewing:

> That night I almost laughed myself into a hernia. Tears were rolling down my cheeks and I was literally on the floor for most of the movie. Luckily, the movie only runs sixty-three minutes; another twenty minutes of watching Ro-Man tune his war-surplus shortwave/bubble

> machine in "one of the more familiar Hollywood caves" and I think I would have laughed myself to death.[4]

Other reactions[5] veered more toward simple disbelief. Gregory Moffett, who as a child played the film's central character, recently responded to interviewer Michael Barnum's assertion that it has a following: "You are kidding. Fans of *Robot Monster*? Oh, please."[6] Decades before, Harry Medved interviewed gorilla suit performer George Barrows—who played Ro-Man in the film—and asked him if he could provide an introduction for potential use in a bad film festival. Barrows stated for the ages:

> *Robot Monster* was a good example of the thriller horror movies of the fifties, and you have to take it in your stride as that. It wasn't trying to be anything overly hokey or anything overly great. It was just entertainment, and you enjoyed it or you didn't enjoy it. That's all.[7]

The bad movie cult was soon mainstream in the eighties, with celebrity acolytes such as Warren Beatty and Tom Hanks, and Paramount Pictures' brief distribution of Edward D. Wood Jr.'s *Glen or Glenda* (1953).[8] Losing some of its luster, the movement survived as the obsessive fanbase for the movie-mocking cable series *Mystery Science Theater 3000*. And as that show began its relentless sixth season in autumn 1994, Tim Burton's loosely biographical film *Ed Wood* debuted in theaters.

But from that high point, the movement soon waned and withered. While weird, obscure, or old films are still available on home video and the Internet, they began to disappear from an increasingly homogenized and indistinguishable television landscape, as good a barometer as any of a mass viewing trend. *Mystery Science Theater 3000* survived a barely released 1996 feature film version of itself and the jump to another cable network before being finally canceled in 1999. Cable channel TNT, which had shown 1940s films in prime time as recently as the early nineties, dropped its Saturday night *Monstervision* series in 2000. The Sci-Fi Channel, initially a repository of everything from classic Universal horror films to old *Doctor Who* episodes, gradually moved toward hours of direct-to-video movie dreck. American Movie Classics, a predecessor and competitor of Turner Classic Movies, changed format completely in 2002 to a commercial-laced mixture of mostly contemporary films that was indistinguishable from so many others. And all of these changes followed on the heels of USA's 1998 cancellation of its Friday and Saturday *Up All Night* blocks of cult films.

Films of the pre-seventies past now had a limited audience, at least in the minds of those in charge of programming, and there was no mass outcry against cable TV becoming an infinite void of *Law & Order* re-runs. As part of that same trend, the classic bad monster movies of the fifties and sixties became a specialty taste, much as silent films had been since early in the talking era. But looking back and squinting hard, one can still make out a barely visible point of contact with that vanished era, and it is the hobbling silhouette of a gorilla wearing a diving helmet.

Whether popular or obscure, most of the bad monster movie era has been well documented, investigated, and even fictionalized. Most of that era has, with the glaring exception of *Robot Monster*. Shrouded in the urban legend of a movie so mocked that its maker attempted suicide, little of substance has been written about its production and even less about those who made it, with director Phil Tucker depicted as a lesser Ed Wood. Tucker believed that *Robot Monster* was brilliant, so the assumption goes, and deserves scorn for his misguided sense of artistry that led to suicidal despair when reality set in. Wood's eccentric personality (a transvestite former Marine with an angora sweater fetish) at least did not include room for suicidal tendencies.

But the urban legend of Tucker the screwball artist begins to unravel as soon as one examines his career in any detail. For unlike the prolific Wood, Tucker made very few films as a writer or director, and only one of them bears much resemblance to his most famous creation. What is more significant is that, by what account he left behind, he did not see *Robot Monster* as a misunderstood work of genius any more than his other extremely low-budget films, such as *Dance Hall Racket* (1955) and *The Cape Canaveral Monsters* (1960). Wood, the most famous filmmaker of the bottom-budget world he inhabited, could reasonably be called the Steven Spielberg of bad monster movies. Like Spielberg, Wood made many films as director, seemed to know everyone, and did things his own way at every turn and made films with a consistent sense of the same personality behind them. But to extend this metaphor, Tucker—who knew Wood and reportedly even worked with him—was very much the fifties fleabag cinema's George Lucas. Like Lucas, Tucker worked in a more indirect pattern, directing occasionally while doing a great deal of editing and other less glamorous work

WADE WILLIAMS DIST.

Edward D. Wood Jr.'s *Plan 9 from Outer Space*, still fondly recognized as the Worst Movie of All Time.

in the background. And much like Lucas, Tucker had a knack for the mechanical that steered him toward editing and post-production. Wood's *Plan 9 from Outer Space* may be the Worst Movie of All Time, but it is Tucker's *Robot Monster* that serves as the master image of an entire genre. What *Star Wars'* Darth Vader is to the later era of *Jaws* and other blockbusters, Tucker's robot-gorilla Ro-Man is to the era of Ed Wood. The point was memorably proved in the *Plan 9 from Outer Space* documentary *Flying Saucers Over Hollywood,* when host Lee Harris asked a man on the street about Wood's masterpiece:

> *We're on the streets of fabulous Hollywood with John the district manager of Pacific Theaters, and he has seen . . .*

Plan 9 from Outer Space, with the main character being a gorilla suit with a scuba diving helmet on.

John, I think you've got that mixed up with Robot Monster.
Oh, *Robot Monster,* right.[9]

When readers of *The Fifty Worst Films of All Time* and *The Golden Turkey Awards* experienced the write-ups of *Robot Monster,* with their occasional fascinating quotes from Tucker, none knew that the interview was an extensive forty-five minutes worth that was left mostly unquoted. Harry Medved's recorded conversation with Tucker is the director's only known interview, apart from sporadic quotations that have shown up in newspaper and trade magazine stories. I am proud to say that Tucker's remarks from the interview are essentially all quoted in this book, minus some stray words and brief sentences. But although an invaluable window into Tucker's life, the interview presented complications, as the transcript was incomplete in some spots and the audio was of poor quality. Tucker's voice recorded softly, and at a few points becomes inaudible. As Phil Tucker Jr. said of the recording, "My father sounds really tired. With the diabetes he had, some days were worse than others, and that sounds like it was a particularly bad day for him."[10]

Complicating matters further was Tucker's increasingly spotty memory, a problem he suffered by his own admission, and further confirmed by his son. Some aspects of Tucker's chronology do not add up when compared to other sources and yet, amazingly, some of his more fantastical memories were corroborated. And as a final ambiguity, Tucker had a natural tendency to embellish or exaggerate his stories, his son noting that there could be times when "with him, you know, you never know whether to believe it or not." This book is a best shot at finding the truth of a very elusive man, filled with an unavoidable amount of maybe, seems likely, should, and probably. It is something like a Phil Tucker film: the best possible under the circumstances.

The epigram quoted at the beginning of this book is a bit of unconventional wisdom too seldom recognized, that "if a thing is worth doing, it is worth doing badly." Prolific English writer G.K. Chesterton did not mean these words as a call to abandon judgments of what is better and worse, but rather to praise the effort of those who do something rather than nothing, and without overly worrying about the approval of the experts. And while I do not know if Phil Tucker ever read Chesterton, I believe that Chesterton's idea is central to understanding Tucker.

Chesterton also once wrote a critical biography of his friend George Bernard Shaw, in which he showed an admirable humility in the midst of picking apart Shaw's ideas and motivations. Chesterton expressed admiration for Shaw's almost spiritual feeling for music, noting that he admired it but could not really understand it:

> Upon this part of him I am a reverent agnostic; it is well to have some such dark continent in the character of a man of whom one writes. It preserves two very important things—modesty in the biographer and mystery in the biography.[11]

Even under the spotlight, Phil Tucker remains mysterious, which I hope has kept his biographer a little bit modest.

1

St. Louis to Hollywood

I was born in Parsons, Kansas. I was raised in St. Louis.

Phillip Jay Tucker was interviewed about his career once, and summarized his youth in two tiny sentences. Conducted in Tucker's Los Angeles apartment in 1976, Harry Medved's interview has been unpublished and mostly unquoted for decades.[12] The Medved brothers' four bad-movie books, published from 1978 to 1986, referenced it only briefly. According to Tucker's son, Phil Tucker Jr., the elder Tucker sounded lethargic in the recording, showing the effects of the Type II diabetes that steadily wore him out and eventually claimed his life in late 1985. The disease also reinforced an ingrained Tucker habit. Tucker Jr. grew up close to his father, knowing him well while learning little about his early years. The elder Tucker consistently "kept a lot of stuff really close to the vest," according to his son, but this reticence seemed to carry over to others who knew him and yet did not have much to say. Actor, singer, and writer Trustin Howard remembered Tucker with affection but also a degree of ambivalence, noting, "It's hard to say. I think that he certainly was a good friend. He seemed to be very loyal."[13] Actor Timothy Farrell at least briefly remembered him as "a war hero and also a heavy drinker,"[14] while Tucker Jr. observed, "I feel there is much about my father that I still do not know." Commenting in more detail:

> *Robot Monster* was made many years before I was born, so I do not have any first-hand knowledge or anecdotes related to its production . . .. My father almost never spoke about the film. I believe that he viewed it as a personal failure and not an accomplishment worth bragging about. He had moved on. Undoubtedly, it was detrimental to his career and probably haunted him to some degree. Despite frequent claims to the contrary, he did not have any delusions of grandeur but recognized the film for what it was. I'm sure he would have preferred that people remember him for his work on *King Kong* (1976), but sadly it is a different monster that will always be associated with his name.[15]

But Tucker Jr. also remembered his father's "workaholic" personality, his "almost manic energy," and such physical details as being "six-foot-five tall with a stocky build," hair that grayed early, a love of food that eventually made him "borderline obese," and his father's status as "one of the most intelligent people I have ever known."[16]

Phil Tucker in March 1953.

Tucker's military records confirm the birth date given him in online sources, May 22, 1927. What they do not reveal is that, by the age of two, Tucker had been orphaned,[17] one fact about his early life that his son could confirm.[18] The 1930 federal census pinpoints Tucker in Precinct 13 of St. Louis, Missouri, an "inmate" of the Christian Orphan's Home. Conducted on April 11, the census lists Tucker's age as two years and ten months, confirming Tucker's identity as his third birthday was imminent the following month. According to Bonnie Stepenoff's *The Dead End Kids of St. Louis,* the orphanage was one of many founded by religious organizations in the nineteenth century to help the city's vast population of abandoned children and runaways.[19] Tucker may have been orphaned in infancy, but if given away closer to the time of the census, then it was at a particularly vulnerable time for a child's development. A toddler is old enough to be attached to his family but not old enough for much independence or ability to reason. Two older Tucker children were also listed in the census, George, age six, and Barbara, age five, the age range suggesting that the three were siblings. Confirming their mutual relation is the fact that, compared to the entries for other children, the three Tucker children were uniquely uncertain in their origins. The "Place of Birth" section of the census form contains three subdivisions for the child, the mother, and the father. But while the other entries on the page have this information specified down to a state or foreign country in most cases, the three Tuckers are consistently listed as from "United States" for themselves and both parents. As for the enigmatic parents, Tucker Jr. had an intriguing clue, noting, "I remember hearing that his parents died in a car crash."[20]

This uncertainty about the parents who orphaned the Tucker children might have left their origins a complete blank, if not for one detail that appeared on Phil Tucker's entry in the California Death Index, 1940-1997: his mother's maiden name was Hastings. According to the census, brother George was six in April 1930, and one family tree record exists that matches the known facts. According to that reference, George Lewis Tucker was born May 25, 1923, in Denver, Colorado, to parents William Tucker and Mabelle Hastings. George enlisted in the Army on September 1, 1942, in Missouri and attained the rank of Sergeant Major. Serving during World War II, Korea, and Vietnam, he amassed two years of high school education, and worked in a variety of mechanical and trade jobs prior to enlistment. George's one descendant, Charles Anthony Tucker, was born in Germany in 1948, mother unlisted, and died in Lexington, Kentucky, in 1989. George died in 1996 and was interred in Nicholasville, Kentucky. The fate of Barbara remains a mystery.

William Alvin Tucker was born March 5, 1890 in Frankfort, Kentucky, and Mabelle Hastings was born June 6, 1889, in Neodesha, Kansas. That George Tucker and his son Charles eventually settled in the home state of George's likely father William may be coincidence, but it also suggests that the orphaned Tucker children knew their family origins. It also reinforces Phil Tucker Jr.'s impression that his father simply chose to not discuss many things. The Tucker name is not only common in America but in the British Isles, a likely connection for a family with origins in the American South. A vocational surname, referring to the job of fulling textiles (cleaning and thickening them), tucker was a variant term for fuller, and both nouns are common English names. According to two surveys of English names, the Tucker variation was common "frequently in western England," and "in some of the southern shires, particularly in the Southwest, the [fuller] would be called a TUCKER." And in a foreshadowing of Phil Tucker's relentless approach to life and career, the name carries ancient suggestions of hardworking stubbornness: "The Old English word *tucian* meant to torment something."[21] Tucker's maternal line may have also been from Britain, the name Hastings being derived from "a seaport in Sussex, situated on the English Channel."[22]

The 1920 census places a William Tucker in St. Louis, occupied as a hotel clerk. Tucker's age is listed as 30, exactly right for a January 1920 survey, and his home state is listed as Kentucky, with also the notation that the same state was the place of birth for both his mother and father. But other points of interest make the situation obscure and even confusing. A 1925 Kansas survey lists both "Mabel" and Carl Hastings as roomers, ages

36 and 37 respectively (listed as married, although not necessarily to each other). Then the 1930 census places 41-year-old "Maybell" in Wichita Falls, Texas as head of a household, owning a radio, from Kansas with the occupation of "Doctor" in the industry of what looks like "Drugless practice"—meaning that she was likely a chiropractic. According to this record, she was first married at 18 with the current status of widowed. Adding more ambiguity is the knowledge that William Tucker may have had a wife prior to Mabelle Hastings. Hildreth, surname unlisted and age 25 on the 1920 census, was born in Missouri of parents born in Louisiana. Hildreth could have died or been divorced but, in any circumstance, William Tucker apparently met the Kansas-born Mabelle and sired their third child, Phillip, born in Parsons, Kansas.

Formally established in 1871, Parsons came into existence because of railroad expansion into the western frontier. Labette County, wedged in the southeastern corner of Kansas, had originated as Dorn County in 1855, and was renamed Neosho County in 1865 as a result of the Dorn namesake becoming a Confederate. The county became Labette in 1867, and the city of Parsons was the result of a post-Civil War competition between three railways to connect Ft. Leavenworth with Ft. Gibson, Oklahoma, a large expanse of Indian Territory in between. The MK & T line (or "the Katy") won the competition, and the Parsons Town Company was established in October 1870, with city government officially organized the following March. Although Parsons was a town that existed for the railroad and, by extension, the military, it was far from utilitarian or transient in its culture. Schools were established in the area as early as 1869, telephone service established in 1882, and a magnificent, three-storey and 1,600 square-foot public library began construction the same year.[23] But the robust "Infant Wonder of the West" was not completely free from the recent Bloody Kansas past. Adjacent to Labette was Montgomery County where during the 1870s, a supposed family of serial killers, the Benders, murdered several unsuspecting travelers, looted the bodies, and buried them on their property. Although discovered, the Benders escaped and were never officially apprehended.[24]

Parsons' economic significance did not diminish until the late 1950s, and a hotel clerk in the Midwest metropolis of St. Louis could logically journey one state west for better prospects. The birthplace of Mabelle Hastings, Neodesha, is just 33 miles from Parsons—the town's county of Wilson is diagonal to Labette County, touching its northwest tip—making it

Historical view of a Parsons, Kansas church and the town's library.

likely that she lived there when she met William Tucker. With George born in Colorado in 1923, William and Mabelle would have met in the very early twenties. Since William Tucker did not likely return to St. Louis merely to orphan his children, the family was probably already there at some point after Phil's mid-1927 birth. The move might have been before or after the 1929 stock market crash, but the abandonment could have easily been related to it (assuming that William and Mabelle did not perish in a car accident). As one Missouri history notes, the effects of the Great Depression were harder felt for many in the state than in previous downturns, because just over half the population had become urban and lived on salaries. Country and small-town dwellers, partially rooted to the old way of maintaining "garden plots, a few chickens, and a fruit tree or two," could often scrape along while those dependent on industry could not.[25] According to Stepenoff, booming cities like St. Louis were heavy orphan producers due to the combination of immigration and "rapid industrialization, urbanization, and the westward movement."[26] More than a few urban children therefore suffered the fate of George, Barbara, and Phillip.

William and Mabelle's story then dries up, their lives apparently undocumented and perhaps cut short. A much later news item from Kansas' *Salina Journal* reported an eerie echo of the family tale that Tucker Jr. heard of his father's parents dying in an auto wreck. As reported on April 28, 1958, "Mrs. Mabelle Hastings, 69, Arlington, Kan., was killed in a one-car accident near Hutchinson. George Worth, 84, of Hutchinson, was critically injured."[27] Arlington is 200 miles slightly northwest of Parsons and, born June 6, 1889, Hastings would have turned 69 that June. Given the rarity of her name's spelling, there is a solid chance that the *Salina Journal* was reporting on the same Mabelle Hastings. She was listed as a "Mrs.," while she did not retain the name of Tucker, suggesting that she and William Tucker were long parted if they were in fact ever a couple. (George Worth, injured in the one-car accident, would die in August 1959. His obituary made no mention of Hastings.[28]) The *Hutchinson News* then published a lengthy classified advertisement for the "Mabel [sic] Hastings Estate" on August 17, a property listed at an Arlington address. The property was described as a "5 room Modern House; 2 enclosed porches; half-basement . . ." to be sold following the sale of "Personal Property," which included some thirty to forty appliances and furniture pieces or sets. The extensive list included an "Independent Gas Heater," "5 Pc Maple Bed Room Suite," "Chrome Chairs," and such health-related items as an "Electronic Medical Unit," along with "Medical Books."[29]

The 1940 census reveals that Phil Tucker was out of the orphanage by the age of twelve, and was then a boarder in the St. Louis home of foundry worker Harry Soppington, along with wife Bessie, two sons, and another boarder. He joined the Marine Corps on January 10, 1945, in time to have possibly seen World War II action before the August nuclear bombings of Hiroshima and Nagasaki, and the September armistice. He maintained a warrior's stoicism about those days, rarely speaking of them any more than other aspects of his early years, although military records provide some details. A July 1945 Camp Pendleton (near San Diego) muster roll reveals that Private Phillip J. Tucker was AWOL from the morning of July

7 until the night of July 9 when apprehended in Los Angeles by shore police, and subsequently given time in the brig. One year later, a Naval Gun Factory (Washington, DC) muster roll noted that he had spent sick time at the Naval Hospital in Bethesda, Maryland. Most interesting is a record from the Department of Veterans Affairs, regarding a "Jay Tucker" with matching birth and death dates. According to this record, Tucker had two Marine Corps enlistments. The first one, which began on January 10, 1945, ended on November 17 of the same year. The second was from June 25 to October 30, 1946. According to the U.S. Veterans Gravesites listings, Tucker made the rank of sergeant. As he told Harry Medved,

> When I got out of the Marine Corps, I went back to St. Louis. [Inaudible.] Then I had to start earning a living. After about three or four weeks, I got up to manager of display advertising. I was doing very well, and I was bored silly.

Tucker was remembered in composite as resourceful, independent, energetic, highly intelligent, fun-loving, and mechanically gifted. He clearly learned early to be his own man since those traits cannot be credited to a stable home life he had barely known, and it is notable that did not follow his big brother into the Army but instead the more infamously grueling Marine Corps. He may have had no choice in which service most needed recruits, but he also may have joined the Marines out of his unstoppable self-reliance. But Tucker also had a lifelong passion that would channel his independence into ever-changing and fascinating avenues. As Tucker Jr. remembered,

"He just loved show business. Ever since day one, he wanted to be a part of it."

While many work the same nine-to-five job day after day, Tucker was psychologically unfit for anything but self-employment. He could not stomach a successful-yet-stagnant sort of existence, and craved something challenging and personally satisfying. He might have been following in the footsteps of the itinerant father he barely knew. It is no surprise, then, that he soon gravitated to his closest available substitute for show business:

> I started producing radio shows for CBS in St. Louis, which is KMOX. At one time, I had as many as four half-hour radio shows on the air at a time. Pretty soon, I was bored silly with that. The work was pretty good. I was making fifty bucks a show, or something. I was making, for those days and times in St. Louis, it was the big money. But [not] in terms of enough money to do anything with or to give you any real picture coverage, at that time.
>
> *"Those days" just referring to, like what period?*
>
> '46.

AM news format station KMOX, the "Voice of St. Louis," had been around since 1925 and largely covered sports. Any job at KMOX would have been above average and, with his enthusiasm for entertainment, Tucker could have easily carved out a niche within the hours of news, sports, and farm reports.[30] As his son remembered:

> He was a pretty charismatic character. He had a larger-than-life personality, which I think served him well as a producer. He could use that to his advantage to talk about a project that he was working on, and maybe get you excited about it and want to be a part of it.

With that ambition and charisma, Tucker would soon leave St. Louis behind entirely, his sights set on something far grander: "So I came out here. I had been stationed in town, and I knew Los Angeles a little bit and liked it."

In a defining comment that illustrates much about Phil Tucker's life by this point, and about what he was about to experience as he left home for good, Trustin Howard remembered, "He fought. He really fought, which you have to do in this business."[31]

2

The Fringe

Movies are expensive, and are only made with collaboration. These are the two essential difficulties of film production, and the basic reason that so few movies rise above average. Technology has recently begun alleviating the first difficulty, but the second will likely always be there. Artistic endeavors tend to be introverted and some are truly selfish, but a filmmaker does not create in calm reflection. Writers, composers, and painters can learn their crafts and practice them at will. If they are never recognized, they have still at least created something. But filmmakers must create in collaboration with others and contend with the second-guessing of financiers. Except for Stan Brakhage's paint-splatter reels, nearly every film made requires some crew and actors to come into being, and few are made with less than a minimal dozen.[32] Visually oriented introverts like Alfred Hitchcock and George Lucas therefore may prefer storyboarding or editing to filming.

Given these realities, many of those who move beyond the daydreaming stage and actually make films have no poet's soul to wound. They are motivated by a sense of adventure, a lust for glory, or a plan to make a quick buck, but the process remains as grueling for them as for a true artist. As drive-in critic Joe Bob Briggs put it, "The wonder is not that we have so many one-hit wonders, but that we have so many people who are able to make more than one film in a lifetime. The reason those guys fight for their multimillion-dollar budgets is not because they want a bigger trailer, but because they don't want to die early."[33] And as a corollary, the wonder is not that there are so many bad movies, but that there are any good ones.

1927, Phil Tucker's birth year, was a favorable omen. The Academy of Motion Picture Arts and Sciences was founded in May, and *The Jazz Singer* premiered in October, ending the silent film era. And just as Tucker came to Hollywood in the late forties, the industry experienced changes almost as great as that epochal introduction of sound. In 1948, the U.S. Supreme Court ordered the five major movie studios—MGM, Paramount, RKO, Twentieth Century-Fox, and Warner Brothers—to divest themselves of their theater chains. Television, developed and refined for decades, was also becoming a nationwide, commercially viable form of entertainment in the early fifties, which posed an even larger challenge to the film industry. According to one history, half of American theaters were in the red in the early 1950s.[34]

Few who come to Hollywood strike it rich, overnight or years later. But with Tucker's love of show business and simple desire to work anywhere, he might have rapidly gained entry into the lesser movie studios, if the transitional late forties and early fifties had not been a uniquely bad time for them.

Besides three intermediate studios (Columbia, United Artists, and Universal), there was a small band of minors that could have provided entry-level opportunity. Later labeled Poverty Row, such studios as Monogram and PRC (Producers Releasing Corporation—but affectionately dubbed Pretty Rotten Crap by some) churned out small films on small budgets that dovetailed in symbiosis with the efforts of the majors. Republic Pictures was a Poverty Row titan, formed in 1935 when Herbert J. Yates merged his Consolidated Film Laboratories with a few small production outfits. Guided with mostly reliable financial acumen by Yates, Republic unashamedly sought to please a mass audience with economic films that entertained and appealed to traditional, small town values.[35] There was comforting reassurance in much Poverty Row product,[36] and this comfort value was also evident in how the films were exhibited.

According to Charles Flynn and Todd McCarthy in their groundbreaking anthology *Kings of the Bs*, by the mid-thirties audiences were accustomed to theatrical double features, a form of exhibition that appealed to the more-is-better mindset of the Great Depression. They noted, "That more than a few moviegoers often failed to sit through the entire program is beside the point." Two films were paired together, one upscale in cast and budget, and the second cheaper and formulaic. Combined with the newsreel, cartoon, comedy shorts, and other odds and ends, audiences at least got bulk for their buck with an assurance of quantity. As Flynn and McCarthy state, "There had certainly been low-budget features before the arrival of the double bill, but . . . it was the double bill that made the Bs a necessity." The majors lacked incentive to produce the bottom-end of the double-bill; they would not waste two expensive star-packed "A" vehicles in one show, and the profit margin from second-string movies was marginal. But that tiny sliver of income ($10,000-$15,000) from cheaply made "B" films was enough to galvanize small outfits like Republic into supplying them. As long as the studios had their own system of distribution (the theater chains that they owned until 1948), there was a guaranteed slot for the work of Poverty Row outfits. These films were rented out on an advance payment basis (a flat fee up front) rather than a profit percentage, as the B films were added value and did not get people into seats on their own. The Poverty Row studios also rented their work out for similarly marginal returns across the "state's-rights" system—an unofficial network of locally owned franchises with no studio affiliation that was unaffected by the 1948 decision.[37]

Poverty Row films were often lowbrow affairs, reliably fitting some easily recognizable genre, their reliable bread-and-butter a spate of cheaply made, unapologetically formulaic Westerns starring such cowboy idols as Gene Autry, Johnny Mack Brown, Ken Maynard, Jack Perrin, Roy Rogers, Bob Steele, Tom Tyler, and (in his early years) John Wayne. But amidst the Westerns, crime, horror, war adventures, and occasional comedies, the small budgets and factory efficiency let an enterprising filmmaker do interesting work. Edgar G. Ulmer created the film noir *Detour* (1945) at PRC, one of the most utterly grim and hopeless movies to escape the Hollywood dream factory. And Yates instituted a four-tier system of movie budgets at Republic that, with the reliable support of cheap Westerns, financed Orson Welles' nightmarish *Macbeth* (1948) and John

Poverty Row studios occasionally released an ambitious project, but most of the time just did what was reliable.

Ford's *The Quiet Man* (1952). While Yates' hankering for sporadic quality was admirable, it did not help his bottom line. In 1948, Republic lost nearly $350,000, a sickening plummet for a studio that had seen years of healthy profits. Although Republic bounced back in 1949, it never again reached its $1,000,000-plus profit of 1946, and it fell back into the red in 1957 and '58 on its way to extinction in 1959.

The Poverty Row outfits were never that robust, and had great difficulty in adjusting to a sudden, massive, and negative change in their market. The Supreme Court's 1948 *United States v. Paramount Pictures, Inc.* antitrust ruling, intended to help the little guy by breaking up behemoth business interests, cut them off at the knees, an epic illustration of good intentions paving the road to Hell when do-gooders collide with the law of unintended consequences. According to Kevin Heffernan, "The long-term effect of the *Paramount* decision was to place the [neighborhood] operator in an even more precarious position in relation to the distribution arm of the film industry."[38] The majors had been happy to let the Poverty Row outfits supply the B feature, as the small profit was not worth the production cost, but as guaranteed bookings in major-owned chains ended, there was no certainty that new theater owners would rent B films in the same numbers, if at all. But also contributing to the end of the B-fueled double feature was the mass licensing of television stations that exploded in the United States in 1947 and was completed by 1953. With the growth of this new broadcast medium, initially fascinating in itself with virtually no content, there had to be more and more material to broadcast. Tucker had left a state that established television broadcasting in 1947 for another which established it the same year, and which would be the epicenter for national broadcasting. He was well aware of the medium's possibility:

> At that time, TV wasn't an entity but it existed, and I thought there was tremendous potential, and I was screwing around with several different things. [It was] the hottest period of my writing. I wrote a few screenplays, none of which did anything, but they taught me things about how you write screenplays.
>
> *About writing the screenplays, [inaudible] films?*
> In my mind, television and movies had never been separated. For me, television was simply movies at home, instead of movies that you have to go out to.
>
> *So did you write screenplays or teleplays?*

I didn't think there was a difference, and I didn't distinguish a difference then when I came out.

Tucker's perspective was extremely prescient. While the film industry resisted the tide of "movies at home" with all sorts of gimmicks to get audiences back, attendance numbers never again reached the high levels of the Depression and World War II. This was partially because times were better and the need for escapism less severe, but also because the means of distribution were mutating to better service consumers at an individual level. From today's perspective of television having led to cable, satellite, home video, and Internet access, it is hard to escape the conclusion that mass theater attendance had never been a truly popular phenomenon. Huge numbers of people once flocked to theaters because they could not experience movies in any other way, and many of them chose to do otherwise when given the chance. Classic era movie-going as a near-holy "communal experience" arguably existed less often in the real world than it does in fan nostalgia. As one survey of the B Western film shows, the long-ago communal movie-going experience often bore no resemblance to the gooey sentimentality of modern writing on old movies: "The matinees were full of screaming children, making concentration next to impossible, while the evening performances were populated by adults, most of whom found it a lark to chortle or satirize the proceedings."[39] As cheap fifties Westerns moved into television, rowdy kids and sardonic grown-ups often got their fix at home.

Tucker remained open to all possibilities, on either side of a film-television division whose legitimacy he did not recognize.

As his later credits show, he would work in any genre, medium, or position.

> I felt I wanted to get into film production. I would meet people who had money and who liked my idea. Gradually, bit by bit, I came closer and closer to the making of a movie. I was shown how it's done. You have to try quite a few times before you get your [chance]. Finally, Dave Kaufman, who is still at *Variety* (at that time, I forget what he was, but he was sort of half-way up on the list), he took a liking to me and encouraged me very much in several endeavors which he may not even remember now (although, probably he would—Dave's that kind of guy).

Kaufman was a crotchety old-style reporter, someone who could logically bond with Tucker. In his pre-Hollywood days, he dug up material such as a quote for the Mason City, Iowa, *Globe-Gazette* from recently divorced Sinclair Lewis that his ex-wife was one of "those damned intellectuals."[40] A *Hollywood Reporter* acquaintance once tried to match Kaufman's casual and relentless Scotch intake and "then went back to his office and nearly passed out."[41] *Variety*'s TV editor beginning in 1951, Kaufman was in the unique position of reporting on the medium in its infant stages, making him an ideal contact with the lower tiers of Hollywood.

> He finally got me together with some people who had money. I was going to do a picture at what was then

General Service Studios, I don't know what it is now, it's 1040 North Las Palmas. (The Nassour brothers worked there, they made a lot of bad pictures.) Of course, the whole thing fell through, it was a terrible fiasco. Not one foot ever got shot.

What was the picture going to be called?
It was something about the South. I think it may have been *The South Shall Rise Again*, or something like that.

General Service Studios was one of the better small locations in Hollywood, taking advantage of the beginning of Hollywood production of TV material. According to a 1951 AP report, "The Hal Roach Studios, Eagle-Lion, the old Vitagraph lot, Nassour studios, General Service studios, and the old Enterprise lot are among former movie sites now busily producing television movies and shows."[42] In September 1951, the *Long Beach Press-Telegram* reported that "a new series of television comedies titled *I Love Lucy*" was "being filmed by Desilu at General Service Studios, Hollywood, where a sound stage has been converted into the nation's first television film-theater."[43] As 1952 press stories noted, the studio was by then making a profit for the first time.[44] This was thanks to the success of *I Love Lucy*, but more generally because its seven or eight sound stages were in constant use for mostly TV production. In this scenario, low-budget films fit easily into an independent studio's schedule. Tucker was of course ready to work on anything at General Service or anywhere else, for whatever medium it was intended.

In that period, I met a cameraman named Gordon Avil, who has died just in the last two or three years. Gordon, in essence, took me aside and taught me eight million things about making pictures. I made about twenty-five or thirty pilots for television.

I see, so you started out in TV.
I was never in TV; I just made pilots. They were bad. But it taught me a little bit about film, *per se.*

Tucker may have been exaggerating or misremembering here. Twenty-five filmed TV pilots would have added up to quite a bit of money, and the financial stake of his investors would guarantee the survival of at least a few of them, while none appear to exist. But some vestige of this earliest stage of his professional career has survived, revealing that he made at least a few of the pilots he remembered. *Daily Variety* reported on March 11, 1952 that "producer Phillip Tucker says he wrapped up 29 mins. of soap opera vidpix in eight hours and six mins. of shooting Saturday," the completed *A Day with Dr. Edith* consisting of three episodes for $1,500 that also covered "music and 10 prints."[45] Filmed at Larchmont studios by Avil, the project starred Charlotte Miedell with other unknowns Dick Norris, Billy Dixon, Colette McMahon, "and Tucker," amazingly implying that Tucker at least once appeared on camera as an actor. *Daily Variety* announced a month later, "Vidpix producer Phil Tucker will shoot a second soap opera series *Jennifer's Husband,* Saturday, with Alan Nixon and Connie Sezanne in the leads. Bankrolling the project is A. Brooks Conklin."[46] While there is no record of Sezanne and Conklin, Nixon is almost certainly

Allan Nixon with his name slightly misspelled, a working actor of the forties to early sixties who starred in *Mesa of Lost Women* (1953), one of *Robot Monster's* few rivals in weird badness. And by implication, this "second soap opera series" makes *A Day with Dr. Edith* Tucker's first pilot, and possibly the first time he completed one of his own projects. Then announced in a variety of late August *Variety* issues, *How Julius Becomes Caesar*—"series of thirteen half-hour telepix"—was to shoot at Quality Pictures Studios on September 1, with Avil on camera, Tucker as producer, and Sam Leacock as associate producer for Lea-Tuck Telefilms, Inc.[47] (Quality Pictures and Sam Leacock were important in Tucker's career, as will be discussed.)

While none of these early Tucker projects seem to have survived, there remains a reasonable facsimile of what they were like. One filmmaker is often seen as Tucker's equivalent, compatriot, or rival, with a reputation that in death became larger than life. Edward D. Wood Jr.—Ed Wood as he is remembered—made a soap opera drama at around the same time as Tucker, and it is widely available. (Tucker's *A Day with Dr. Edith* also included Ann Wilner in its cast, who later appeared in Wood's *Bride of the Monster* [1955].) *Variety* reported on December 26, 1951 that the filming of "15-minute dramas" would continue on January 17, entitled *Five Minutes Before Eternity* and *Cindy is Dead.*[48] While these were supposed to be the "first two," it may be that only one was filmed, for one 14-minute Wood drama has survived, *The Sun Was Setting*, with a cast that matches the three persons listed in *Variety*: Angela Stevens, Tom Keene (as Richard Powers onscreen), and Phyllis Coates. Either title listed in *Variety* could have been a working title for *The Sun Was*

Setting, a completely set-bound tale of a terminally ill woman deciding to go out for a night on the town, even if it kills her. The entire short drama consists of she and two friends endlessly talking around this situation, along with a very ham-fisted bit of symbolism at the end. Wood's lack of experience is evident in the presentation of the story. Shots go on forever and when there is an edit the effect is poor, with disconcerting cuts to barely different angles and weird inserts of the main character saying nothing. While it is impossible to know if Tucker's TV pilots were better or worse than Wood's, they were likely similar because of the time and location in which they were made, and the inexperience of those involved. And as Tucker himself summed them up, "They were bad."

But even if Tucker's soap opera was of the same quality as Wood's, Gordon Avil would have been an excellent mentor.

WADE WILLIAMS DIST.

Ann Wilner in Ed Wood's *Bride of the Monster*. Wilner is one of the few recognizable actors who appeared in Phil Tucker's early TV pilots.

His Hollywood career began with that of director King Vidor, collaborating on four of his films, including the Oscar-winning boxing drama *The Champ* (1931). Vidor remembered promoting Avil to "first cameraman . . .. I liked his personality and I thought he was worthy of it." Avil shot *Billy the Kid* (1930) for Vidor in a rare early use of 70 millimeter film, before it became a popular format in the fifties and sixties. It was also shot in 35 millimeter, Vidor said; "Both cameras were right alongside each other when we filmed."[49] Tucker's mentor rose through the ranks, and did not hesitate to film in an uncommon and cumbersome format. He was therefore very technically skilled, and was exactly the kind of person Tucker would relate to and learn from.

While Avil's Hollywood credits are strangely uneven from the mid-thirties to late forties, showing years of apparent inactivity, this seems to be because he craved a challenge wherever he could find one. In 1933, the Kroger grocery chain promoted their *Thought for Food* short film in a "Kroger Section" newspaper advertisement. It noted the film's impressive "photographic effects," and that "Gordon Avil, chief photographer who filmed it, has a number of 4-star pictures to his credit . . .."[50] Avil later collaborated at least seven times with Western specialist Lesley Selander, and worked on many TV shows after his Hollywood career picked up for a second time. In 1961 he was again attached to a short requiring experimental photographic technique. The Oscar-nominated *The Face of Jesus* depicted "likenesses of Christ from the age of 12 through the Resurrection," according to a *Greeley Tribune* report. "The featurette presented many problems in photography embracing proper use of light and shadows but the difficult task has been surmounted by Gordon Avil and the finished product has been awarded plaudits by all who have seen it."[51] And Avil was willing to go into rugged locations, which Tucker no doubt admired. In 1957, he was in Tahoe City, California, "making trail and background shots" filmed "over a wide area" for the *Sergeant Preston of the Yukon* series.[52] His eagerness to help and educate others was a lifelong trait. The director of photography on *Hogan's Heroes* until his 1970 death, Avil spent weekends teaching actor Ivan Dixon directing skills[53]; another cast member, Robert Clary, remembered him as "the sweetest man."[54] But according to Gerry Dooley's history of the Disney *Zorro* series, director William Witney found Avil too laidback, and preferred to work with Lucien Ballard.[55]

Tucker not only absorbed the technical acumen of men like Avil, but soaked up the entire aesthetic of early television and Poverty Row filmmaking. To understand why an intelligent and competent man like Tucker would have made some of the odd filmmaking decisions that are forever preserved in *Robot Monster* and *Dance Hall Racket,* it only needs to be understood that such decisions were increasingly common the lower the budget, and the shorter the schedule. Flynn and McCarthy describe how the cheap studios would remove as much detail from scripts as possible, starting scenes with characters already on set and avoiding the complications that could ensue from the characters arriving. All such simplifications were made to save time and money, but their cumulative impact could have an unintended effect on the feel of cheap movies. "This elimination of stage business, of entrances and exits, gives most Bs a strange, almost cryptic air of flatness and unreality," they write, also noting the B film tendency for massive re-uses of stock footage that sometimes resulted in the kind of surreal continuity errors associated with Ed Wood.[56]

As *Plan 9 from Outer Space* documentarian Mark Patrick Carducci told prolific interviewer Tom Weaver, "There's an area of filmmaking that I call 'the universe of the unintentionally surreal,' . . .. defined by things like hollow post-production sound; very little dialogue in sync sound; stiff acting; a lack of exteriors (maybe just stock shots); dark camerawork, etc."[57] And, as noted, filmmaking is an intrinsically grueling art, where hiding the seams is difficult precisely because it takes money and the cooperation of many others. So whenever movies are made under conditions where they can barely be finished at all, they will very often play a little strangely when assembled. Film is the most realistic art, capable of showing the sights and sounds of life just as they are, but also the art that quickly becomes the most dreamlike. When night and day are edited together, when ridiculous monsters cause terror, when characters abruptly disappear, react to sounds that were never dubbed in, or arrive at illogical conclusions, then the apparent reality of the recorded image becomes an irrational dream. And this is the reason that derided low-budget works like *The Beast of Yucca Flats* and *Glen or Glenda* have a funny kinship with surrealist art films like *Eraserhead.* Anyone working with ultra-low budgets will sooner or later create effects similar to the acclaimed and bizarre styles of directors like David Lynch, Luis Buñuel, or Alain Resnais; the cheap monster epics of Tucker, Wood, and their contemporaries located the ideal of absurd weirdness better

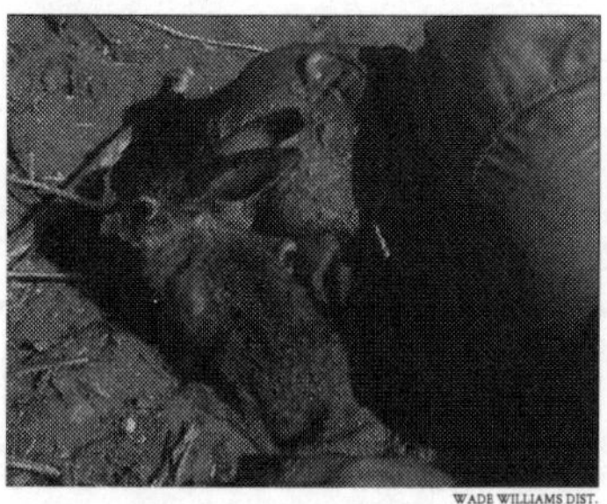

WADE WILLIAMS DIST.

***The Beast of Yucca Flats* and *Eraserhead*, films which demonstrate that the line between so-bad-it's-good movies and art films can be very thin. The common denominator is surrealism.**

than most who braved making a movie with few resources. As Carducci put it, "If you like *avant garde* cinema, I think you'll be able to easily make the switch into Ed Wood's universe, 'cause I think he's unintentionally a bit closer to an *avant garde* filmmaker than he is to a narrative storyteller in any kind of a commercial mode."

Tucker was accumulating excellent knowledge, but his opportunities to put it into practice were limited. Within Poverty Row, he could have found a logical niche in better times, but he had to make do with things as they were and if his only opportunities were at the bottom of the barrel, he would settle there for a time. At the outmost fringe of Hollywood was a shadowy band of independents that survived the changes that rocked the post-war movie economy. They made movies but they were not movie studios, their names were unknown, their companies consisted of two or three individuals, they lacked any notion of artistic seriousness, and they probably spawned more accidental surrealism than any of the Poverty Row studios. Cheap horse-opera factories like Republic made their most cut-rate B Westerns for $30,000, while these undesirables only hit that low level at maximum. Whereas the majors survived the times through sheer size tempered by a grudging willingness to change, these cinematic bottom-feeders survived because they spent virtually nothing to make their films, and they continually adapted to trends. Their trade was exploitation. As one of them explained:

> . . . [Professionals] equate technical ability with an ability to entertain people. There is no correlation at all. None. . . . The only film that an independent can make and survive with is a film that the major producers cannot or will not make. I regard that as a physical law, I don't regard it as a theory.[58]

These are the words of Herschell Gordon Lewis, a former English professor with a stake in a small film company. He realized that he could shock audiences with graphic, repulsive color violence that had never been seen on film, starting with the 1963 *Blood Feast.* While this form of exploitation was over a decade away in the post-war era, Lewis' summation of how to survive in a pre-digital, no-budget film world is the formula always followed back to the genre's carnival sideshow origins in the twenties.[59] Whether the films' subjects were drug abuse, mental illness, nudist colonies, prostitution, teenage pregnancy, or venereal disease, they were made for very little money and distributed independently, were of terrible quality, and were represented by advertising that promised the audience unimaginable debauchery.

In reality, exploitation films only went a short distance beyond what was acceptable in mainstream film. Before the 1957 *Roth v. United States* Supreme Court decision, there was little legal ambiguity about obscenity, and the law was strongly enforced against blatant pornography; therefore, exploitation swam in a safe direction within the murky currents of the potentially obscene. To this end the secular religion-substitute of progressivism—less popular with the masses, but highly influential within the intelligentsia—was invoked to give such films respectability, a handy appeal when an exploitation man found himself in hot water with local authorities. Just as some Biblical epics were arguably displays of cruelty and lust legitimized by a veneer of religion, exploitation films skirted illegality by appealing to the progressive shibboleths held sacred by America's elite.

A consistent part of the exploitation game therefore was the transparently fake assurance that it was regrettably necessary to discuss the films' lurid subject matter. To leave it unrevealed, the rationalization went, would be to be complicit in a societal ill.[60] Movies therefore began with a moralistic prologue (or "square-up") and never strayed from punishing sinners at film's end.[61] Along the way, the audience could glean a few cheap thrills if they happened to live in a "hot" distribution territory, which might allow a few brief flashes of nudity. If they lived in a more restrictive "cold" territory, the gulf between the suggestive lobby art and the actual film onscreen was even wider, as the very same films would play in edited form and sometimes

This poster for 1954's *Girl Gang*, directed by Robert C. Dertano and starring Timothy Farrell, exemplifies the ludicrous, exaggerated quality of exploitation film publicity.

under completely different titles.[62] The exploitation filmmaker did not care one way or another as long as there was profit, movies operating on the we-already-have-your-money business model. As a 1953 advertisement from Mack Enterprises of Dallas proclaimed in the trade magazine *Box Office*: "For exhibitors who need money! . . . Exploitation Pictures!" The accompanying art of a coquettishly smiling burlesque dancer said the rest.[63]

But despite the reliable, lowest common denominator pull of sleaze as a means of separating fools from their money, an exploiter's money was never in great abundance. According to Eric Schaefer's survey *Bold! Daring! Shocking! True!*, they were middle-class people, respectable enough on the surface but not wealthy.[64] While their films were made for as little as $10,000,[65] the profits were modest and the shifty nature of many state's-rights distributors complicated matters further. Faced with the choice of a low upfront payment or a potentially greater box-office profit percentage, the exploitation filmmaker often chose what was low but reliable. It had the virtue of avoiding any creative accounting. According to low-budget filmmaker Fred Olen Ray:

> Under the right conditions, the states-rights sub-distribution method of reaching the public was ideal, as it was nearly impossible for a small company to set up bookings in the thousands of theaters that dotted the country. By arranging a deal with a [sub-distributor] the independent would have to contend with only one group for a given geographical area.[66]

But while the state's-rights system was reliable enough, releasing films through it was an unpleasant, hardscrabble process that would sap the patience of most. Cinematographer Bri Murphy, former wife of cheap monster movie maker Jerry Warren, relayed to Weaver her vivid memories of dealing with "state's-righters" as

> . . . the most *painful* thing you could imagine. . . . You're in the screening room with these distributors, and they're answering the phone and they're talking to each

> other and they're smoking, and they get up and leave for a while and then come back. And then they ask, "What do you want for this piece of shit?"—*that* kind of stuff. Really terrible.[67]

Warren could get $14,000 out of such deals—if he had obtained a 14% profit agreement from telling the lie that his no-budget film had been made for $100,000! And according to Ray, the state's-rights system was very slow. An independent producer could not afford to make a large number of prints, which insured a long time for films to play their way across various territories.[68] No wonder then that any who made product for this system, even those who were not makers of exploitation, were fanatical cost cutters. Victor Adamson, an Australian cowboy turned maker of American Westerns in the twenties, reportedly kept budgets down in the four digits. According to Robert S. Birchard, "The economies involved in these efforts included purchasing food for the location shoots at the damaged canned goods store in east Los Angeles. . . . In an effort to avoid making opticals, [Adamson] was known to lower a piece of black cardboard over the lens to simulate a wipe."[69] And producer Sam Sherman states that through 1934, Adamson made Westerns "for $2,500 each," their star getting "a whopping $250 each."[70]

In crime writer Jim Thompson's 1949 novel *Nothing More Than Murder*, the protagonist runs a small town movie theater, and the entire second chapter provides a close look at the exhibition end of the state's-rights system. Despite its "projectors that should have been in a museum, and a wildcat sound system," the little theater does okay, "particularly on Friday and Saturday, the horse-opera nights." The narrator discusses many ins-and-outs of the business, such as arranging inescapable "stinker product" for maximum advantage within his schedule, distributors who can provide "a sex picture or two," and the practice of inserting tiny clips of movie stars like "Gable and Bergman" into cheap movies. "A ten-frame shot of them sitting in the Stork Club," he scoffs. "And what it has to do with the picture nobody knows." There is even a mention later in the novel of "the big city houses that play product on percentage instead of at a flat rate."[71] In other words, the big guys are not so much at the mercy of creative accounting and fickle audiences.

Exploitation sometimes just focused on things that were unusual, without any hint of smut. According to Sherman, "People today who are just involved with content really limit themselves as to the possibilities in the exploitation field, because the exploitation field was selling an idea, selling a concept, not selling content (how well done it was)."[72] Silent film veteran A. Harry Keatan, in some sources believed to be the brother of Buster Keaton, would work with Tucker but made the pages of the January 1953 *Reporter* with *Trails of Marco Polo,* an alleged documentary "filmed by an expedition in Iran, Afghanistan, India and Tibet."[73] Far weirder was a September 1954 *Reporter* item about a movie starring celebrity psychic Criswell: "Actor Wayne Berk and cameraman George W. Richter . . . plan to start shooting immediately on a feature titled *Criswell Predicts to 1999.* . . . the producers plan to exploit it as an attraction that will 'never' be seen on TV."[74] This gambit was clearly aimed at the idea that TV was "movies at home."

Tucker paid many of his cinematic dues in this world of exploitative filmmakers and distributors, learning the rudiments of filmmaking in the hope of moving into better things. Unlike many who came to Hollywood and failed to become an overnight sensation, he worked relentlessly for whatever slim opportunities he could find. As he continued from his reference to Avil:

> Then I met a guy named George Weiss who made main street pictures.
>
> *Do you want to explain what main street pictures are?*
> Pictures that are intended to play on the main streets where the twenty-cent theaters were in those days, now I guess it's five bucks or whatever it was all throughout the country.

The term "main street," though its origins are unclear, was another way of saying exploitation. Schaefer writes, "The origin of the term Main Street theaters remains something of a mystery, perhaps a reference to the low-end theaters on Los Angeles' Main Street."[75] Weiss, according to Ed Wood biographer Rudolph Grey, described himself as one of the few who "were making that type of picture that could play the Main Street houses around the country,"[76] which he did mostly from the late forties to the late fifties. And on the set of *Glen or Glenda,* the Wood-directed sex-change film he financed, Weiss told a reporter, "We do exploitation pictures." Weiss emphasized that Wood's film contained "nothing censorable whatsoever."[77] Censorable, sensible, or otherwise, Weiss' films fell often in the exploitation sub-genre of *vice,* movies about the criminal underworld that were the dull, bottom-feeder cousins of the often wonderfully creative film noir films. The diminutive Weiss was, as Weaver noted, nothing like the "fat, vulgar slob" version of him portrayed by Mike Starr in the 1994 film *Ed Wood* (understandable as it may be to assume this image of the producer of *Test Tube Babies, The Devil's Sleep,* and *Racket Girls*).[78] By the same token, most who toiled in the lowest substrata of Hollywood were nothing like the infamous Wood, who remembered Weiss as "a delightful, gutsy little fellow."[79] (Actor Conrad Brooks also liked Weiss, calling him "a good man" but "tight with the dollar!"[80])

Because of Wood's cult status as the Worst Director of All Time and his distinction in being the subject of a Hollywood film, he casts a large and distorted shadow from the great beyond. When most people think of this dingy, subterranean type of filmmaking, they think of the legend of the cross-dressing former Marine who made the Worst Movie of All Time. It is true that most in the cinematic netherworld cared about their work enough to do their best within the means available to them. Even career exploiters had to worry about hitting certain basic points of audience appeal. But a crucial difference between Wood and his contemporaries was that they maintained a realistic sense of the shortcomings of their work. In contrast, Wood considered his movies important enough to merit continued viewing, a belief that allowed him to act like an obnoxious relative subjecting a family reunion to hours of home movies as he called friends at odd hours to remind them of his films appearing on TV. But Phil Tucker Jr. remembered exactly how his father viewed his movie work:

> He didn't make these films because he thought he was creating art. It was just to make a buck, and to survive, and do what he loved and that was really about the only option back then to do it.

And however Weiss initially got involved in exploitation, he was also just making a buck. Timothy Farrell, smooth-voiced narrator of *Glen or Glenda* and prolific actor, remembered Weiss' constant pacing, a towel draped around his neck to absorb perspiration, and his worry over the "nine cents a foot" cost of film.[81] Weiss called himself "the only guy I can remember [who] used his own money and made pictures."[82] While not the only one, few chose a life of marginal self-employment that must have reinforced Tucker's own inclinations. Just as cheap and important to the beginning of Tucker's career was William Merle Connell, sometimes billed as W. Merle but often by the middle name alone, who did camerawork on five surviving films that Tucker directed, of which Weiss produced at least two. Much Los Angeles exploitation filming took place at the absurdly named Quality Pictures, located near an alley on Santa Monica Boulevard, at which Connell had some poorly defined supervisory role and where Tucker was scheduled to shoot *How Julius Becomes Caesar* in late summer 1952. Whether the location's owner or steward, he was, as Brooks remembered, "the boss,"[83] and he did, according to Farrell, "a lot of the set work." There were many other cheap little studios sprinkled around Los Angeles, but only Quality would earn any cult recognition, thanks to *Plan 9 from Outer Space.* As Farrell remembered, some of Weiss' films were done at "the Jack Miles Studios in Larchmont, but mostly [at] Quality Pictures . . . ."[84]

(Wood, writes Grey, remembered it as nothing more than a "stinking little studio with sacks across the ceiling."[85]) Between Weiss and Connell, Weiss seems more a financier and Connell more a worker. Weiss' credits rarely stray past producer, while Connell moved between cinematography, directing, and editing. Additionally, Farrell and Tucker remembered their exploitation careers primarily around Weiss with only brief mentions of Connell.

Connell produced, directed, photographed, and edited exploitation projects in varying combinations, after an apprenticeship in Los Angeles' arcade peep show business in the mid-forties.[86] A January 1944 issue of *The Billboard* noted that Connell had "signed with Standard Pictures Corporation to make movies for movie machines," while not mentioning him in connection with the news that "Quality Pictures along with Les Lorden" was also making them.[87] A profile of the Standard company in the same issue interviewed president Fred Walker, and went into technical detail about Standard's product and process, including a note that Connell was in charge of films shot on 16 millimeter.[88] But in February 1947, the same trade magazine listed Connell as a partner in Quality Pictures Co., noting that the outfit produced "six new subjects monthly" for Panoram machines (music video jukeboxes).[89]

All evidence indicates that Connell was a particularly smart and ambitious exploitation man and, from that point of view, the Quality name had the appropriateness of lousy product that fit its intended purpose. While Schaefer notes that this world of early arcade peek shows is "even more clouded than that of classical exploitation,"[90] another 1944 article featured the thoughts of Lorden ("formerly an orchestra leader" and "one of the pioneers of the peek machine") and two other arcade moviemakers on the future of the business. Lorden's optimism that the business would keep booming after the war, allowing for future use of attractions like 3-D and color, was tempered by the skepticism of Tony Brill, who noted that 75% of business was from servicemen and wondered, "Do you think they will continue to be as rabid for pin-up girls after the war?"[91] Into the post-war void stepped Connell. Schaefer notes, "One of the most prolific and professional of the peep producers was W. Merle Connell's Quality Pictures. By 1947 Connell had created no fewer than twenty-five reels of strip films, each one featuring six numbers that used dancers from Los Angeles burlesque theaters."[92] And as his surviving films indicate, Connell recognized that the value of arcade burlesque entertainment was limited. By 1947's *A Night at the Follies,* he was dabbling in feature-length strip films for showing in burlesque houses and anywhere else that would play them. If such material was going to continue to be profitable, it would have to be outside of arcades that relied on the fleeting attention of soldiers and sailors on leave. Vindicating Connell's move out of the arcades, a 1955 "factory closeout" classified ad revealed that the originally $275 machines were being blown out for $45 each.[93]

One of the earliest surviving references to Connell is from *Daily Variety* in July 1940, where he is listed as one of three associates with boss Billy Evans in Educationettes Distribution Co., a Hollywood outfit "launched to handle 16mm shorts for classrooms . . . ."[94] Soon after in the 1941 *Film Daily Year Book of Motion Pictures,* Connell was listed as Secretary-Treasurer of Modern Movies, Inc., a company "organized in 1935" that produced "musical shorts" and "coin machine shorts" on 16 millimeter.[95] Listed as President above him is Jean R. Connell, who was identified on the previous year's federal census as Jean V. Connell (the Lady Macbeth behind his success in the smut racket?), the census also listing their twelve-year-old son James R. Connell.[96] But farther down in the *Film Daily Year Book* listing as a production department head was Boris Petroff, another significant player in the Connell-Quality circle. A former ballet dancer[97] and supposed "former Russian nobleman,"[98] Petroff went from managing large ballet shows in the early twenties to becoming part of Mae West's inner circle for a time in the mid-thirties. His duties included overseeing West's 1934 visit to an American Indian high school, in which some 350 young men were paraded around for her leering examination for parts in an upcoming film.[99] He also once purchased a boat for her use that she refused to board, for fear that she might get tan.[100] Eventually out of West's orbit, Petroff hired a young Samuel Fuller to write a script that, as Fuller disgustedly remembered, was pruned of everything satirical and became the silly comedy *Hats Off* (1937).[101] Petroff did not produce or direct any features for a decade, but in the meantime partnered up with Connell, who shot a three-minute 1940 film that Petroff directed, *The Daughter of Mademoiselle from Armentieres,* credited to Featurette Films.[102] (The title is from a risqué World War I song, suggesting that Connell was doing exploitation from his earliest years in film.) In January 1944, *The Billboard* mentioned Connell's work in the arcade-peep movie business with the note that he was "formerly with Boris Petroff," but there is no other evidence that the two drifted apart.[103] They released the folk-dancing documentary *The World Dances* in 1954, an example of exploitation by way of targeting a narrow audience without any need for raciness. The film was reportedly intended for "art theaters, churches, colleges and auditoriums."[104] By the time that Petroff was making low-budget features in the fifties (he unsuccessfully tried to get the *Peyton Place* movie rights[105]), Connell was involved at least twice, and Petroff's last directorial effort, *Shotgun Wedding* (1963), was scripted by Wood. A profile from around the same time noted, "The 30 or so films in which he has had a hand have two things in common. Hardly anyone, outside the industry, remembers most of them and all have made money."[106]

Weaver's interview with *Star Trek* producer-writer John D.F. Black illustrates the down-and-out milieu of Tucker's professional life. When Black was a mid-fifties drama student, his ad-writing job gave him an eye-opening introduction to the movie fringe courtesy of Petroff, Connell, and Quality Studios:

> The place was located near Western Avenue on Santa Monica; at that time, it was like the boondocks of Hollywood. . . . it was between a small saloon and a borax furniture store. . . . I walked down the alley and through the door of this little studio, and there behind a desk in this very dingy, small office sat Boris Petroff . . . the stage was *not* really what you would call a huge film stage. The ceiling was a little higher than your average ten-foot ceiling, it was about 14 feet. . . . it was a really small place, used primarily to make porno pictures. And screen

> tests—when some guy wanted to make a screen test of a beautiful young lady he wanted to get next to quickly, he could (for 20 bucks or 50 bucks or whatever) get the guy who ran the place, Merle Connell, to shoot a test of the girl. . . . [Connell] was a sweet man, but he wouldn't talk story with me, all he said was, "Do whatever Boris asks. And that way he'll be very happy and everything'll work fine."

Petroff had a story idea and was buying an ad for writing help. Because he was in reality trying to get a complete script written below professional rates, Black obliged and got his first screen credit, though not without difficulty. Petroff's wife had typed up the script and claimed credit for actually writing it but, unfortunately for her, Petroff had written a contract for the script and had to pay Black the Writers Guild minimum. Black wasted no time cashing the check.[107]

Directed by Petroff as Brooke L. Peters and released in 1957 as *The Unearthly,* it was an inferior and uncredited ripoff of the previous year's *The Black Sleep*; both films featured John Carradine and Tor Johnson. In Petroff's version, Johnson plays his Lobo character, as he did in two Wood films. The original version, *The Black Sleep,* even has its own separate connection to Tucker, with camerawork by Gordon Avil. And a few other reports of *The Unearthly*'s production are worth mentioning, for their perspective on the experience of working with Connell and Petroff. Makeup artist Harry Thomas disgustedly recalled in *Filmfax* his detailed work that was never seen in close-up, was poorly lit, or only shown for brief seconds. Said Thomas,

"Believe me, I raised hell, but it didn't help."[108] And actor Arthur Batanides had this to say to Weaver:

> We drove the director absolutely fuckin' ape-shit. The whole cast was uncontrollable . . .. a lot of horsing around and playing around. That was one way of *dealing* with [it]. . . . *The Unearthly* was one of the few times I've ever been drunk doin' a show. The *only* time, really. . . . I don't think I got $400 for that movie.[109]

The exploitation world sustained a dozen or so like Connell and Weiss at any point between the early twenties and mid-sixties, when there was soon very little left forbidden and thereby exploitable. But besides providing a marginal but challenging opportunity for them and new hopefuls like Tucker and Wood, exploitation was a retirement fund for some who had seen better days. William C. Thompson, allegedly one-eyed cinematographer of *Plan 9 from Outer Space*, had been lensing features since at least 1914. Some were respectable, but Thompson was not averse in early years to taking on grungier projects like Dwain Esper's *Maniac* (1934), a nonsensical "study" of mental illness that must be seen to be believed. But though half-blind, Thompson was a competent cameraman and his mysterious, high contrast images are the best part of Wood's movies. Thompson's cinematography was also better than the one narrative film he directed, an obscure piece of the cheap thirties Western tsunami called *The Irish Gringo* (1935), described by Don Miller as "a debacle of such blatant ineptitude that it is a source of wonder the footage was ever assembled for public showing."[110] Even more wondrous was a 1953 *Variety* note that

WADE WILLIAMS DIST.

A representative sample of the 1950s low-budget movie world in which Phil Tucker toiled. On the *Night of the Ghouls* set, Harry Thomas applies makeup to Tor Johnson while William C. Thompson checks the light and Ed Wood stands by (*at right*).

he "declared yesterday that he was in no way connected with" the exploitation film *Side Streets of Hollywood.*[111] Some things were apparently beyond the pale for Thompson.

Such old-timers as Petroff and Thompson were a valuable source of knowledge for newcomer Tucker, and brought with them an array of acquaintances. Given the multiple hats usually worn by exploitation filmmakers and everyone else in the low-budget world, the experience must have been like going to a sleazy film school, before film schools even existed. Tucker had taken this sub-entry-level work because it was all he could get, and now had to watch for the right opportunity to parlay his learning into professional filmmaking. As he summarized these days:

> I worked two years for him.
>
> *I see. Which two years?*
> Probably '48 and '49, [or] '47, '48, I don't know.
>
> *"Him" referring to?*
> George Weiss. In that period I learned how to use a camera, to some extent. I learned how to boss a crew around, to some extent. I learned how to choose, [to] select the equipment.

By 1952, the opportunity was ever clearer. Ever since the pulp magazine explosion of the thirties, science fiction had been inching closer and closer toward the mainstream. This was partially just a matter of its readership expanding, as evidenced by the success of Ray Bradbury, a pulp author who made the jump to writing bestsellers in hardcover for a major publisher. But it was also a reflection of the real world beginning to resemble science fiction in various ways. Many of those alive in the early fifties could remember a time before radio, the telephone, and cars, and World War II had ended with the detonation of nuclear weapons. Given the ongoing scientific experiments with rocketry and the advent of television in the home, it was logical that science fiction would make its first big move into that most popular medium, the movies. In 1952, some notable new science fiction films already existed (*Rocketship X-M*,

The Thing from Another World) and many movies that would become genre classics were either being filmed (*Invaders from Mars, The Beast from 20,000 Fathoms, The War of the Worlds*), or were in some stage of pre-production (*Creature from the Black Lagoon, 20,000 Leagues Under the Sea, Forbidden Planet*).[112] Science fiction was everywhere in 1952, and Tucker expressed an affinity for it that will be explored in more detail. He would soon find an opportunity to latch onto this movement and seize it for all its worth.

> When I set out to make *Robot Monster,* I was accomplished and knew the tools of directing. Whether or not I was able to use them well is a different matter. I did not use them properly.

3

Robot Killer

In later 1952, half a year before filming *Robot Monster,* Phil Tucker succeeded in making a name for himself. Soon following the late August announcement of his *How Julius Becomes Caesar* series, he made the front page of the September 4 *Daily Variety* with this headline: "SWG Charges Phil Tucker With Paying His Telepix Scribes Under Minimum." The Screen Writers Guild (SWG) planned to convene the next day a "hearing to determine whether he shall be put on the Guild's 'unfair' list." The project in question was a Lea-Tuck Telefilm Co. TV pilot, *Fabulous Murphys,* completed on September 3. Despite lacking any "pact with Tucker," the Guild disapproved of his paying an unidentified writer "$250 a week" rather than its preferred "$500 minimum."[113] Given that *How Julius Becomes Caesar* was intended to shoot on September 1, it almost had to be the same project as *Fabulous Murphys,* but the interesting point is Tucker's reaction to the Guild.

The September 9 *Daily Variety* announced on the front page that Tucker had started Hollywood's fourth "producer's association," the Independent Producers Guild. (Already existing were National Society of Television Producers, Television Film Producers Association, and Alliance of Television Film Producers—this one "now being struck by SWG . . ..") Tucker had been placed on the "'unfair' list" prior to starting the new group, and he complained, "I cannot find out if a writer can do the kind of work I want until after I pay for it." Tucker did not shy away from detailing his frustration, stating, "I think that it's high time that the producers of this town started making the same demands on unions. We have just as many mouths to feed as writers do. We have just as many expenses, in addition to which we have to take the gamble with our money." And in describing the purpose of the Independent Producers Guild, he was especially blunt. Tucker's Guild would "maintain equitable standards in working conditions throughout the industry for all people involved, not just a minority that has long outworn its welcome."[114]

Tucker's direct and unapologetic confrontation with a powerful film industry union may have stalled his career more than any other factor that was against him. It is to his credit that he had the confidence to buck the odds and not care about the imbalance of power between the Screen Writers Guild and himself, but it also shows that he may have misinterpreted the situation and the likely result. And only one week after it had announced Tucker's new Independent Producers Guild, *Daily Variety* reported that it had disbanded. The September 16 issue stated that Tucker's decision followed "his return from Alaska," where producer Sam Leacock "advised against the new setup and favored peace with SWG . . .." Tucker would "approach the

Guild to seek a basis for 'understanding;' that he was ready to comply with Guild terms."[115] While in retrospect Tucker may not appear better off as a result of his decision to play ball with the Guild, his career would at least continue on an even keel in relation to where it had already been.

Apparently having had enough of TV pilots, Tucker got himself right back on the front page of *Daily Variety* with an explosion: "Phil Tucker said yesterday he has made tentative plans to leave next week for Italy, to discuss with Charles 'Lucky' Luciano a projected biopic of the deported gangster." The October 15 story noted that the film "would be financed by Luciano to the tune of $300,000," and Tucker "said script would seek 'to show society was to blame' for Luciano's wind-up in the clink, but at the same time would not white-wash him."[116] *Daily Variety* reported on October 21 that Tucker claimed that his passport request had been turned down by the State Department, but that the project would continue anyway with Luciano still involved in scripting and planning to appear as narrator, including an introduction and moralistic ending (to warn youngsters away from crime). Tucker was in "negotiations for studio space at Eagle Lion and California Studios," was producing under the Lea-Tuck Telefilms, Inc. banner, and had "inked Joe Karnes for second lead in the bio-pic."[117] Karnes had a minor acting career with a few bit parts in the forties and fifties. Even more obscure was lead actor Matt Barlow, reported just two days later, who was "formerly known as Frank Marta" and took the role after it was "nixed by seven thesps to whom it had been offered."[118] Nothing is known about this actor as Barlow or Marta, beyond a February 1955 reference in *Daily Variety*, that Marta was cast in *Sicilian Bandit,* an apparently unmade independent production to be directed by veteran editor Arthur Hilton.[119] For Tucker's Luciano film, it was also announced in the October 23, 1952 *Daily Variety* that Tucker would direct at Quality Pictures, with Gordon Avil on camera and Lyle Willey handling sound.[120] (Willey did sound on many low-budget film and TV projects, including *Robot Monster.*)

But the October 29 weekly edition of *Variety* reported, "Indie producer Phil Tucker reveals that Charles (Lucky) Luciano, deported gangster, has chilled deal whereby the deportee was going to angel a biopic to tune of $300,000, with Tucker producing and directing." Tucker considered the project off because he had to either provide half the budget, or make it entirely with Luciano's funding and go along "with a set of conditions" that "would have pretty much white-washed" him.[121] Tucker's former plans had been noticed by Hollywood gossip heavyweight Louella Parsons, who scoffed at the idea that the project would get "past the Johnston office. There's too much bitterness against the ex-vice lord . . .."[122] Much more revealing was an item from columnist Leonard Lyons' late October "Lyons Den" column:

> I wrote to Luciano about it, and he replied from his home in Naples. "In reference to that story about me making a deal to make a movie of my life, I assure you that there is no foundation whatsoever to it."[123]

The following week saw reiterations of the news that the project was shelved. Entertainment writer Erskine Johnson reported on November 3: "'I thought maybe I could film it my way,' Tucker told me, 'and tell the truth. But Luciano insisted on showing that he was framed and this I couldn't do.'"[124]

Many mobsters loved the glamour of show business, and Luciano was one. Orson Welles remembered running into Luciano in Europe, the gangster buttering him up about making a movie of his life before Welles improvised some excuse to disappear. According to Welles, "'Wouldn't you like to make a picture about me, Orsten?' he used to say. 'The real-life story of me?'"[125] But even with no reason to put much stock in his word, the likeliest scenario is that Luciano was not bluffing when he denied being associated with Tucker. He would have been unhappy with anything but a big Hollywood treatment, and he would not have sought out the services of an unknown. Tucker was getting press for himself by attaching his name to Luciano's; he knew that the film would never be made in the studio system, and recognized an easy opportunity for publicity, and a long-shot chance at making a movie.

Whether or not Tucker's stunt attracted undesired attention from the law (or other parties), he did not stay down long. While his late-life recollections do not include the Luciano project, he remembered something else up his sleeve at what must have been the same time. Asked whose idea it was to use a gorilla suit and a "diving helmet" for the costume, Tucker had a detailed memory of how *Robot Monster* began:

> In one of my in-between pictures, there was a situation where I was delivering telegrams for Western Union. At that time, Chavez Ravine had been abandoned for later clearance. At that time there were still a lot of houses

> standing. I had never heard of the place. The telephone at the telegram office that I was working out of serviced a number of [a] few people still living there.

Chavez Ravine, a section of northern Los Angeles, was home to working class families, the majority of them Hispanic. It was annexed by the city in the late forties as part of a national public housing movement; part of the area had been depopulated and torn down by the early fifties. But after enthusiasm for public housing cooled, the city looked at other plans and, after years of wrangling, made a deal for the property with the Brooklyn Dodgers baseball team. Rod Serling, a native of New York state, snuck some barbs about the Dodgers move into *The Twilight Zone*. The second season episode "The Whole Truth"

WADE WILLIAMS DIST.

The ruins of Chavez Ravine, as seen in *Robot Monster*.

ends with a sardonic reference to being "at Chavez Ravine watching the Dodgers" in Serling's closing voice-over. And in season four's "On Thursday We Leave for Home," one member of a marooned space colony asks a rescuing space pilot, "What city has the Dodgers now?" and is answered, "Still Los Angeles." But even when the city-controlled Chavez Ravine was intended for housing, the project was questionable. In a depressing and revealing comment, architect Richard Neutra spoke with condescension of "the present charm of rural backwardness" that he was going to remove, and won praise and emulation for the thirteen-storey structures he proposed with colleague Robert Alexander.[126] It is difficult to imagine how life in a thirteen-storey concrete block would be an improvement over life in a real home, no matter the improvement in sanitation. One man raised in Chavez Ravine remembered, "With all the studies I see about what people need to grow up healthy, what psychologists say, that's what we had."[127]

Phil Tucker recalled,

> One night, I had a telegram to deliver there, and I *really* got lost. And I got so lost I had to come back and leave the car there, and go back the next morning to get the car. When I got back the next morning, I looked around and I thought, "Wow! Shit! This is fantastic! It looks like a war-torn [country]. I'll make a picture for it." And I sat down that morning and came up with the basic design for *Robot Monster.*

Tucker's reaction was no personal eccentricity. Interviewed by Harry Medved in the early eighties, gorilla suit actor George Barrows remembered the area with as much amazement as Tucker:

> And we also shot it where Dodger Stadium is now.
>
> *Chavez Ravine.*
>
> That's right. And what they did, when we went into it I didn't realize it, but they had been razing all these homes of these people to get 'em out of there to put in Dodger Stadium, and it looked like a bomb had hit through there. It was the most amazing thing I've ever seen. They didn't quite get everything, the effect that you see by your eye, but that was the idea was it was supposed to have been devastated by these robot monsters from another planet.[128]

By Tucker's own recollection, *Robot Monster* came to exist because he found an opportunity. It was perhaps something of an artistic inspiration, but it was far more the logical recognition of a means to better pursue his show business dream. But although Tucker remembered creating the concept of the film, he did not end up with writing credit, an honor that went to another name simultaneously unusual and unremembered. Wyott Ordung is a largely forgotten figure who amassed a modest number of writing and acting credits, most of them in the years immediately following *Robot Monster*. Born May 23, 1922 (five years older than Tucker, nearly to the day), in Shanghai, China, Wyott Bernard Ordung's background was a great contrast to

Tucker's, yet mixed with notable similarities. His father was a career Navy man who died soon after the outbreak of World War II, and was posthumously awarded a Gold Star.[129] As the *Los Angeles Times* reported on April 6, 1942:

> Wyott Thomas Ordung, who enlisted in the United States Navy 27 years ago, has been reported missing in action following the sinking of the Langley, his wife and son have been informed in a telegram from the Navy Department. Ordung, 44, served aboard the aircraft tender as chief quartermaster.
>
> The first news of the sinking of the naval craft, released Friday afternoon, did not reach the wife, Mrs. Bella Ordung, or her son Bernard, 19, and it was not until Saturday afternoon when the Navy Department's telegram reached them that they knew Ordung was missing. . . . Mrs. Ordung last saw her husband in Manila in November of 1940, while the son visited his father last in September of 1939 on a trip to Hawaii.
>
> "It's been my ambition for quite a while to serve in the American Volunteer Group in China," the son said last night, "and now I'm more certain than ever that I want to get in. It's a personal war for me."[130]

The February 1942 sinking of the USS *Langley* was foremost a tragic loss of Navy personnel, while also an illustration of how rapidly seacraft had evolved in a few decades. According to author Dwight R. Messimer, the once radically innovative

USS *Jupiter*, decommissioned in March 1920 for refitting, was commissioned two years later as the *Langley*, then a slow and bulky prototype for landing airplanes at sea that would be badly out of date by the late thirties. Mobilized after Pearl Harbor, the *Langley* was expected to have a slim chance against the Japanese. The ship's crew enjoyed some frivolity in the tense first weeks of deployment when anti-aircraft gunners shot at a stubborn white dot in the sky, amusing those aboard the nearby USS *Pecos* with their ineffectual attempt to fire at the planet Venus (one officer noted that ammunition was likely insufficient for "interplanetary target practice"). But as Messimer notes, the lighthearted incident was a grim foreshadowing of the ship's impending fate; its inability to hit real targets proved fatal in combat.[131]

Young Bernard soon joined, enlistment records identifying him as "Wyott B. Ordung." Recorded as single with no dependents, he had completed high school and was occupied as a "nurse, practical," at 120 pounds and five feet, two inches. He enlisted in the Army on July 28, 1942, with the notation "Branch Immaterial—Warrant Officers, USA."[132] (*Daily Variety* once referred to him in 1953 as the "smallest flame thrower in World War II . . .."[133]) His father's death may have caused Bernard to list himself as "Wyott Ordung" on his film credits, but he was known socially as "Barney" from the middle name that he favored. While some have mockingly wondered if the name Ordung meant "gilded excrement," it is also a German word meaning law or rule, used by Quakers. (Walter Winchell gave Ordung a one-sentence mention in a 1954 column for his "odd" name.[134]) Likely related, there was an Ordung family in

Wyott Ordung in a 1951 *Dick Tracy* episode.

Massachusetts since at least the 19th century, including a Thomas Ordung, listed in a reference on Leominster, Massachusetts. Thomas was "a native of Sparneck, Germany," who "has kept a fish market here for the past seven years."[135] This nautical connection was probably not coincidental, as news of Wyott Sr.'s posthumous 1946 Gold Star was reported in the *Fitchburg Sentinel*, listing him as one of "90 Leominster boys who made the supreme sacrifice in World War II."[136] (Missing in action since 1942, his official death date was December 15, 1945.)

Evident in his film and TV performances, Barney Ordung had exotic features for the era and played a variety of ethnic types. As his long-time buddy and occasional collaborator Ewing Miles "Lucky" Brown remembered with a chuckle, "We used to call him 'Buddha Head.'"[137] Ordung's diminutive stature and somewhat Eastern appearance was the result of his Russian mother ("a little, tiny thing," according to Brown), who was reputedly a refugee from Soviet communism. According to the State of California's death index, she was born Bella Rahmulev in Russia in September 1892. She and Wyott were listed on a ship manifest for "alien passengers" headed for America in December 1935. Son "Boris Ordung" was 13 years old on this report, which matches his May 1922 birth. Bella was listed here as "Bertha Voitzman Helenius Ordung," age 42, which is only a year off from her official birth year. Heading for San Francisco, both were interestingly listed as of Finnish nationality and ethnicity, and both previously living in Hankow, China. (Wyott Sr. is listed on a naval record as having enlisted in Hankow.) Both were listed as speaking English and Russian, with Wyott also a Chinese speaker. "Mother and father deceased no other relatives," the manifest stated regarding his mother's residence in China.

While his father's military career greatly influenced Ordung, his mother's interest in the supernatural was just as important. As Brown remembered, "She was very much into the occult and she was a piece of work; she was very funny. She could read tea leaves for you." Ordung was the same, with strong beliefs in past lives and psychic phenomena. His Eastern origins also gave him a broad background in Asian culture, evidenced by his lengthy, unproduced TV miniseries script *The Yangtze Pirates.*[138] As Brown remembered, Chinese restaurant workers were often pleasantly surprised by Ordung's ability to converse with them in their own tongue. But he also had a streak of sheer eccentricity:

> In my last lifetime, vultures ate me up . . . if you say "Hawk!" or "Eagle!" or anything with a beak, I'll go through that window. . . . I am a professional psychic, and I went to college. There are only seven Esoteric Esotericians in the world. I am a Master of Esoteric Science. The Dai Lama of Tibet is also one.[139]

Ordung was not just having a bad day when he made the above comments, as the same sort of impressions colored the recollections of many who knew him. Various parties later described him as "a screwball," "a strange person," and "truly one of the most unusual characters in Hollywood."[140] Interviewed at length by Johnny Legend in his only published complete interview (*Fangoria*, 1984), Ordung spoke about his belief in reincarnation, corresponding fear of birds, vivid near-drowning and mass-vomiting experiences, all while obsessively using the number seven. As Legend noted, Ordung was fiercely individualistic, fast-moving, and intense, "a short, stocky, two-fisted 'get-the-lead-out' type of guy."[141] Ordung's Western he-man and Eastern mystic binary personality was unique, and the interplay of this psychological yin and yang may have hurt his career more than anything else. After the war, Ordung was one of several veterans studying at the Actors' Lab in Los Angeles, which had famous faculty and students but specialized in G.I. Bill recipients. One was Audie Murphy, the most decorated U.S. combat soldier of World War II and later movie star. Deceptively small and boyish, Murphy had killed 250 or more enemy combatants and suffered from post-war nightmares and bouts of depression. While the Lab was part of the growing trend toward naturalistic method acting, the faculty avoided exercises where veterans reenacted war experiences.[142] But actor Philip Pine later remembered Murphy performing combat skits, and recalled that Ordung was his accomplice.[143] And as Ewing Brown remembered one production:

> We needed uniforms and equipment. Wyott went over to Fort MacArthur, and we wound up with a truckload of uniforms, weapons, belts, webs, K rations, [and] C rations. We were the best-dressed soldiers on the stage.[144]

And likely a few years later in 1951, Ordung was part of the cast of Samuel Fuller's *Fixed Bayonets!*, the combat veteran director surrounding his actors with flashes to stimulate some realistic performances. "I've never set off explosions closer to the actors than on this picture," stated technician Larry Chapman.[145]

Ordung's bonding with the natural warrior Murphy reinforces the strong individuality that Johnny Legend detected, and the importance he placed on his military service. If Ordung also had difficulty reconciling his war experiences with the domestic aftermath, that trait could explain his eccentric qualities, and it may also explain how he became *Robot Monster*'s screenwriter. In addition to being interviewed by Legend, Ordung was interviewed in July 1983 by the late Ray Zone, 3-D expert and author. Briefly quoted in Zone's 2012 book *3-D Revolution*, Ordung specified, "Tucker came to see me in 1952 when I was living in Sun Valley. I acted in a picture for him. I had done 18 pictures by the time I had met him."[146] Minus a few details, Ordung remembered largely the same story for Legend's interview, recalling that he met Tucker "at a studio," acted for him and was paid "straight." It could have been an exploitation project, or one of his long lost TV pilots, but the important point is that Tucker chose Ordung out of the many he met in Hollywood to write a script from his idea. With Tucker's own time in the Marines, he and Ordung had wartime experiences in common and easily could have become friends around them. But if they were too similar—independent, stubborn, and plucky—the clash of similar personalities may have wrecked their partnership.

Ordung reminisced to Legend,

> [Tucker] came to my house with his wife, Francine, and said, "I have a picture I want you to write. It's called *Googie-Eyes.*" Francine said, "Wyott, I don't think he's making any sense." He was talking to me about a comedy, a monster comedy. I said, "Phil, I think you've got the wrong guy. I cannot write comedy." Phil said, "It's this Googie-Eyes, a guy with big protruding eyes . . ." Francine explained, and this is how *Robot Monster* started, she said, "Wyott, Phil wants to produce and direct a picture about the last four people on the face of the Earth after an atom bomb attack." And I said, "That's not funny. Especially if you're the one who gets your ass blown off!" She said, "That's what I've been trying to tell him since last night." Then Phil said, "Ro-Man." I said, "What the hell's a Ro-Man?" Phil said, "That's short for Robot-Man!" I said, "Okay, what's he gonna look like?" Phil said, "I don't know."[147]

Tucker's wife, Francine, was only named in Ordung's memories of the old days although, as will be discussed, George Barrows also remembered a wife on the set. Writer and performer Trustin Howard met Tucker around this time, but remembered this aspect of Tucker's life uncertainly. Said Howard, "I don't know if he had just gone for a divorce. When I went to Phil's home, there was never a wife around."[148]

By Ordung's account *Robot Monster* was Tucker's idea. It sounds just like what must have gone through his mind while wandering in the ruins of Chavez Ravine, yet he did not know how to bring it to the screen. But it is genuinely surprising and bizarre that Ordung claimed that Tucker wanted the film to be a comedy, appropriate as it is in light of the finished film. The monster movie craze first kicked into gear in the early fifties, and there was likely little audience for a spoof.[149] The one sensible explanation for why Tucker wanted to turn his "war-torn country" drama into goofy comedy lies in his plan to call the film *Googie-Eyes.* Googie-eyes—white plastic circles with a small, loose black dot covered by clear plastic—were cheap, dime-store amusements and the title's implication is clear: Tucker knew that he could not create a convincing monster for no money, and had to find some way to sell audiences on a ridiculous one. Therefore, the film would be a comedy right down to the title.

But the concept simply did not make sense as Ordung and Francine knew and, more than likely, even Tucker knew that it would not work. He could not resolve the concept into a coherent story, and sought Ordung's help, suggesting greater writing abilities and experience. The concept may have soon died with

Ordung's reaction but another part of his account is fascinating, for it implies a distinction between "Googie-Eyes" and an additional monster already called "Ro-Man." Tucker did not know what this "Robot-Man" would look like, a distinct contrast to the "big protruding eyes" of the first monster. Googie-Eyes might not have been a conventional monster at all, as Tucker described him as a *guy*. Tucker may have had a bug-eyed actor like Jerry Colonna or Jack Elam in mind for the role, which could have been a bumbling human main character trying to survive the activities of Ro-Man in this supposedly funny situation. It was forward-looking of Tucker to turn such material into comedy. The first detonation of atomic weapons was less than a decade in the past, and few comedies were yet made about life after a nuclear war. (A Jack Broder comedy about a man's fear of the bomb, *Run for the Hills,* would in fact play on a double bill with *Robot Monster* when *Hills* debuted in Los Angeles in June.) When Stanley Kubrick's *Dr. Strangelove* (1964) satirized worldwide Armageddon a decade later, it was startling. Tucker's Googie-Eyes concept illustrates his resourceful imagination, and the lengths he was willing to go to make a film.

Jerry Colonna (*left*) and Jack Elam.

But Tucker asserted that Ordung's involvement was almost non-existent:

> *Okay, so first of all, Wyott Ordung. How did he get the story on the film, and you came up with the idea?*
> He had nothing to do with it, he typed it for me. In return for typing I told him I'd give him writer credit, and if I ever got any money from the film, I'd give him some.
>
> *I see, but you really wrote the film, he just typed it up?*
> Right.

If *Robot Monster* was going to be his first directing credit, Tucker might have happily spread around other credits. Some famous directors, such as Howard Hawks and Alfred Hitchcock, contentedly went uncredited for extensive script contributions, but Tucker had clearly not reached their level. In the ultra-frugal world of exploitation filmmaking, it is unlikely that he would have been unwilling to do his own typing. He may have believed that Ordung's contributions were minimal or unusable, but retained his credit as a payment for effort, or just out of friendship. But Ordung was already beginning to get ahead in acting, and such a rugged individualist would not have wanted charity. As the March 26, 1952, *Hollywood Reporter* noted, he had been cast in the Cold War shocker *Invasion U.S.A.,*[150] most likely as one of the Soviet attackers in a film that would soon lend bombed city footage to *Robot Monster.* Then on September 25, not long before Tucker initiated his Lucky Luciano project, the *Reporter* noted that Ordung had "been signed by Talent Associates for a top role in a Family Theatre *Life of Christ* telefilm."[151] Tucker might have been doing Ordung a favor, but Ordung was at no obvious disadvantage.

How likely is it that Tucker wrote the entire script himself? The years leading up to *Robot Monster* were the "hottest period" of his writing, and he remembered writing and selling science fiction stories at around the time of *Robot Monster*:

> At that time, I was writing a lot of science fiction, most of which, if not all of which, was selling very well in the little magazines (and you get two-fifty, three hundred a story, and so forth like that). I was very much into science fiction. I used a different name for everything I ever wrote, which I'm now sorry about. Because some of it was pretty good stuff; some of it, I can't even remember. Once I read a story, and didn't realize that I wrote it.

As Tucker Jr. remembered about his father's interest in science fiction, "He was a fan of the genre." The above would make it seem that Tucker was ideal for writing a sci-fi screenplay, but the claim is still hard to take seriously. For as Tucker Jr. also admitted of his father, "With him, you know, you never know whether to believe it or not." His penchant for exaggeration, combined with diabetic exhaustion, was probably getting away from him when he made this claim. Young, unknown Ray Bradbury made his first professional sale to the short-lived *Super Science Stories* for $27.50 in 1941 (at a rate of a half-cent per word),[152] and Tucker would not have easily earned as much as $250 for a story sale in the forties. Says Bill Warren, "I'm skeptical about the amount paid; I don't think anyone but the top writers got anything like $250 in that period."[153] According to extremely prolific science fiction veteran Robert Silverberg, "The magazines would pay you anywhere from one to three cents a word: a 5,000-word story therefore would bring you $50 to $150, before such things as your agent's commission and the exactions of the Internal Revenue Service were figured in."[154] Silverberg began publishing in the fifties but Frank Gruber, high-volume craftsman of mystery and Western tales, noted that in the mid-thirties, "The base rate of pay at the majority of the pulp magazines was one cent a word."[155]

With the continued frequency of penny-per-word rates into the fifties, Tucker was very unlikely to earn $250 for a story. He would have been a busy pulp writer to beat the odds and manage such a large sale, yet he has no fiction credits to this day, even with such contemporary aids as the Internet Speculative Fiction Database. Tucker's claim to have used pseudonyms seems a thin disguise for having never published. With his name on several exploitation films, it is hard to believe that he did not want credit in the more creative and respectable field of writing. Authors are desperate to establish an identity and a paying audience, for which a recognizable name is essential, even if a consistent pseudonym. Silverberg admits that he wrote under several pseudonyms along with his own name because he worked at a lightning pace and made a living from his stories, but he is an exception.

But while Tucker is hard to believe on the question of authorship, Ordung added a fascinating additional twist: "How can I tell people I didn't write this piece of crap? . . . I didn't recognize [the finished film]." While he and Tucker had very different memories of the film's origins, they were in agreement on three important points. First, both agree that Tucker and no one else had the basic, original idea for the film. Second, Ordung says that Tucker wanted to make a movie about life in the aftermath of nuclear devastation, and Tucker said his inspiration for the film was an abandoned neighborhood that looked "like a war-torn country." Third, both men state—in very different ways—that the finished film was not the product of a script by Ordung. In fact, if one ignored Tucker's assertion that Ordung did nothing but type the script, everything in their statements gels. Even Ordung's claim that Tucker initially intended it to be a comedy is only unmentioned by Tucker, not contradicted. Both men were probably telling the essential truth about the genesis of *Robot Monster.*

And both men may have also been unaware of a third party involved in that writing. According to his 1992 *Variety* obituary by professor Joseph McBride, blacklisted comedy screenwriter Frederic I. Rinaldo worked on the *Robot Monster* script. While McBride did not remember much about that tidbit of Rinaldo's career (which included a notable string of Abbott and Costello movies), he picked it up while interviewing Rinaldo's writing partner Robert Lees.[156] "His scriptwriting during the blacklist era was sporadic," McBride noted, "including work on the British *Robin Hood* and *Lancelot* TV series and on the 1953 3-D feature *Robot Monster*."[157] Although Rinaldo's involvement is not established beyond this reference, it is likely. As will be discussed, the use of blacklisted talent is a recurring element in the *Robot Monster* production.

Tucker was ready to film by the beginning of 1953. The *Hollywood Reporter* printed the following notice on January 29:

> **Tucker Shooting *Robot***
>
> Tucker Productions, headed by producer-director Phil Tucker, will start shooting *Robot Killer* next week at Quality Studios.[158]

The title *Robot Killer* suggests that Tucker accepted Ordung's advice that the film could not be *Googie-Eyes,* or anything else comedic. It would be an unapologetic monster movie, even if there was no money for a good monster onscreen. As Tucker was producing as well as directing, and could not have had deep resources, the budget was either incredibly low or supported by a backer or two (in which case it was probably still incredibly low). And like an exploitation filmmaker, he went to the trouble of forming a production company that probably consisted of himself alone: "Tucker Productions." But the fact that the production was scheduled for filming at Quality Studios (or Pictures) is surprising and a little strange. The finished *Robot Monster* was filmed on location and, apart from a few shots of the boss Ro-Man and infrequent special effects, none of it could have been done in a studio.

Was *Robot Killer* a completely different movie than *Robot Monster*? Filming at Quality Studios is logical in the sense that his connection with the exploitation world of Merle Connell and George Weiss preceded his most famous credit at least as far back as August 1952, but it also casts his fascination with Chavez Ravine in an odd light. Tucker was resourceful enough to dig into a difficult filming location, and the family scenes in the finished film were shot in Chavez Ravine, with the Ro-Man scenes in Bronson Canyon. Tucker could not have saved money by constructing a fake cave or ruined house on Connell's soundstage, so he probably listed Quality Studios in the press because it sounded better than not filming at a studio at all.

The next day's *Hollywood Reporter* included *Robot Killer* in the weekly Friday list of "Pictures in Preparation," with a start date of February 6.[159] The project appeared once more, two weeks later in the February 18 *Reporter,* before disappearing completely.[160] (*Variety* made no mention of it.) On the same page that featured a story on Hollywood's emerging fascination with "3-D Production Going in High Gear," *Robot Killer* was included in a list of "Three-Dimension and Wide-Screen Production[s]." The company, producer, and director credits were unchanged, and for color process "Black & White" was listed. But under the heading of "Process," the word was "Realdepth." Whether or not *Robot Killer* was *Robot Monster,* Tucker was already working in a three-dimensional process, or at least creating that impression. Probably not so much as a foot of *Robot Killer* was shot, but the important point is that Tucker succeeded in getting his name and that of his project in print. All he needed now was an interested party to put up the money.

4

Class-Exploitation

> **Independent Producers**
>
> Can furnish cash financing for number of first class independent productions. Submit your package by detailed letter . . ..[161]

Whether or not this ad from the March 4, 1953, *Hollywood Reporter* was placed by producer Al Zimbalist and whether or not Phil Tucker responded to it as a way of resurrecting his recently scrapped *Robot Killer* project, something like that scenario must have played out. In one month, Tucker went from *Robot Killer* dropping off the *Reporter* schedule to being filmed in a head-spinning four days as *Robot Monster.* If Tucker had never been filming *Killer* but only seeking the attention of an investor, the effort paid off.

Zimbalist's filmography might not suggest that he got into the movies because he just loved show business from day one, but the evidence is that he did. At the very least, he loved

WADE WILLIAMS DIST.

Al Zimbalist in March 1953.

working in publicity. The 1954 *Motion Picture and Television Almanac* states that Zimbalist joined the Warner publicity department in some capacity in 1929, but with the erroneous birth year of 1916. The Social Security Death Index places his birth at March 3, 1910, but it may have been 1909, according to the 1940 federal census. Albert Zimbalist was 31 in 1940, according to the census, born in Russia but living in Los Angeles with parents Nathan and Rebecca and his younger brother Max. He had completed his education through the eighth grade, had been living in the same residence five years previous and was married, officially employed as a "Technician Laboratory."[162] For a time during the late forties he was employed by Irvin Shapiro's distribution company Film Classics, leaving it in early 1949, according to the 1954 *Almanac*.[163]

As will be seen through the course of this book, Zimbalist was friendly with Hollywood's elite, despite the fact that his career skated on the bottom of the studio system, when it was not outright involved in independent distribution. One reason for this connection may have been MGM producer Sam Zimbalist, whose relationship with Al Zimbalist has never exactly been clear. Gabe Essoe in *Tarzan of the Movies* states that

Sam Zimbalist was Al Zimbalist's father,[164] while Harry and Michael Medved said that Al "tried to encourage confusion between himself and Sam Zimbalist of MGM (no relation) . . .."[165] Entertainment columnist Mike Connolly agreed that they were "no kin,"[166] while that is disputed by the *Reporter*'s July 1960 statement that "Nathan Zimbalist, 74, father of independent producer Al Zimbalist and uncle of the late MGM producer Sam Zimbalist, died yesterday of a heart attack . . .."[167] If they were not cousins, it is nonetheless true that Al enjoyed an arrangement with MGM for a time. As the *Reporter* noted on October 9, 1959, he was given "a new non-exclusive contract with MGM as an independent producer . . .."[168] Sam was born in Russia in 1901, making their relation possible, but what seems certain is that neither Al nor Sam was related to Efrem, Efrem Jr., or Stephanie Zimbalist.

Soon after Al Zimbalist's 1929 start at Warner Brothers he appeared in *Variety* in connection with the studio's "third annual boat ride up the Hudson . . .. Young Al Zimbalist is publicizing the affair, and figures attendance by 1,000 boys and girls."[169] By 1933 Zimbalist had left a position at the Newark Warner office and by 1934 was the studio's publicity director in St. Louis. He was also married by this point to Bernice Higgins, who would later have a single film credit for "research" on *King Dinosaur* (1955).[170] By 1936, Zimbalist had resigned from a publicity job with St. Louis Amusement Co. and was working in Philadelphia in early 1941.[171] Described by *Variety* as a "Warner exploiteer," Zimbalist organized a stunt at Philadelphia's Karlton theater with "a man dressed as Ferdinand, the Bull, picketing the house protesting against 'unfair competition' of

Elsie, the Borden Cow." But everything else in Zimbalist's career pales next to the gall of one particular bit of publicity that soon followed. According to *Variety* in April 1941, "Zimbalist sent a letter to Prime Minister Churchill asking him to endorse the picture *Little Men,* which opened at the Karlton three weeks ago." With the harrowing Battle of Britain just won in October and the war against Hitler still raging, a response came from "Churchill's secretary" that Churchill "has considered your suggestion, but he has asked me to explain that, owing to extreme pressure of other work he regrets it will not be possible for him to do as you suggest."[172]

Still in Philadelphia, Zimbalist in October was "elected president of the Warner Club," and in December 1942, with the United States firmly entrenched in the war, Zimbalist helped organize the Philadelphia branch's "Warnerettes," a group of "gals in the office" who would be pen pals with servicemen.[173] In January 1943, Zimbalist told *Variety* that "Warner Club members have purchased more than $120,000 worth of war bonds . . . ."[174] But Zimbalist left Warner Brothers for RKO Theatres by February 3, and in summer 1944 was paid $1,000 for a story idea. Perhaps unrelated to RKO was *Radio Canteen of 1945,* a prospective show that was "making the agency rounds" and was "based on an idea and script by Al Zimbalist."[175] *Variety* reported in 1947 that Zimbalist "was allocated a budget of $100,000 to handle exploitation campaigns" by "Film Classics, formerly a reissue outfit" that was "moving into the distribution field with new product." Film Classics had also just "filed for an injunction . . . to restrain Astor Pictures from advertising or selling" a film competing with their *The Spirit of West Point.* Featuring Army football stars Felix "Doc" Blanchard and Glenn Davis as themselves, the Film Classics drama faced competition from Astor's planned *The Game of Games,* reportedly with the players "seen only from a distance in hazy outline. Short was enlarged from U.S. Navy pictures of a game which were originally shot in 16m."[176] Six years later, Zimbalist would sell distribution rights for *Robot Monster* to Astor.

Leaving Film Classics in 1949, Zimbalist was an assistant on a pair of Edward L. Alperson releases in 1951 and '52 and, as Phil Tucker was riding the coat tails of Lucky Luciano and pondering an apocalyptic landscape, Zimbalist unleashed his own plans. As covered across several months of the *Hollywood Reporter* beginning in August 1952, he moved aggressively into film production—or at least into creating the impression of it:

> Alfred N. Zimbalist and Harold Nebenzal have formed Motion Picture Artists, Inc., and have established headquarters at Motion Picture Center for the production of films. Zimbalist is president, and Nebenzal is v.p. Also associated in the venture is George Moskov.[177]

Then on September 12, the *Reporter* ran a more detailed look at the same basic story, noting that the plan of Zimbalist and friends was

> . . . to specialize exclusively in "class-exploitation" pictures in Eastman color. The films will be designed for top billing in exploitation houses and lower half of double bills in houses playing duals.

> First to roll, in about ten days, will be *Miss Robinson Crusoe,* by Ricardo Yriondo, from a serial published in Spain. Amanda Blake and George Nader head the cast. George Moskov is production supervisor.
>
> Two other properties being scripted are *Half-Caste Girl,* by Major K.W.L. McDonald, and *Virgin of Cadiz,* by Yriondo.[178]

Zimbalist was likely aware that he might have to start on the bottom, while his career shows evidence of wanting to be part of respectable Hollywood. With decades of working in Hollywood publicity under his belt, Zimbalist nonsensically described his projects as "class-exploitation," a paradox that allowed him to hold his nose while slumming. The venues he intended for these proposed films were realistic, and the titles listed at the end were perfectly exploitation-ready (*Virgin of Cadiz* could have been intended with religious connotations, but it probably was not). But the above story is especially invaluable for its early view of the template that Zimbalist followed through decades of using the press to gin up interest in his projects.

First and most significant is the fact that Zimbalist was announcing a film whose title riffed on that of another current production. The October 9 *Reporter* noted that producers the King Brothers had hired director Kurt Neumann (who would later work with Zimbalist) to direct "Robinson Crusoe," an American-British production to include location shooting in the Canary Islands.[179] While the King Brothers' film was announced later, Zimbalist's was likely announced with it in mind for he had a habit through his career of capitalizing on current properties going on around him. Second, Zimbalist revealed a tendency to jump on the current bandwagon for new ways of presenting films, such as making them in Eastman color. Third, Zimbalist's press image was one of always having several projects stewing in the pot with different authors involved, and preferably with "class" names. It is not clear, for example, if Major K.W.L. McDonald ever existed or wrote a screenplay, but his name was perfect for a well-traveled British Army officer with a hint of Scottish ruggedness. Zimbalist itemized some projects in the press that seem to have had no outside existence and were likely verbal window dressing, but *Miss Robinson Crusoe* was filmed and eventually released as *Miss Robin Crusoe.* Female lead Amanda Blake, then little known, would become beloved as Miss Kitty on the long-running *Gunsmoke.* But more pertinent was her co-star in Zimbalist's film, George Nader, who would soon star in *Robot Monster.*

On October 14, the *Reporter* announced that *Miss Robinson Crusoe* was wrapping that day at Motion Picture Center, and reaffirmed that it was in color.[180] Eventually, the *Reporter* and *Variety* printed essentially interchangeable reports on January 13, 1953. *Variety*'s headline noted: "Geraghty, Al Zimbalist to Make Indie Film." The new partnership, between Zimbalist and "Maurice Geraghty, director-writer" (the *Reporter*'s description) was called Shamrock Productions and was housed at Goldwyn Studios. According to the *Reporter*:

> Their first picture, *Miss Robinhood,* written and directed by Geraghty from his published story, is slated to roll in Pathecolor about Feb. 23. Zimbalist will produce.[181]

To emphasize, this new project with a new partner and a new production company was called *Miss* ***Robinhood****,* not to be confused with the previous *Miss* ***Robinson Crusoe****.* Zimbalist was just maybe pummeled by fate into taking on a project with a similar title as the previous one, but it seems more likely that that was not the case. (And it also seems non-coincidental that a British film titled *Miss Robin Hood* had been released in 1952.) Zimbalist had at least one more ambitious announcement, unveiled in the February 27 *Reporter*:

> Al Zimbalist, who just produced *Miss Robinson Crusoe,* has bought a published magazine story, "Adam and Eve," by Guy Reed Ritchie, for filming in color at the Goldwyn studios.[182]

With the name Guy Reed Ritchie (not to be confused with contemporary British director Guy Ritchie), Zimbalist was packing as much upper-crusty class into three names as possible. There is no more evidence for the existence of Guy Reed Ritchie than for the previously employed McDonald, but Ritchie's virtual career outlasted that of the major, an association that continued with Zimbalist for years and had an important bearing on *Robot Monster* itself. Zimbalist's next reported project was not illusory. Just one day before filming began on *Robot Monster,* the *Reporter* announced:

> **Zimbalist-Tucker Start First Film**
>
> Another 3-D process—this one using one camera without mirrors and which can be shown with only one projector but requires audiences to use viewers—makes its

> bow this week, when Third Dimension Pictures, Inc., headed by Al Zimbalist and Phil Tucker, starts filming of *Robot Monster* in the Trudepth system. The process was worked out secretly and Tucker, who will act as producer and director on the feature, was instrumental in its development.
>
> A new type of viewer is required for Trudepth, according to Tucker, who said an order for 20,000,000 has been placed for showings of *Robot Monster*, which rolls tomorrow. Patents on the glasses have been applied for, and, pending notification from Washington, no details of the process will be divulged.
>
> Cast in the film on which Zambalist [sic] will be executive producer are George Nader, John Mylong, Selena Royle, Gregory Moffett, Pamela Paulson. It will be shot in black and white, although the Trudepth process also can use color.
>
> Clarence Eurist is assistant director on the film, headquarters for which are at the Samuel Goldwyn Studios. The picture will be finished without a release being set.[183]

Why did *Robot Killer* become *Robot Monster*? *Killer* was maybe too brutal, or just more horror than science fiction; perhaps *Monster* was more commercial, with the words "robot" and "monster" together perfectly selling the film's essence. (Wyott Ordung told Ray Zone that he "gave the script the title *Robot Monster*."[184]) And Zimbalist may have noticed in the March 10

Reporter that writer Crane Wilbur had completed two scripts for 3-D films at Warner Brothers (including *House of Wax*), and was negotiating to direct *The Monster* in 3-D.[185] Foremost of details in this announcement is the certainty that the production was put together in extreme haste. Television, the much-feared arrival of "movies at home," was increasingly popular by 1953, and according to the November 21, 1952, *Reporter*, the American film industry's condition was astonishingly dire, with all but a tiny handful of movies consistently losing money. The studios avoided complete disaster thanks to re-distribution of older titles, particularly to a solid foreign market, but still faced a grim situation:

> It is the general belief throughout the industry that, on current film operations every major company is losing money; that every Hollywood studio with the possible exception of Universal and Warners is operating in red figures and that the cuts in production costs have been negligible because of the big load every studio is carrying. All this and more must be a cause for some direct and decisive action in the immediate future and Hollywood should not be surprised to get an axing such as it has never before seen in the business.[186]

The pinch was not felt merely by the studios, but inevitably spread through the rest of the business. A January 3, 1953, feature in the exhibitors' trade publication *Harrison's Reports* quoted at length the disgusted reaction of many exhibitor heads to the recent decision by Republic Pictures to sell some of its back catalog to television. As one president noted, "One of the most important factors in the sales equation is goodwill and with one move Republic may have destroyed that factor." Another put it differently:

> Take heart, boys! You are not the only ones who apparently need to augment the old income with a few filthy bucks from outside activities. Republic Pictures just took on some outside activities too. . . . They must need the revenue desperately to keep on selling what they sell to us to our mortal enema—and we didn't misspell it.[187]

In the midst of unprecedented bad times, Hollywood would try anything to woo the fickle mass audience, but an outsider had to show them the solution. Sid Pink had been trying to break into show business here and there, including running a burlesque review in Los Angeles for a time during the late forties. He noticed radio writer Arch Oboler's *Five,* a barely released 1951 post-nuclear apocalypse drama and, impressed by the movie's odd feel, gave it a new ad campaign. In a brilliant move, he arranged to give it a premiere and have it covered on local television with (because some studio executive threatened her not to) Bette Davis hosting. The TV premiere and the movie were hugely successful, which lead to Pink producing Oboler's disastrous comedy *The Twonky* (about a malevolent, alien TV set). Leaving *The Twonky* unreleased until 1953, Pink and Oboler were both interested in, but hard-pressed to finance, a film about the hunt for the bloodthirsty lions known as "The Maneaters of Tsavo" (also depicted in *The Ghost and the Darkness* in 1996). It might have never been made, if not for

Arch Oboler promoting *Bwana Devil.*

more foolishness from Hollywood's elite studio bosses. Turned away by the major studios, Milton Gunzberg and his ophthalmologist brother Julian provided Pink and Oboler with a gimmick that got the project financed and made it massively successful.[188] By the end of 1952, the 3-D sensation *Bwana Devil* was so successful that Oboler was positioned to sell the $400,000 film to distributor Edward L. Alperson for as much as $2,000,000 thanks to its nationwide "record-breaking grosses."[189]

3-D movie fever, covering the entire fifties in the retroactive consciousness of pop culture, in reality gripped Hollywood only from late 1952 to mid-1954. But 3-D had long been a part of American culture, and did not enter the movies solely because of the Hollywood downturn. The stereoscope viewer was hugely popular in the 19th century, evolved into further variations in the 20th (including the View-Master for children), and eventually led to a post-World War II fad for stereoscopic photography as a hobby. Many celebrities got in on the craze, none more than General Dwight Eisenhower who was elected president right as Hollywood adopted 3-D in November 1952.[190] Despite the Hollywood elite's reticence, 3-D movies were a logical development, and there is every reason to believe that Tucker was eager to practice the format.

According to Jeff Joseph of the 3-D Film Preservation Fund, there was a 3-D rig that somehow wound its way through the hands of exploitation filmmakers during these years.[191] Dan Sonney and possibly others made some 3-D shorts during this time, and the circumstantial evidence is compelling that this could have been the equipment used to shoot *Robot Monster.* With Tucker's connections to exploitation filmmakers Merle Connell and George Weiss already well-established, it is worth noting that Sonney produced Connell's *A Night at the Follies* (1947) and was credited for "art direction" on Weiss' *Racket Girls* (1951). Sonney knew Tucker's exploitation bosses, and knew them exactly when Tucker was getting to know them.

Because of these connections, it is even more likely that the *Reporter* announcement's extravagant claims about the Trudepth 3-D process were only ballyhoo. And not only was the technology employed likely borrowed and well-used, there were really few technological innovations in 3-D film during the brief 1952-1954 craze. According to Hal Morgan and Dan Symmes' *Amazing 3-D,* the one notable innovation of the era was the printing of both left and right eye images on the same film frame. This improvement, debuting with 1954's *Creature from the Black Lagoon*, eliminated the need for interlocked projectors and the subsequent eye strain that could result when synchronization was off.[192] *Robot Monster* had no such innovation for, as can be seen on the Image DVD, it contained an intermission card.[193] In what might seem like just one more bizarre touch in a movie filled with them, *Robot Monster* needed an intermission for a completely logical reason: 3-D films playing on synched projectors needed intermission time for changing reels. Tucker and Zimbalist were pulling everyone's collective leg with their assertion that the Trudepth viewer was going to be patented, and that it would allow the use of only one camera. Remembering the shoot for a far superior 1953 science fiction 3-D film, Universal's *It Came from Outer Space*, actor Russell Johnson described the camera:

> A strange contraption, as I remember it. There were two mounted cameras facing each other with constant adjustments necessary. Anyway, each scene was staged with an imaginary line over which an actor or anything crossing it came off the screen into the audience [in] 3D.[194]

If Universal was using a bulky, two-camera 3-D rig, then chances are that so were Tucker and Zimbalist.

3-D was not being used as a means of presenting *Robot Monster* so much as *Robot Monster* existed as an excuse to showcase 3-D. And as Tucker remembered it, his homemade 3-D process was just as budget-savvy as every other aspect of the film:

> . . . to give you an idea of the kind of corners we cut, we shot it in 3-D . . .
>
> *You did shoot it in 3-D?*
>
> We did shoot it in 3-D. But we never printed up the second camera. We only printed the first camera, did the whole thing with one camera, and then simply matched slates [clapboards]. We made an indication on the soundtrack where the slates started for the other camera. And when we were all through, all we did was cut the negative to match that and so we never made a print, *ever*, of that second thing until we made a release print of it. And you'd be amazed how much money you saved right there. But that's the kind of techniques that were used throughout the making of the picture to cut down cost.

While Tucker's method was savvy it was, according to Joseph, nothing unusual in 3-D production. But Tucker's fond memory of saving money in this way nonetheless reinforces how well he understood the mechanics of filmmaking for being an outsider struggling to break into the closed shop of Hollywood.

Like the seemingly absurd intermission, Ro-Man's nonsensical bubble machine is explainable by way of the film's 3-D process. Drifting all over, this way and that, floating bubbles were an inexpensive but expansive 3-D effect. Tucker in fact did not remember the machine in terms of its slightly silly screen credit ("Automatic Billion Bubble Machine" by "N.A. Fisher Chemical Products"), but for what it brought to the film:

Who supplied the Automatic Billion Bubble Machine?
I don't remember now . . . it was a . . . [inaudible].

What did it actually do? Did it actually make bubbles, did it look like this?
Uh-huh.

[Referring to picture.] *This is not a TV antenna?*
Oh no, no, this is not the real bubble-making machine. The bubble-making machine I don't think was ever seen, but it supplied a vast amount of bubbles.

How was that constructed?
. . . it was a long time ago. It's a minor prop thing that you have a prop guy make for you. But the actual bubble-producing machine was made by somebody else who let us use it for the picture.

Tucker could not remember specific details, but nonetheless significantly remembered the bubble machine's role in the production; this indicates that the role of its cheap 3-D effect in the production was important to him. Actor Gregory Moffett recalled in a *Classic Images* interview with Michael Barnum, "It was the same bubble machine that Lawrence Welk used at the Aragon Ballroom. . . . I remember it not working one day and there was a significant amount of profanity about the fact that someone had forgotten the bubble material. It was at somebody's house and nobody had brought it." Moffett's memory verifies the importance of the effect; whether or not Lawrence Welk's bubble-maker was called an Automatic Billion Bubble

Machine and manufactured by N.A. Fisher Chemical Products, its use in the film was essential enough to cause "a significant amount of profanity."[195]

Along with Avil's "Stereo-Director" assistance on *Robot Monster,* Tucker was assisted in his 3-D exploration by director of photography Jack Greenhalgh, another seasoned veteran from the thirties, who did at least assistant work in the silent era. A World War II veteran, Greenhalgh appears to have been as competent and tough as every other hardcase from the Tucker milieu. *Daily Variety* reported in May 1950 that Greenhalgh had been trampled by a horse, an accident that did not seem to slow him down and did not prevent him from working on *Robot Monster* in 1953.[196] But most notably, Greenhalgh was cinematographer on the infamous 1936 exploitation classic *Tell Your Children,* far better known as *Reefer Madness.* Director Dwain Esper had made the even worse *Maniac* (1934), which Sonney produced. With these connections, it seems inevitable that Greenhalgh would work with Tucker, although it is uncertain just how large his contribution was. Avil's involvement was presumably just to help with the 3-D process, with Greenhalgh left mainly in charge, but accounts of the shoot suggest (as will be discussed in detail) that it may be impossible to know who was the dominant influence. What seems certain is that Greenhalgh was no less able than any of the other low-budget camera men like William C. Thompson. In *Poverty Row Horrors!,* Tom Weaver noted that in *Dead Men Walk* (1943), "Jack Greenhalgh's lensing is persuasive in lending a gray dankness to Fred Preble's sets."[197] Likewise, Don Miller explained that for Tim Holt's early forties cowboy movies, "Harry Wild was no longer the 'house' Western photographer, but picturesque contributions were offered by J. Roy Hunt, Nicholas Musuraca, and even Jack Greenhalgh, on the lot on loan from PRC."[198]

As a result of so successful an independent production as *Bwana Devil,* the major studios eagerly embraced the gimmick that propelled it and, by late January, *Variety* was reporting "Major Studios in 3-D Race," with technical details and news on various projects.[199] On February 2, *Variety* reported "10 Studios Prepping Variations of 3-D,"[200] and on February 18, the front page of the *Reporter* declared that 48 Warner Brothers-owned theaters were 3-D ready, or were in the process—the studio-owned theaters apparently not yet completely sold off.[201] (A March report on big studio 3-D projects in the *Pacific Stars and Stripes* even took time to note, "Producer Phil Tucker is employing Realdepth for *Robot Killer.*"[202]) But while there were soon high quality 3-D films such as *Kiss Me Kate* (1953) and *Dial M for Murder* (1954)—and even superior 3-D horror (*House of Wax* [1953]) and sci-fi (*It Came from Outer Space* [1953])—there were immediately dissenting voices on the wonder of three dimensions. Among them was Hollywood lion Cecil B. DeMille, his opinion summarized by *Harrison's* that early 3-D success was "due mainly to novelty appeal." Likewise, Dore Schary of MGM emphasized, "If somebody produces a great motion picture, you will go to see it whether it's in black-and-white, in color, round or flat."[203] There was also *Variety*'s George E. Phair, in a late January "Retakes" column:

While scientists are turning out miraculous inventions
The time is nigh when TV sets will picture three dimensions.
And you can sit at home and see, between dramatic scenes,
A three-dimension portrait of a can of pork and beans.[204]

Exhibitors and audiences had their own misgivings, many of them focused on the fact that to trick the human brain into seeing a 3-D image, the wearing of either polarized or anaglyphic glasses was unavoidable (at least with the technology of the time). The February 7, 1953, *Motion Picture Herald* ran a feature on 3-D with a picture of two Chicago women mass-sterilizing glasses, and promised that it "will be a familiar scene . . . ."[205] But the practice of cleaning glasses, done to eliminate the unappetizing and unsanitary aspects of sharing them, had its own downside. *Boxoffice* on March 28 reported the testing of an "odorless 3-D sterilizer" to eliminate the "odor which has annoyed patrons."[206] In late June, a Texas exhibitor complained in the *Reporter* about frustrated families leaving his drive-in early because of the dissatisfaction of children wearing glasses meant for adults, noting that "parents have actually been urged by their children to leave the drive-in theatre."[207] It was apparently no help when an advertisement from National Film Service appeared in a late March *Reporter*, promising, "Now you can get expendable 3-D glasses that are adjustable!"[208] In May 30, *Harrison's* had run similar comments from a Midwestern distributor:

THE WASHING OF THE GLASSES. This will be a familiar scene, the sterilisation of the Polaroid spectacles for third-dimension. Here the job is done in Chicago.

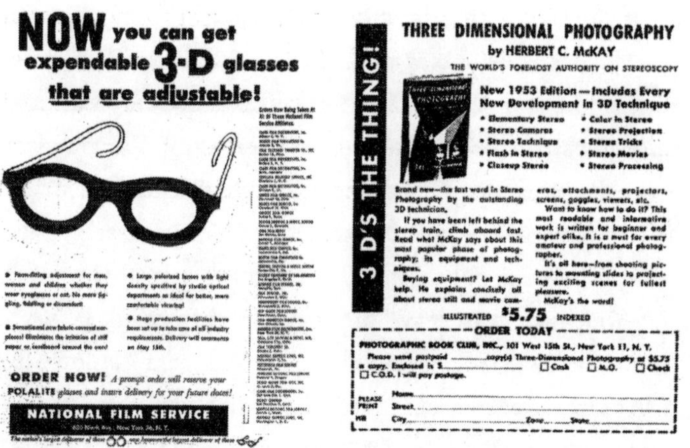

The fifties 3-D movie trend was short-lived, but intense within the film industry while it lasted.

> We'll bet a cigar box full of carbon stubs that, once we start getting a supply of 3-D pictures, and the novelty wears off, the theaters catering to family trade hears nine thousand complaints a week about how the kids can't wear the specs . . . any new system of projecting pictures has to be one without glasses . . ..[209]

Much of Hollywood already felt the same way in the midst of 3-D fever. Something was necessary to get audiences away from "movies at home" and back into theaters, and that something had to give them a viewing experience that was bigger, deeper, or wider than television. But with the illusion of depth constrained by a cumbersome filming process and an obnoxious viewing process, it was best to drop it altogether and concentrate on expanding the screen's other dimensions.

On Thursday, March 19, 1953, the very day that *Robot Monster* began its four-day shoot, Hollywood was in a state of incredible excitement. The Academy Awards were that night, but something far more unusual was in the air. *Variety*'s front-page headline was "CinemaScope Wins H'W'D Favor,"[210] while the *Reporter* trumpeted "Industry Hails CinemaScope":

> **THROW AWAY THE GLASSES**
>
> We've seen CinemaScope.
>
> We've heard the new Stereophonic sound.
>
> We've viewed the new crystal-clear Eastman color stock.
>
> The combination of the three, as shown at yesterday's test press showing of CinemaScope, is the answer to every exhibitor's prayers.

> This is it, boys. You can toss away the polaroids and relieve yourself of that worry because what was shown yesterday by 20th-Fox—and is available to all producers, distributors, and theatres—is as great an advance as the picture business, or any business, could stand in a century of progress. It's all any audience could desire when coupled with a good picture.[211]

Based on technology that went back to cinema's very origins, Fox's CinemaScope was the most significant of the many widescreen formats that would be trumpeted in movie advertising for the next two decades. While widescreen formats can be classified into a few basic types, CinemaScope was the first of any of them to enter the mainstream and set the pace for everything that followed after. While early filmmakers experimented with a number of different shapes, Hollywood had early on adopted a standardized ratio of 1.37 to 1, meaning that the screen was nearly square, just a little bit wide by one-third of its height. Television had been set at a barely different ratio of 1.33 to 1. But with the use of anamorphic lenses—by which an image twice as wide as standard film was compressed onto it, and then projected the same way—CinemaScope presented viewers with an image shape of around 2.5 to 1 (often 2.35:1 after matting). This astonishing expansion of width allowed filmmakers to create immersive and lifelike compositions by capitalizing on the reality that, with eyes set side by side, human range of vision is more wide than tall. It was a far more subtle and effective way of exploiting vision to its limits than 3-D, and required no glasses.

Even more immersive than the use of anamorphic lenses were the large frame widescreen formats of the late fifties and sixties, in which the lenses remained normal while the 65 or 70 millimeter film was wide-shaped and about four times the size of regular 35mm film, producing astonishingly sharp detail in epics like *Lawrence of Arabia.* (The 1959 *Ben-Hur* combined 65mm film with anamorphic lenses.) For lower budgets, a less dramatic widescreen effect could be achieved by simply matting (in camera, or in projector) movies shot on 35mm to a shape of around 1.85 to 1 (most often 1.66 to 1 in Europe). By the second half of 1953, Hollywood adapted the use of widescreen formats across the board in one form or other and subsequently only a handful of independent films were intended for projection at 1.37:1. As Harrison's noted on May 30, MGM was set for a widescreen aspect ratio of 1.75:1, Paramount for 1.66:1, and Universal and Columbia for 1.85:1; Warner Brothers was at the moment still undecided.[212]

Because Hollywood was in the midst of such upheaval in early 1953, there was room for an enterprising independent to find an exploitable angle and make a buck. If Tucker and Zimbalist were as convinced as many that 3-D was going to only be a novelty, then they were only that much more motivated to hit the ground running and get their movie into distribution before the market bottomed out.

5

Oscar Weekend 1953

Wyott Ordung told author Mark Thomas McGee about the aftermath of Phil Tucker's strange proposal for a post-apocalyptic comedy:

> A couple of days later we shot some 3-D tests, Phil, me, and a cameraman named Gordon Abel [Avil]. I wore a fire suit and had a fish bowl on my head with TV rabbit ears. Phil kept blowing his whistle which was the signal for action and I stumbled around this vacant lot in East Los Angeles shoving my hand at the camera. We used Arriflex cameras and a mirror box. Phil thought we had better 3-D than Warner Brothers but I never saw the footage.[213]

Telling the same anecdote to Johnny Legend, Ordung said that he had to keep up this buffoonery for "seven or eight hours." He also soon after wrote the script, but was never paid, and believed that getting the screen credit might have actually hurt his career.[214] And according to Ray Zone, Ordung said that their efforts yielded "about 25 minutes" of 3-D experiments, with the detail that the test was shot in an area of "broken buildings and things."[215] The test suit he wore was amazingly a cheap substitute for a cheap substitute. Tucker either did not have access to a gorilla suit, or had not yet decided to use one, but the test version is a reasonable facsimile for not having the suit or the helmet. And Ordung's account reinforces Tucker's memory of cobbling together his own 3-D setup, a challenge that the mechanically gifted director probably enjoyed figuring out.

The *Hollywood Reporter*'s announcement listed the cast accurately except that it omitted two of eight performers. John Brown, voice of both Ro-Men, never appeared onscreen and was probably hired in post-production. But the absence of Claudia Barrett—female lead, hero's love interest, and monster's obsession—is glaring. To judge by the *Reporter,* the role was up in the air only a day or two before filming began and, according to Tucker, there was a reason:

> . . . Amanda Blake was a friend of Al Zimbalist's, and I wanted George Nader.
>
> *Did you know George Nader for a while?*
> Oh yeah. George and Amanda would have been perfect together. We signed George, but at the last minute Amanda couldn't do it—of course, that was before she became anything, she wasn't a name [but] she was up for something. Might even have been [inaudible] that she was up for, I don't know. Anyhow, she couldn't do it.

Claudia Barrett

Since Zimbalist's *Miss Robinson Crusoe* had starred George Nader and Amanda Blake, this was clearly the reason they were intended to reunite in *Robot Monster.* Tucker remembered it as though using Nader was purely his idea, but the actor's association with Zimbalist is a fact.

> So I wanted somebody who played as well against George as she did. And we held an audition. Claudia Barrett was one of four or five. She wasn't the best actress of the bunch, but she looked the best, relative to George. And [the part] didn't really call for that much acting. I figured it's good. So the price was right—scale—and she looks well with George, and she can get by acting.

Since the *Reporter* neglected to mention Barrett, auditions could not have been held long before the day the story ran. Born Imagene Williams, Barrett suffered from crippling shyness at a young age, which led her parents to have her study acting. Given a one-year Warner Brothers contract, perhaps because she fit the pixie-ish Anne Baxter look of the time, she took her screen name (also taken legally), and did screen tests and small movie roles, including a bit part in *White Heat.*[216] Barrett's looks were no more lost on the public than on Ro-Man, as Mike

Connolly observed in *Daily Variety* that she "makes Jane Russell and Dagmar look like this: ________________ . . . ."[217] She was devastated when Warner dropped her, and found it difficult to even get through interviews effectively but she eventually became, like Blake, a horse-opera player on television and for Republic on film. (Tucker no doubt approved.) She was in fact already in this phase of her career by the time of *Robot Monster*, which explains her participating in it.[218] *The Hollywood Reporter* stated on June 18, 1952, that "Republic [had] signed" her for *Desperadoes Outpost*.[219] Barrett retired from acting in the sixties and later worked for the Academy of Motion Picture Arts and Sciences. Her *Robot Monster* co-star George Barrows remembered her as someone who could not endure the rat race:

> It was heartbreaking, because the kid was a real swell little gal and a very dedicated little actress, but she got very discouraged in the business. She couldn't make it. I think she was too insecure. She couldn't handle Hollywood.[220]

Barrett recalled a few *Robot Monster* details to interviewer Paul Parla:

> I met director Phil Tucker at the first interview. Al Zimbalist was the producer. Mr. Zimbalist had me read for the part. I'm not sure, but I think Mr. Tucker read with me, playing the other parts. They both liked me and decided to use me as Alice. The picture was low-low-low-budget and my agent at the time was not too pleased

that I decided to take the part. But I was an actress and I just wanted to act.[221]

To take Barrett literally, there were multiple interviews for the low-low-low-budget film, indicating that the director and producer were at least shrewd enough to worry about the quality of the leads. A good screen couple could not save a cheap film, but that film would have no prayer with unappealing stars. As news items continually attested, Zimbalist was heavily involved in the production, further muddying the question of who was responsible for the strange quality of the finished film.

That George Nader took the *Robot Monster* lead while Blake declined was appropriate on multiple levels. Little remembered now is the fact that Nader had already co-starred with Barrett as husband and wife in a 1950 Allan "Rocky" Lane Western, *Rustlers on Horseback*. As Barrett remembered, "I had made one Western feature with George Nader a year before, so, it was nice working with him again."[222] And besides his established connection with Zimbalist, he had one tenuous connection with Tucker besides Tucker's memory of knowing him. The *Reporter* noted the day after Christmas 1952 that he had a part in a January "Boris Petroff TV film" to be made at General Service Studios.[223] And making *Robot Monster* might have

George Nader

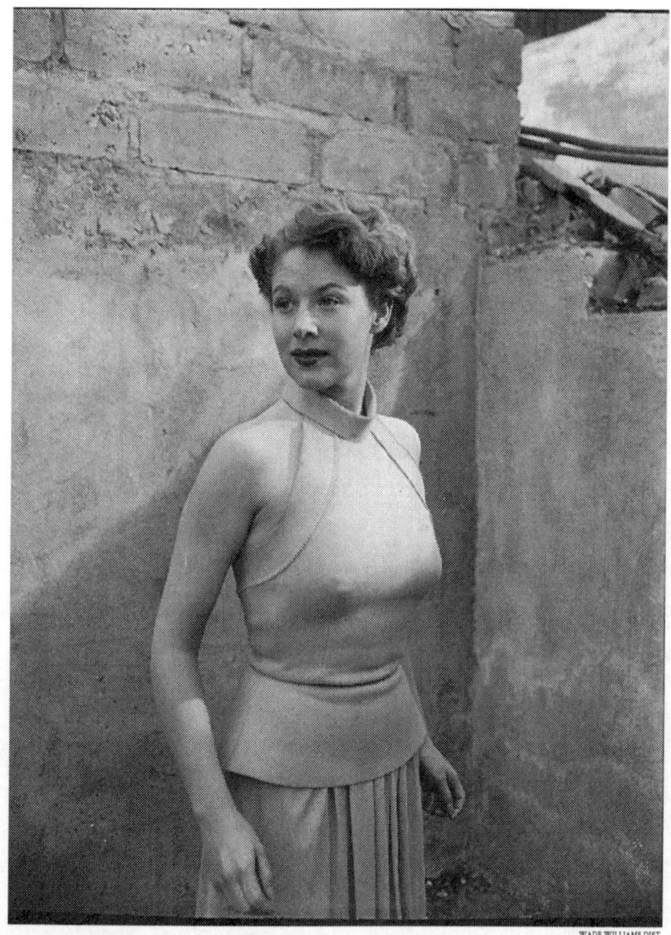

WADE WILLIAMS DIST.

Claudia Barrett and George Nader in a pair of previously unseen *Robot Monster* publicity stills.

connected him to more work; *Daily Variety* reported in May 1953 that he was cast in the Lippert production *Sins of Jezebel.*[224] Directing it was Reginald LeBorg, who was more than once a collaborator of Tucker's mentor Gordon Avil. But Nader was in

WADE WILLIAMS DIST.

general one of the hardest working performers in Hollywood, as a February 1952 *Reporter* shows: "George Nader of 20th-Fox's *Phone Call from a Stranger* cast returned yesterday after completing the leading role opposite Ursula Theiss in *Monsoon* in India and a TV pilot film, *Passport to Danger,* in Sweden."[225] The *Reporter* noted in April that, post-*Monsoon,* Nader was heading back to Sweden "to co-star with Anita Bjork in Robert Spafford's *Memory of Love.*"[226] Early August brought Nader a part in "Republic's current untitled musical,"[227] while October found him co-starring with Joan Crawford in a TV film (his role in *Miss Robinson Crusoe* was "just completed" at that time).[228] Amidst all of this film and TV he found time for the stage, as indicated by a December 30 report that he "returned yesterday from New York where he conferred on a Broadway legit stint."[229]

Nader showed the same drive through mostly second tier Universal contract work in the fifties, followed by regular television roles and low-budget European films, including the Jerry Cotton series of spy thrillers. The *Reporter* noted in November 1960 that he "wraps up shooting today on five TV commercials, all in Spanish, for Goodyear-International."[230] But Nader could be annoyed into dropping a job; in early 1959, he announced that he would leave NBC's *Ellery Queen* series if the show's production shifted from Hollywood to New York City: "I signed to do the series because I was assured the show would originate here. I live in Hollywood, I like Hollywood, and I'm satisfied to keep on working here."[231] By November of the same year, while starring in *Man and the Challenge,* he lamented that TV stars received very little support from producers compared to movie stars of old, and insisted that they were "entirely within [their] rights" to insist on a larger chunk of the profits.[232]

Nader was forced to retire in 1974 because of eye damage and subsequent glaucoma, which made him unable to endure the glare of set lighting. Slightly later, a 1976 reference work noted that Nader "remains a bachelor,"[233] while his homosexuality was still a secret to the public. According to a *Filmfax* profile by Howard Johns, Nader had been with former stage singer Mark Miller since the late forties, the pair also being close friends with Rock Hudson (neither intimately involved with him). After Nader's forced retirement, Hudson hired Miller as his personal secretary and made each of them beneficiaries; they were both loyally taciturn during the media frenzy that surrounded Hudson's 1985 death. Re-ignited at this time were old rumors that Nader's career never achieved full stardom because Universal dropped him in reaction to a gossip rag's threat to reveal the truth about Hudson. But Nader emphatically denied being the victim of such an arrangement and if he had been, his personal life could have easily been public knowledge long before his retirement.[234] It was within the science fiction genre that Nader outed himself with his 1978 debut novel *Chrome*. It was an explicitly homoerotic futuristic adventure novel and *Best Sellers* gave it a measured but ultimately negative appraisal, noting Nader's penchant for often "tediously elaborate" description.[235] Reaction was mixed within the science fiction field, to judge by critic Baird Searles' appraisal that the novel was "pretty naïve," but at least had "ideas and moments here which do have that new and oblique view that an outsider can bring to any field."[236]

One member of the *Robot Monster* cast was far more prestigious than the rest, and was the only one with a misspelled name in the credits. Billed as "Selena Royale," perhaps intentionally, Selena Royle was a respected performer on stage and screen who was essentially born into her art. Her father, Edwin Milton Royle, was a successful playwright of the early twentieth century theater, whose best-known work *The Squaw Man* jump-started the film career of Cecil B. DeMille. Transforming Royle's play into his first feature in 1914, DeMille re-filmed it in 1918, and again early in the sound era in 1931.[237] DeMille never forgot the importance of *The Squaw Man* to his career; almost two weeks before the filming of *Robot Monster*, the *Reporter* noted that he "celebrated the 40th anniversary of the production of his first picture," describing the 1914 release as a "a box office sensation and a model for all Westerns filmed for many years."[238] DeMille took the opportunity to remind technology-crazed Hollywood of the need for a good story as the foundation of a good movie. Royle had long before commented on the 1914 version, "I will make it a condition in my next contract that I am to have the privilege of being around when the work of direction is going on. . . . I believe that the man with a considerable stage experience may be permitted to offer suggestions."[239] One can only savor the thought of how DeMille would have responded to Royle's advice on how he should direct.

Selena Royle

Selena Royle, born 1904, appeared in over two dozen Broadway productions from 1921 to 1937, before establishing herself in Hollywood in the early forties. Appraising the Brooklyn, New York theater scene in 1924, Arthur J. Busch related that Royle was to "be the leading lady" for the Montauk Players, a group about to present a mixture of new and old plays.[240] And in a 1926 *Variety* short review of the play *Yellow*, Mollie Gray praised Royle's performance as "the young wife," also noting her as "dignified and well gowned," sporting "a frock and hat of Chanel red" with "a handsome silver fox scarf."[241] Royle was responsible in the mid-twenties for recommending a struggling Spencer Tracy to theatrical producers William Wright and George M. Cohan, breaks that proved essential for him. As the melancholy Irish actor told Royle on the set of *Cass Timberlane* (1947), "Selena, if it hadn't been for you I would probably be driving a truck, and happy."[242]

Between playing the mother of *The Fighting Sullivans* (1944) and her involvement in starting the Stage Door Canteen, a dinner and entertainment revue for soldiers, Royle had a very positive image. But her career spiraled downward after she was listed in the June 1950 publication *Red Channels* in connection with eight groups, causes, or petitions that were allegedly communist front activities.[243] A copy of a legal filing (date unlisted) with the New York Supreme Court against its publisher, American Business Consultants, exists in Royle's papers at the University of Wyoming.[244] Represented by Arthur Garfield Hays, Royle sought $150,000 in damages against the *Red Channels* publisher.[245]

Better known is Royle's open letter to the American Legion that appeared in the July 8 *Daily Variety*. Royle asserted that the Legion had been influencing studios to not hire her, denied ever being a communist, and affirmed her patriotism.[246] Ivan Spear praised the letter in the July 26 *Boxoffice*[247] and in August,

AN OPEN LETTER TO THE AMERICAN LEGION

Hollywood, California

American Legion
U. S. A.

Gentlemen:

I am told that someone purporting to represent your organization has been calling prospective employers of mine and suggesting that it would be unwise to hire me.

I know, of course, that there is a list issued by you comprising the names of those you deem unworthy of employment. I am sure, before you took such drastic action as to send such a list to the Motion Picture Studios, you must, of necessity, have made a thorough investigation of each and every charge against each name.

Therefore, I find it hard to believe that you would be in any way responsible for my blacklisting. An honest investigation would have shown that I am not now, nor have I ever been a Communist, and that I have never done anything which could be considered as un-American—on the contrary!

Further, that I have a long record of service to the men you are organized to represent . . . the servicemen. I was, as you know, Co-chairman of the New York Stage Door Canteen and, for five years, Vice-chairman of the Entertainment Committee of the Hospital Division of the Los Angeles Chapter of the American Red Cross. I am sure that you are also aware that while I was associated with these two organizations they both received citations of merit, while I personally was several times so honored.

I heartily disapprove of whispering campaigns, so I feel it only just to give you this opportunity to deny or affirm your responsibility for the rumor campaign against me.

Sincerely,

Selena Royle

Selena Royle

Selena Royle's open letters, calling out the American Legion (*above*) and subsequently making peace with it (*facing*).

AN OPEN LETTER

To My Friends In The Motion Picture Industry

This letter is addressed to those who expressed such warm interest in my open letter to the American Legion published in DAILY VARIETY July 8, 1952.

In that letter I stated in part:

> "I am told that someone purporting to represent your organization has been calling prospective employers of mine and suggesting that it would be unwise to hire me."

Convinced that the American Legion would not knowingly participate in such illegal action, and receiving no reply to my open letter, I have addressed additional communications to the American Legion.

In reply to one letter the Hollywood Post of the American Legion stated categorically that it had not used any influence which could have resulted in my losing employment.

In a personal interview with me Mr. John Home, Americanism Chairman of the Hollywood Post, admitted that my name was not on any list, that the American Legion possessed no such list, and that no Legion member could have officially made any phone calls to employers of mine.

I am therefore happy to state that the calls which were placed to prospective employers must have been made by irresponsible individuals and not by the American Legion.

I am happy to clear the American Legion of the charge that they have participated in the un-American activity of fostering a blacklist with respect to me and to take this opportunity of so informing the motion picture industry.

Selena Royle

Royle exchanged letters with the Hollywood Post of the Legion, which denied her accusations.[248] Something changed in the ensuing months, because Royle published a second open letter in the December 23 *Daily Variety* in which she was "happy to clear the American Legion of the charge," and attributed her career problems to "irresponsible individuals" alone.[249] And Royle was not completely without other friends during this time. During 1952, she received letters of support from Stanley Kramer and Eleanor Roosevelt,[250] and during August 1953 she was even managing a small comeback. Co-written with husband Georges Renavent, the play *September's Morn* was a comedy about an egotistical star's inability to accept his age. Starring John Hoyt and playing at the Laguna Summer Theater, the play got five positive reviews from *Variety* and local newspapers.[251] With the filming of *Robot Monster* almost half a year in the past, Royle might have been optimistic at the time.

A former MGM contract player did not appear in *Robot Monster* out of enthusiasm, and obviously took the job because her career had gone from Chanel red to *Red Channels.* Royle seems uncomfortable in her scenes, her line delivery somehow both melodramatic and uncertain while she often fusses with her hands. She carries a pained expression that works for the part but, it can almost be assumed, was a sign of how she felt about being in such a production. To judge by *Robot Monster* alone, one would not know that she was a professional. She had a few more parts, such as an early 1954 TV drama about the Red Cross, *The Good Samaritan* (one newspaper TV section called her a "distinguished American actress"[252]), and did a stint on *As the World Turns.* Royle eventually emigrated to Mexico with Renavent, wrote books, and was active in the arts.

In regard to his father using a blacklisted actress, Tucker Jr. noted, "The fact is that with the blacklisting going on, he was able to hire good actors at bargain basement prices because they were all out of work and would do just about anything. So actually the blacklisting thing was an opportunity for low-budget films, not a threat."[253] Tucker said,

> Well, the blacklist was an unofficial thing, and it had to do more with major studios than with independents. There wasn't any kind of a thing that you weren't allowed legally to use somebody on the blacklist. It was something that if you were a member of the MPPA [sic], [or something] like that, you'd be going against their wishes. Well, since I wasn't a member of anything, I could do what I want.
>
> *I see, but since you were employing a blacklisted actress, wouldn't that further prevent you from working in a major—*
> No. If I had made a fuss about it—if I had asked somebody's permission, and they'd said "No," and I had said "[Growling noises] and I don't care how blacklisted she is, it's unfair!"—yeah. That could do it. But to just go ahead blithely, and do it, and then say later, "Well, I don't know what all this blacklist bullshit is about," [would be okay]. Because there weren't any really formal blacklists, very much, and they certainly didn't pass 'em around to me, if there were.

And American society was not as humorless about communism and anticommunism as is sometimes assumed. A "Grin and Bear It" cartoon by Lichty from early 1953 shows one college boy complaining to another: "Pop's taking this talk about communism in our colleges seriously . . . makes me sign a loyalty oath every time I write home for money."[254]

While those on the blacklist had limited sympathy at the time, they were within a decade seen as unconditional victims and were eventually a subject for Hollywood films such as *The Front* (1976). But as Tucker's memory of the period indicates, with his subtle sense of how to use a blacklisted actress without getting in trouble, the political situation was never black-and-white. No one's life better illustrated the gray of it all than director Edward Dmytryk, a communist from 1944 to 1945, who hated the autocratic mind-control of communism while disliking the high-handedness of the Congressional committee that investigated its presence. Staying silent did not save him from jail time when others called to testify before Congress in 1947 adopted a belligerent, confrontational stance that tainted his own appearance. Then when Hollywood communists made an effort to publicly embarrass him after his six months in prison ended, Dmytryk had had enough of backstabbing friends and cleared his name by testifying against them. But with his career rebounding, he then lived with the sneers of Hollywood's respectable left and the residual dislike of others on the right.[255] A socialist, Dmytryk noted that his Republican friend Dick Powell was one of the few who stood by him throughout the whole mess.[256]

Dmytryk also pointed out that one anticommunist group he disliked, and whose influence on the blacklist he believed to be grossly underestimated, was the American Legion: "The only part of the cleansing rites of 1951 that I truly regret is my appearance and soul baring, meager though it was, before the Hollywood chapter of this chauvinistic organization." He held the publication *Red Channels* in similarly low regard, and noted widespread sympathy "for those who fled to Europe or Mexico rather than face the music" (he had more empathy for those who stuck around).[257] Put all of those factors together, and it is a composite portrait of Royle's situation in the blacklist.

Billed fourth in *Robot Monster*'s cast was John Mylong as the Professor. Born in Austria (though he may have been Russian) in 1892, his birth name is unclear.[258] Some early promotional portraits list him as Jack Mylong-Münz, although he was credited in early years under some ten variations. After years of German work from as early as 1921, Mylong's career stopped short in the mid-1930s, restarting in Hollywood by 1941. He appeared in a remarkable number of American films and television series, including such high points as *For Whom the Bell Tolls* (1943), *The Clock* (1945), *His Kind of Woman* (1951), and *Magnificent Obsession* (1954). Yet for having a long and respectable career, Mylong left scant impression on the histories of German and Hollywood cinema, perhaps the result of playing minor supporting roles in so many films; being ubiquitous somehow made him invisible. Even in his early years in Germany, his credits show no collaborations with famous German directors like Fritz Lang, F.W. Murnau, G.W. Pabst, or Robert Siodmak. However, Mylong was in Alfred Hitchcock's extremely obscure

John Mylong

Mary (1931), the German version of *Murder!* (1930) (filmed simultaneously). Hitchcock blamed his own lack of finesse with the German tongue for its reputed deficiencies.[259] Mylong's distinctive, heavily accented English provided some of *Robot Monster*'s more subtle humor. Often when addressing Ro-Man, he pronounces it "Roman," as if addressing the director of *Chinatown.* Mylong's voice was ribbed in *The Fifty Worst Films of All Time* as "a German accent so outrageously bogus that it couldn't even qualify for *Hogan's Heroes.*"[260] But while Mylong's native accent was the same across many performances, the comment is still somewhat right—Mylong apparently did not hail from Germany. Tucker knew as much about Mylong as anyone, which is not much, calling him "a very prominent actor. Far more famous than Selena Royle, except his day had been passed by twenty years," with the note that "he would work for scale."

Billed next were *Robot Monster*'s two child stars, Gregory Moffett (as Johnny) and Pamela Paulson (as Carla). Neither had big careers, and Tucker remembered little about them as individuals:

How about the two kids, Gregory Moffett and Pamela Paulson? Were they also . . .

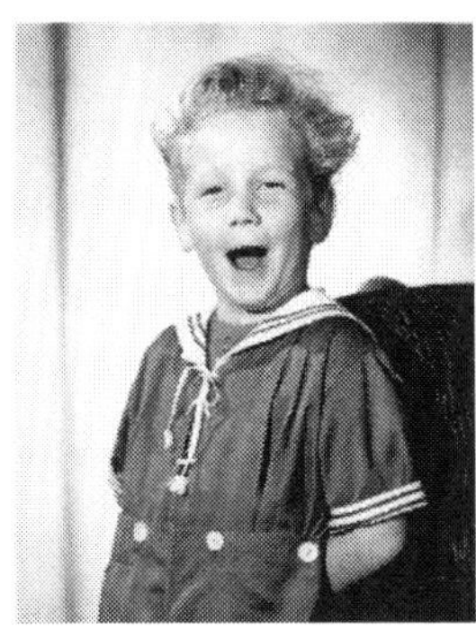

WADE WILLIAMS DIST.

Gregory Moffett and Pamela Paulson

I don't remember, I . . .

It seemed that Pamela Paulson, she was so nervous that during the film she was about to wet her pants, and constantly Selena Royle would have to hold on to her and make sure that she would face the camera.
Yeah, we had a lot of problems with them. I don't know whether they were professionals, [it's] really been much too long. Although they were in the film a lot, they really had very little to do. And I don't imagine that the care was taken with the casting of them.

What were some of the problems that you did have?
I can't remember. The one you mentioned. Selena always had to hold [her] so you could see her. It seemed to me that the boy wasn't bad.

Yeah it seems to me, though, that just about every one of his lines was dubbed later.
No.

Really?
It wasn't in the budget.

Pamela Paulson had literally no other screen credits. According to a "Cinepan, Shlock [sic] in the Cinema" column by Dean Chambers, Paulson "became a housewife in San Francisco, where she once discussed the picture on Bob Wilkin's [sic] local TV horror show."[261] Gregory Moffett's brief career was comparatively glamorous. With both parents in show business, his older sister Sharyn was already a child actor by the time he had his first small role in one of her movies. He was in two big features (with Joel McCrea and then Fred Astaire) prior to *Robot Monster,* and followed it with a variety of television and other parts, including an episode of *The Adventures of Superman.* Moffett enjoyed his acting career but let it go as he hit adolescence, by his own account not missing it, and remembering *Robot Monster* somewhere between amusement and embarrassment.[262]

No one in the cast contributed more to the iconic nature of the film than George Barrows, the physical presence of both Ro-Men. Son of singer and silent film actor Henry A. Barrows and one of the best of Hollywood's small fraternity of gorilla suit men, he usually wore his costume with a gorilla mask and was only laughable when the part required it. Bob Burns, the world's leading collector of classic horror memorabilia, was a gorilla actor himself and ranked Barrows as second only to the

George Barrows

legendary Charlie Gemora (and Burns considered the three of them "the only gorillas who could do comedy"). Burns recalled, "George did a pretty darn good gorilla, and he was probably the only one of the latter-day guys that *tried* to do a real gorilla." Barrows went to the trouble of making his mask from a cast of

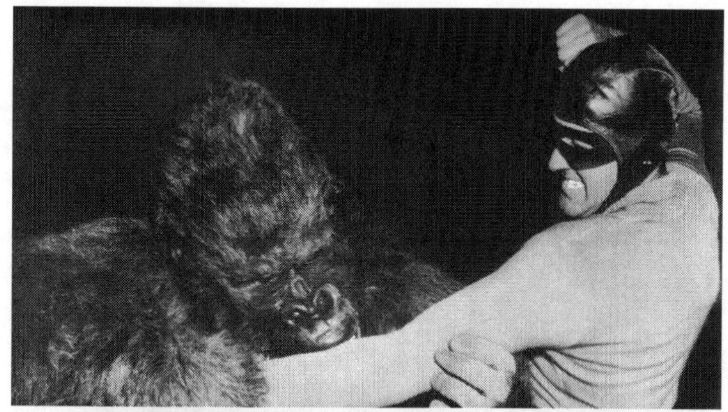

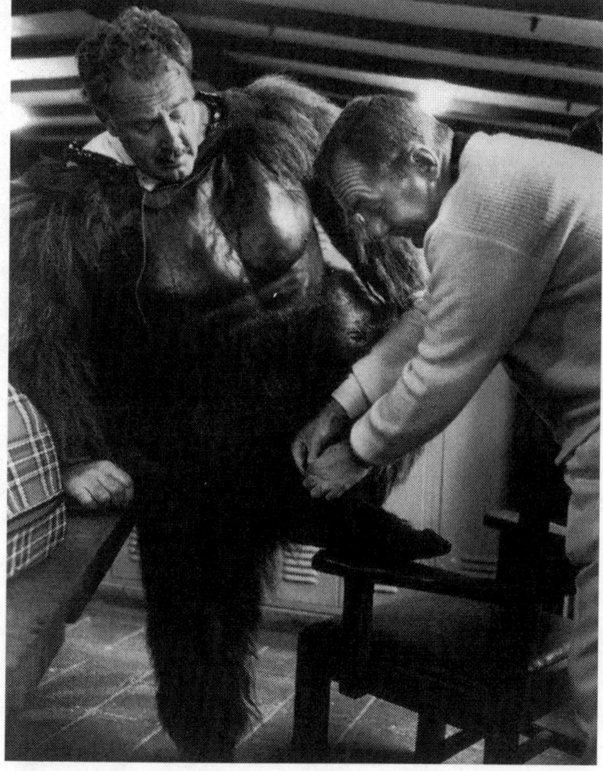

(*Above*) ***Adventures of Captain Africa***

(*Above*) ***Black Zoo***

(*Below*) ***Gorilla at Large***

his face, using arm extensions to simulate simian proportions, and studying gorilla behavior at the zoo. He made his own suit for "around $400," covering it with yak hair that he "sewed in like a wig." Burns noted, "Ray Corrigan and Emil Van Horn had had theirs made *for* them; Janos Prohaska always *said* he built his own but I know John Chambers made it for him." The tall, thick Barrows had a "perfect 'movie heavy' face," according to Burns, but "was a sweetheart—such a sweetheart that I saw him quite a few times after that." Burns not only socialized with Barrows, but benefited from his advice and brotherly care in developing his own gorilla man career.[263]

Despite having a show business father, Barrows got into movies accidentally:

> The first movie I did was, I think, *Cleopatra* (1934) with Henry Wilcoxon. I was strictly an extra, holding a spear or something. They came to the YMCA, and I used to work out. I used to wrestle and lift weights and all that, and they wanted some kids with good bodies. So they came up, "How would guys like to come in and work for ten bucks a day?" Oh man, in 1934? That was a lot of money during the Depression. So we came to work on it for three weeks. Then I didn't do any more because I was working in a furniture building shop, and I didn't want to quit that. They'd say, "Come on, Barrows, take off for a few weeks." I came back, and then I was working out again and someone said, "You know, they're looking for someone to double [Johnny] Weissmuller in a couple of shows." . . . Johnny was about three inches taller

> than I, but proportionate weight . . . proportionally, you couldn't tell us apart. . . . I did everything; I did Westerns, part and stunts . . . at Republic, I used to do back-to-back stuff over there . . . doing heavies on it, doing cowboys, doing Indians, doing every goddamn thing.

Barrows morphed readily from an extra into a stuntman ("Most of those guys, I've seen them grow old in the business [beside] myself."), and he moved on to bigger projects like *The Adventures of Robin Hood* (1938) ("there were twenty of us on it . . . for twenty, twenty-one weeks"). Barrows traced the craft of gorilla imitation back to the only one greater than him, Gemora:

> Charlie, I knew him back in 1932 or '33. . . . And then he was the only guy that had a suit that was realistic, but it wouldn't do too much. Mine, the lips open and the nostrils dilate and all that sort of thing. . . . He did a number of shows, he had it sewed up. Then I built my suit, when I got out of the service . . . I built that, figured it would supplement income, and all of a sudden this thing starts to snowball once I started to use it. And, Jesus, they wanted it because it had expressions. And I not only did the serious thing, but I also did the comedy, and Red Skelton used me on about eleven or twelve shows. And I used to play off him in so many of those things—George Gobel—and I did an awful lot of comedy with it. And of course straight stuff and all that, like *Gorilla at Large* (1954).

According to Weaver, Barrows' *Gorilla at Large* cast-mate Charlotte Austin ranked his gorilla work more believable than that of Steve Calvert, who played an ape opposite Austin in both *Gorilla at Large* and *The Bride and the Beast* (1958). She recalled Barrows as "a lovely man,"[264] kind sentiments echoed in Parla's interview with Barrett: "He was easy-going, and I felt perfectly safe in his arms. Running up and down those hills, George could have dropped me several times. Fortunately, he didn't."[265]

Tucker was fortunate that Barrows had a thrifty, blue-collar approach to his various skills and was not above projects like the amateurish *Mesa of Lost Women,* where his name was misspelled "Burrows" in the credits. ("I've used the suit in so many of those . . . 'epics,'" he stated.) In this uncommon dramatic role out of his gorilla suit, Barrows is an effective performer. (The cast, including Dolores Fuller and Katherine Victor, is a bad movie perfect storm.) And although Barrows could be as dismissive as anyone when it came to looking back on *Robot Monster* ("It was so bad I automatically obliterated it from my mind."), he was—in Tucker's account—unintentionally responsible for the film's central bit of weirdness. Tucker's exploitation film training indisputably served him well in at least one area. When he set out to make his *Robot Monster,* he completely understood what he was up against:

> In those days, the only way an independent could get money for making something was to indicate that what you were going to do was going to cost zero.

And costing zero was exactly the situation at hand. Zimbalist's Hollywood connections did not give him the means, or perhaps even the desire, to start producing films on a moderate budget. It seems that his motivation, conscious or not, was to follow in the footsteps of exploitation filmmakers like George Weiss, but on a more respectable, visible, near-Hollywood level. While Tucker's memory of how much *Robot Monster* cost was cloudy, it was still richly detailed:

> I don't know if I really can remember exactly—diabetes affects your memory, by the way, that's one of the side effects it has—but I would guess it was somewhere around, well under $20,000, a figure sticks in the back of my head: $16,000 plus whatever it cost for . . .
>
> *Lab? Prints?*
>
> Well, yeah, but see prints shouldn't be included in the cost of the picture because that's not part of it, that's part of distribution. I remember a conversation that took place between Ed Mosk and Al Zimbalist and myself, relative to revealing the cost of the picture, that they felt it would damage the picture if people knew how cheaply it had been made, and I agreed. But also I felt that you couldn't quote a high price, because people look at that and say, "Jesus, what a terrible picture, you didn't spend that much money on that piece of shit." And I remember vaguely agreeing that, when they asked, we would all say "somewhere under $50,000."

Whether or not Zimbalist was a relative of Sam Zimbalist, he had friends in the highest Hollywood ranks. Mosk was a famous Hollywood lawyer, often handling divorce and custody matters between celebrities such as Bette Davis and Gary Merrill,[266] and Blake Edwards and Patricia Walker.[267] The younger brother of California attorney general (and later state Supreme Court justice) Stanley Mosk,[268] he worked for liberal causes and was very involved in Progressive Citizens of America.[269] Among other groups, this one was listed in *Red Channels* under the entries for both John Brown and Selena Royle, raising the possibility that both got parts in the *Robot Monster* cast out of blacklist sympathy. Royle received a letter dated September 9, 1952, from attorney Arthur Garfield Hays advising her on legal options (the cause unspecified, but presumably in reference to the American Legion). Hays affirmed her approach on the matter, noting that she and someone named Mosk were in agreement.[270] Likely then, Ed Mosk was representing or at least advising her, and it may be through him that Zimbalist cast her in *Robot Monster.* But Edward Dmytryk remembered Mosk as a once helpful, fair weather friend, too respectable to be seen with him after his testimony against communists. Mosk invited Dmytryk to lunch soon after his 1951 appearance to tell him that "he could no longer represent" him.[271]

The more or less $16,000 budget that Tucker, Zimbalist and Mosk agreed to was about as cheap as a film budget could possibly be. Republic's bottom tier of cheap Westerns averaged a cost of $30,000-$50,000, which shows how cheap a small studio was able to get and have a releasable product.[272] But in a demonstration of inexcusable incompetence, a young Ed Wood managed the independent cowboy movie *The Outlaw Marshal,* allowing the budget to balloon from $20,000 to a ludicrous $57,000. Besides shedding light on Wood's career-long difficulty in trying to survive in Hollywood, the production resulted in a heavily litigated film and an angry pool of investors who had to be persuaded to let the film be released for it to have any prayer of earning its money back.[273] Tucker clearly understood these budget subtleties far better than his contemporary Wood to have completed *Robot Monster* for as little as $16,000, and to have then understood the negative impression that could be created by the bald-faced truth of that budget.[274]

For by the early fifties, there was really only one type of film regularly made for *Robot Monster*'s budget, one with which Tucker was well-acquainted. Exploitation films—with their threadbare sets, static camerawork, and often amateur acting—had nearly 100% of their value in their over-the-top advertising and could afford to be as cheap as $16,000. The films were in themselves largely worthless, only viewed in the hope of illicit thrills, and were the ultimate in the bait-and-switch business technique. But to push a slightly better type of film into that rock bottom level was to risk making a movie that would be truly un-releasable. No audience would tolerate a science fiction movie without a spaceship, a monster, or at least a ray gun. No audience would patiently sit through seventy minutes of stilted actors talking about nothing on cheap sets, in the hope of glimpsing a quick shot of a spaceship. Society did not prohibit the display of robots and space creatures, and a filmmaker promising them had to deliver and not merely tease.

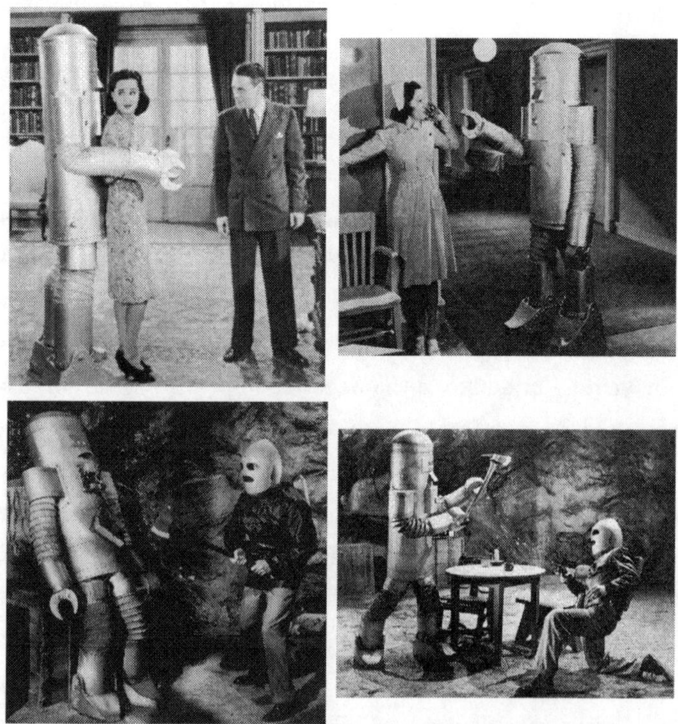

Republic's robot costume, as seen in *Mysterious Doctor Satan* (*top row*) and *Zombies of the Stratosphere* (*bottom row*). This is likely the only recycled robot costume from the time of *Robot Monster*.

Tucker had to figure out how he was going to pull off his robot invader on a budget like that of the exploitation films he had trained on. His free location for a destroyed Earth awaited him, but he had to somehow create the monster that would inhabit it and terrorize the survivors.

> . . . I talked to several people I knew who had robot suits—I originally envisioned a kind of a robot—but it was just out-of-the-way, money-wise, just no possible way to do it.

Reinforcing Tucker's point, there seem to have been no regular robot suit guys in early fifties Hollywood, in contrast to the gorilla performers. Republic had a robot costume that appeared in multiple adventure serials, including *Mysterious Doctor Satan* (1940). Tucker theoretically could have rented this suit, and likely tried, but it must have been unavailable or "just out-of-the-way, money-wise."[275] (A more recognizable recycled robot only appeared years after *Robot Monster*, when Robby the Robot debuted in MGM's *Forbidden Planet* [1956] and was thereafter loaned out for several appearances in TV and movies.) So with the conventional option of making or borrowing a suitable costume out of reach, Tucker did what any clever exploitation man would do: He made the best substitute he could manage for as little money as possible.

> So I thought, "Okay. I know George Barrows. He's got a gorilla suit. I know George will work for me for [nothing]. I'll get a diving helmet, put it on him, and it'll work!" So that's how it came to be.

It is easy from the vantage point of hindsight to laugh at Tucker's solution, and the results onscreen were of course absurd. But to make a non-exploitation movie on an exploitation movie budget, he had to be brave enough to pursue whatever insane solution would get the film made. Perhaps someone with great design sense could have creatively combined cardboard and paint in some effective way, but Tucker's robot-gorilla concept is still less crazy than has been acknowledged. In summer 1952, RKO successfully reissued *King Kong* (1933) and Tucker must have noticed a re-release so fantastic that it was featured in *Time* and far out-grossed its initial release.[276] The return of *King Kong* was packing in audiences right about when Tucker was pulling the Lucky Luciano stunt and when he discovered the ruins of Chavez Ravine. His use of a gorilla suit as part of the monster costume was therefore not a random, casually chosen substitute for a true robot. With a conventional robot impossible, Tucker chose an alternative that had true audience appeal. With *King Kong* a hot property, it is clear why Tucker used a robot-gorilla (and in the opinion of Mark F. Berry, *Robot Monster* is essentially "a *King Kong* remake"[277]). If he could not provide a robot or a giant gorilla, he could at least manage a gorilla wearing a diving helmet.[278] Little wonder that with it featured in gigantic proportions on the poster, *Kong*-crazed audiences made the film successful.

But according to Barrows:

> It wasn't Phil Tucker's idea. Zimbalist, it was more or less his brain child, I understand. Because I was interviewed before the thing, and he asked me about it. "What do you think?" he says. "You have this gorilla suit, and it's a terrific suit and all that," and I said, "Yeah, yeah, it is; wonderful suit." "What do you think of creatures from outer space being gorillas?" I said, "I guess it would be the same as if they were green monsters. Who knows?

> We've never seen 'em. Your imagination is as good as anyone's." So they went with that.

But while Barrows' account reinforces Zimbalist's central role in guiding the production—clearly on display in trade papers up to the film's release—it does not contradict Tucker. Zimbalist is not depicted with coming up with the idea, and his inquiry to Barrows suggests that he was as skeptical of the robot-gorilla concept as anyone who would later see the film. Zimbalist was in charge, but what Barrows says makes it seem *less* likely that he created the idea. But he may have had input in refining the costume to be as good as circumstances allowed. Barrows said,

> They were going to first use the head, and have horns or something, antennae, and all that sort of thing.
>
> *So how did they get to the diving helmet?*
> They didn't want the gorilla head, they thought it would look more "out of this world" if it were some kind of space helmet, where they actually couldn't breathe our atmosphere so they had this special thing on where they had to breathe their own atmosphere.

This ambiguity about how to make the monster seem alien extended all the way to the film's release. The poster famously shows Ro-Man with a detailed skull face within the faceplate of the helmet, which fits in with the varying ideas thrown around in the planning stages. It may have been the case that Zimbalist decided to go for broke and advertise Ro-Man in all his stunning, surreal glory. The audience thereby knew what it was in for and might even have been intrigued; there was not much else to put on the film's poster anyway, and undiscriminating ten-year-old boys might have made an association between the gorilla monster and the still popular *King Kong*. Whether the artist came up with the skull or Zimbalist ordered it, the on-screen face was murky enough to plausibly make such an embellishment on the artwork.

Tucker would began filming *Robot Monster* the very day after it was announced in the Wednesday, March 18 *Reporter*. By the Friday issue, when the film was listed in the weekly "Pictures Now Shooting" section, the second day of shooting may have found it half completed:

> *How many days did it take to film?*
> Four.

A copy of the script has survived, consisting of 56 pages (nearly matching the old screenwriter's rule that one page of script equals one minute of screen time) plus three additional pages of production schedule and a cover page.[279] Among other details, the pages specify three days of shooting. The *Reporter* announced on Wednesday the 25th—exactly one week after initially announcing the project—that "*Robot Monster* 3-D Film Brought in for $50,000," and that the film had finished shooting the day before.[280] Sunday may have been a day of rest for cast and crew, and filming may or may not have taken place on Monday. *Robot Monster* was therefore completed in a delirious six days at most, and Tucker's memory of four days could be exactly right. This very brief schedule is in proportion for a movie made for far less than $50,000, on a budget more like that of an exploitation film. According to James King in the anthology *Hollywood Corral,* "The shooting schedule for the B Western of the '30s and early '40s was often no more than ten days."[281]

The script further listed locations for the planned three-day shoot, with three schedule pages at the end. Thursday and Friday were scheduled for "Shooting at 8 A.M.," specifying "Location at Chavez Ravine – Effie and Bishop Road," and that cast and crew "Leave from parking lot Formosa Grill – Santa Monica and Formosa – 7:00 A.M." After these two pages with thirty-five-and-a-half script pages scheduled for shooting during the two days at Chavez Ravine, the final page itemized fourteen-and-three-quarters script pages for shooting at

WADE WILLIAMS DIST.

One of the three Bronson Caves, as seen in *Robot Monster*.

"Location Bronson Canyon" on Saturday the 21st. While likely few watched *Robot Monster* and knew with certainty that Chavez Ravine was the location for the onscreen ruins, many recognized the film's other location, Bronson Canyon. According to Harry Medved:

> Griffith Park's Bronson Canyon was once a quarry where rocks were gathered to pave the streets of Hollywood and the San Pedro Breakwater. The canyon is best known for its Bronson Caves, three passages drilled through the base of a rugged mountain.[282]

It was one of the screen's most famous and repeatedly used outdoor settings; *Robot Monster* specifically used one of the three caves that have been seen repeatedly in everything from cheap Westerns and cheap monster movies to *The Searchers* (1956) and TV's *Batman* (1966-1968). Barrows poetically described the location's appeal:

> It used to be a rock quarry, years and years ago, right after World War I, and it looks like a piece of ground taken out of the moon. They've taken a lot of these moon shots, these motion pictures where all these astronauts . . .? And it's tremendous. It's the most rugged piece of ground, and it has caves in it that won't stop. Big deep caves that go back where they're actually quarry deep, stone and all that.

Perhaps by coincidence, Ordung had a double connection to Bronson Canyon that week. According to the March 16 *Variety*,

"Recent fire in Bronson Canyon turned out to be beneficial" for "Jack Broder's *Combat,*" saving the production time and money in creating a war-torn setting.[283] *Combat* was from an Ordung script and released that fall as *Combat Squad.*

While Barrows appreciated the mystery of Bronson Canyon, he did not enjoy the filming, noting, "I think I made $500 a week on it, and I carried Claudia Barrett around until I almost got a hernia." Furthermore:

> Because I had to carry her one time for about a hundred yards. That's a long ways in that suit, and going up over this ground that, it's not like slough or pavement or something. This is all ruts and holes and grass and clumps and things, and all that. But, that's pictures, what the hell.

The difficulty of walking on this unpleasant terrain may have contributed directly to the bizarre quality of the film. According to filmmaker Larry Blamire,

> I would go out on a limb and say that Ro-Man is entertaining primarily because of his walk. . . . [Barrows is] not playing a gorilla, so he doesn't walk like a gorilla. He just kind of walks like a guy, and so he just kind of plods along. And a lot of the time it's in this tremendous wide shot, which makes him even smaller. . . . The way he walks, it's just so everyday, it's like a guy going to work. . . . He's the working stiff alien.[284]

But Barrows had a keen mind and a strong work ethic, by which the experience became a little more difficult still:

There are several shots in the film of the robot monster just walking up the hill and then walking back down, and it seems like, under the hot, blazing California sun that it would have been very sweaty. How sweaty were you in the suit?
Well, let me put it this way, Harold, in that suit—now that particular show, I never particularly measured it—but when I did *Gorilla at Large* I would lose ten pounds a night. Next day you'd pick it up by drinking water, fluids, anything, but you could lose, ten, twelve pounds a night. Now that's a lot of fluid content and I'm sure on that show, I lost that much. Then, not only that—

You mean, just by sweating?
Sure, dehydration. It's terribly hot in that suit. It's a very, very enervating, difficult thing to wear, believe me. Not only that, but I had that helmet on my head. With a gorilla head, you can breathe through the mouth, you have air coming in and out of it, and under the neck, which doesn't show of course, due to the hair and all that. But with that thing, you have the helmet. Then—which was my idea, like an idiot—I said, "How are we going to cover up his face inside it?"

Right, because the helmet you just see right through.
So I said, "Why don't you just put a stocking over it?" So all it showed was the nose projection, but you couldn't

> see the eyes, you couldn't see what it was, it didn't look human. And it did give a hell of an effect. They were going to put some kind of a mask over me, and I said, "That'll be hokey." You know, like a Halloween mask, or some kind of monster thing. I said, "This way it looks like nothing, it looks like nothing human or animal." But I suffered for it, believe me.

And this "Halloween mask" detail further hints at why the poster version of Ro-Man had a skull face. This idea of taking a cheap shortcut of a masked face for a monster effect must have stayed with the filmmakers even after they had dropped it from the film itself. The poster would not have been painted until postproduction, and likely the skull-face effect was reinstated because the open and faceless quality of the onscreen Ro-Man was too abstract for movie publicity.

And, to settle an important point for all time:

> *Was it a real diving helmet, a real deep-sea diving helmet, because those are pretty weighty?*
>
> No, it was aluminum, some kind of aluminum ball that they constructed, cut a hole in the bottom, then built some kind of thing on the outside of it that fit down over my shoulders. It was a costume, strictly a piece of costume work and [Zimbalist], and Henry West—who was a good friend of mine, who was the wardrobe man on it—devised it. Henry I'd met years ago on [*The Adventures of*] *Robin Hood,* he handled all the wardrobe on *Robin Hood* with [Errol] Flynn. Old Henry West, he worked on it

with me, says, "George, you're going to die in this thing." I said, "I know. But, in the long shots we can leave this plastic thing off the head up here, take it off, so I could breathe through it." But in the close-ups, you had the round plate in it, like a diving helmet. But I made it so you could take it off in the long shots where you saw me walking, carrying her.

Four views of the Ro-Man helmet.

The Ro-Men "diving helmets" are of course very similar to other spaceman helmets of the era, such as those seen in *Destination Moon* (1950) and *Radar Men from the Moon* (1952). (This brings to mind one of *Robot Monster*'s alternate titles, *Monsters from the Moon.*) But most importantly, Medved referred to a single helmet, and Barrows continued in that vein, never remembering plural helmets. This implies that both Ro-Men were perhaps portrayed with the same helmet along with the same gorilla suit, despite some cosmetic differences in the look of each. Great Guidance's helmet has some kind of suction cup attachments in place of Earth Ro-Man's more traditional antennae, and lacks the front disc and gear attached to the back. Most notably, Guidance's helmet is dented on the left edge of its opening. The Guidance helmet could have been a re-dress of the same helmet or (less likely because it would have meant more trouble) a hastily made second helmet. But in any case, it is unfortunate that Guidance has the dented helmet, because the damage would have been a good externalization of Earth Ro-Man's unbalanced nature. The more perfectly un-dented, round opening of Earth Ro-Man's helmet would have better represented the unsympathetic and unyielding nature of Guidance and the tight, closed, circular logic of "the Plan."[285]

And as for the director who had first thought up the gorilla diving helmet scheme, Barrows had no affection:

> This director was a madman, and he had a wife who was a madwoman. The minute you stopped shooting, she says, "Don't take anything off, I want to sketch you." And when she first sprang that on me, I said, "Wait a minute,

WADE WILLIAMS DIST.

***Robot Monster*'s woman on the hill (*top center*), who could have been Phil Tucker's then-wife Francine.**

what are you talking about, sketching me?" I'm taking the helmet off by this time. I said, "You want to take a photograph, go ahead, be my guest." "No, no, I want to *sketch* you." I said, "Forget it, honey, you're going to have to do that on the wing, while I'm working." And he got mad at me, said [inaudible]—I said, "I don't give a—I have to breathe. You want me to go in the next scene, you better let me get some *air*, right now." Yeah, Phil Tucker, or whatever his first name was, he was a nut. . . . He was a madman. He could [not] care less for anyone or anything, just get the scene. And I said, "Come on, Tucker,

> I've been in the business too long for this, you've got to give the actors a break somewhere."

Tucker's mysterious wife, mentioned by Ordung as "Francine," reappears here, making her existence undeniable if her identity still elusive. (She is a good candidate for the woman visible at the top of a hill in the background, when Johnny meets Ro-Man halfway through the film.) Regarding the way Barrows remembered Tucker, it is notable that most people who knew Tucker found him likable, and Barrows is the major exception, perhaps because of the circumstances in which *Robot Monster* was shot. But Tucker Jr. confirms that his father was relentless in getting things done:

> He was kind of manic at times, he had an incredible work ethic where if he was doing something, he would just push and push and push and drive, he was like a bulldog. He would do whatever it takes, and if he had to get on the phone and call people or try to cajole them into helping him out. He would just work at it until it happened.

Somewhat confirming Barrows' negative memories of the experience, Barrett remembered a confused set, with directions coming from both Tucker and the two cameramen: "It was my understanding that Mr. Tucker was a first-time director. He was not familiar with camera techniques." Barrett also made this revealing remark: "It's too bad the original producer and director didn't have a good sense of humor."[286] As neither Zimbalist nor Tucker were remembered as particularly grouchy people (and Tucker Jr. remembered his father's love of laughter), this comment says a great deal about the mad, rushed quality of the shoot. For his part, Moffett told Barnum that he had no memories of Tucker, while remembering Barrows' overheated discomfort and difficulty breathing, resulting in the fact that "the filming of his scenes didn't go on too long."[287] Responding to my own questions, Moffett wrote:

> As you might guess, 58 years later matters. You must remember that as a juvenile, I had four hours of school every day, so I wasn't on the set as much as Mr. Barrows. If I remember correctly, the whole shoot took only seven or eight days, maybe less. That said, I do have memories of someone sketching, don't know if it was Mr. Tucker's wife. Who was in charge? I have no distinct memory. Cast and crew photos, I don't think so, my mom would have had them, and she didn't.
>
> I wish I could have helped fill in more details, but, alas, I cannot.[288]

Tucker must have been thrilled by the confluence of so many major events in Hollywood as he was filming *Robot Monster.* To answer Ro-Man's question, this is truly the point on the graph where cannot and must meet. The Academy Awards were given out the night of Thursday the 19th, after Tucker completed his first day of filming. The Academy voters awarded honors to a varied bunch—Best Picture *The Greatest Show on Earth,* Best Director John Ford (*The Quiet Man*), Best Actor Gary Cooper (*High Noon*), Best Actress Shirley Booth (*Come Back, Little Sheba*)—but the event was also the silver 25th Anniversary ceremony, and far more notably was the first televised ceremony. As *Variety* reported the next day, attendees contended with the discomfort of rainy weather and the knowledge that viewers of that first TV broadcast were arguably getting a more intimate and varied view of the proceedings. (Those in charge even went to the trouble of tinting the frosting of the oversized anniversary cake blue, so that it would show up better on black-and-white television.[289])

It is easy to picture Tucker, who wanted so badly to be part of show business, luxuriating in the glow of his first day of filming while enjoying that first broadcast.[290] Even if he had been scrambling to prepare for day two, he would have been buoyed by the knowledge that he was finally starting to make it. Perhaps he imagined himself at the ceremony he was watching a few years down the line, and enjoyed the fact that television was becoming so mainstream that film awards were finally broadcast through it. The medium that was to him just movies at home was now the medium that gave those at home an unprecedented window into the movies. The future was television, and he had already been aggressive in pursuing it. If *Robot Monster* did not open up the movie world for him, he could still make it in TV.

On Saturday the 21st, *Harrison's* ran a front-page account of the enthusiastically received "CinemaScope Demonstration," the process that soon ended the 3-D craze and made movies wide.[291] Monday's *Reporter,* stuffed with congratulation notices to Oscar winners, had the front page headline "Exhibitors Swarm Hollywood; Raves for CinemaScope and 3-D." Also on Monday were the many enthusiastic reactions of those in attendance, while tucked away on page 41 of the overlong special issue, it was finally noted that Claudia Barrett was co-starring with George Nader on the "now shooting" *Robot Monster.* But that report's final sentence accidentally foreshadowed what was imminent: "Producers are Al Zimbalist and Al Tucker."[292] Phil Tucker, half-mentioned in the write-up, would soon find himself not mentioned at all for the film he directed.

WADE WILLIAMS DIST.

(*Above*) Rare, little seen cast and crew photo from the *Robot Monster* shoot. (*Detail, below*) The 3-D rig used to film *Robot Monster*.

WADE WILLIAMS DIST.

6

Monster

Al Zimbalist wasted no time. Tuesday, March 24, was the final day of filming and by Friday the *Hollywood Reporter* announced that he had acquired "Master Tone Sound's newly developed stereophonic sound system" for *Robot Monster.*[293] On April 4, the *Motion Picture Herald* announced that Zimbalist was branching into a 3-D film service for independents. The report claimed that he only that week announced the debut of Tru-Stereo Corporation, that would supply "equipment and technical staffs" for a mere $15,000 plus 2½ percent of the profits, with the alternative of an outright payment of $30,000.[294] From the previous chapter's discussion of *Robot Monster*'s $16,000 cost, it is obvious that an immense chunk of any low-end film's budget would be wiped out by renting Zimbalist's 3-D services. But hot as 3-D was, some may have convinced themselves that the investment was solid. The *Herald* also noted inaccurately that last week Zimbalist had *started* filming "*The* [sic] *Robot Monster* in the Tru-stereo Process."

The April 24 *Reporter* mentioned Zimbalist with more substantive news, this time closely related to *Robot Monster.* Composer Elmer Bernstein signed with him for a multi-film deal, with *Robot Monster*—"now in final editing stages on the Goldwyn lot"—his current assignment.[295] (*Variety,* often dry on low-budget film news, reported Bernstein's contract the same day with the headline "Giving *Robot* Rhythm.")[296] By Tuesday the 28th the *Reporter* noted that *Robot Monster* was "currently being edited"[297], and on May 14 it reported that the film would be "scored tonight by Elmer Bernstein."[298] Phil Tucker took no credit for Zimbalist's house composer:

> *How did Elmer Bernstein get assigned to the project, of all people?*
>
> It was Al Zimbalist.

Bernstein's archived papers at the University of Southern California include three cues for his *Robot Monster* score, each date-stamped May 1953.[299] Most of each score sheet's eighteen bars are divided in half for two convenient sections of nine bars, two score pages of music thereby crammed onto each page. As Bernstein's music budget was likely as small as everything else in the production, he would not have had a large ensemble to work with, but this disadvantage allowed him the efficiency of making each score sheet do double duty. The score's nine parts are written for flute, trumpet, trombone, cello, bass, treble and bass parts for Novachord (an early electronic instrument), and first and second percussionists. (Wyott Ordung told Ray Zone that Bernstein used an "eight-piece orchestra" and that Capitol Records was interested in releasing the score up to the point when "somebody went to see the picture and we got laughed out of the record business."[300]) There is no mention of how many of each instrument was intended, though a paltry one of each would have fit the budget. Bill Warren aptly criticized the score as "under-orchestrated but overemphatic,"[301] but it could have hardly been otherwise. Bernstein could only afford a small group, but he intelligently chose a broad variety of orchestral colors with winds, strings, a variety of percussion effects, and electronics. This was one way to get around the budget limitations, and another was to make the music reasonably bombastic. Bernstein gave the movie the music it needed to seem like a grim, apocalyptic alien invasion, even if its majestic quality just brings out Ro-Man's absurdity all the more.

One unexpected aspect of the score is the lack of a piano part, for the instrument is notably audible throughout the film. It seems that what was written is therefore possibly far away from the final score, and this is explained by a closer look at Bernstein's early musical development; he was an accomplished pianist at a young age, giving an entire solo recital while in his teens.[302] He was also from this early time already beginning to be musically creative, and improvising little compositions along with his practice. His piano teacher brought him to the attention of Aaron Copland, who was sufficiently impressed to recommend a composition teacher.[303] Given Bernstein's talent, he likely did not bother writing a piano part because he had one in his head that he could have performed while directing the other musicians. This also explains the briefness of the score pages, and that they do not read as if they exactly contain the score as heard in the film. Bernstein's score also sounds as if he

MUSIC CUE SHEET

MARLEN MUSIC COMPANY
40? N. Rodeo Drive
BEVERLY HILLS, CALIFORNIA

ASCAP

ollowing is a list of the music used in THREE DIMENSION FILMS, INC. (TITLE OF CORPORATION) production of "ROBOT MONSTER" (TITLE OF PICTURE)

Description of Picture FEATURE/FILM Produced by AL ZIMBALIST Date 1953

GOLDWYN Studio MARLEN MUSIC CO. A.S.C.A.P. Musical Director ELMER BERNSTEIN

RE L CUE

1. Title of Composition: MAIN TITLE — Extent of Use: 1:47
Composer: ELMER BERNSTEIN (ASCAP) — Instrumental X
Publisher: MARLEN MUSIC CO. (ASCAP) — Instrumental Visual
Rights Secured From: " " " " — Vocal — Vocal Visual

2. Title of Composition: PLAY IN THE RAVINE — Extent of Use: 1:12
Composer: ELMER BERNSTEIN — Instrumental X
Publisher: MARLEN MUSIC CO. — Instrumental Visual
Rights Secured From: " " " — Vocal — Vocal Visual

3. Title of Composition: GREAT GUIDANCE — Extent of Use: 3:45
Composer: ELMER BERNSTEIN — Instrumental X
Publisher: MARLEN MUSIC CO. — Instrumental Visual
Rights Secured From: " " " — Vocal — Vocal Visual

4. Title of Composition: MORE GUIDANCE — Extent of Use: 2:20
Composer: ELMER BERNSTEIN — Instrumental X
Publisher: MARLEN MUSIC CO. — Instrumental Visual
Rights Secured From: " " " — Vocal — Vocal Visual

5. Title of Composition: FIX SCREEN — Extent of Use: 1:28
Composer: ELMER BERNSTEIN — Instrumental X
Publisher: MARLEN MUSIC CO. — Instrumental Visual
Rights Secured From: " " " — Vocal — Vocal Visual

6. Title of Composition: MORE FIX — Extent of Use: :30
Composer: ELMER BERNSTEIN — Instrumental X
Publisher: MARLEN MUSIC CO. — Instrumental Visual
Rights Secured From: " " " — Vocal — Vocal Visual

7. Title of Composition: JOHNNY & ROBOT — Extent of Use: 1:02
Composer: ELMER BERNSTEIN — Instrumental X
Publisher: MARLEN MUSIC CO. — Instrumental Visual
Rights Secured From: " " " — Vocal — Vocal Visual

8. Title of Composition: MORE JOHNNY & ROBOT — Extent of Use: :47
Composer: ELMER BERNSTEIN — Instrumental X
Publisher: MARLEN MUSIC CO. — Instrumental Visual
Rights Secured From: " " " — Vocal — Vocal Visual

9. Title of Composition: MAD ROBOT — Extent of Use: 1:57
Composer: ELMER BERNSTEIN — Instrumental X
Publisher: MARLEN MUSIC CO. — Instrumental Visual
Rights Secured From: " " " — Vocal — Vocal Visual

10. Title of Composition: GG PALAVER — Extent of Use: 1:27
Composer: ELMER BERNSTEIN — Instrumental X
Publisher: MARLEN MUSIC CO. — Instrumental Visual
Rights Secured From: " " " — Vocal — Vocal Visual

WADE WILLIAMS DIST.

(*Above and facing*) Elmer Bernstein's *Robot Monster* cue sheets.

had some stock ideas in mind; the music for the playing children seems to have its roots in Carl Orff's "Schulwerk" pieces, and there is a creeping, ominous section that calls to mind Igor Stravinsky's *The Rite of Spring* (see the latter part of the opening

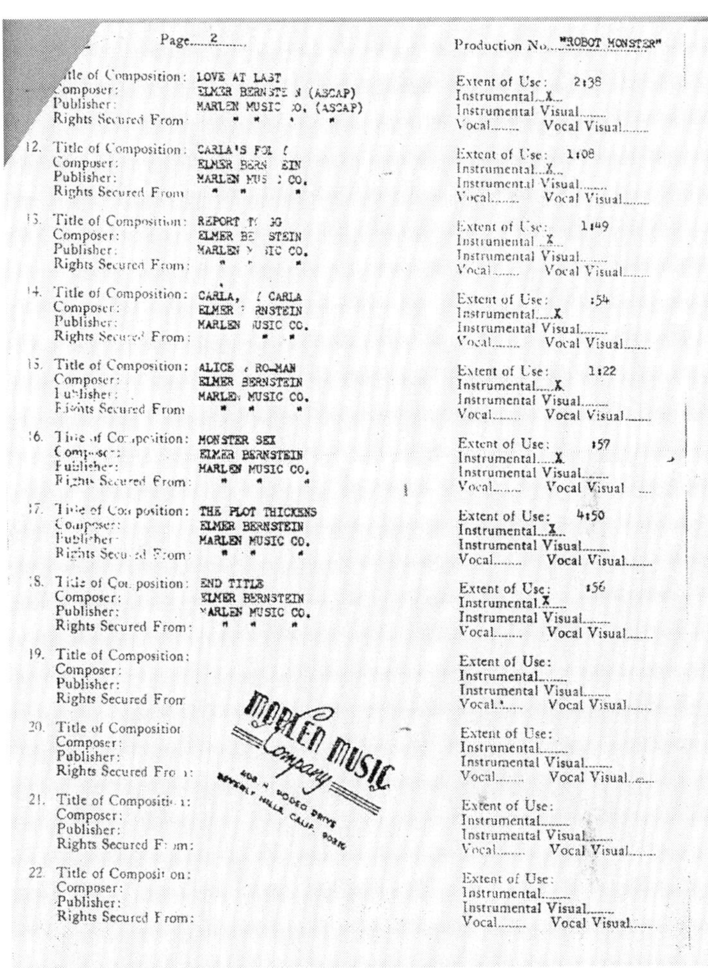

Page 2 Production No. "ROBOT MONSTER"

No.	Title of Composition	Composer	Publisher	Rights Secured From	Extent of Use	Instrumental	Instrumental Visual	Vocal	Vocal Visual
11.	LOVE AT LAST	ELMER BERNSTE N (ASCAP)	MARLEN MUSIC CO. (ASCAP)	" " " "	2:38	X			
12.	CARLA'S FOI	ELMER BERN EIN	MARLEN MUS CO.	" " "	1:08	X			
13.	REPORT T G	ELMER BE STEIN	MARLEN SIC CO.	" " "	1:49	X			
14.	CARLA, CARLA	ELMER RNSTEIN	MARLEN USIC CO.	" "	:54	X			
15.	ALICE RO MAN	ELMER BERNSTEIN	MARLEN MUSIC CO.	" " "	1:22	X			
16.	MONSTER SEX	ELMER BERNSTEIN	MARLEN MUSIC CO.	" " "	:57	X			
17.	THE PLOT THICKENS	ELMER BERNSTEIN	MARLEN MUSIC CO.	" " "	4:50	X			
18.	END TITLE	ELMER BERNSTEIN	MARLEN MUSIC CO.	" " "	:56	X			
19.									
20.									
21.									
22.									

MARLEN MUSIC Company
408 N. RODEO DRIVE
BEVERLY HILLS CALIF.

WADE WILLIAMS DIST.

credits). The written score was possibly just an initial sketch at what it would sound like, for it was well within his abilities to have changed things around by the time of that May 14 night of scoring (likely the soundtrack's only recording session), and to tell the musicians to adjust things here and there. Furthermore, while each page of all three cues are stamped "robot monster" at the top, the first page of one of them has a notation written across that title, "1006 'CAT WOMEN.'" Writing the *Cat-Women of the Moon* score later in 1953, Bernstein apparently went back to the same well of ideas from which his *Robot Monster* score arose. Two cue sheets itemize the actual completed score, consisting of eighteen tracks running a total time of thirty minutes and fifty seconds.

Bernstein remembered these beginning years of his film career with humor, noting that he had leftist associations that were stalling his career while not quite blacklisting him.[304] The June 1952 *Reporter* announced that he would soon "score his own composition at Republic," for the film noir *Sudden Fear,* showing that some of his early projects were better than Zimbalist quality.[305] It must have nonetheless been eagerness to stay employed that persuaded him to go along with a bit of eyebrow-raising *Robot Monster* publicity, preserved by *Daily Variety*: "Thesp John Brown and composer Elmer Bernstein will plug *Robot Monster* when they guest on Bill Ballance's KNX airer tonight."[306] (If only *that* particular piece of old time radio history had been preserved!) Bernstein told interviewer Elise Christenson in 2003 that before Cecil B. DeMille gave him his big break scoring *The Ten Commandments* (1956), "I found myself doing things like *Robot Monster* and *Cat-Women of the Moon,* and I didn't know what the devil was going on. But if you're going to do a really bad movie, at least you do one that is at the top of the all-time bad-movie list."[307] Bernstein found some value in scoring terrible films, as he told interviewer Nick Joy, "I had as much fun working on those films as I did on *The Ten*

Commandments."[308] But Harry Medved told me, "I interviewed Elmer in person as part of a series of evenings with film composers that I hosted a few years ago . . . When I mentioned [*Robot Monster*], he slapped his hand to his head (as if to say, 'Oy') and basically said, 'Why would you want to talk about that one? I was so young...' . . . He clearly groaned when I brought up the title."[309] Phil Tucker Jr. likewise remembered attending "Jeff Joseph's event at the 3D festival, [where] a seat had been reserved for [Bernstein] . . . and remained unoccupied throughout the screening. I think that, like my father, he went on to do bigger and better things and did not want to dwell on a low point in his career."[310]

By April 28, Zimbalist was announcing two new 3-D Tru-Stereo projects, *Pirate Women* and *Baby-Faced* [sic] *Nelson*, the *Reporter* also noting that *Robot Monster* was "currently being edited."[311] It is interesting that the film was still being cut together over a month after being shot. As brief and straightforward as it was, it seems that the editing should have been straightforward and quick as well. But special effects had to be added, the 3-D process could have added complications, and there may have been problems inherent in the footage. Zimbalist also cut costs of his Tru-Stereo process to "as little as $5,000 and a small percentage."[312] On May 13, the *Reporter* stated that Zimbalist was preparing *Robot Monster* "for release," and was planning another 3-D Tru-Stereo production, *Conquest of Space*, to be made in color.[313] The "original" script by Guy Reed Ritchie, previously reported as the author of the magazine story "Adam and Eve" that Zimbalist had purchased for adaptation, concerned "adventures on the moon." Perhaps original, it was undoubtedly titled to cash in on the popularity of science author Willy Ley's 1949 nonfiction bestseller of the same title, which was ultimately adapted into a 1955 film by producer George Pal and director Byron Haskin. The next day brought the news that agent Walter Kohner would represent Zimbalist's "True-Stereo Corp.," headquartered at, of course, the Goldwyn Studios.[314]

These Zimbalist-focused reports connect the dots of *Robot Monster*'s post-production process without mentioning Phil Tucker even once. Likewise on May 20, the *Reporter* noted that "more than 1,500 feet of special effects in 3-D were completed yesterday by Jack Rabin's Complete Film Enterprises at Eagle Lion for inclusion in Al Zimbalist's 3-D science fiction feature,

ALL IMAGES ABOVE - WADE WILLIAMS DIST.

(*Clockwise from upper left*) **Among the movies that *Robot Monster* borrowed footage from are *Flight to Mars, Invasion U.S.A., Lost Continent*, and *One Million B.C.***

Robot Monster."[315] (If factoring in the double use of footage for the 3-D process, 1,500 feet of 35-millimeter film equals over eight minutes of special effects, which seems exaggerated.) But Tucker may have contributed a great deal un-credited, for the stock footage that nonsensically shows up in *Robot Monster*—its most surreal element, next to Ro-Man and his speeches—was richly connected to Tucker's background. Stock footage was peppered into *Robot Monster* at moments where effects were needed, and given Tucker's background and Zimbalist's subsequent reputation, it could hardly have been otherwise. According to Richard Maurice Hurst's history of Republic Pictures, "In order to realize and maintain these heavily emphasized economies, the studio utilized efficient and often clever means to save money. Republic relied heavily and very professionally on such devices as expert use of stock footage . . .."[316] Stock footage was part of the lifeblood of Poverty Row, and exploitation makers never hesitated to reuse material either (they re-released entire movies under different titles, after all).

Robot Monster took hurtling asteroids from *Flight to Mars* and bombed-out city shots from *Invasion U.S.A.* and *Captive Women*, but the film's most obvious source of borrowed footage was the Hal Roach production *One Million B.C.* (1940). While it now plays as an unadventurous prehistoric adventure it was, according to Mark F. Berry, one of very few "dinosaur-oriented feature film[s] to appear since the *Kong* pictures." "No one," Berry says, "had seen anything like it." But much more significant was the wealth of "scenes, test footage, and outtakes" from the film that were repeatedly recycled into other films and TV shows at least until Al Adamson's *Horror of the Blood Monsters* in 1970.

Berry lists nearly twenty such titles, but notes that "this list is surely incomplete."[317] Though not the first, Boris Petroff's *Two Lost Worlds* (1950) and Merle Connell's *Untamed Women* (1952)[318] had already recycled *One Million B.C.* footage, and so Tucker was well-acquainted with the practice of raiding the old Roach film by the time he made *Robot Monster.*

Tucker and Zimbalist were unique for using footage from Lippert's recent *Lost Continent* to supplement the other dinosaur footage. These stop motion effects were inferior to others (and inferior to the real animal performers from *One Million B.C.*) but, according to Berry, they were the first onscreen since 1933's *The Son of Kong,* making it clear why they were at the time desirable for recycling.[319] In relation to *King Kong,* which looms in the background of *Robot Monster* on multiple levels, Tucker discussed it in this somewhat incoherent exchange:

> *Very interesting how these just put this still from* One Million B.C. *in there, and stuck it right on.*
> Well, we incorporated some of that.
>
> *I know that. Who in fact bought the stock footage from* One Million B.C.*?*
> Well, I don't understand what you're saying.
>
> *First of all, whose idea was it to use the footage of the dinosaurs? Did you write that in the script?*
> No, it was never in the script, but it was always explicit in discussions that we had.

The idea of the calcinator death ray exploding the Earth and [then] dinosaurs . . .
I didn't know what footage was going to go with the other, so I think at that point we set stock footage here [inaudible].

One review said it was from King Kong.
Well, it was in a sense.

No, I mean the stock footage wasn't used from King Kong.
In the sense that all the *One Million B.C.* footage was used from *King Kong*, yeah.

All right.

While *One Million B.C.* did not use footage from *King Kong*, the confusion is understandable given Tucker's health problems, and the scarcity of big special effects movies in that era.[320] Furthermore, his jumbled memory on this point reinforces the certainty that *Robot Monster* was in many ways influenced by the resurgent popularity of *King Kong.*

The common denominator of some of the effects stock footage was the man credited for effects on the film itself, Jack Rabin. While he shared credit with David Commons, whose credits were relatively sparse, Rabin was incredibly prolific during this era, often in partnership with Irving Block. While calling them "those semi-reliable craftsmen of low-budget SF films," with "many good ideas and some bad ones, too," Warren credited them for being "usually way ahead of others working on their budget level . . ..."[321] Likely no one could have pulled off a better job for the money on *Robot Monster,* and Rabin in fact considered himself uniquely qualified for the challenges of what he termed "restraint budgets":

> I've always wondered if a man gave me a million dollars and I could bring back 800 trees from the High Sierras, for how long it would take to ship it, I would rather take something like a piece of string on a low-budget picture and do the same thing. There must be some relationship between that challenge and no money—the juices flow for me that way. Why? You'd have to go to a doctor to figure that out.[322]

Rabin's career began in the silent era, and he gained effects experience throughout Hollywood before going independent "in the mid-40s" and soon after teaming with Block, according to a profile by special effects artists Robert and Dennis Skotak.[323] In this partnership Rabin was generally in charge, with Block the main designer and specific tasks sometimes doled out to such associates as Gene Warren, who remembered Block as "a really good matte painter." (Block's story "Fatal Planet" was bought by MGM and eventually became *Forbidden Planet,* the legendary film also benefitting from his design suggestions; he eventually became an art professor at California State University.)

One of *Robot Monster*'s most frequently mocked original effects, in which the spinning and sputtering "space platform" blows up (thereby taking out the never seen "Jason and McCloud"), shows an unfortunately visible black-gloved arm holding the ship aloft. Rabin was surely as aware of that shot's shortcomings as anyone, but of course it was probably left as is because there was no money to make and blow up another model on this "restraint budget" production. A simple, cheap, and successful effect native to the movie was the use of brief flashes of negative film to represent the effect of Ro-Man's calcinator ray, although it could have come as easily from the mechanically gifted Tucker. But although Rabin sparked the idea for Roger Corman's *War of the Satellites* and Block contributed to *Forbidden Planet,* their abilities may have been mostly limited to their effects and design work. Actress Marilyn Nash told Tom Weaver about working on their 1951 production *Unknown World*:

> . . . I felt they didn't have any talent. I couldn't imagine how they became producers. I just thought that they didn't know what they were doing. . . . They were really nice fellows, but, oh, my God . . .![324]

The James Earl Jones to George Barrows' David Prowse, John Brown is probably the most underappreciated of the underrated cast and—for reasons that will be explored—was likely hired in post-production. Brown brought life to both Ro-Men's absurd dialogue, which defines *Robot Monster* almost as much as the diving helmet and gorilla suit. Brown was a highly prolific radio actor with occasional film and television credits. Born in England in 1904, he grew up in Australia and then New York City. He was later working in a New York mortuary while trying to break into radio, which he did in 1934; he would become one of the most talented and busy vocal actors in radio history. Adept at various accents, his favorites included regional dialects of his

John Brown

native land, and he appeared in literally thousands of radio productions, legendarily appearing in seven programs per week in 1941. Working in all genres, he was highly desired as a comedy stooge and was a regular member of Fred Allen's ensemble.[325] Brown had one regular part that connected with the general public. *The Life of Riley* (1944-1949) had been cancelled early but returned, and blossomed, thanks to Brown's portrayal of "friendly undertaker" Digger O'Dell. As creator Irving Brecher remembered, "I want[ed] a very sepulchral voice, quavering, morbid, and [Brown] got it right away."[326] The former mortuary worker brought Digger to life, repeatedly terrifying William Bendix's Riley with his creepy salutations. The character remained over initial sponsor objections, generating fan mail and ratings.

Brown had a smattering of film roles but some were noteworthy, including *The Day the Earth Stood Still* (1951). His final onscreen appearance in 1953's *The Wild One* brought the notice that "Comedian Goes Straight" from *Daily Variety* in February 1953.[327] In 1952, he guest-starred on the TV series *Biff Baker, U.S.A.*, a show that also hired John Mylong and Wyott Ordung for one episode each (none of them together, alas). But Brown's best onscreen showcase was Alfred Hitchcock's *Strangers on a Train* (1951). He shows his vocal mastery in the small, pivotal role of a math professor, drunkenly singing "Bill Grogan's Goat" on a passenger car to Farley Granger's amusement, later not remembering it sober in a police interrogation. Brown changes his voice between scenes, switching from soused, stretched-out working-class vowels to a sober affectation of mid-Atlantic diction. His performance throws in the subtle suggestion that the professor's memory is not so much faulty as selective. What might have cut Brown off from more film and television was his listing along with Selena Royle in *Red Channels.*[328] Tucker did not remember blacklisting in connection to Brown:

Wasn't John Brown also . . .[blacklisted]*?*
I don't know.

I think he was in the hearings.
Very possible.

Brown died May 16, 1957, of a heart attack.[329] With his radio-honed talent and work ethic, he was perfect for the *Robot Monster* voice-overs, likely a one-day job. Towering over the film's many shortcomings, his performance is one thing that goes decidedly right. It is never obvious that both Ro-Men are vocalized by the same actor, and no one could have done a better job with the ridiculous dialogue. The effect of Brown's performance is absurd, but only because of the material.

Befitting a movie with so many unique properties, the *Robot Monster* credits showed more imagination than most threadbare credit openings for no-budget monster epics. A background shot of comic books was a cheap and simple way to provide some visual interest, keep ten-year-old boys distracted, and establish the theme that little Johnny had monsters on the brain.

The credits sequence was even prescient for, by coincidence, the first 3-D comic had been in preparation for some time and debuted in July.[330] As Moffett remembered, "Those were the days of those 3-D funny books and kids loved them—I know I did."[331] Following logically from the American craze for 3-D photos and now movies, 3-D comics were however burnt out and abandoned within less than a year.[332] The distinctive sans-serif font Futura Extra Bold Condensed (in white, with a darker shaded, 3-D "perspective trail" variation for the title) contributed to the unique feel of the sequence, along with a series of headshots of the six recognizable onscreen performers. Given the marginal value that the film had for their careers, perhaps cast members would have been happier *un*identified by face in the credits, but at least Ro-Man was not pictured yet, and entered the film later with some chance of surprise.

Medved questioned Tucker about one clearly noticeable comic in the upper right side of the frame:

> *. . . I saw in the title credits of the film, it starts out with an array of comic books, just assorted different titles. One of the titles was Robot Monster. I was wondering, did you print that for the film, or was there a comic book Robot Monster before the film came out?*
> No, that was made just for that shot.
>
> *So the film wasn't based on a comic book?*
> No.

Noticeable with home video technology and a little gazing effort is that the doctored *Robot Monster* comic is based on a comic that appears almost directly below it.[333] *Strange Suspense Stories* #5 appeared in 1953 and was the last issue of the Fawcett series that began the previous year. The cover depicts a witch gleefully stabbing pins into a voodoo doll and imagining the results on the victim. While doctoring up a *Robot Monster* comic shows admirable ambition, this supernatural horror cover was not an ideal choice. A better one, visible in on top and left of center, would have been issue #6 of Dell's short-lived *Tom Corbett, Space Cadet.* A spaceman, up to his waist in a torrent of water leaking from a damaged wall, furiously cranks a water valve in the colorful cover painting. Along with the hero's mostly clear, bubble-like helmet, it would fire the imagination of little Johnnies everywhere, even without a monster. But horror comics, popular from the late 1940s until controversy choked them out of existence in the mid-fifties, would have

WADE WILLIAMS DIST.

***Robot Monster*'s comic book credits collage.**

been readily available at the time and loosely fit the monster theme of the film; this is probably why they dominate the comics on display.

Another supernatural Fawcett title, *Beware! Terror Tales* was well represented in the credits. There are at least three copies of issue #6, two on top of each other lower left and another on the right edge. The cover shows an exaggeratedly frightened man, hair standing on end, facing a skeleton while the cover text promises "tales conjured up by the devil and written in blood!" Issue #7 (bats and a ghost on a full moon night) and final issue #8 (witches stirring a cauldron) appear near each other in the center. A few other Fawcett horror titles torment the credits, including *This Magazine Is Haunted* #11, this one with another frightened man and another skeleton carrying a noose; two copies are partially buried on the center and right edge. Issue #10 of *Worlds of Fear* carries a striking painted cover image of a man wearing silver reflective glasses amidst a landscape of giant eyeballs, and appears in the lower center and again barely visible on the left. Another notable painted cover appears on *Strange Stories from Another World* #5, depicting yet another frightened man surrounded by a woman, giant hands, and all manner of ghouls. This one appears very noticeably in the upper left, as well as upper center, but also appears largely hidden lower left, with the word "COPY" visible in a light ink on the cover. While horror comprises the bulk of the *Robot Monster* comics, there are a few more titles just visible in the credits shot. *Underworld Crime,* another Fawcett title, is represented by two copies of issue #5 (with a fedora-wearing thug, visible on left and upper right corner) and one barely visible copy of issue #6 (lower right corner). One last comic, Dell's *John Carter of Mars* #375, can be spotted in the lower right corner, just poking out from under *Underworld Crime* #6. This one would have also made a better choice for a *Robot Monster* comic book than *Strange Suspense Stories,* but with the possibility of incurring the wrath of the wealthy Edgar Rice Burroughs' estate (which retained control over properties licensed from his characters), it may have been smart to not feature that cover too obviously.

Enterprising as ever, Zimbalist had a new ware to hawk. Noting on May 25 that *Robot Monster* was "recently completed," *Variety* reported that he was for $10 also selling a widescreen converter for standard ratio projectors.[334] With *Robot Monster* filmed right as CinemaScope converted the entire industry to widescreen, he was smart to try and cash in. But this also illustrates the fact that, for aspect ratio purists, *Robot Monster* is a puzzling case. It was likely filmed at 1.37:1 with no care for the widescreen issue, as the filmmakers were wrapped up in getting the desired 3-D effect and were probably unaware of the CinemaScope demonstration through at least the first day of filming. Even if it crossed their minds, they probably ignored it; it would be months before Hollywood made official decisions on the matter. Tucker and Zimbalist did not know if 3-D would die out in favor of widescreen, or if widescreen would stick around as the new default setting for movies. But by the time the film was released a few months later, widescreen had become the industry standard and theaters were in some proportion already converted to its use. *Robot Monster* therefore must have been projected inconsistently, anywhere from 1.37:1 to 1.85:1. While the only objective choice for the film's correct ratio would be the 1.37:1 it was filmed in, it looks good zoomed into 1.78:1 on widescreen TV. While some shots become compromised and the opening credits are partially unreadable, the film's often bland compositions sometimes benefit from the cropping, creating more dynamic framing.

In the same report, *Variety* mentioned that Zimbalist had made "his" Tru-Stereo process available for any project at a much more economical $5,000, suggesting that his original budget-busting offer went unappreciated. With these favorable new terms, interest in his services might have risen dramatically; the completed *Robot Monster* would soon be previewed for critics. Both the *Reporter* and *Variety* weighed in on Thursday, June 11, with strikingly similar appraisals. The trade paper kingpins noted the leaden acting and general un-believability, but were pleased by the quality of the special effects and 3-D imagery, each complimenting it as "easy on the eyes" and mercifully free of cheap tricks like objects flying into the camera. *Variety*'s Neal was particularly impressed that the film was made for "under $50,000" (confirming Tucker's memory precisely) while describing Tucker's direction as "off"; the *Reporter* noted that it "does little to inject vitality." The bottom line was that the bottom line was looking good, as both sources predicted good business for a production with little budget but much exploitation potential.[335]

According to the *Reporter*'s review, the "picture [had] no release as yet," but the next day announced that it would "open locally June 25 at the Hollywood Paramount, Manchester, Globe, and four other Fox West Coast theatres," with a nationwide deal being pursued.[336] Zimbalist (Tucker was not mentioned) also had a project filming in July, *Conquest of the Moon*, which may or may not have been written by Guy Reed Ritchie (of *Conquest of Space* fame), but was "based on a story by Roy Hamilton." The same day as this news in the *Reporter*, June 12, *Variety* noted that Zimbalist had made Eddie Barrison sales manager of Three Dimension, and that he would be going to work on *Robot Monster*.[337] Further down in the report was the news that Zimbalist's *Conquest of the Moon* would begin filming September 1, not at some point in July, with *Baby Faced* [sic] *Nelson* starting "late fall." It is difficult to imagine just why the same project was reported as having completely different starting points in reports that appeared on the very same day, other than that Zimbalist perhaps had no definite starting point in mind and did not care if what was printed was accurate. By June 18, Zimbalist was sharing his profit arrangement for *Robot Monster*'s debut, *Daily Variety* noting that his arrangement with "the Hollywood Paramount, Orpheum and Manchester theatres" will also be made with national distributors, Zimbalist receiving "35% of the gross up to an undisclosed 'split' figure after which he and the house split 50-50." Zimbalist also planned to "sell his film abroad in all markets."[338]

Boxoffice got around to printing the local release news on June 20 (the national release was still being worked out)[339] and, more pertinently, the film surfaced in the *Hollywood Citizen-News* on June 22, finally putting it in view of potential customers. Along with a write-up, *Robot Monster* was represented by an ad promising an "exclusive one-week engagement" to start Wednesday the 24th. Paired with the Sonny Tufts vehicle *Run for the Hills*, the film promised "'Robot Monsters' from outer space . . . fire can't burn them . . . bullets can't stop them . . .will they destroy the human race?" The ad utilized the famous poster image, in what must have been one of its earliest appearances, with the skull-face Ro-Man carrying a long-haired glamour girl who does not much resemble Claudia Barrett. (The ruined buildings, dinosaurs, and rocket ship that Ro-Man towers over bear far more similarity to their onscreen counterparts than do either he or Alice.) Her name and Nader's made the ad, as well as that of Zimbalist. Not surprisingly, Tucker was unmentioned.[340]

The June 23 *Citizen-News* hyped the film once again with a little more focus, throwing in the eccentric detail that it was about "an assault on Earth by electronically-controlled monsters launched against this planet from the moon." The next day's paper brought a larger version of the ad, appropriate for opening day, using the same image but with a pretty accurate portrait of Nader and Barrett now visible in the lower left corner. The new ad line read, "Moon Monsters Launch Attack Against Earth!"[341]

About the robot, [from] *where did you actually plan for him to come? I noticed that the alternate titles of the film have been Monster from Mars and Monsters on the Moon, did anybody actually decide—*
Well, I had nothing to do with alternate titles.

Did you plan for the monster to come from the moon?
No. I planned for the monster to come from . . .

Planet Ro-Man?

. . . some place, some other star.

Tucker claimed at this point to have been a writer of science fiction short stories, and then emphasized, "But I would never have claimed that Ro-Man came from the moon. I would have had him come from some other solar system altogether, simply because that would have been my thinking."

Opening day, Wednesday the 24th, the *Citizen-News* had another short write-up, noting that that film was the "first three-dimension motion picture to be offered at popular prices."[342] The film's release, then, was shrewdly geared to have broad appeal to the masses, and not ten-year-olds only. (Zimbalist, or someone involved in the production, must have understood the old rule of economics that more units of something sold at a lower cost will usually be more profitable than fewer units at a higher cost.) The report also noted that a 3-D short was attached to the release, *Stars* [sic] *in Your Eyes*, a filmed performance by impressionist Slick Slavin, stage persona of Trustin Howard. The short was actually titled *Stardust in Your Eyes* and, according to Jeff Joseph, ended with Howard introducing *Robot Monster*.[343] The addition of this short may have been influenced by the May release of Universal's *It Came from Outer Space*. In *Amazing 3-D*, Hal Morgan and Dan Symmes state that this film had an accompanying 3-D musical short, featuring Nat King Cole performing with extra 3-D visual support from acrobats.[344]

On Thursday, the *Citizen-News* reviewed the film.[345] Writer L.E.R. avoided the industry perspective that colored reports from the trade papers, and instead found the movie competent but obviously cheap, with appreciation for the effects shots and the looks of Claudia Barrett, and the conclusion that the film was best for uncritical kids. Most interesting in the review was the writer's unwillingness to accept that the creature onscreen was in fact a man in a gorilla suit, noting that it "wears a coat of hair like a gorilla and a sort of deep-seat [sic] diving helmet." (Tucker was right that his no-budget robot costume would work.) Likewise, it is a toss-up as to whether it was more the fault of the critic or the film that certain details could not be recalled accurately, as L.E.R. noted that the monster was commanded by the "Great Mind in Mars."

But while the location of Ro-Man's home world became increasingly vague, his destination was becoming steadily clearer. Trumpeting "State-Right Moola for Indie Product," the June 29 *Reporter* outlined Zimbalist's plans for widening the film's release.[346] Aided by salesman Edward Barison (as he was now listed, minus the second r), he claimed to be expecting $500,000 by selling the film directly for 500 engagements at $1,000 a crack. Subsequently, the film would be tied up for two years in state's-rights releases, in "exploitation houses exclusively." (Tucker may have taught Zimbalist a thing or two about bottom-end distribution.) J. Arthur Rank was allegedly in talks to buy the British rights, and Zimbalist had been recently in New York on business, with *Conquest of the Moon* beginning in "eight weeks."

Shortly after on July 11, *Harrison's* reviewed *Robot Monster,* and this review closest to the paying customer found almost nothing positive to say about it.[347] (The Los Angeles-based trade papers may have condescendingly thought the film good enough for the rubes out in the sticks.) Theater owners "may be able to use this 3-D science fiction picture on the lower half of a double bill, but [they] should not expect [their] patrons to like it, for it is the poorest 3-D picture that he [sic] been made so far." Shedding no tears that no distribution deal was yet in place, the reviewer called the story "illogical" and noted that the "the supposed monsters from another planet are laughable." Just about the only positive comments were reserved for the acting of young Gregory Moffett. Predicting that other films like *Robot Monster* would end public interest in 3-D permanently, the reviewer ultimately summed it up as "Harmless for the family." Meanwhile, Phil Tucker was once again cut out of any credit: "Al Zimbalist produced and directed . . .."

On July 28, the byzantine complexity of Zimbalist's speculative release plan dissipated in the light of a new press item. "Astor Pictures has acquired worldwide distribution rights" for *Robot Monster*, the *Reporter* noted, as well as "an option on worldwide rights to *Cat Woman on the Moon*," a film that would begin "in six weeks" and film in Tru-Stereo 3-D.[348] Zimbalist's next project had mutated all the way from *Conquest of the Moon* to *Cat Woman on the Moon*, and the Roy Hamilton-scripted project later in the year became *Cat-**Women of** the Moon.* In the meantime, *Robot Monster* had a solid, blood simple release schedule in place, as befitted the experienced and thrifty Astor Pictures. Smaller than a Poverty Row studio, but more professional than an exploitation outfit like George Weiss' Screen Classics, Astor seemed to release virtually anything if it was cheaply acquired and had some built-in audience. According to Don Miller, it was "an independent clearing house for assorted oldies and shoestring independent productions."[349] In 1947, Astor released *The Road to Hollywood*, a compilation of early Bing Crosby shorts titled to encourage confusion with the popular *Road* series of

R. M. (BOB) SAVINI, Pres.

130 W. 46TH ST. N. Y. 36

ASTOR PICTURES CORP.

(31 DISTRIBUTING EXCHANGES — U.S. & CANADA)

ATLANTIC TELEVISION CORP.

(PRODUCERS-DISTRIBUTORS and SALES)

PRECISION FILM EDITOR CORP.

(PREVIEWING-CUTTING — INVESTIGATE — HAS NO EQUAL)

NOW—ASTOR 3D FILMS, INC.

(PORTABLE-ONE CAMERA 3D EQUIPMENT)

NOW AT THE KNICKERBOCKER HOTEL, HOLLYWOOD

A 1953 Astor Pictures publicity ad.

Crosby and Bob Hope comedies. Trade reports of the time reveal such other bits as an April 2, 1952, *Reporter* note that Astor was preparing a "new feature," the anticommunist drama *Seeds of Destruction.*[350] This film was in reality a recycled 1949 Roland Reed production, then distributed by the Lutheran Laymen's League as *The Sickle or the Cross.* The August 22 *Reporter* revealed that Astor was releasing worldwide the "three-reeler" (a roughly thirty-minute short) *Argentine* [sic] *Mourns Evita,* presumably showcasing documentary footage of the recent funeral of Eva Peron.[351]

Astor's consistent game plan did not factor in quality. According to Bill Warren's *Keep Watching the Skies!,* "Astor Pictures developed an unenviable but justified reputation for releasing the very worst science fiction and horror films." Warren also noted in a later section, "Astor turned out the worst science fiction/horror movies of the late '50s . . .. Their releases . . . are nearly unwatchable . . .." And if that was not consistent enough, he invoked another's low opinion in his review of *Giant from the Unknown*: ". . . Don Willis thought it was 'not as bad as some of Astor's pictures, but then again, nothing is as bad as some of Astor's pictures.'"[352] But according to Eric Schaefer, Astor sometimes even functioned as a semi-exploitation outfit. "Relatively innocuous motion pictures were sometimes given a full exploitation treatment long after their original release," he noted. One example was Astor's fifties reissue of "a cache of pre-Code independent films" with racy new titles and the option of adding "exploitation shorts or burlesque reels distributed by Astor."[353] In *Kings of the Bs*, Charles Flynn and Todd McCarthy noted that this ratty outfit was one of the "more important independent distributors" using the state's-rights system during the forties.[354]

Heading this little empire was longtime movie exhibitor Robert M. Savini, who had been working in film distribution since before the Great Depression. In April 1929, the "Atlanta motion picture man" was involved in the production of filmed sermons by evangelist Billy Sunday, whose preaching thereby continued into the future.[355] According to Kevin Heffernan's *Ghouls, Gimmicks, and Gold*, "Astor Pictures had been in business as an importer and distributor of supporting features since 1933."[356] But a September 1954 *Reporter* item suggests that his career went back even before 1929 with the news of a "50th anniversary drive honoring Bob Savini, president of Astor Pictures . . . ."[357] Writer-director Oliver Drake recalled meeting Savini in the early fifties when he made an unannounced visit to the outdoor set of a Sunset Carson Western:

> The driver opened the rear door, and a portly, middle-aged, well dressed man stepped out and strolled importantly toward the camera setup . . . He had only taken a few steps when he was stopped abruptly by my first assistant director, Charlie Gould. . . .
>
> The portly gent straightened up to his full height and tried to eye Charlie down. "I'm Bob Savini," he replied rather stiffly.
>
> "I don't care if you're the devil himself," Charlie roared. . . .
>
> A big smile spread across Savini's face as he stared at Charlie, then he turned and nodded to the driver . . . Still smiling, Savini gave Charlie a mock salute and walked around him . . . "You've got quite an assistant director," [Savini] commented. "He really put me in my place."[358]

As the *Reporter* noted in November 1953, he was smart enough to get out of a lawsuit with a settlement that cost money but gained him "the rights to five Westerns."[359] It was probably just that economical side of Savini that led to the following announcement in the April 1954 *Reporter*: "He just purchased the Florida Keys Driftwood Industries in Islamorada, which manufactures household furnishings made from driftwood."[360] But maybe he realized how hilarious it was for a merchant of cinematic driftwood to take over a driftwood furniture company.

Savini's interests went beyond film distribution into logical areas for partnering with Zimbalist. In February 1952, the

Reporter noted that he was staying the better part of a month at the Knickerbocker Hotel, and was taking advantage of his Hollywood visit to promote the imported Editola, a supposedly versatile and accurate piece of editing equipment.[361] By the spring of 1953, Savini had been advertising his diverse enterprises in the trades. An ad that ran within a few days of itself in the *Reporter* and *Variety* indicated that Savini was president of four companies: Astor Pictures, Atlantic Television, Precision Film Editor, and the new Astor 3-D Films.[362] This last outfit, incorporated in Arizona and "capitalized at $200,000" according to the May 8 *Reporter,* was a one camera 3-D format, "with two prints being taken off the single negative for projection."[363] With Savini already in the 3-D projection business, acquiring *Robot Monster* was logical and, with its rock-bottom production cost, everyone involved should have profited. Astor also had a connection with the Hal Roach company at least as early as February 1953, when the *Motion Picture Herald* noted that Astor had "six new productions now being filmed at the Hal Roach Studios" along with its usual reissues.[364] The *Reporter* and *Variety* also stated in March that Savini had agreed to distribute new product by Roach's new company Lincoln Productions, Inc.[365] With this connection, Astor's distribution of Zimbalist's Roach-footage-infested production seems almost inevitable.

Astor released a press book for the film, uncredited but possibly the work of Tucker and Zimbalist.[366] It is a pile of undiluted equine excrement that is almost as astonishing as the film, and is really the last word on the lengths movie producers go to in underestimating audience intelligence. No further comment is necessary:

OVERWHELMING! ELECTRIFYING! BAFFLING!

WILL "ROBOT MONSTERS" COME TO DESTROY THE WORLD BY FEEDING ON THE BODIES OF THE HUMAN RACE?

SEE THE UNFOLDING OF THE MYSTERIES OF THE MOON AS MURDEROUS ROBOT MONSTERS DESCEND UPON THE EARTH AND CONTAMINATE THEIR VICTIMS! YOU'VE NEVER SEEN ANYTHING LIKE IT! NEITHER HAS THE WORLD!

SEE . . . The Moon's sinister crew of killers!

The thrilling, three dimension melodrama has its locale on an open ruins in America where these deadly robots descend to earth in their mysterious Spaceship and immediately disappear into the earth's caves.

Not since the atom bomb project was launched had there been the hushed curiosity which met the making of Al Zimbalist's Three-Dimension motion picture of man's first contact with Robot Monsters in "Robot Monster" . ...

"How will they do it," curiosity seekers asked.

Shooting the film required the help of outstanding scientists of the day, pioneers in rocket research, astronomers, physicists, etc.

. . . there is something that augurs to make the picture rank among the all-time thrill-greats in the film world. It is the dramatic presentation of the invasion from space of Robot Monsters zipping through space at 7 miles per second and defying all the laws of the universe.

In addition to the sheer dramatic impact of the film is the fact that here one will get an actual preview of the first successful contact from space, which, according to the best-known authorities, will be made within the next 10 or 15 years.

. . . it is a known fact that if we had today's V-2 rocket on the moon, and could fire it, it would reach the earth. Less gravity from moon to earth. Therefore, the obvious military fact that he who controls the moon controls the earth. . . . it has been proven scientifically, that life exists on the moon. What type, scientists must prove. Just such a situation, in the abstract, is brought on the screen in "Robot Monster" filmed in Three-Dimension, which was directed by Phil Tucker, for in it, the audience is brought to contact for the first time with "Robot Monsters", who are said to closely resemble moon inhabitants. This you must see for yourself.

"Robot Monster" Big 3 Dimension Hit

A sensational, True "Three-Dimension" spectacle made its screen bow yesterday at the — — — theatre when the Science-Fiction thriller, "Robot Monster" opened to give local audiences the thrill of their lives.

Scene 200

George Nader and Claudia Barrett are attacked by one of the many Moon Monsters that invaded Earth, in Astor's thrilling 3 Dimensional film, "Robot Monster". This science-fiction thriller opens at the.......Theatre on..........................

SYNOPSIS

(NOT FOR PUBLICATION)

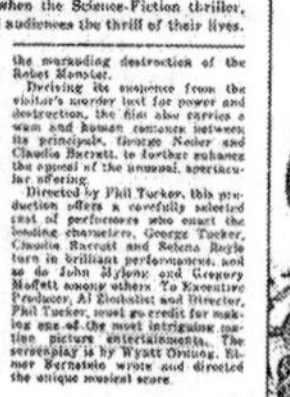

Al Zimbalist's sensational production tells a strange, thrill-packed tale of a fearsome invader cornered in a huge cave.

One of the most suspenseful tru-stereo three dimension pictures ever made, "Robot Monster" offers a cast of brilliant actors in an amazing story of terrifying Robot Monsters from space.

The thrilling, three dimension melodrama has its locale on an open ruins in America where these deadly robots descend to earth in their mysterious Spaceship and immediately disappear into the earth's caves.

The thrilling developments take a form of conflict between the last remaining Americans who realise these creatures and their contaminating rays poses a threat to all remaining civilization.

Dealing with the dramatic discovery of Robot Monsters from space, the picture achieves conviction that makes its amazing story tremendously vivid and suspenseful in Three Dimension. It wouldn't be fair to reveal the plot here, but it can be said that the crises of the gripping drama is brought about in the contamination of the world and the marauding destruction of the Robot Monster.

Deriving its suspense from the visitor's murder lust for power and destruction, the film also carries a warm and human romance between its principals, George Nader and Claudia Barrett, to further enhance the appeal of the unusual, spectacular offering.

Directed by Phil Tucker, this production offers a carefully selected cast of performers who enact the leading characters. George Tucker, Claudia Barrett and Selena Royle turn in brilliant performances, and so do John Mylong and Gregory Moffett among others. To Executive Producer, Al Zimbalist and Director, Phil Tucker, must go credit for making one of the most intriguing motion picture entertainments. The screenplay is by Wyatt Ordung. Elmer Bernstein wrote and directed the unique musical score.

Scene-Art 2

The above art-still is available in release set.

Natural Thrill-Film Awaited by Local Movie Fans

Three Dimension Science-Fiction Film Gets Scientific Aid

Not since the atom bomb project was launched has there been the hushed curiosity which met the making of Al Zimbalist's Three-Dimension motion picture of man's first contact with Robot Monsters in "Robot Monster", which is slated to open here next — at the — theatre.

"How will they do it," curiosity seekers asked.

Surely the first requisite of a successful motion picture is entertainment.

"Robot Monster" was directed by Phil Tucker, and stars George Nader and Claudia Barrett.

Thrills Keynote Sensational Three-Dimension Picture

The problem of what to do with deadly and terrifying visitors from space forms the theme of startling new Tru-Stereo Three-Dimension Science-Fiction production, starring George Nader, Claudia Barrett and produced by Al Zimbalist. Phil Tucker directed from a story by Wyott Ordung.

Hailed as the most sensational screen offering of the decade, the film has as its locale an open countryside in America, where a group of last remaining Americans battle robot monsters for life, while the world is contaminated and destroyed by the mysterious robots.

The subsequent happenings make for a breathless climax of the unusual picture.

Three Dimensional Pictures, Inc.

presents

"ROBOT MONSTER"

in

THREE DIMENSION

Photographed in Tru-Stereo Process

starring

GEORGE NADER • CLAUDIA BARRETT

SELENA ROYLE • GREGORY MOFFETT

PAMELA PAULSON • GEORGE BARROWS

JOHN BROWN

Executive Producer

AL ZIMBALIST

Produced and Directed by

PHIL TUCKER

Story and Screenplay by

WYOTT ORDUNG

(Running time—62 minutes)

Camera..........JACK GREENHALGH

Music..........ELMER BERNSTEIN

Editor..........BRUCE SHOENGARTH

Released thru

ASTOR PICTURES CORP.

TRUE THREE DIMENSIONS ALIVE BEFORE YOUR EYES!

* * *

NATURAL or SUPERNATURAL? WHERE DID THEY COME FROM? HOW DID THEY GET HERE? WILL IT DESTROY US ALL?

* * *

ARE THEY HUMAN OR INHUMAN? WHAT DOES SCIENCE KNOW ABOUT THEM?

* * *

OVERWHELMING! ELECTRIFYING! BAFFLING!

* * *

FIRE CAN'T BURN THEM! BULLETS CAN'T KILL THEM!!

* * *

WILL "ROBOT MONSTERS" COME TO DESTROY THE WORLD BY FEEDING ON THE BODIES OF THE HUMAN RACE?

Scene 100

One of many prehistoric monsters in Astor's 3 Dimension "Robot Monster".

SEE THE UNFOLDING OF THE MYSTERIES OF THE MOON AS MURDEROUS ROBOT MONSTERS DESCEND UPON THE EARTH AND CONTAMINATE THEIR VICTIMS! YOU'VE NEVER SEEN ANYTHING LIKE IT! NEITHER HAS THE WORLD!

* * *

A NEW WORLD OF THRILLS! A WORLD OF HORROR! A WORLD OF TOMORROW? IN THREE DIMENSIONS!

* * *

UNBELIEVABLE ... the deadly Robot Monsters. UNIMAGINABLE ... in live Three Dimension! UNUSUAL ... are these the wonders of the Moon?

* * *

SEE ... True Three Dimension. SEE ... Robots from space in all their glory! SEE ...

Scene-Art 1

The above art-still is a-

HE WHO CONTROLS MOON CONTROLS EARTH

In Wyott Ordung's story of "Robot Monster", the first black and white Three-Dimensional Science-Fiction picture, which is soon to make its debut at the — theatre, the contention is made that occupation of the moon is a military "must."

This is a highly potent problem among scientists and army specialists and will continue to be for some time.

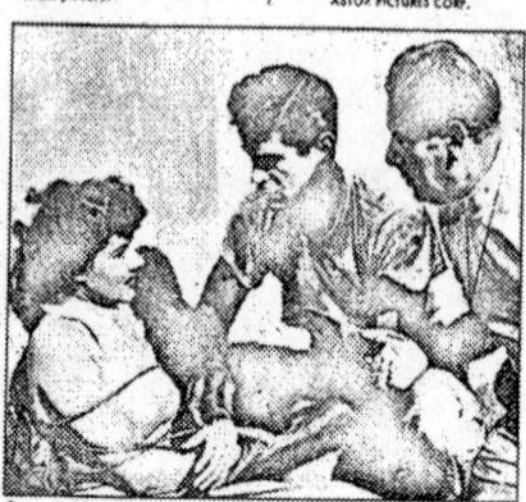

Scene 201

Claudia Barrett is saved by George Nader and John

WADE WILLIAMS DIST.

Astor's creatively worded *Robot Monster* press book.

7

Script vs. Film

Robot Monster fascinates, amuses, and haunts viewers primarily because of the monster's costume and dialogue. The nonsensical dinosaur footage, alternate titles, sometimes stiff acting, and generally shoddy look of everything are also notable factors—along with the knowledge that the people who made the movie must have known and accepted what they were doing. But with much production history pieced together, one final *Robot Monster* mystery remains: *Who* made the movie what it is? Credits only narrow the issue down to a director and a writer. Phil Tucker claimed sole credit for the film, while Wyott Ordung allowed little beyond the fact that his name appeared onscreen. Ordung also assigned rewriting to an unknown third party, connected to Al Zimbalist (perhaps a relative or blacklisted comedy writer Frederic I. Rinaldo), while he was not around for the filming or post-production, and presumably knew less about what happened than Tucker.[367] But the film's shooting script has survived and, while it is essentially similar, it contains discrepancies large and small. These differences offer a fascinating window into *Robot Monster*'s production, and into the question of how it got as crazy as it did. Much of the finished film does not exist in the script, and many details within the script are missing from the film.

> FADE IN:
>
> 1 EXT. WOODS – DAY – MED. SHOT – SPACE HELMET APPEARING FROM BEHIND BUSHES
>
> It is of the traditional plexiglass kind with antennae on top of it. At first CAMERA sees only the top part. On SOUND TRACK we hear a persistent "Beeeep-boooop" sound.
>
> The wearer scuttles behind bushes a moment, then appears in open. He is JOHNNY, a seven year old, completely outfitted in Spaceman's costume. He has a Spaceman's gun. He is making the "beep-boop" sounds orally.
>
> Johnny sees something offscene, raises his gun and fires, imitating the "sssss" effect of a ray gun.

The script opens much as the film does, the quoted section could be called close enough, but there are many discrepancies in the opening alone and they are significant. The initial notation "EXT. WOODS" contrasts with the dry, rocky onscreen setting, and many subsequent script notations reaffirm that the action takes place in a wooded area. This raises the possibility that the writer visualized deep tree shadows for Ro-Man to weave in and out of, a much scarier environment than sun-scorched rocks. In the film, Johnny appears from behind a hill and with helmet appearing first, but it has little effect as there is no space age sound beyond a faint mechanical whirring; there is no potential for the initial suspense that it could actually be a robot walking over the hill. What is more, neither script nor film begin with close-up details of the helmet which, combined with a suitable electronic noise, might have created some doubt. Further, Johnny does not scramble behind a bush, a detail that would have improved a very pedestrian shot. But most importantly he is not wearing a full costume, merely a piece that covers his head and chest. With that change, there is no chance that he could have been mistaken for an extraterrestrial as the film opens.

The script's opening is rich with detail that the film omits, and the cumulative lack of these details result in a scene that is routine and competent, but which lacks flavor. If the film had been shot with attention given to these details, and had been storyboarded in advance, there could have been multiple shots from different perspectives and distances that would have brought out the scripted details and created suspense (as Johnny walks over the hill) and humor (as he hides behind the bush). As a detailed analysis will make clear, many of the film's shortcomings follow the same pattern in relation to the script, and could have been avoided with more preparation and attention to detail.

The next shot is described as a medium perspective of Johnny's sister Carla that plays mostly like the movie. One minor script detail—"Johnny enters to her"—was changed in the film, which uses the duller option of keeping them both in frame the entire time. Shot three, described as "CAVE SECTION OF WOODS," accurately describes the kids hearing a "chipping" sound from a nearby cave and moving there. Shot four does not appear in the film:

> **4 INT. CAVE ENTRANCE – DAY**
>
> **as Johnny and Carla enter. They look off curiously.**

The description of this lost shot is notable for its classification of the inner part of the cave as an INT., or interior. In screenwriting, the terms EXT. or INT. are used in relation to whether a scene will have to be filmed on an outdoor location or an indoor set. This notation connects the script with the January 1953 *Hollywood Reporter* news that *Robot Killer* would film at Quality Studios, and so a constructed set had at some stage been planned for the cave scenes. Tucker at least influenced the script on this point, even if someone else wrote it. Shot five is essentially what appears on film:

> 5 MED. SHOT – PROFESSOR AND ROY
>
> The Professor is sitting on a stool examining a rock. Roy is chipping away at a picture on the wall. They do not see Johnny and Carla enter to them. Johnny raises his gun.
>
> JOHNNY
>
> Spacemen—you must die!

Note that Roy is specifically working on "a picture on the wall." (The Professor's stereotypically German wearing of a monocle in this scene is not in the script.) This chalky picture is barely visible onscreen and only fleetingly referred to in the film. But one minor discrepancy is positive and worth noting as evidence that the filmmakers were paying attention. In the script, the Professor says to Johnny, "We're archaeologists, son . . .," while in the film "son" becomes "boy." This establishes that everything about to happen in the main part of the film is a dream, and that the Professor is not Johnny's father.

Nothing printed in bold in the following section (and throughout the chapter) occurs onscreen:

PROFESSOR

. . . the only way he could pass on what he knew was through pictures like this one here.

He points to picture. Kids look up.

6 CLOSE SHOT – PICTURE

SEEN clearly for first time. It is of an ape-like creature. The face is missing.

ROY'S VOICE

Did you kids know this was in here?

7 MED SHOT – GROUP

Kids shake their heads.

CARLA

My mother told us to stay away or we could get hurt.

WADE WILLIAMS DIST.

JOHNNY

(indicating picture)

Is that what would hurt us?

PROFESSOR

If it was alive it could. But this picture was painted almost a million years ago.

ROY

Our job is to chip it carefully out and take it to a museum so people can study it.

At the end of the Professor's speech ("like this one here"), he nods at the picture but does not get to point, and the kids do not look up. There is instead an awkward, abrupt cut to Roy's line, "Our job . . ." The loss of this shot six material devastated the film's believability. If included, it would have provided a clear and close view of the cave drawing that is only obliquely visible in the finished film, and this drawing would have given the film a logic it has never had: "It is of an ape-like creature. The face is missing." As written, Johnny had a very logical reason for dreaming up a robot-gorilla. His monster-addicted mind would have internalized a headless primate—all the more mysterious for being real and from an ancient, forgotten time—and turned it into something like Ro-Man. It would be the most natural thing imaginable for a boy to dream of the cave drawing and replace that missing head with the head of a robot. But without that brief, clear view of the drawing, the film lost that crucial chance for logic and rushed headlong into the accidentally surreal.

The extended dialogue of shot seven contained more dialogue missing from the film:

PROFESSOR

So far as we know, there weren't Spacemen in those days.

CARLA

(bored glance at Johnny)

I wish I'd been born then.

JOHNNY

But what <u>was</u> he?

ROY

The Missing Link perhaps. If we knew what his head looked like we could judge better.

JOHNNY

(big shot)

He looks like some of the people I saw last time I was on Pluto.

Though this omission is not as significant, it additionally hurt the film's believability. Johnny expresses the curiosity that logically leads into his dream, and Roy further encourages him to wonder about the missing head.

The film's next deviation from the script was less important, but still contributed to the dullness of the opening scenes. Shot eight was listed as "EXT. WOODS – CAVE SECTION – MED. LONG SHOT – JOHNNY'S MOTHER AND HIS SISTER ALICE," with dialogue that was on film merely included in a cave shot. Thus, *Robot Monster* was denied another point that could have added variety and flavor. Also of interest in the lost shot is the script's introduction to Roy's love interest: "Alice is a pretty, intelligent looking girl. She carries a box of Kleenex." Alice does no such thing onscreen but, as even the film makes clear, this little touch made some sense. It is the Professor's "super serum" that, as Johnny unthinkingly tells Ro-Man, keeps them safe not only from "real bad bugs" but the calcinator ray. So, Johnny thought up the serum because of his sister's sniffling and nose-wiping. This is another logical detail that would have helped ground the film in reality, left stranded in the script and absent in the film. More dialogue is soon after lost:

ALICE

. . . And off you scoot.

CARLA

I didn't want to go. I wanted to play house.

JOHNNY

And I'm too old for naps. Besides these men are <u>real</u> scientists. I want to watch awhile.

ALICE

(sarcastic)

I'm sure they'd love that.

(to Roy)

I hope he hasn't given you any trouble.

She wipes her nose with Kleenex.

ROY

Not at all.

The cold-sniffling motif continues, as does the fact that kid dialogue is largely what is missing. ("We had a lot of problems with them," as Tucker said.) These lost lines would have added some poignancy to Johnny's later lament that he did not play with her more, as well as adding the interesting detail that the boy has learned from his comic book reading to look up to scientists as something like superheroes.

More missing lines reveal more missing nuances of character:

PROFESSOR

If we are, you're welcome to join us.

(to Martha)

Goodbye. Nice children you have.

MARTHA

Thank you.

Professor and Roy return into cave. Johnny looks after them.

ALICE

Come on, come on. Stop stalling.

In the film, not much reinforces the fact that the Professor and Martha have only met, which further weakens the fact that the bulk of the movie is Johnny's dream. The Professor's missing line and Martha's missing response would have cemented the sense that there was the potential for he and Roy to become part of this family. Additional details in this scene differ from the film: the Professor and Roy do not return to the cave because they have never left it, and it is Roy—not Johnny—who is shown looking away at the others.

The final missing script section of the pre-dream part of the story is another blow to the film's credibility:

JOHNNY

. . . I hope he's a big scientist, making rocket ships, things like that.

ALICE

(sniffing; taking another piece of Kleenex)

If he finds a cure for the common cold he'll be the biggest man of all.

JOHNNY

Really?

ALICE

Oh come on!

Reluctantly Johnny and Carla follow them.

WIPE TO:

11 MED SHOT – JOHNNY AND CARLA TAKING REST

The Kleenex motif reaches its peak here, and as scripted greatly clarifies that the bulk of the film was a dream. Alice expresses her wish for a common cold cure and, hearing it soon before napping, Johnny would have easily incorporated it into his sleeping monster fantasy. The film quickly fades to black (there is no wipe), right after Johnny's first line above and before Alice can talk about the cure. She can, however, be seen touching her nose onscreen and giving out a near sneeze right before the fade. Whether or not the common cold lines were filmed, the idea must have at least been discussed before filming (even though the tissue box described in the script never appears on screen).

Also noteworthy in this section is Selena Royle. She has one line to deliver, but spends the scene fussing, fidgeting, huffing, and sighing. She seems incredibly uncomfortable, perhaps a measure of Tucker's limitations as a director. The other actors, with not much more to work with but less to lose, come across far better and, again, nothing in *Robot Monster* would lead anyone to believe that Royle was a professional.

The script follows the non-wipe with a medium shot of the two children napping on a picnic blanket (the two women, visible onscreen, are unmentioned), when Johnny "opens one eye" and scampers off. This picnic scene is where the pre-fade scene in the film ended, and the angle after the fade-in onscreen is almost the same. Tellingly, there is no close-up in the film emphasizing that Johnny is opening his eyes to be sneaky and get away. Like so much of the film, it plays out in a pedestrian shot with no cuts to emphasize any finer points. Then, the film omits more extremely precious detail:

> **12 MED. SHOT – WOODS – NEW ANGLE**
>
> **Johnny makes a dash for it, looking back. He doesn't see the gully ahead of him. He falls into it.**
>
> **13 INT. CAVE**
>
> **It is deserted now. We hear Johnny running toward it. He enters, looks disappointed men are gone. Then he studies picture. He grabs a piece of rock to climb closer. The rock comes loose. Another piece of rock hits him on the head. He falls.**
>
> **14 CLOSE SHOT – JOHNNY ON GROUND**
>
> **On sound track we hear the Vibrator noise associated with loss of consciousness. Johnny lies**

still. CAMERA MOVES IN, BLURRING, AS NOISE INCREASES.

BRIEF FADE:

FADE IN:

15 EXT. WOODS – NIGHT – MED. SHOT – ENTRANCE TO CAVE

There is a light inside the cave. CAMERA STARTS TO MOVE IN.

LAP DISSOLVE TO:

16 INT. CAVE – CLOSE SHOT – JOHNNY

He is painting a picture on the wall. He is dressed now just in shorts. He works feverishly. His space-gun is on the floor.

Almost none of this happens onscreen. Johnny makes no mad dash, does not fall into a gully, and there is no emphasis on his face to register disappointment at the absence of the scientists. Furthermore, he does not fall from trying to climb a little higher to the cave drawing (that incredibly important detail is once again denied anything that would emphasize it), and he falls on film in an almost arbitrary way. This occurs onscreen in conjunction with post-production added lightning flashes, and the film immediately switches to its first, bewildering montage of lightning flashes and dinosaur footage. The film completely omits the tantalizingly logical events of scenes 14 through 16, where sound effects and camera losing focus make the transition to a dream state definite and obvious. There is no sudden switch to night as there is when the dream begins in scene 15, with the eerie potential of a "light inside the cave." Only in scene 16 does the film begin to again resemble the script, as Johnny reappears on the ground after interminable shots of dinosaur battles.

When Johnny awakes, there is the sense that he was knocked out by the weird lizard lightning montage, as he is in the same spot but with Ro-Man's equipment tables and bubbles now visible. Regarding the direction from scene 16 about Johnny being "dressed now just in shorts," his clothes onscreen have changed, although it would be easy to never notice. His toy gun and a can of paint with brush are by his feet. Johnny then takes the paint brush and very briefly applies some paint to the cave drawing—but again, only from a side angle with no view of what he is painting or why. He runs almost immediately, sensing the impending presence of Ro-Man, about to make his screen debut.

Tucker and others involved must have had some notion of including this crucial detail in the film as they created the cave drawing, used a paint can and brush for props, and had Johnny touch up the drawing. But it is continually bewildering that they brought no emphasis to this detail when the script did, repeatedly:

17 CLOSE SHOT – PICTURE

Johnny is filling in the face – and it is the face of a Spaceman – that is to say, the heavy features of the

ape-man are there, but covered by the plexiglass hood and the antennae.

This missing scene—an emphatic "CLOSE" shot no less—is perhaps the worst loss of all for the film. The cave drawing is that of an ancient primate, something more than ape and less than human, and Johnny vandalizes it with the space technology that is constantly on his mind. The ludicrous, exploitation quality solution that Tucker improvised for getting his cheap movie off the ground ("I'll get a diving helmet, put it on him, and it'll work!") was in fact *completely logical* in the context of the script. A boy like Johnny would dream of turning the primitive human ancestor into a robot, would therefore realize it completely in his mind, and a gorilla suit man wearing a robot head was a perfectly good way to bring the monster to dream-life. While Tucker would have preferred to do a movie about a real robot and use a real robot getup, he, Ordung, Rinaldo, or whoever else wrote the script did an outstanding job of justifying the cheap costume. Tucker and Zimbalist then snatched defeat from the jaws of victory by not following the script's emphasis on the cave drawing. Even if the expository dialogue in the opening cave scene had gone un-filmed, a few postproduction insert shots of the drawing would have made all the difference. *Robot Monster* would have never been a great film, but it could have easily avoided being a laughingstock with a little effort.

18 CLOSE SHOT – JOHNNY

Suddenly he listens. Faintly we hear a "beep-boop" sound. It comes from the rear of the cave. . . .

There is never a "beep-boop" sound in the film, whereas it appears twice by this early point in the script. It is the sound of Johnny's space-man gear at the beginning, and it reappears in the dream as the sound of the monster. But onscreen there is no relation between the sizzling electric hums that accompany Ro-Man, and the cheap mechanical whirr of Johnny's ray-gun. Yet again, a very easy way to cement the dreamed nature of the film was thoughtlessly abandoned.

19 INT. CAVE

with space-gun in med. foreground. The SOUND GETS LOUDER.

THEN RO-MAN APPEARS. He is just like the drawing on the wall and we can see what parts of him Johnny has failed to paint in – particularly an adding machine type gadget inside the plexiglass helmet that has wires connected into Ro-Man's ears.

Ro-man looks at the space-gun, then at the painting. His "calculator" begins to work and we hear the faint click and clunk of bolts falling into place. Then Ro-Man turns toward entrance to cave and raises his hands. From his long fingers come sparks accompanied by a droning, static sound.

Tucker had not abandoned all hope for an ambitious robot onscreen. The adding machine he intended to be visible through plexiglass would have probably not had moving parts,

As scripted, Ro-Man was less of a gorilla wearing a diving helmet, with a head that predicted *Forbidden Planet*'s expensive Robby.

but it might have seemed as if it had thanks to the sound effects described. But the aluminum-papier-mâché ball used onscreen was what could be done in the real world on $16,000. Paying for a sculpted piece of plastic would have been prohibitive, but it is notable that the description is not unlike what would be seen a few years later on *Forbidden Planet*'s Robby the Robot. Another detail is extremely important here: Ro-Man gets to shoot lightning from his fingers, a power left up to his superior in the film. It is in fact at this point that Great Guidance first appears on film, as Ro-Man contacts him via his scrap-wood view-screen, but the movie again deviates from the script. At this point Johnny runs away and is united with his dreamed family members, hiding in ruins. But this initial scene with Great Guidance never appears in the script, nor do any of the character's subsequent five appearances. Ro-Man's boss, central in the film to establishing his humanizing internal conflict, appears nowhere in the script and is never so much as referenced.

When Johnny arrives at his destroyed home, the script largely mirrors what ended up onscreen. But there was striking detail in the script, richly described, that has no counterpart on film:

21 EXT. FAMILY "CAMP" SITE - NIGHT - MED. LONG SHOT

WADE WILLIAMS DIST.

We see the wire barricade, behind it the ruins of the house. CAMERA MOVES IN SLOWLY.

The Professor comes to the wire barricade, peers out, troubled. He hears the sound of Johnny's approaching footsteps. He tenses.

22 MED. SHOT – BARRICADE

Johnny comes running up to it.

JOHNNY
(breathless)

Pop!

The Professor reaches through wires and clamps his hand over Johnny's mouth. He pantomimes vigorously for him to come inside the barricade without speaking. Johnny nods, indicating he understands. As he climbs through wires, Professor calls back toward ruins.

There is not much evidence of a wire barricade in the movie. There are some strange and seemingly pointless shots of current wiping across electrical wires, but the idea was never taken to the extent of showing the ruined house in its entirety or showing a wire structure protecting it. The slowly advancing camera direction in the script is especially compelling, painting a mental picture of a foreboding and mysterious night image. The Professor lifts Johnny into the concrete ruin (in broad daylight; the film has no night sections), but there is nothing so specific as the character-enhancing pantomime between father and son that is scripted.

The next few pages of script flow largely in synch with the film, with some variation in the dialogue. Notably, the Professor has a missing chunk about the barricade:

PROFESSOR

You know the terrible things that have happened since this "Ro-Man" landed on Earth. **The only reason we are still alive is that his directional beams are bent around this house by these syntochron wires.** He cannot hear us. . . .

Bizarrely, the film does here throw in a brief insert shot of the wall wires, despite the fact that the Professor's dialogue explaining them was excised, and that he explains that he and Alice had "worked out a way to deflect [Ro-Man's] deadly beams."

The screenwriter(s) intended more detail about life in the aftermath of alien invasion:

25 MED. SHOT – RUINS

We see now more clearly how the family is living; mostly in the open, a few rude lean-tos; dishes on a broken table; a few open cans in evidence. Carla sleeps on a pallet. Her mother covers her. Then the family comes and sits wearily at the table. Behind them is the Viewer Screen and associated gadgets.

These details would not have been hard to capture, but were apparently also too much for the film's breakneck schedule.

Notable, if minor, discrepancies continue to pile up. As Martha pours Johnny a tiny portion of water to drink, the Professor pounds his fist on the concrete basement wall of the ruin, rather than the script's direction that he "pounds the table in frustration." Why the change? Pounding a wall will show up more easily in a long shot than pounding a table, and requires no insert shot. Likewise, John Mylong as the Professor seems to have some difficulty at one point, largely skipping an entire chunk of dialogue:

> PROFESSOR
>
> **We can hope so. If someone could only get through to them—**
>
> (hopelessly)
>
> Ah but why should they succeed when so many have failed?

Ro-Man soon after makes his first communication with the survivors:

> After a brief flicker, the horrid face of Ro-Man appears on [the] Viewer Screen. **Behind him we see the wall of the cave and many scientific gadgets.**

Ro-Man onscreen gets nothing more impressive than a bare cave wall, and his subsequent taunting of the survivors plays fairly close to the script, but very much out of sequence.

RO-MAN

Humans! Listen to me. **I have calculated your tele-screen wave lengths, so if you have a set you must be watching . . .**

In keeping with the fact the Guidance Ro-Man is never even mentioned in the script, Ro-Man's threatening monologue is, while in the same spirit as the film, almost completely different in word. While he does not promise in the script that "your death will be indescribable," he does assure the survivors that if they continue their defiance, they "will suffer infinite torture infinitely prolonged." He also never mentions in the script the infamous "calcinator ray," but instead references a "catatomic ray" (an atomic ray that causes catatonia?). Ro-Man's threat speech is no more or less interrupted by the family in the script than in the film, but chunks of dialogue have switched positions. Onscreen, Ro-Man's taunts soon switch to Alice, Martha, and the Professor lamenting the near-total destruction of life on Earth, and the presumed death of Roy. But this exchange, produced very accurately from the script, appears there a couple of pages after its corresponding point in the film, in fact after Ro-Man has switched off the Viewer Screen. Likewise, the Professor and Martha discuss the potential value of surrender in the film after their conversation with the tormenting space gorilla has ended, but this stretch of dialogue occurs in the midst of his threats as scripted, and are specifically addressed to him:

PROFESSOR

(to screen)

No thank you, Ro-Man. If you want us, calculate us.

WADE WILLIAMS DIST.

On film, the Professor and Martha lean against the ruined basement wall on the right (which functions as their front door throughout), and his line is specifically about Ro-Man in the second person: "If Ro-Man he wants us, he should calculate us." This script change was therefore unambiguously decided on during filming, but the motivation remains unclear. Perhaps it was decided to direct less of the dialogue toward communicating with reaction shots that would have to be added later, and thereby make the footage more versatile in the editing stage.

Adding to all this confusion is the fact that sleeping Carla appears with the family when Ro-Man's transmission begins, and then is not visible in some shots. As for the script, she is not mentioned at any point in this section, but left to doze on the pallet the entire time. Before cutting to Ro-Man's cave, the script ends this section with Alice's lament about Roy, and a stage direction that did not happen onscreen:

> **She leaves the table and throws herself on a pallet in b.g. The others look at each other glumly.**
>
> **WIPE TO:**

Once again, there is no wipe effect but instead a straight cut. Both film and script move to Ro-Man's cave, but with significant difference. As written, the scene had potential to be a good piece of mysterious and subtle suspense as Roy walks by in the "woods" at "night." He hides as he hears Ro-Man's "buzz sound" and "reacts in horror" in close-up as he gets his first sight of the monster. Then:

> **39 CLOSE UP – RO-MAN**
>
> **He senses something. The calculators click. Then his hand goes to his head. He shakes it, returns to cave.**

Roy then enjoys a "triumphant smile" as he escapes the area. Again, this is a silent scene that could have been greatly effective. But nothing in the film was shot at night (or processed as day-for-night), nothing so subtle happens, and everything is shot with flat, dull medium shots and no close-ups. The film goes in about as unsubtle a direction as possible, though not a bad direction in all points. It is here that Great Guidance appears for the second time, as Ro-Man calls him for advice and is chewed out for miscalculating the eight surviving humans as five. The scene adds bombast as stock shots of space and destruction are thrown in, along with the bubbles floating around in Guidance shots that surely stood out in 3-D. (The folded pleats of the sheet hanging in the background were perhaps an additional 3-D effect, though not likely intended.) While Ro-Man's bubble machine is not working at this moment (did the wing nuts[368] visible in side shots of the Viewer Screen stand out in 3-D?), he has become increasingly multidimensional in an important way. Ro-Man's difficulty in accurately performing a head count of survivors and his boss' impatience with his inadequacy foreshadow his impending quandary, where he is unable to act according to either desire or duty.

And on that point, the film shows a degree of intelligence that the generally superior script lacks. Ro-Man was written as a one-dimensional monster and, from the point of view of Johnny's dream, this is logical. But from an audience point of view, it is dreadfully dull. Many films work well with unsophisticated villains, but *Robot Monster* would not have been one of them. It is so threadbare that without Ro-Man's scenes of conflict with his superior and with himself, it would have been boring, the one sin that an audience can never forgive. The concept of Guidance was clearly developed in post-production: Despite observing Ro-Man communicating with Guidance in the film, Roy never mentions it, and never refers to multiple monsters—almost certainly because the assembled film was too dull. With a few shots of a second Ro-Man thrown in, this conflict was easily created with the assistance of such a good voice actor as John Brown. There was no need to match lip movements, and virtually any dialogue could be plugged in

WADE WILLIAMS DIST.

during postproduction. Though some have commented that Johnny clearly "had issues" from the fact that he dreams about a monster's erotic feelings for his sister, it is not so weird in the context of the script alone. Fatherless, he is anxious about becoming the man of the house and, monster-obsessed, he dreams about such a monster threatening his beloved sister. He does, after all, defy the monster a good deal on-screen. Ro-Man's desire for Alice only seems odd in the film because it goes so far into the monster's point of view; as written, Johnny is just being a protective brother.

Half the film's surrealism comes from the robot-gorilla costume, cemented by the filmmakers' repeated flubbing of one script opportunity after another to justify it. The other half comes from the monster's absurdly eloquent expressions of angst, with an assist from utterly inane uses of dinosaur footage. But the nonsense of it all does not negate the fact that the filmmakers were trying to make the movie better than they had filmed it. They would at least not let it be boring.

At this point in the film, we are introduced to Roy's bleeding right ear. Graphically displayed in a publicity still of Roy and Alice in a kiss, but less noticeable in the course of the film is a trail of dried blood running down from the right ear opening. It is not scripted, and never explained onscreen. But it is visible at this first appearance of Roy in Johnny's dream and, given his torn shirt, it is a logical part of his disheveled appearance, even though it is frustratingly never explored. (Did he puncture an eardrum?)

From Roy's near encounter with Ro-Man, the film returns to the survivors asleep in their ruin. At this point, the film returns to a shot of wires on a brick wall, which was perhaps a desperate attempt to create the impression of the barrier that the Professor refers to in the script. (The shot bizarrely freezes toward the end, fixing the electric current in position, perhaps just to make the shot seem different or indicating that the protection system tensed up because of Roy's approach.) The family is asleep in what appears to be broad daylight (again, was a day-for-night effect intended to be done in the lab?), and soon awakens to the pleasant surprise of Roy's arrival that largely follows the script, but with some missing dialogue.

In the script, Carla awakens right after the others exclaim their joy (written in as ad libs by the cast) over Roy's arrival:

CARLA

What of it: He always hangs around.

She goes back to sleep. The others gather around Roy.

ROY

Of course I made it. Do you know who's in . . .

Of the two children, Carla's presence is more inconsistent. She has less to do than Johnny (it is his dream), and her purpose seems to be merely to give him someone to disagree with and, later on, the audience someone to feel pity for. As Tucker noted, he thought Gregory Moffett was the better of the two kids, and Pamela Paulson's career began and ended here. This brief bit may have been cut out because of difficulties with the young actress. Also of interest is the fact that "Roy's face falls" after he finds that the others already are aware of Ro-Man's presence. It is a small detail, but would have been a good one.

As Roy soon describes how he and the others survived—not because of the Professor's shield, but because of the all-curing serum he developed—the sparring of Roy and Alice loses some detail:

ROY

. . . Thanks to his wise choice of assistants, he achieves his goal.

ALICE

"In spite of," not "thanks to."

ROY

(giving her a mock bow)

So upon whom . . .

During this section of the film, there are three cutaways to Alice, all of which cover missing sections of the script. Also missing soon after is a single crucial line from Roy, when the Professor admits he thought "it was the barricade" that saved him, and Roy snorts "Alice's Folly?" This is one of the most subtle bits of illogic in the film, as it is hard to believe that a medical cure would be better protection from a sort of death ray energy than an electrically generated shield. But it does make sense from a filmmaker's point of view: If the opposite was true in the script, the cast would have been restricted to their ruined basement home.

Another detail wiped over with a redundant cut to Alice occurs soon after:

ROY

. . . I didn't bring it.

He sits at the table and leans back, satisfied.

ALICE

It's a stage wait. We're supposed to ask, "Why?"

ROY

Ask.

ALICE

(in bored tone)

Why. [There is no "?" in the script.]

These lines, like so much that is missing, are minor but would have been nice bits of character building. Roy then enthuses about their ability to take a rocket to the "space platform," exclaiming in a missing line, "We'll give Ro-Man the biggest surprise of his life!" (These cuts do not just patch up missing stuff, but look like they were thrown in from a completely unrelated part of the film.) A cutaway to Roy obscures another missing chunk:

ALICE

. . . blast the ship right out of the sky.

MARTHA

She's right, Roy.

WADE WILLIAMS DIST.

ROY

(troubled)

I don't know what else we could do. Jason and McCloud are taking off in two days. On foot it would take me longer than that to get back there.

ALICE

Big genius.

ROY

All right! What do you suggest?

ALICE

We'll have to get word to the space platform, that's all, and rewire the circuits on the Viewscreen so we can broadcast without Ro-Man picking it up.

PROFESSOR

In theory it's possible. But such a complicated job in two days?

With these cuts, more of the sense of sniping affection between Roy and Alice is lost. But far more fascinating is that, in the midst of much cutting, are a couple of lines that remain in the film but slightly later. Roy's reference to the mysterious "Jason and McCloud"—never depicted in script or film—became part of Alice's response to Roy's despondency. On screen, these are Alice's lines:

We'll have to get word to the space platform, that's all. Jason and McCloud are taking off in two days. On foot it would take me longer than that to get back there. We'll have to rewire the circuits on the Viewscreen so we can broadcast without Ro-Man picking it up.

Note that Alice's reply flows just as logically in response to Roy in both versions of the scene, and that some care must have been taken in order to preserve the lines removed from Roy. But why the change was made at all is unclear. It may have been to build up Alice's character and, at the same time, prevent Roy from dominating the scene. Roy's line, "You're so bossy you ought to be milked before you come home at night," appears soon after on film, but was not in the script, and was perhaps an ad lib by George Nader.

The script moves into what onscreen is a soldering montage—shots of the hands of Roy and Alice manipulating a soldering iron over circuitry, accompanied by some off-screen, overdramatic line readings. But as written the scene was substantially different:

44 CLOSE SHOT – ALICE AT WORK ON INNER WORKS OF VIEWSCREENER – DAY

It should look like a brain operation in progress. Highly specialized tools to hold highly specialized tools. Alice is chief surgeon; Roy her assistant. He has a two days' growth of beard; Alice looks pale and drawn. She is breathing heavily as she makes

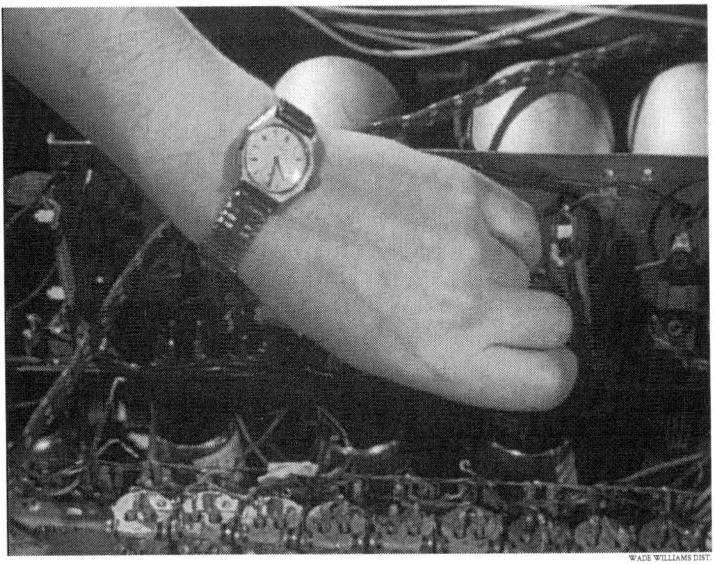

WADE WILLIAMS DIST.

a minute, delicate adjustment. Suddenly she pulls her hands away. They are trembling visibly.

As scripted, the film should now have been switching from night to day, and it should not have been continually focused on close-ups of a bank of circuits. We see Alice and Roy at work, and Roy's assistance would have been especially changed with his growth of facial hair. These elements were no doubt dropped due to time, but the most damning change for the quality of the film was the lack of any "highly specialized tools." This was probably why the circuitry close-ups were devised: Showing them working on such material would have been unimpressive, and the only hope for making it seem technologically advanced was to show it in detail to create the impression of being part of a larger whole. The overdubbed dialogue ("You're either too beautiful to be so lovely, or too lovely to be so beautiful . . .") is not in the script. Some of it is amusing if one's mind drifts into an adolescent gutter, and perhaps Tucker and Zimbalist were laughing themselves silly as these fill-in scenes were hastily put together.

Alice and Roy soon begin to display affection for one another in their exhaustion, though not as expressively as written. She never "collapses dejectedly against Roy." There is, no surprise, yet another chunk of dialogue that was somehow just left out:

ALICE

But I didn't.

ROY

I'm so proud of you I could kiss you.

ALICE
(wearily)

Go ahead.

ROY
(suddenly feeling the weariness in himself)

I'm too tired to enjoy it.

ALICE
(dropping off to sleep)

Know just . . . how . . . you feel . . .

Suddenly the light and buzzer on the Viewscreen begin to operate. . . .

But the young scientists in love do not seem particularly worn-out onscreen, and the missing section would have made their later marriage flow more logically, as their affection has so far remained in the teasing stage. They just stand around in the film, and do not look any different from the previous scene, despite Johnny's astonishment that they had been working for two days and thereby missing their chance to contact the ship leaving for the space platform.

The Professor then loses a couple of lines ("Maybe they made it. This might be them.") as the Viewscreen lights up and Ro-Man taunts them with the destruction of the space platform. This scene could be called close enough between its scripted and filmed versions, but as usual Ro-Man's dialogue is almost completely different:

RO-MAN

Humans . . . I thought I would tell you that I made a mistake. But my automatic calculator caught it. . . .

Whatever an "automatic calculator" is—another prime example of the pseudoscientific jargon that pops up throughout the script—why would Ro-Man be ready to admit to them that he had made a mistake? Perhaps it foreshadows his weakness in his inability to eliminate Alice, though he is much more of a robot killer in the script than the waffler he becomes onscreen. The language of his speech about destroying the space platform is much more elaborate and interesting in the film, where even simple repetition ("Negative, negative, negative!") plays better than the scripted lines read. But most important is the fact that the unscripted Great Guidance appears in this sequence ("Great One himself sends the cosmic blast."), and that Ro-Man refers to him three times. Again, the second Ro-Man must have only been thought of later on, as the survivors never refer to the invaders in the plural. There is only one Ro-Man in the script, and in the film's dialogue; Guidance could be a figment of Ro-Man's imagination for all we know (like the ambiguous nature of the ghost of Hamlet's father). Whoever's idea it was to add the second Ro-Man, Tucker was clearly involved, remembering a great amount of thought that went into making the character interesting:

> *What about the impassioned speech that Ro-Man delivers when he's about to be taken back, or destroyed, from his superior Ro-Man? He says, "I want to be like a human. I want to laugh, to sing, to hear children's voices. Why aren't these human qualities incorporated in the plan?"*
>
> Well, that was part of the basic concept. I knew that I was going to have very few days to shoot it. I knew I was going to have at best second-rate actors and actresses. At that time I was certainly a third- or fourth-rate director, and I knew it. What I wanted to do was give conflict within his character, but within the framework of what could actually be shot and shot well. I felt that it was a natural place for conflict to be that somehow or other

> he had been contaminated by his superior [while] on Earth, that even as bad as things were on Earth, they still found things to be happy about, and hopeful about, and that to a robot this would either seem strange, or wrong, or terribly right, and why wouldn't he be included? One of those three things. I arbitrarily picked the third because that was a point of conflict which would establish [inaudible].

But as the script shows, it is unlikely that Tucker had thought all of this through prior to filming (as his words indicate).

One of the most laughably cheap moments in the film is when the space platform is confusingly exploded. To depict this event, V-2 rocket film and shots of the two Ro-Men are mixed with new footage of a spaceship prop carrying a lit sparkler

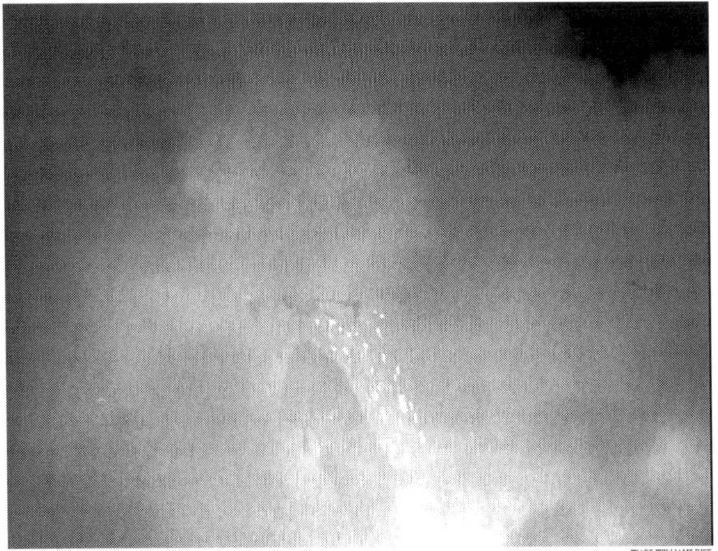

WADE WILLIAMS DIST.

in its back end. It is difficult to discern just what is happening in this sequence, but it is easy to see a gloved arm hurling the spaceship prop around in darkness and smoke. The script handled this sequence in a much more straightforward manner:

> **51 CLOSE SHOT – VIEWER**
>
> **An object approaches it, explodes it. Then Ro-Man's face appears again.**

In truth it may have been unlikely that this sequence could have avoided confusion—as the space platform is never introduced earlier, it is going to be unavoidably unfamiliar when it is destroyed. But the elaborate-yet-ludicrous scene on film was clearly not the best approach.

In another lost detail, Alice is scripted as collapsing soon after Ro-Man signs off, with the other adults setting her down on the pallet and Roy "[covering] her tenderly." From here the film dissolves to another equipment sequence, where Roy tells the non-crumpled Alice that one "can't connect these two circuits," perhaps foreshadowing in regard to their marriage. This scene is completely unscripted, which is logical. There is no reason for Roy and Alice to be doing more equipment work (their reason for doing it now wiped out by the destruction of the space platform), and it is not certain why it seemed necessary to add more of it to the film.

From Alice's written collapse, the script does a dissolve to Ro-Man, "puttering around with his logarhythm [sic] tables" just as his Viewscreen comes to life. In a very interesting detail, "Ro-Man chuckles" as he switches it on. The laughter has some logic, as he is expecting a surrender, but he never displays enough confidence in his onscreen version to indulge in the superiority of laughing at his defeated opponents. The only superiority he displays in the film is of an angry, threatening, bombastic kind; the brittle surface confidence of one who masks inner weakness. A confident chuckle on his part would have undermined the weakness that is all too apparent when he is unable to fulfill his mandate, and thus it never happens. It almost seems that a great deal of thought had gone into the character by the time the film was done; he not only has the best lines, but is by far the most interesting and rounded character.

The Professor then declares the survivors' defiance of Ro-Man, in a scripted scene on the whole like the film. But we are denied the following spectacle:

56 CLOSE SHOT – RO-MAN

He starts calculating like mad. The tumblers roll, he writes rapidly.

PROFESSOR'S VOICE

If you are trying to calculate our position, you are wasting your time. **We are not fools. We only called you because we have solved the problem of high frequency dispersal. Given a little more time, we earth people would have known as much as your people -- and used our knowledge more wisely.**

Ro-Man stops calculating.

RO-MAN

(angrily)

I'll get you yet: None shall escape me. . . .

In this interesting and unused bit, the film would have showed Ro-Man in close perspective, doing scientific or mathematical calculations while the Professor spoke. It is amusing to imagine George Barrows trying to imitate writing with the fingers of his gorilla costume, but it is also intriguing that the film would have showed Ro-Man behaving recognizably as a scientist (it is left to implication in the film). (The Professor's mostly unused speech was partially scratched out in the script copy.)

In his defiance, the Professor then shows off the survivors one by one. It is not obvious onscreen how the Viewscreen grabs different perspectives, but the script at least has the Professor "turning a dial" to make it happen. Ro-Man's verbal reactions to the individual family members (which sound comically obligatory, as if he is being polite by making threats because of an expectation to say something) are not scripted, and adding them in broke up what would have been a tiresome parade of familiar faces. (Once again, there is great dubbing advantage in using a character without a mouth.) Johnny's defiant tongue-wagging ("The boy is impertinent!") is specifically noted in the script as a contrast to Carla's uncertain shyness.

It is only to Alice that Ro-Man reacts in the script: "Let me see the girl again." And Alice identically in each version uses the phrase "peace with honor" (famously later used by President Nixon in ending the Vietnam War). The script is not too far from the film as Ro-Man declares his desire to meet with Alice, but his note on film that "It is not in The Plan . . ." does not appear in the script. "The Plan" was every bit as much an invention of post-production as was Great Guidance. Ro-Man's dialogue, across the board more poetic in the film, gets earthy in at least one scripted spot as the Professor insists on being representative for the survivors:

61 (CONTINUED)

RO-MAN'S VOICE

That's not very smart, Human. The girl could accomplish more.

There was also some script detail for the meeting place that had to be changed in filming. Ro-Man's proposal to meet at "the fork of the two dry rivers" was scripted as "the area of the two sewers." Why there would be two sewers at a location, rather than one big one, is baffling and the film did well on that point. Also strange is a line cut out from the kids, not from Carla this time, but Johnny:

64 CLOSE SHOT – CARLA AND JOHNNY

CARLA

(to Johnny)

Is Alice gonna have a date with Ro-Man?

JOHNNY

How can you figure girls?

Perhaps Johnny was cut to build up Carla. It is too bad, as his lack of self-awareness in complaining about females to a female could have been very funny. Much of this section is close to the film, as Roy, Alice, and the Professor argue (both in script and movie, Martha often has very little to do). In an excised bit, after Alice has argued that she should be smart and submit to the monster's affections, Roy's intentions become explicit at last:

ROY

(grimly)

You're not going anywhere, kiddo. I'm holding on to you – now and in the future.

ALICE

(weeping hysterically)

You fools, you fools!

At this point Johnny sneaks off, just as he does onscreen, but he gets a quiet scene all to himself that was unfortunately not included. Good in itself, suggesting the thoughts that children entertain when adults are wrapped up in themselves, it also helps cement the dreamed quality of the film:

66 CLOSE SHOT – JOHNNY

He watches the struggle thoughtfully. Then he backs toward the barricade, slips through and hurries away.

DISSOLVE TO:

67 EXT. DISASTER AREA – DAY – MED. CLOSE SHOT – TWO SEWERS

Hold on this shot until Johnny's legs come in.

68 WIDER ANGLE

Johnny stops and looks at the two sewers. CAMERA PANS as he looks around, taking in the layout. CAMERA goes to a flight of stairs that lead to the sky as the building is no longer there, then PANS back to that spot. Johnny walks up to the stairs and triggers it to let loose when he kicks the support from under it. He then sits down on a ledge.

The amount of thought that went into the script for this cheap little monster movie is again impressive. On film, the camera pans right as Johnny escapes from the squabbling family and then cuts to Ro-Man, walking for no discernible reason and apparently just out for a stroll. Then, as preserved on the Image Entertainment DVD release, an intermission title card appears. Done over the familiar comic book potpourri from the opening credits and in the same font, it was there for the technical needs of a 3-D film. But Johnny's lonely, taciturn course of action in the script is much more interesting, as he reasons out how to eventually entrap Ro-Man.

Most notably, the script writer "directed" with great intelligence, with a close perspective on Johnny and the use of a dissolve to make certain the audience understood the passage of time and distance. The sense of journeying is further increased by Johnny's walking into shot 67. Unfortunately, the grammar of film is never used so intelligently in the movie and its overall lack of interesting camera angles is perhaps its ultimate

WADE WILLIAMS DIST.

weakness. Some aspects of the script were too much trouble for the time and budget, but a better basic visual sense would have helped it to no end. On that point, Phil Tucker shared something with his contemporary Ed Wood. As producer Alex Gordon recalled to Tom Weaver, "The thing about Eddie is that he really didn't know how to direct. If you look at *Bride of the Monster* (1955), you'll see that he had these long-shot scenes which *screamed* for some close-ups and over-the-shoulder shots and other things. But he didn't 'sell' the picture in any way, he just got it on film the best way he could."[369] Gordon's description reads like an apt criticism of Tucker's direction. But whether Tucker, Ordung, Rinaldo, or someone else wrote it, the script contained some poetically suggestive language with "the two sewers" and "a flight of stairs that lead to the sky," word images that the film does not equal.

As scripted, scene 69 picks up right where the shot of Johnny sitting down left off:

69 SAME AREA BUT DIFFERENT PART – FULL LENGTH SHOT

Ro-Man comes around the corner of a destroyed building and moves toward CAMERA. CAMERA PANS WITH HIM as he misses CAMERA by a few feet and passes on. CAMERA PANS HIM TO steps. Johnny gets up slowly and faces him. Ro-Man stops.

Ro-Man walks near the camera, but there are no buildings for him to weave around, just an expanse of grass. (At this point in the film, a mysterious figure can be seen stopping, standing, and looking down in the extreme background at Johnny and Ro-Man. Was it just someone strolling by and understandably curious, or someone from the film? Did Tucker think it would be cute to give his wife a little cameo?) More missing material pops up as Johnny banters with Ro-Man:

RO-MAN

Now I will kill you.

JOHNNY
(on qui vive)

You'd have to catch me first.

Ro-Man raises his hands. Electric sparks shoot from his finger tips. There is a weird humming sound. But Johnny stands his ground.

More interesting in the script is that once again, Ro-Man has the power to shoot lightning. Almost certainly the idea was dropped because it was too much trouble. As the effect seems to have been created by scratching onto the film itself, it was probably not expensive, but it would have been time-consuming. More to the point, it was probably difficult to do with realism from one character to the next. If the shots were filmed with the wrong perspective, the effect might look unconvincing. When the lightning-fingers effect is recycled onscreen by Guidance, it is notable that he fires solo in camera, the lightning landing somewhere off-screen. This eliminated the difficulty of making a convincing effect for the object of the lightning strike. What is more, the technique used on film—developing a few film frames negative and dubbing in an electronic noise—would have been very easy in comparison.

Thankfully, this sequence explains one of the most baffling elements of the movie. Johnny immediately tells Ro-Man, "You look like a pooped out pinwheel," on paper just as he does on film, but it actually makes sense in the script. Ro-Man might take offense to being likened to a device that has run down, and if he was intended to have whirling fans and blades inside his plexiglass head, then the pinwheel reference is logical.

RO-MAN

So. The calcinator ray really cannot harm you. Your father must be a brilliant **man**.

JOHNNY

He's smart enough.

RO-MAN

Did I understand him to say that medicine is his special field?

JOHNNY

He's got a super serum . . .

The bolded "man" in Ro-Man's first sentence becomes "scientist" on film. The sequence's conclusion also loosely mirrors the final film, but again loses an excellent detail:

RO-MAN

You have told me all I need to know, **stupid boy**. I will now calculate the spectrum dust in the calcinator to counter-attack this antibiotic. **But there is a much easier way of killing you.**

He starts toward Johnny. Johnny prepares to trip trap at the top of the stairs. As Ro-Man gets to first step Johnny lets the trap fall and runs away. Ro-Man tries to sidestep the trap and as he does he trips on a bit of rubble and falls down as the trap misses him. He gets up burning with anger and climbs the steps. CAMERA sweeps the area but Johnny is nowhere to be seen.

70 CLOSE UP – RO-MAN

RO-MAN

(shaking fist)

I'll destroy you yet. I'll get you all.

71 FULL CLOSE – RO-MAN

He walks toward CAMERA.

FADE OUT:

The lines "stupid boy" and "much easier way of killing you" were perhaps eliminated because they were thought too mean directed at a child. George Barrows could have easily done the fall as scripted, but did not as the business with Johnny setting up a trap did not remain in the film. Ro-Man does ineffectually chase him and shake his fist, so his final line was perhaps meant to be included. It may have also been thought another excessive threat aimed at a child (the monster already gets to say, "Now I will kill you" onscreen).

The film preserves the final bit of camera direction quoted above that Ro-Man walks into the camera. As scripted, this was intended to create suspense:

FADE IN:

72

PROFESSOR'S VOICE
(calling)

Johnny! Johnny!

The Professor's back moves away from CAMERA.
He runs several steps, stops, looks around wildly.

Perhaps suggested by similar, but less intense transitions in Alfred Hitchcock's *Rope* (1948), this excellent fade in/out would have given the film a good dose of vitality, but it does not exist onscreen and there is not even a shot beginning on the professor's back. At this point in the script, the family notices Johnny's absence and Roy and Alice set out to find him, a sequence that plays out largely as written on film. However, another gigantic change is apparent here. As written, Johnny's running off, setting the trap, and encountering Ro-Man take place in uninterrupted succession. But the film works much differently. As the film goes right from Johnny's escape to a shot of Ro-Man to the intermission, it then resumes with some more shots of Ro-Man bobbling around and then straight to the Professor's concern over Johnny. (It should be acknowledged that there is here a brief shot of Johnny walking through what appear to be woods.) Then Roy and Alice depart, and Johnny's encounter with Ro-Man on film does not occur until after this point.

Because of this scene-jumbling, the nicely conceived script transition could not have been pulled off, and an especially good bit of visual flair bit the dust. But Tucker and Zimbalist may have been wise to rearrange things as they did. The weakness of the nicely scripted Johnny sequence is that it is extended. There is little sense of time passing between his setting the trap and

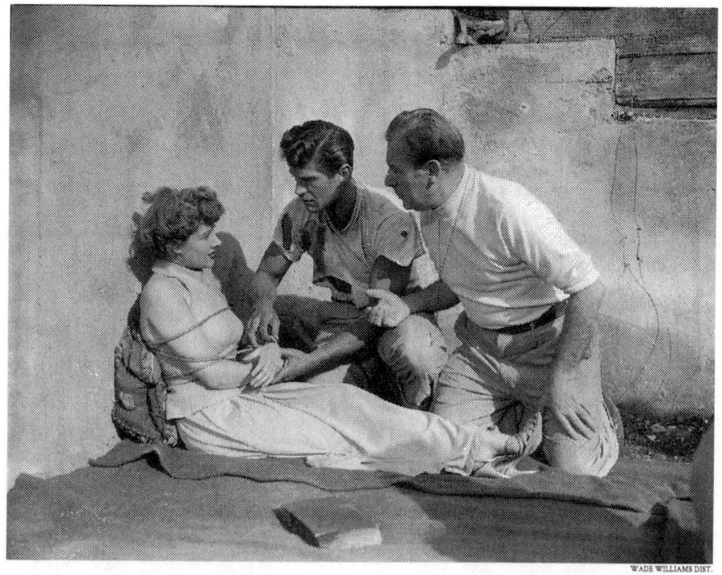

WADE WILLIAMS DIST.

Ro-Man's arrival, and the events seem more believable by cutting back to the family's ruin.

As the family panic scene is written, there are details deleted from the film:

> **PROFESSOR STORMS ACROSS AREA to where Alice sits, bound hand and foot. Roy is beside her, calmly reading a torn, partly burned book. Alice eyes her father with resentment. He kneels beside her and starts untying her bonds.**

Roy has a book onscreen, which he is shown tossing aside. The Professor, however, does not untie Alice while Roy does. The Professor's dialogue as they leave is reasonably close to what was scripted, with some minor differences:

PROFESSOR

Be careful. Ro-Man will be stalking the woods too. If Johnny comes back, I'll set off a flare.

From that scene the script goes into an extended sequence that has very little parallel in the film:

73 MED. SHOT – JOHNNY IN WOODS

making his way home cautiously but rapidly.

74 MED. SHOT – ROY AND ALICE

searching. He pantomimes for her to take one direction. He goes in another.

75 MED. SHOT – JOHNNY

He stops as he hears noise of footsteps near him. He hides carefully. CAMERA PANS UP to Roy as he hurries by. After he passes, Johnny gets up and moves on again.

76 MED. SHOT – ALICE

She stops dead in her tracks, shrinks back against a tree.

On SOUND TRACK WE HEAR THE APPROACHING BUZZ-BUZZ OF Ro-Man.

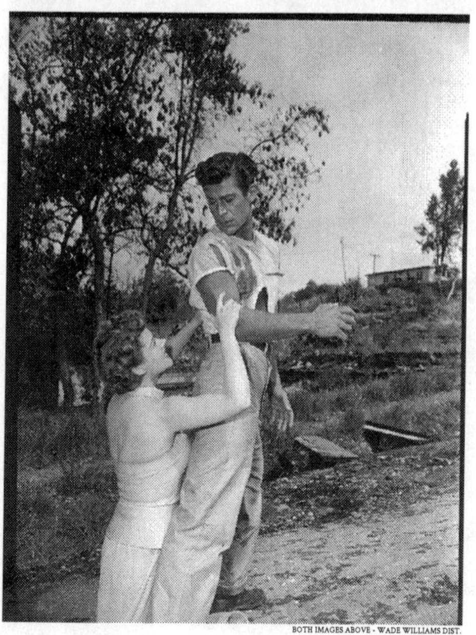

BOTH IMAGES ABOVE - WADE WILLIAMS DIST.

WADE WILLIAMS DIST.

Alice turns and runs. She comes smack into Roy. She pulls him behind a rock.

77 OVER-SHOULDER ALICE – MED. SHOT – RO-MAN

He goes through the woods, saying something to himself. As he passes the hideaways we hear it:

RO-MAN
(rolling it
over his
tongue with
relish)

Al – ice . . . Al – ice . . .

78 CLOSE SHOT – ALICE AND ROY

She gives an involuntary shudder and hides her face on Roy's chest. He strokes her hair, but cannot resist grinning down at her. Alice looks up, catches the grin. Annoyed, she breaks away from him, hurries through woods.

The sequence of shots here quoted comprise all of page 36 in the script, and the lack of this sequence in the film brings to mind the urban legend of John Ford, informed that he was behind schedule, ripping ten pages out of a script to get his production up to speed. (There is a large check mark written next to scene 77, suggesting that the scene was the first to go? Or was it considered very important before being dropped?)

The teasing edge of Roy's affection for Alice comes out most clearly at this point. He misdirects her, knowing that Ro-Man could show up at any moment, and cannot deny finding it humorous that she is the uncomfortable object of robot lust. Combined with the lack of some of the earlier eliminated dialogue, there is contrast between the devil-may-care cockiness of Roy in the script and Nader's relatively muted personification of him. But most disappointing is the cleverness in the script of having Johnny nearly intersect with Roy in the midst of his game with Alice, and the detail of Ro-Man muttering Alice's name to himself as he stalks the woods. There are many shots of the monster stumbling around the countryside in the film, but they are not accompanied by dialogue to clarify what the monster is doing at the moment. At this point in the film, there is only the most skeletal approximation of this sequence when Alice and Roy walk along; he removes his shirt and carries her away. There is nothing so complex or interesting as the intercutting with Johnny that is in the script.

In both versions, the story moves to Johnny's return to the ruin, and his lament over giving away their secret. The script directs that he cries but, though Martha and the Professor comfort him, he does not actually cry in the film. The scene ends as scripted with the Professor taking action to get the attention of Alice and Roy:

PROFESSOR

(absently)

Yes, darling, of course.

He gets a flare gun and fires it.

In the film, the Professor says the line but does nothing else. There is an abrupt cut to black screen, and then right to an abrupt fade-in to a weird, shiny object in the sky that has perpetually baffled viewers. It is extremely bright, twirls around and makes an odd noise. Did Ro-Man do something to the sun? Is Guidance arriving on Earth? As the script makes certain, it was supposed to have been the flare that the Professor has just fired. But he never gets to fire it onscreen and, yet again, the film suffers from a problem that should have been easy to avoid. (A quick shot of the Professor pointing *any* gun to the sky, even without firing, would have suggested a flare gun). Furthermore, the script made the effect even clearer:

WADE WILLIAMS DIST.

80 INT. WOODS – EDGE OF CLIFF

Alice and Roy are searching. There is a whistling sound overhead followed by a series of sharp pops. They look up, look at each other and sigh in relief.

81 EXT. CAVE – CLOSE SHOT – RO-MAN

He too is looking up. The calculator noise works briefly. Then Ro-Man shakes his head slightly and enters the cave.

These two scenes are completely absent from the film. No one notices the so-called flare onscreen, just as there is no explanation given for it. What is truly odd here, given that Tucker and Zimbalist chose to leave in the shot of the flare, is that it is not only unexplained but does not look anything like a flare (purely on the basis of what appears onscreen, it is easiest to conclude that it is supposed to be the sun, although even then the shot has no point). If they knew when filming that they did not have footage that made the flare effect logical, then why attempt it? In any case, the money had apparently been spent, and the shot was not going to go to waste. But in contrast to the film, at least one point of this part of the script is hard to fathom: Why does Ro-Man dismiss an object in the sky that would allow him to "postulate" the location of the survivors?

The script then moves to Roy and Alice having a quiet interlude that is almost identical to the film, as Roy does more pantomime to affirm his love for her. Described over six paragraphs, it accurately describes the action onscreen: "Roy puts his palm over his heart, then holds it out to her, indicating that it is hers." It is also worth noting that this emphasis on silent communication is very intelligent given the situation they are in: "Roy opens his mouth to speak. Alice puts her fingers to her lips quickly; Roy remembers." This is one of the best parts of the film. The actors get to behave as believable characters, and have more interesting things to do than spout pseudo-scientific jargon. They are also completely successful in communicating and expressing their emotions while saying nothing.

There is a cut to black, a cut to Ro-Man entering his cave, and then the return of Alice and Roy to the ruin. The script does basically the same, while eschewing the intervening shot of Ro-Man. The script is here again guilty of tedium, as it goes straight from Roy and Alice courting to them getting married. Another large chunk of the script is missing:

PROFESSOR

(to Roy; kidding)

You're quite sure there's no one else, son?

ROY

I'll be the most faithful husband this world has ever known.

PROFESSOR

(clapping Roy
on shoulder)

In that case, let's get to it.

(in high
spirits)

And I want you to know this is the biggest social event of the year. The whole darn community is going to turn out **for my daughter's wedding, so I want it done right. Martha, scurry up a veil and a handkerchief to cry into. Carla, you're the flower girl. John, you be best man. Hop to it now.**

Each one dashes about his business. Carla searches the compound for flowers. Johnny tries to make Roy look as presentable as possible. Martha digs up an old piece of cheesecloth and drapes it over the back of Alice's hair.

WADE WILLIAMS DIST.

PROFESSOR

Everybody set?

CARLA

(agonized)

I can't find any flowers but these!

ALICE

That's all right dear. We'll pretend you have a basket of rose petals.

PROFESSOR

All right. Places.

Two important things happen at this point. If shot as scripted the assembled film was obviously dull at this point, and the filmmakers took necessary steps to maintain audience interest. The Professor only gets out the beginning of his directions before the film cuts to Ro-Man communicating with Guidance for the third time. (Johnny's paint gun and toy ray gun are still sitting in the cave.) Also of great important in the deleted section is the Professor's direction to Carla to be the flower girl, and that she is then "agonized" that she cannot fulfill the role. This script element soon has great resonance.

Soon after the third appearance of Guidance, the Professor performs the wedding ceremony and, while it is reasonably close on film to the script, John Mylong plays it better than it is written. What was not scripted was that the Professor initially tries to perform a traditional wedding ceremony before he stops uncomfortably, and then addresses himself to God in a personal manner, acknowledging his own inadequacy:

PROFESSOR

(looking upward)

Dear Lord. You know that I'm not trained for this job. **I guess you know I haven't even been too regular in my attendance at church.** But I have tried to live by . . .

The Professor comes across as rather pious onscreen with this line gone, and perhaps it was removed with some thought toward building up the character as a patriarch and role model. Or perhaps Mylong just had a long speech to memorize and forgot a line. There is another missing chunk later in the same speech:

. . . give to Roy and Alice a long life, and a fertile one, **that Men might sing Your praises, and do Your work.** But no matter how . . .

Carla's tragic fate comes soon after the wedding scene, and was scripted with far more emphasis than the film's treatment of it:

84 **CLOSE TWO SHOT** – CARLA AND JOHNNY

CARLA

She ought to have some flowers. It isn't right.

JOHNNY

(carelessly)

So hop down to the meadow and pick her some.

He leaves her. Carla considers this, then hurries off. CAMERA PANS TO ALICE AND ROY as they leave the barricade, amid ad lib farewells.

DISSOLVE TO:

The film does not emphasize this moment with the close shot described, and Johnny's indifferent response to her need to do something well was completely excised. The film does not show Carla scurrying away, but instead cuts to yet another view of Ro-Man, now leaving his lair. Film and script are then fairly similar when Carla catches up with Roy and Alice to give them flowers, but the film dropped a nicely conceived shot from the script:

86 MED. LONG SHOT – CARLA – DOLLY

She runs toward the CAMERA and CAMERA PULLS BACK SLIGHTLY to let her meet with Roy and Alice directly in front of CAMERA. She jumps into Alice's arms and kisses her generously.

On film this part is more pedestrian, stationary shots. The camera movement described may have been too difficult on uneven terrain under the film's budget and conditions, but the film keeps deviating from the script in ways not so easily excusable:

90 FULL ANGLE – GROUP

WADE WILLIAMS DIST.

CARLA

Aw . . . awright.

Carla turns away, waves goodbye and starts down the hill. Roy and Alice watch her.

91 TWO SHOT – ROY AND ALICE

ALICE

Do you think she'll be safe or had we better go with her?

ROY

Ro-Man has never come around this part yet.

They continue on their way.

The script gave Roy and Alice a logical reason to not worry about Carla; they are boneheads for assuming that things would work out okay, but they at least have an excuse. Carla soon enough runs into Ro-Man, and the material missing from the film is a detriment to keeping Ro-Man interesting:

CARLA

My Daddy won't let you hurt me. **He said so.**

RO-MAN

What are you doing here alone? **Did they send [you] out here to trick me?**

CARLA

I picked some flowers for Alice and Roy. They just got married.

RO-MAN

(angry)

Married?

CARLA

I have to get back now.

RO-MAN

Wait. Give me those flowers.

CARLA

(hesitant)

If you want.

She holds them out.

In the film, Ro-Man's anger and lust for Alice are much less defined. He is denied boiling rage over the uncomfortable truth that Alice cannot possibly want him. Although he has his interactions with Great Guidance, they define his Hamlet-like lack of resolve. Ro-Man's aggressive side follows a straight and dull rise in the film, with no point such as this one in the script that represents his going over the edge into a full-blown rampage. It should also be noted that, onscreen, Carla's line "My Daddy won't let you hurt me" occurs after Ro-Man's line "What are you doing here alone?".

Carla's death scene as scripted is another thoughtfully planned sequence that did not make it to the screen:

96 MED. CLOSE – FLOWERS

All we can see is [sic] **the hands of Carla handing the bouquet toward Ro-Man. Then we see Ro-Man's hands come out toward the flowers. At first it appears as though he is going to take them. Then his hands go on past and we hear Carla scream. Then Ro-Man pushes in until the CLOSE-UP is on him. (CAMERA MUST NOT MOVE DURING THIS SHOT.)**

DISSOLVE TO:

On film, Ro-Man just grabs Carla and kills her off-screen. The shot described in the script was both extremely simple and effective, perhaps even one that would linger in viewers' minds. George Barrows was uncomfortable with his character murdering a child, according to Bob Burns, and had to be persuaded that the scene was acceptable since the story was a dream.[370] Also of interest is the fact that, according to Weaver, *Robot Monster* is one of only about six horror films in the decades following *Frankenstein* (1931) to imitate its gruesome plot point of a child being killed by a monster.[371] *Robot Monster* obviously lifted this story element straight from the horror classic, since in both films a little girl plays with flowers and is murdered by the monster. The connection to *Frankenstein* is even more appropriate in that Ro-Man is also an awkward patchwork of

WADE WILLIAMS DIST.

spare parts, both as scripted and in terms of the costume used in the film.

The script directs a dissolve to Roy and Alice from the subtle death scene quoted above, but the film instead cuts straight to the fourth appearance of Guidance, and from there to Ro-Man ambushing the newlyweds. This gives the tubby alien invader

WADE WILLIAMS DIST.

a rather awkward, zigzag trajectory at this point in the film, while the script had the benefit of logically dissolving straight to his attack. This sequence is roughly the same in both versions but, yet again, there are significant changes:

97 CLIFF AREA – NIGHT

BOTH IMAGES ABOVE - WADE WILLIAMS DIST.

By moonlight, CAMERA PANS OFF SOME **TREES** to pick up Roy and Alice kissing.

ALICE

(as they break)

At this rate we'll never get there.

Roy pantomimes that she shouldn't be talking. Alice reacts contritely. She takes his hand to lead him on. But he pulls her back. He pantomimes that he wants one more kiss. She comes to him. As they embrace . . .

98 MED. CLOSE SHOT – RO-MAN

He parts some bushes and watches balefully. Then he starts to move forward.

Again, the film is supposed to be taking place at night but it did not work out that way. Likewise, the camera pans in this shot and Ro-Man emerges from trees, while there is no dialogue from Alice or pantomiming from Roy. This is unfortunate because it would have created some character continuity from their earlier big scene to this later part of the film. The script here is again written with the sharp precision that the film lacks, as Roy and Alice move toward one another to be split asunder right as they make contact.

Also noteworthy is the description that the scene is occurring at a "cliff area." There is even less of anything in the film that could be called a cliff than there are woods, and this point is crucial. As Ro-Man grabs Alice and Roy battles him, more details contrast with the film. It is Roy in the script who takes a boulder and "crashes it over Ro-Man's head," whereas onscreen Alice attacks the monster in this way. And although Ro-Man pushes Roy over an edge of some sort, it is never visually set up as a cliff, or depicted as specifically as it was written:

> **103 MED. SHOT – EDGE OF CLIFF**
>
> **Ro-Man, carrying the struggling Alice over his shoulder, drags Roy to the edge of the precipice and drops him over.**
>
> **104 CLOSE SHOT – EDGE OF PRECIPICE**
>
> **Roy manages to grab hold with his fingers and hang on.**
>
> **105 CLOSE SHOT – RO-MAN – ALICE OVER HIS SHOULDER**
>
> **He looks down at Roy.**
>
> **106 CLOSE SHOT – ROY HANGING ON FOR DEAR LIFE**
>
> **Ro-Man's HEAVY foot comes into scene and crushes Roy's fingers. He loses his grip and falls. His agonized cry gets fainter as he falls.**
>
> **107 CLOSE SHOT – RO-MAN AND ALICE**

WADE WILLIAMS DIST.

Ro-Man listens until the cry is broken by a heavy thud. Then he shifts Alice so he can hold her in both arms.

RO-MAN

Now you are mine.

This would have been much more captivating than the finished movie, where Roy seems to be rolling into a ditch. But the well-scripted sequence might have not happened simply because Tucker had not planned out how to accomplish it without having his star hanging on the edge of a cliff. As Barrows remembered:

> [Tucker] even had Nader, who was very frightened at certain scenes in which he had to go along on the edge of this wall—and it was a drop of eighty feet down there—and he wanted him really close to it, and he didn't want to do it.

As written, Alice immediately begins to try to beat Ro-Man by appealing to his attraction to her, asking him how he can be "so strong." His reply strays slightly from the film:

RO-MAN

We have atomic energizers that instantaneously repair any damaged part.

This dialogue was less silly than the film's insistence that "We Ro-Mans obtain our strength from the planet Ro-Man, relayed through our individual energizers," and there is some loss of logic. If the alien invaders used some sort of remote power source, having it located nearby is more believable than relaying it from another planet. As in the film, Alice asks where the power source is located and Ro-Man replies that it is in the cave. (It is stupid of him to give her this information, of course, but he is smitten.)

In the film, that scene occurs after the following script scene, in which Martha and the Professor discover Carla's lifeless body. This cross-cutting was probably wise, for the ever-needed reason of mitigating monotony, and because it gives Alice some bit of time to become collected enough to try getting information out of her captor. Script and film are almost identical at this point (and Royle comes across better here in her emotional outburst than she does in most of the movie) with one large exception:

> **The Buzz-Buzz of Ro-Man is heard. The Professor quickly gathers Carla in his arms and hurries away. CAMERA PANS TO PICK UP RO-MAN as he hurries toward CAMERA, carrying Alice.**

As mentioned, this scene leads into the earlier scripted scene of Alice using her wiles on the alien invader. And presumably (the script does not make this clear) Martha gets up and leaves with the Professor. No electronic Ro-Man is heard on the soundtrack but, more importantly, there are some thoughtful details packed into this brief description. The Professor carrying Carla and Ro-Man carrying Alice in the same shot is a nice bit of symmetry and contrast that would have created some visual flair. Likewise, the monster's walking into the camera is a repeated motif in the script that is just as absent onscreen. The lack of this detail is a shame, as it would have given the visually static film not only dynamism but continuity. And it is especially surprising that it was left out as the film was made in 3-D. It is such an obvious 3-D effect that its presence in the script is evidence for the argument that Tucker had exploitation film connections for stereoscopic equipment, and had plans to use the format even before Al Zimbalist was involved. It may have been a pitch about 3-D to Zimbalist that got the production going.

In the script, there is now a dissolve to the scene of Carla's burial, where Johnny laments not playing with his sister as often as she wanted. As a sound is heard and the group tenses, there is another intelligent piece of business in the script:

> There is a sound of something dragging through the bushes. They freeze. It keeps coming closer. **The Professor rushes for his ray gun. He holds it trained against Johnny's head, ready to fire if it should be the Ro-Man.**

WADE WILLIAMS DIST.

A badly beaten Roy shows up instead of Ro-Man, but the film differs in not having the Professor ready to give Johnny a mercy killing. This aspect of the script, like other previously deleted parts, might have been thought too brutal. What is hard to comprehend is that when Roy soon collapses, the script indicates that he faints while the Professor pronounces him dead on film. Probably added to make clear what happened to Roy, it seems less logical in comparison. In the script Roy gets dropped a significant distance and should be dead, while on film his fall is not obviously lethal and he could believably just be exhausted.

While the film briefly cuts to Ro-Man carrying Alice to his cave, the script continues with Johnny and the parents discussing their next action in words that closely mirror the film for about a page. Then, never very far away on the horizon, more changes occur right as the Professor agrees that Johnny's plan "might work" ("reluctantly" agreeing in the script, though on film much more enthusiastically):

MARTHA

It <u>would</u> work. But with <u>me</u>, not Johnny.

112 CLOSE UP - JOHNNY

JOHNNY

No, Mom. We're gonna win this fight. And when we do, Alice and Roy's children will start coming along and somebody will have to teach them.

MARTHA

Alice is smarter than I am dear.

JOHNNY

Maybe about some things. But can she plant rose bushes like you? Or make a feller feel better when he's feeling bad? Gosh there's a lot more to knowing than blueprints and formulas.

113 TWO SHOT – JOHNNY AND MARTHA

Martha takes him to her bosom and cries over him.

MARTHA

Johnny, Johnny . . .

JOHNNY

It's all right Mom. I'm only a sort of a caterpillar still. It don't matter so much if I get stepped on.

114 MED. CLOSE – PROFESSOR

He makes his decision.

PROFESSOR

The boy is right, Martha. There's no time to lose.

He rises with determination.

This missing section is affecting and, unlike the film, Johnny plans with the assumption that he will die. He thinks, at his young age, of the good of others and comforts his mother. Touchingly, he may even be trying to atone for guilt over giving up their location, and perhaps blames himself for the death of Carla. And Martha (like the Biblical Martha witnessing the resurrection of Lazarus, about to witness the resurrection of humanity?) gets a moment of parting with her somewhat Christ-like son that would have made her character far better onscreen. In reality, Johnny's parents would have sacrificed themselves in Johnny's place but—as the script reiterates so much more effectively than the film—the story is a dream, and a red-blooded boy's wish fulfillment fantasy. On film the entire family leaves once the decision is made, rather than the Professor simply rising up with determination. When the film gets to the Professor's line ("There's no time to lose."), it arrives by a very abrupt edit. As with other parts of the film where chunks of script are missing, the editing is choppy, as if it were the best possible patch for covering a hole.

Both versions then get to Ro-Man carrying Alice to his cave, while in the film he mauls her somewhat, pulling down the halter straps of her dress. According to interviewer John Beifuss, Claudia Barrett said she "was surprised at that, too, but Phil Tucker liked that . . .. I grabbed my top pretty fast. Phil Tucker was a character."[372] (The Rhino VHS edition of the film jokingly added a black censor bar over her bust at this point.) As Barrett remembered in Paul Parla's interview, the sequence "was a case of too many cooks." Contradictory instructions from Tucker and the two cameramen "really made things difficult. I was supposed to be screaming and beating on Ro-Man but after we took the long shot, Tucker got the idea I should try to seduce Ro-Man to find out his secrets. The finished scene is a bit confusing."[373] The script differs in some details:

WADE WILLIAMS DIST.

115 INT. CAVE – MED. SHOT – RO-MAN AND ALICE

She is about as undressed now as the law allows. She is backing away from Ro-Man who pursues her, breathing heavily with passion.

ALICE

(desperately)

But Ro-Man, you must try to understand us women. Before I can really love you, I must know all about you. And you haven't told me yet where the energizer is kept.

RO-MAN

Tomorrow – maybe. Now –

116 INT. CAVE

> Ro-Man enters it, carrying Alice. He sets her down, she starts to escape. In the struggle her clothing is torn. At the last moment, as he has her cornered the Viewer—screen lights up and buzzes. Ro-Man pauses a moment, then lumbers over to it, holding Alice.

Alice is not "as undressed as the law allows" onscreen (the strap-ripping does not much expose her), and the written sequence is far kinkier than the film. Whether or not Barrett was comfortable with how the scene was written, Tucker would have realized that it could cause trouble. We fortunately do not have to hear robotic heavy breathing, nor is there as much struggling as described here; there is no moment when "he has her cornered." Likewise, he does not possessively grasp her when speaking to the Viewscreen, having knocked her unconscious and barely tied her up before answering it in the movie. The film's great continuity error is here as Alice is suddenly seated and thoroughly tied up, with no indication that Ro-Man had time to finish the job in the midst of being chewed out by Guidance. Ro-Man does not have the problem of an unreasonable boss in the script, and he is also specifically described as chaining her to the cave wall before going to kill the survivors. (Alice not only predicted a famous saying of President Nixon, but the name of grunge band Alice in Chains.)

Ro-Man on film shows a slightly tender and lonely side to his abduction. He asks her if she would love him if he was a man, and begs her to not hate him for his impending murder of her brother. It makes him a little less of a selfish brute and slightly humanizes him, and is in keeping with his indecisiveness that builds throughout the film. But the scripted Ro-Man pushes this sequence beyond what would be releasable; an unequivocal destroyer until this point, he is now a one-dimensional violator. Ro-Man maybe became indecisive, wordy, and unintentionally comical onscreen because the scripted Ro-Man was so unlikable and simplistic.

At this late point in the script, the parallel scenes on film become very confusing. Ro-Man is contacted by the survivors that they wish to meet him for an easy death, and is directed by Guidance to finish off the humans. He then emotes in his infamous, great soliloquy ("At what point on the graph do 'cannot' and 'must' meet?"), and is again contacted by Guidance to kill Alice. Finally having enough of his melancholy Dane of a Ro-Man, Guidance strikes him down right as he is about to kill Johnny, and unleashes a nonsensical barrage of lightening, dinosaurs, and suddenly high-pitched, echoing dialogue: "Explode the Earth out of the universe!" Johnny soon awakens as Roy carries him into the cave, with blood on his forehead to show that he fell and knocked himself out. That point was, again, well established in the script but shown only in the vaguest way onscreen. The newly larger family now happily walks away together and a succession of Ro-Men (the Guidance version of Ro-Man, judging by the helmet, which has a certain logic) advance slowly into the camera. The ending is just about the only time that the obvious 3-D action of the monster trudging into the camera occurs outside the script.

The script ends similarly but as there is no Guidance, there is no surrealistic silliness of dinosaurs and explosions. (This dinosaur business is not completely unbelievable in the context of a Monster Kid's dream, but it is nowhere in the script.) There were instead some nicely planned details, but one that was as silly as anything in the film:

119 VIEWSCREEN

PROFESSOR

Now! Hurry. We will meet you halfway – in the ravine.

120 CLOSE – RO-MAN

He looks puzzled a moment.

How is a gorilla wearing a diving helmet supposed to appear puzzled, especially in a close-up? Perhaps he could cock his head like dog? But Johnny's encounter with him in the script is far more than a perfunctory skirmish before Guidance's saurian destruction:

125 MED. SHOT – JOHNNY COMING TO OPEN SPOT

He stops.

JOHNNY
(calling)

Here we are. Hold my hand, Mom. Hold my hand, Pop. Here we are!

126 PAN SHOT – RO-MAN

He hurries toward voice. CAMERA HOLDS ON BUSH. RO-MAN EXITS FROM SCENE, PROFESSOR COMES FROM BEHIND BUSH, HURRIES TOWARD CAVE.

Once again the writer invented excellent visual detail. The action described, with the Professor hiding and then exiting from the bush just as the monster goes past, was another simple but effective piece of visualization.

127 CLOSE SHOT – JOHNNY He peers into the darkness. Then his eyes widen.

128 REVERSE – RO-MAN COMING TOWARD HIM

Nothing so specific or suspenseful happens in the film's climax, and it would not have been difficult to film. The scripted scene does not have strange explosions and dinosaurs but it has a more gut-wrenching conclusion. This final confrontation between Johnny and the monster is especially important because it cements the point that the story is from his point of view, and it also is the culmination of his atonement for his guilt. There is no such thematic resolution in the filmed climax, which plays as a non-sensical and arbitrary blast of sound and fury. Johnny has a self-justifying strength that the script carries through to its logical conclusion. But the script's greatest strength is reserved for Alice:

129 INT. CAVE

Professor rushes in.

WADE WILLIAMS DIST.

ALICE

The keys – on the table.

Professors grabs them, frees her.

PROFESSOR

Run.

ALICE

No. Help me.

She starts wrecking the joint. Professor joins in.

While a conventional feminist interpretation would tut-tut that Alice is portrayed as a helpless female in a male-dominated world, she actually shows incredible gumption and is the strongest character in the film. One does not have to agree with her offering herself to Ro-Man to acknowledge her cool, unemotional logic in deciding on it as the best way to survive. Furthermore, she suffers being abducted on her wedding night, her husband tossed away and likely dead, and pretty well immediately has the guts to think through how to manipulate her captor to her advantage. Then put in a degrading situation by the monster, she keeps her cool and is smart enough to not escape but stick around and destroy his equipment. Alice is not helpless; she is simply put in near-impossible situations but has the toughness to survive them. Johnny thinks highly of her to dream about her that way, rather than imagine that he would come in and rescue her. From this scene—a pretty suspenseful use of cross-cutting—the script goes back to the resolution of Johnny's hopeless encounter with Ro-Man:

130 RO-MAN COMING TOWARD JOHNNY

He is quite close now. He raises his arm to strike his blow.

131 CLOSE – JOHNNY

He shuts his eyes and lowers his head ready for the kill.

132 INT. CAVE

Professor and Alice are tugging at a heavy, black metal object, wired to the sides of a cabinet. This

is the energizer. Suddenly it comes loose. Both go out of scene. Tongues of flame lick toward the CAMERA.

133 MED. SHOT – JOHNNY AND RO-MAN

Johnny's back is to CAMERA. Ro-Man reaches him, is about to strike when the skyline behind him is lit up like summer heat lightning. We hear the sound of explosions. For a long moment Ro-Man freezes in his upraised arm position. Suddenly he topples forward on Johnny.

From that impressive point, the script ends the dream much as the film does, but with a little ambiguity that would have been beneficial.

134 CLOSE SHOT – JOHNNY

He struggles to get out from under.

ROY'S VOICE

Take is easy, kid. You're all right.

CAMERA RETREATS TO REVEAL JOHNNY IN INTERIOR OF CAVE WHERE HE FELL AND KNOCKED HIMSELF COLD . . .

The film uses no mysterious voice and the camera does not pull back in such a creative manner. Instead, the film's dream section ends in an orgy of saurian professional wrestling and a shot of the ground splitting in two, apparently representing Guidance's final destruction of the Earth. At the end of a brief dissolve, Roy carries Johnny in toward the cave and it is not clear just where he was supposed to have fainted, as the film is not clear about his fainting in the first place. The closing reunion scene is largely the same with minor differences in dialogue. But just as Johnny's waking from a dream would have brought the imaginary element of the story full-circle, a missing chunk of dialogue from the final scene hurt the film's believability every bit as much:

JOHNNY

. . . Boy, was that a dream! Or was it?

He looks toward the picture.

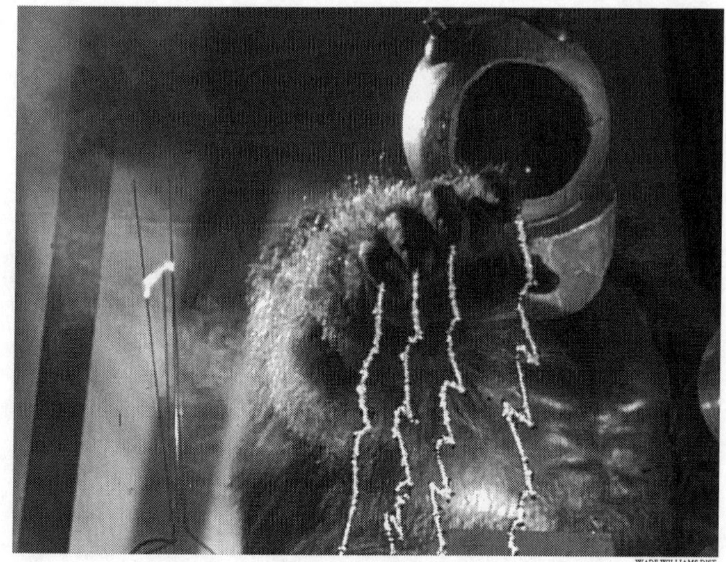

WADE WILLIAMS DIST.

135 CLOSE SHOT – PAINTING – RO-MAN WITHOUT THE FACE

136 REVERSE – GROUP

JOHNNY

That's him, all right: the worst thing that ever happened to the world. But we licked him anyway. And we'd lick him again if he came again.

ALICE

(to Roy)

Don't think he's like that all the time – because he is.

MARTHA

(to Professor)

I really must try to repay you . . .

The script's conclusion could not make it clearer that the ridiculous gorilla wearing a diving helmet was fully explainable as the dream of a monster-crazy kid. Why the filmmakers chose to obscure this point into non-existence is not something so readily explainable. Perhaps they chose to sacrifice believability in the hope that the film would be more exciting if it was apparently all really happening.

In sum, script and film tell essentially the same story but with a chain of small differences that add up to two very different versions. Each is the alternate universe, mirror version of the other. The film has the virtue of being more exciting than the script: Ro-Man has arguments with his boss and conflicting emotions over his purpose, dinosaurs rampage, and the film crosscuts at points in which the script remains statically in the same setting. But the script was thoughtfully written and is more intelligent than many films of its type. It describes camera setups that would have been easy to accomplish, and yet be effective and distinctive onscreen. More importantly, it makes it absolutely clear that the body of the film is Johnny's dream and should not be construed as real. Only the ambiguous final shot of Ro-Men advancing into the camera so much as hints at any doubt on this point. And the script even provides an unambiguous, clear, and logical reason for the film's monster to be a ludicrous robot-gorilla. For the purposes of unintentional humor and accidental surrealism, it is fortunate that the movie deviated from the script as it did. But it is lamentable that so much of value in the script was lost, especially when it would have been easy to achieve.

Nevertheless the low-budget feature did well for what it was, *Variety* reporting that the *Robot Monster/Run for the Hills* double feature had raked in a "Slim $12,000" for its first week at the Orpheum and Hollywood Paramount theaters.[374] While characterizing that return as marginal and noting that despite "Four new 3-D pix . . . most of attention is going to conventional-dimensioned *Beast from 20,000 Fathoms*," *Robot Monster*'s marginal budget of $16,000 had it already almost in the black and likely profitable in the near future. As Tucker remembered it in that context:

I thought that, financially it did—
Well; I'd say rather well. It did a little over a million dollars, which in those days was a lot of money. *Wax Museum,* which opened in the Hollywood Paramount just before we did, did around six million. So—

Wait, House of Wax?
Yeah.

With Vincent Price?
Right.

And for all his disdain for Tucker, Barrows fondly remembered the film's theatrical reception:

How did it look? Did you ever go to the movie theater and see it? What was the reaction of the audience? Did people enjoy it?
Oh yeah. They loved the picture. We had all this stuff, like where I came in, reached into the camera with my hand. They're wearing all these glasses. Oh, we got a lot of screams and squeals, they liked it. It was one of the hokey movies, but no hokier than a lot of them were. Because they made a lot of them. Have you seen some of John Wayne's originals? They were pretty hokey too, you know.[375]

Wade Williams, Monster Kid and eventual owner of the film's copyright, remembered its initial run:

> I bought the rights to *Robot Monster* from John Ettlinger of Medallion Films who owned the property for many years. John bought the film from Zimbalist . . ..
>
> *Robot Monster* was released first in 3-D and a few months later in 2-D in 1953 . . . That was the same year *Invaders from Mars* and *War of the Worlds* were released and science fiction was big business, so some of the distributors changed the title to *Monster from Mars* by splicing a new title section on a few prints, hoping to fool anyone into buying a ticket. Never mind the gorilla was from the moon? Very few prints were struck. I would say less than twenty-five for the USA. It was also distributed in Mexico.
>
> It played here in Kansas City . . . As a 9 year old I saw the film at the Pic with *The Flying Saucer,* another B movie which I liked. However I recognized footage from *Rocketship X-M* and *Lost Continent* . . . I thought the film was stupid at the time but loved anything dealing with outer space. . . . The running time of the film was only 58 minutes so it could be called a featurette and not a full length feature.[376]

Barrett remembered it appearing in 3-D at the Paramount. According to Parla, "My husband and I sat directly in front of Phil Tucker. . . . [who] teased my husband about the problem he had getting me to kiss George Nader."[377] She later described to Beifuss that Tucker had "made a little comment" that she "didn't appreciate."[378]

Bob Burns was there when the film debuted:

> I never met Phil Tucker but I did run into a fellow named Wyott Ordung who wrote *Robot Monster.* The funny thing about it was that I met him at the first 3-D screening of the film at the Paramount theater. Just before the screening he came down the aisle and asked if I was Bob Burns. I have no idea how he knew who I was but he sure seemed like a nice guy. He told me that he wrote the story and script and that it was supposed to be a kid's dream or nightmare so it had a lot of fantasy and weird type things in it. I told him that one of my favorite gorilla men was George Barrows who played *Robot Monster.* I asked him what the helmet was from and he said that it was made at Western Costume. Unfortunately, I didn't see him after the screening and never saw him again.[379]

As for Tucker, he remembered that at the time he seemed to be only going up:

> *What exactly happened after the film release?*
> I'll give you an anecdote first.
>
> *Okay.*
> On the night it was opening, a friend of mine and I went to Aldo's (which is the same Aldo's that's still on Hollywood Boulevard, only maybe it's not Aldo's now).

> We were sitting, having a cup of coffee, when two guys in front of us were talking. One guy said to the other that he was a friend of Phil Tucker—"He's got a picture opening right across the street"—and if the project was any good, he'd take it to Phil Tucker and talk to him about it. And Ronnie [Tucker's friend][380] looked at me and I said, "Well, that means that I finally arrived, right?" The picture opened and it was held over for three or four weeks, which considering how bad a picture it was and how good of a theater it was in, was kind of remarkable. It subsequently was released all over.

As for the value of the film and of his own abilities, Tucker looked back with a mixture of pride and realism:

> *One last question: what did you think of the film, personally, when it was released? What was your opinion, did you like it?* First of all I invented—I shouldn't say I invented—but I made my own system for three-dimension. And at that time, people were more concerned about three-dimension than they were about the picture involved. I felt, and *Variety* felt, and the *Reporter* felt, that my three-dimensional process was far better than anything that anybody had used. I was certainly proud of that. I was very proud in [the] vein of the fact that I'd been able to bring the picture in at a ridiculous budget. I felt that for the budget, for the time, I had achieved greatness. And I still believe to this day that there did not a soul exist

who could do as well for as little I had been able to do. Whether that's good or bad becomes now a matter of viewpoint. There are some people who say, "If you can't raise a million dollars, you shouldn't try to make a million dollar movie." And they may be right. I'm not saying they aren't; [it's] very possible they are.

But what about the content of the film, apart from the 3-D process?

Well here's a script that I spent maybe four days on, that was never meant to be anything but a quickie. I think if you will examine quickies of that day, for instance the B string at Republic is a good example. That's a major studio in those days. It had more merit than most of the pictures that they were putting out that cost—

Vera Hruba Ralston,[381] *right.*

Right, well those were A pictures, the Vera Hruba Ralston, I'm talking about the B string.

Well, Republic, even their A pictures were B—

But, look at their lower level, and I think that you'll find that *Robot Monster* had more going for it as entertainment than most anything in the 100, 250 thousand dollar level.[382] I don't think you can really weigh apples against oranges. I think you have to weigh apples against apples. And apples against apples, it was the most outstanding picture of the year, in my opinion. Put it up against an orange, you got a problem. In fact, I'm proud of anything that I do that is difficult to do, but I still achieve it. I always achieve as much as I possibly can with what I have to work for. If I waited until I had enough to work for to make it easy, I would never have achieved anything. I would have done nothing. Maybe it's better I shouldn't have.

WADE WILLIAMS DIST.

A striking but little seen *Robot Monster* publicity photo.

8

Return to Earth

By mid-summer 1953, with *Robot Monster* in wide release from Astor and Al Zimbalist's name popping up all over the trades, the man who directed the film was not basking in glory. As Phil Tucker remembered:

> Al personally made enough money off of that picture by stealing from me.
>
> *You mean he paid you donuts?*
>
> Well, it wasn't up to him to pay. I didn't get anything from that picture. I owned 25% of it, but I didn't have the money to pay for attorneys to insure my getting 25% of it.

If Zimbalist had shut Tucker out of what should have been his for directing and initiating the film, it would be in keeping with the lack of emphasis on him in the trades. But while rumor has long had it that Tucker was suicidally despondent over the situation, the surviving evidence suggests otherwise. In the May 26 *Hollywood Reporter,* almost precisely one month before the *Robot Monster* premiere, he was already announcing his next project:

> *Return from Mars,* science fiction screenplay by Cecille Reynolds, has been purchased by the newly formed American Artists Film Corp. Latter's officers are George Housch, president; R. R. Lee, v.-p.; Phil Tucker, v.-p. in charge of production, and Richard Rykoff, secretary-treasurer.
>
> Tucker will produce and direct the feature, to be made in Pathecolor. . . .[383]

Cecille Reynolds was apparently gifted with the same luck as Zimbalist's protégé Guy Reed Ritchie, since his name is nonexistent in the credits of finished movies. Likewise, most of the other members of American Artists Film Corp.—Housch, Lee, and Rykoff—have no credits to their names. The project went unmentioned for weeks, but then boldly reappeared on page one of the June 24 *Reporter,* the very day that *Robot Monster* premiered in Los Angeles:

> *Return to Earth,* a science fiction feature to be produced and directed by Phil Tucker in 3-D, will be made in three sections—black-and-white, red, and green, Tucker announced yesterday. The story of space travel will have the Earth sequences in black and white, the Mars sequence tinted in red and the Venus section tinted in green.

> The picture will be made under the banner of American Artists Film Corp., of which Sam Leacock is executive producer. It rolls July 10 at Eagle Lion.[384]

Return from Mars' Pathecolor film process was noticeably absent as the project metamorphosed into *Return to Earth.* The option of using monochrome film with alternating tints for different locations was economical, and was a technique that went back to the silent, pre-color era when it was a common way to add color to black-and-white.[385] Knowing Golden Age movie men like Gordon Avil, Tucker had likely put the technique away in his mental bag of cinematic tricks to be deployed one day. But there were also very recent uses of color tints in theaters, and their connection to Tucker's new project is unmistakable. The atmospheric 1950 Lippert release *Rocketship X-M* told the story of a doomed moon mission that instead reaches Mars, the black-and-white film featuring a red-tinted section when the crew arrives on the red planet. Then in 1951 Lippert released *Lost Continent,* and while that monochrome film did not take place on the planet Venus, the lost continent scenes were tinted green. Both films featured the same V-2 rocket footage used in *Robot Monster.*

Whether or not Tucker might have gotten into a jam with Lippert Pictures over a close appropriation of a gimmick from two of their biggest releases is a moot point. *Return to Earth* was never again mentioned in the 1953 *Reporter,* and Tucker was never mentioned in any capacity in all of 1954. (*Daily Variety* gave *Return to Earth* a brief mention, when George E. Phair noted, "With all those science fiction films hopping to Mars, Venus and other express stops, up comes a picture titled

Return to Earth."[386] Phair apparently did not know—or care—that *Return to Earth* was scheduled to "hop" to Mars and Venus.) But although no such movie survives, the trail does not dry up. Tucker solved the riddle of this mysterious film when he recounted the aftermath of *Robot Monster*:

> It did considerably over a million. At one time, I was going to sue Al Zimbalist to get the money, but I couldn't find an attorney who would [help]. That's pretty much the whole story on that, other than I subsequently went up to Alaska and made the worst picture that's ever been made by anyone, anywhere.
>
> *What is that?*
> *Space Jockey.*
>
> *Space Jockey? What was the film about? Remember the story?*
> It was about a brave crew of men who go to Mars and Venus. And although they don't make it back, they manage to send back enough information so that the lead can say at the end of the picture, "Now the stars are ours."
>
> *Who acted in it?*
> I haven't the foggiest idea.

Given the time frame, and Tucker's brief summary of the film concerning a Mars-Venus mission, *Return to Earth* was another name for his infamous lost film *Space Jockey*, mentioned tantalizingly in *The Golden Turkey Awards*. Lest there be any remaining doubt, consider how Tucker describes the end of the film ("they don't make it back") and compare it to the tragic-heroic conclusion of *Rocketship X-M* (where the crew dies on impact as they "return to Earth"). In both films, the silver lining on the gloomy cloud is that the doomed mission has enabled a future of more space exploration. Tucker had not merely borrowed the red-tinted Mars from the still fresh *Rocketship X-M,* but blatantly copied the ending.

Those intrigued by *Robot Monster* have pined to see the lost *Space Jockey.* As Bill Warren wrote, ". . . I for one would very much like to see it."[387] Alas, almost all Tucker said about it is quoted above, where he spoke of it less colorfully than as indicated in *The Golden Turkey Awards*:

> "My other films are okay," he modestly declares, "but this *Space Jockey*—now that was a real piece of shit. In fact, I'd say it's probably the worst film ever made."[388]

The Medved brothers were, to judge by the book introductions, exhausted by the process of watching bad movies at odd hours and locations and then writing about them, and this may be why Tucker was referenced with a statement that was at least accurate in substance. (Tucker also later in the interview referred to *Robot Monster* as a "piece of shit.") And as the book reported it, *Space Jockey* was made slightly **before** *Robot Monster* but, as the actual quote from Tucker shows, it was made **afterwards**.

Having disappeared from the pages of the *Reporter* as *Return to Earth*, the project did not reappear there as *Space Jockey.* But the story of Tucker's infamous lost film continues, thanks to the fact that he made it in Alaska rather than, as the *Reporter* had it in June, Hollywood's Eagle-Lion studio. The decision to switch locations must have been made rapidly, because news of *Space Jockey* began to appear in the *Fairbanks Daily News-Miner* on July 6:

> Plans to start the production of moving pictures in Fairbanks have been announced by the newly-formed American Artists Film Corp., which has established headquarters in this city.
>
> According to Phil Tucker, who is in charge of production for the studio, work will start on a movie to be filmed in Fairbanks starting July 15. The first movie filmed here will be of the "science fiction" type with an Alaska background.
>
> Tucker said that he sees no reason why the production of movies can't be carried out in the Fairbanks area. He emphasized that the new company hasn't intentions of filming "Alaska pictures."
>
> "We are starting a studio here that will film all types of moving pictures, possibly making use of the abundant scenery that is available. However, our plan is to start a standard film studio that will film every type of movie, not just Alaska pictures," Tucker said.[389]

The first notable thing here is that Tucker kept the same production company name mentioned in the *Reporter*. The second is that he must have become completely disenchanted with Hollywood in order to bother filming a (probably set-bound) science fiction movie in far-off Alaska.[390] And the third and most amazing point is that he explicitly spelled out an ambitious long-term plan for making many movies there, far into the future. While others might have spun their wheels for months in the hope that Zimbalist would develop a guilty conscience, Tucker had learned early to judge people by actions and moved swiftly. Zimbalist had what he wanted from him, and Tucker had no power to make him cooperate. While Tucker remembered enjoying the June *Robot Monster* premiere, press report dates show that his next project was already planned. He likely discovered the rip-off soon after the film opened, inquired about the money, and made a rational decision about his circumstances. By July 6, an Alaska newspaper was already reporting his arrival.

Why was Tucker smitten with Alaska? With the Marine Corps being connected to the Navy, he could have easily visited the area while in the service. He briefly mentioned it when interviewed, and Tucker Jr. remembered it as one detail of his father's early years that actually crept up in conversation:

> He claims to have won some land in Alaska in a card game. Now with him, you know, you never know whether to believe it or not. But that's what he claims to have done, he won some land up there in a card game, he had a really good hand. And so that was his reason for going up there and coming back.

Tucker's friend Trustin Howard provided more clues about Tucker's fascination with the future 49th state, for it led to his Hollywood career:

> I met him in Alaska. I would think it might have been around the mid-fifties, and I was basically working a nightclub there and he just wandered in. He said that they were there for—I don't know if he was looking for a location or something, and that was it.[391]

Howard had no memory of the title *Space Jockey*, emphasizing that he did not know why Tucker was there, while stating that it may have been location scouting. But in a fascinating twist, Howard stated, "He was there with I think a guy by the name of Al Zugsmith, or something like that." While one of producer Al Zugsmith's first productions was *Invasion U.S.A.*, a film with some small connections to *Robot Monster*, Zugsmith was a relatively mainstream producer in comparison to Al Zimbalist, and soon worked frequently at Universal. It is unlikely that Zugsmith was palling around with Tucker, and far more likely that Howard was confusing his name with that of Al Zimbalist. And this implies that not only had Tucker considered making *Robot Monster* in Alaska, but that Zimbalist had taken the idea seriously enough to visit the area with him. *Space Jockey* was therefore put into production in Alaska from a backup plan.

> We had talked about my act. He said, "If you ever get back to Hollywood, look me up," but I never did. When I got back, I got a couple of movie agents, and they sent me out on a cattle call and an awful lot of people were there. And oddly enough the guy that I met in Fairbanks ended up being the producer of this movie *Robot Monster*, which they were going to do as a . . . In other words,

> during the 3-D period everything was sent out with a musical short. And so like everybody else they wanted to do a short with their movie *Robot Monster.* And so when I went for this cattle call, I think he came up, or something, or we saw each other and reminded each other that we met in Fairbanks. And he said, "Could you just do your act?" And I said, "Yeah, I guess I could." And so I put the other 990 actors away, and I did it. And that was it.

Remembering Tucker warmly with great loyalty, Howard said, "Yeah, I saw him after that. We became fairly good friends, and he got me into the Screen Actors Guild." And in his opinion, Tucker was a firm influence on *Robot Monster* all the way to its release, noting, "It seemed like Phil really took the lead with that movie. He was with, I believe it might have been Zimbalist or Zugsmith, I'm not sure now, that somehow or other they were like partners with him. But it just seemed like Phil really pushed it through."

But as to why Tucker was so convinced that he should make movies in Alaska, there were some important precedents in the low-budget movie world. Actor Mikel Conrad directed and starred in 1950's *The Flying Saucer,* a cheap Cold War adventure with little science fiction and a lot of Alaskan wildlife footage, borrowed from 1949's *Arctic Manhunt.* Conrad also starred in that film and its director, Ewing Scott, worked on Petroff's *Red Snow*; Conrad was also in Merle Connell's *Untamed Women.* According to an extensive article on *The Flying Saucer* by Wade Williams, it was while making *Arctic Manhunt* in Alaska that Conrad and associates shot "thousands of feet of film . . .

hopefully as a backdrop for several feature films."[392] This plan led to *The Flying Saucer,* which cleaned up impressively thanks to its then-novel concept. But Tucker almost certainly had another, greater influence who was likely also an inspiration to Conrad. Mixed into Boris Petroff's early fifties credits was another film veteran of decades past.

Born in Argentina in 1884, Norman Dawn was described as an American in accounts of his move into Australia's film industry in the 1920s. As early as 1919, Dawn was praised for his "quadruple exposures and clever trick photograph work [that] has aroused a great deal of interest."[393] Based on a 19th century novel, Dawn's *For the Term of His Natural Life* (1927) was Australia's biggest production and was made in spite of resentment within the local industry for its director and imported American stars. Dawn was a master technician and early trailblazer of matte shots and miniatures on film, which enhanced the natural grandeur he put into the expensively produced story of the Australian penal system. *Variety* faulted the film for "patchy acting and poor captions" along with a "drawn out" plot, but praised the film's impressive visual qualities.[394] By January 1928, Dawn was praised in a *Variety* profile of "important cameramen" for "a number of innovations connected with the camera," such as his patented "process for double exposing one scene on another" that was bought by the "Producers' Association."[395] After another Australian adventure, *The Adorable Outcast,* also in 1928, Dawn left but soon returned to establish Australia's first sound film company, Australia Talkies Ltd, in August 1929. This venture lead to yet another "rugged

A 1922 ad showing Norman Dawn's career in its prime.

outdoor narrative" (Dawn's "ideal" choice for Australian movies), *Showgirl's Luck*, in 1931.[396]

By 1949, Dawn had been reduced to working with Petroff on *Arctic Fury*, an adventure set in Alaska that cannibalized stock footage from his own 1936 production *Tundra* (to the point that actor Alfred Delcambre starred in the later movie in stock footage only).[397] In 1950, Petroff released another collaboration with Dawn, *Two Lost Worlds*, a slightly crazy adventure that begins with pirate ships, continues with the hero stranded in Australia, and wraps up with dinosaurs. The explanation for the loopy, meandering plot is of course that it was an excuse to use stock footage. The opening sequences did an excellent job of integrating new footage with material from two swashbuckling Hal Roach productions, *Captain Fury* (1939) and *Captain Caution* (1940),[398] while the Australian sequences used clearly native footage (with a cowboy riding through kangaroos). The final section of stock footage was from another Roach source, *One Million B.C.*, using some of the very same shots that would be seen two years later in *Robot Monster*. (And Clarence C. Eurist, production supervisor on *Robot Monster*, had the same credit on this movie.) In a situation very likely parallel with the *Robot Monster* production, leading lady Kasey Rogers stated that she "didn't realize at the time they . . . were matching things . . . and were going to intercut."[399] The same year, Dawn also cranked out his final feature *Bowanga Bowanga*, which was sadly a stock footage fest with a jungle women story like many others of the time, including *Untamed Women*.

But while the end of Dawn's career points relentlessly to an association with the same people Tucker was involved with, his earlier association with Fairbanks is explicitly spelled out and undeniable over the course of several years. In his earliest years he was in the same ranks as others who were better remembered decades later. In 1919, Dawn was filming "stampede scenes" for one and "marine scenes" for another Universal production, while "Harry Carey's company, under Jack Ford's direction, is getting desert scenes . . . ."[400] Only a few weeks before, "A photodrama has just been completed at Universal City, under the direction of Norman Dawn, in which dogs are the only actors."[401] Filming location scenes and directing animals was probably a short step to his 1921 outdoor film *Wolves of the*

North, praised for "Dawn's use of scenery to suggest emotion."[402] And as early as August 1923, Dawn was getting his snowy footage specifically in Fairbanks. But more tellingly, he was trying to start his own movie studio there, just as Tucker would do three decades later, nearly to the day.

On August 14, 1923, the *News-Miner* reported "a promise contained in a letter" that Dawn was "coming to Fairbanks for the purpose of investigating location[s] here with a view to establishing a studio and laboratories."[403] *News-Miner* reports of Dawn's local activity appeared steadily through November 1924.[404] In May that year, Dawn had written New York stockholders that the resulting film, *Lure of the Yukon,* was "too good a picture to sell outright" and would be most profitable if released independently.[405] Dawn's affiliation with Fairbanks continued long after his Australian adventure. A May 1937 report noted that he was back there doing "ice scenes" for Republic.[406] In only another decade he was working with Petroff, and could have been a perfect formative influence on Tucker. He was independent, tough, hands-on, part of the same circle, an expert on filmmaking technique, and he wanted to make movies in Fairbanks. He probably taught Tucker a great deal, and could have easily put the idea in his head that would lead to *Space Jockey.*

As the *News-Miner* report from July 6 continued, Tucker was looking for "'a pretty blond,' as well as character actors, and all types of acting talent." American Artists was being "partly financed by local money," and was looking for a "permanent location, such as Weeks field, to set up a sound stage," and Tucker was planning to "work through the winter" in such a location:

"I see no reason why films can't be produced economically right here in Alaska." On Saturday the 11th, the *News-Miner* reported that the film's cast had been decided.[407] Tucker had signed a number of locals for the film, including 23-year-old Maxine Settles, professionally billing herself as Helen Hill, a "blue-eyed blonde who originally hails from Idaho." In the male lead was Jeff Noble, who "plays the part of a 'Space Jockey,' new title of the picture which starts shooting the 26th of this month." With no title reported in the earlier story from July 6, this mention of *Space Jockey* as a "new title" implies that the project might have still been called *Return to Earth* until sometime that very week. Donnis Stark, originally from Indiana, had always wanted to be an actress and was here realizing her dream by playing the comic relief part of "Mamie Dazell." The remaining parts would be cast soon and Tucker was reportedly "surprised and gratified" that, disproving a few initial scoffers, he was able to cast the film locally and was "up to his ears in talented Fairbanksians." Then on Saturday, July 25, the *News-Miner* announced that filming was imminent: "Shooting on the new motion picture, *Space Jockey*, will start Sunday at the corner of Second and Cushman streets in downtown Fairbanks."[408]

From that first day of shooting on Sunday, July 26, the film would be finished eleven days later on Thursday, August 6, according to a massive feature on the film on page three in the August 5th *News-Miner*.[409] Credited to Florence Strand (unlike the previous, anonymous reports), the piece went into exhaustive detail on the project and Tucker's ideas and opinions on filmmaking, as well as featuring four photos of cast and crew. Tucker was "fed up with Hollywood's hamstringing," and had arrived in Fairbanks three weeks previously (placing his arrival the week right after the first two *News-Miner* reports appeared). Cameraman John Mattias was described as the one other Hollywood visitor involved in the project, with the rest of the crew "drafted by Tucker through 'half grit and half hokum,'" while "holding down their regular jobs" for average days of "18 to 20 hours." The all-Fairbanks shoot included a small quantity of streets, along with such locations as "the Drop Inn Cafe, the Squadron Bar, Dr. John I. Weston's medical office, the Lacey Street Hotel and an apartment in Fairview Manor."

According to the report, Tucker had initially wanted to film on "Second Street and Cushman" (the first location for shooting, according to the third *News-Miner* piece) in broad daylight with passersby none the wiser. But many stopped, took photos, and caused Tucker to reshoot the sequence "at 4:00 a.m. another day." Then when shooting at Fairview Manor "last Sunday," a drunk curiously wandered into frame to get a closer look at Noble, just finished with the tender smooching of his co-star. The inebriated critic looked into the camera and demanded, "What the blazes is he doing with lipstick all over his face?"

Though not yet completed, the movie would run 75 minutes, with Tucker calling it a "gem" that is "geared for the audience that likes to be screamingly transported into another world." Tucker further eliminated any doubts for posterity that he did not see himself as Ed Wood saw himself: "It's not art. I'm not trying to create art. I'm trying to make money." Strand's report describes the plot of *Space Jockey* as a "watery, patched-together bit" about the conflict between the title character's desire to "conquer infinity" and his pregnant, "all-suffering" wife's desire

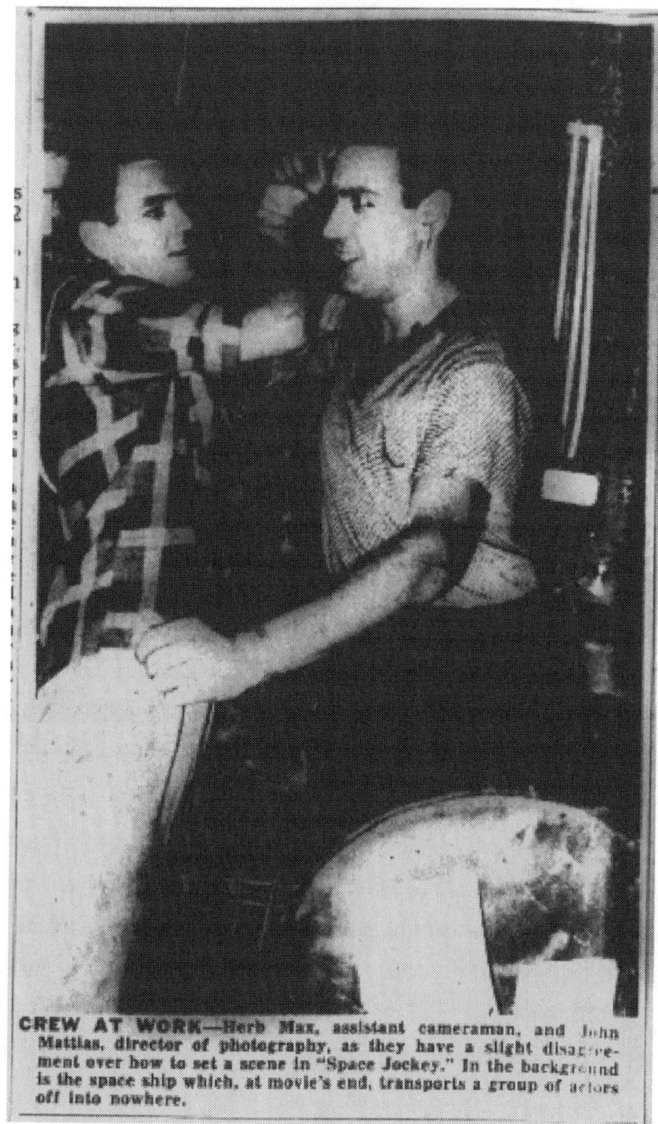

CREW AT WORK—Herb Max, assistant cameraman, and John Mattias, director of photography, as they have a slight disagreement over how to set a scene in "Space Jockey." In the background is the space ship which, at movie's end, transports a group of actors off into nowhere.

Press clippings of the summer 1953 *Space Jockey* production.

SPACE JOCKEY—Leading man, Jeff Noble, sits in the rocket ship, thinking about a trip to Saturn which he never makes. The space ship, made of masonite and boards, is located in Hangar No. 1 at Weeks field. The equipment was gathered from surplus stores, generous merchants and various and sundry junk shops.

ACTORS RELAX—Principals in "Space Jockey" during a rare moment of relaxation in between scenes. Right to left: Helen Hill, feminine lead; Jeff Noble, male lead, and Liberty Heleninhi, make-up supervisor. In real life, Miss Hill is a draftswoman at Ladd; Mr. Noble is a truck driver, and Miss Heleninhi is a dance instructor.

for a stable home. The report also vaguely states that the film contained additional "subplots" relating to love and rockets, and also reveals that Tucker preferred to keep the names of the local backers of American Artists quiet (which Strand speculated was to save them from shame should the whole thing go south). According to the article, *Space Jockey* was the first movie to ever originate completely out of Alaska (in reality, Ewing Scott's *Harpoon* [1948] was first),[410] and it seemed puzzling to Strand that anyone would attempt such an unlikely feat. Tucker spoke at length on his motivations:

> The movie industry is stifled in Hollywood. They tell you what to write, how to produce it, when to direct it, who [to] put in it and when to try and sell it. It's a tight little island of rulers and it's a hard place in which to breathe free. I've been to Fairbanks a couple of summers in the past and I decided that here is where I would try to make movies. This is only the beginning. The cost of production here is about the same if not a little lower than in the States. The area is a wonderful sound stage. There's very little interruption by noise. The workers here are more willing. You're not tied up body and soul by the union. There's a union here—the United Motion Picture Workers of Alaska—but the same regulations don't apply as stateside. The scales are higher but there's no minimum. If you don't need a worker, you don't have to take him. If I need Tom on location, I don't have to take Dick and Harry along too.

FEMININE LEADS—The two Fairbanks women who were selected by Director Phil Tucker to carry on the beauty end of "Space Jackey" are, right to left, Ann Lawrence, a hostess at the Squadron club, and Heiep Hill, a draftswoman at Ladd field. The two ladies, as well as the rest of the crew, have been working at their regular jobs plus putting in many hours daily on the movie. It's the first movie-making experience for both of them.

Tucker "just loved show business," as his son remembered, and the ironic proof was his willingness to leave it.

As Strand's report continued, Tucker was taking the film back to Los Angeles for editing by "the end of this week, as soon as it's finished," with the hope of one day having editing equipment and a sound stage at his disposal in Fairbanks. The cast and crew took a philosophical approach to being paid for their work, apparently not expecting much but working in the knowledge that they might get some money when the film was sold to a distributor. Tucker forthrightly described the pay situation as "a little now, a little then and the rest when you can catch me." He also noted a stream of interested potential investors in American Artists that he had to turn away, as those on the inside were content to keep their "shares," but also stated that "if they want to give me personally some money, that's different. That's fine."

The one detail sadly lacking from the report is the budget, which had to have been in the $16,000 *Robot Monster* range, given these details:

> A spotlight is used instead of a regular light. The microphone boom is hand-made. The spaceship, held together by masonite and boards, is equipped with such gadgets as old dentist chairs and paper cup containers, camouflaged to look other-worldly. It took three weeks to build, with many trappings donated by the International Equipment Company.

Also notably lacking is any mention of exterior shots of the ship, or of miniature model work. Any film about space exploration must show some spaceships, if only briefly, and space adventures do not convincingly live on stock footage alone, especially with few such movies yet made.

With the film nearly complete, Tucker looked toward distribution with some uncertainty: "I may sell it to distributors in Hollywood or I may states-right it. I know it will be sold but I don't know to whom yet and of course, what kind of a reception it will have." Strand's report further noted that Tucker had been seasoned with the making of "a science fiction movie, as well as with radio and TV script writing . . .." He summed up the project as a "real nervous A" film, a low-budget effort where "the director got inspired."

Strand's article included more about the cast and crew. Besides Noble, Settles, and Stark, the cast included an Army man named Ron Tomme and a dance hostess named Ann Lawrence. The crew contained a few members who, while not Hollywood, were notable locals. Credited with set construction was Don Pruhs, a Fairbanks personality who often appeared in the pages of the *News-Miner* for such activities as presenting "nine continuous hours of musical entertainment running from 8 p.m. 'til 5 every morning" in April 1951, at the Cowtown "all-Western playhouse." The "congenial" Pruhs was manager of the Cowtown, at which a 1952 ad claimed he would "act as host and serve moose milk." In the fall of 1953, just as *Space Jockey* was being cut together and searching for a distributor, Pruhs was chairman of a USO benefit and running for a seat on the utility board. In April 1954, he had become president of a company to search for uranium in the area, and by 1953 had been managing another nightspot called the Polaris Lounge.[411] Pruhs may have been the same Don Pruhs who made the sports page of *The Fresno Bee* in October 1945, a "220-pound ex-Marine" who sustained the loss of "two front teeth" in a local college football game.[412]

Doing makeup was Honolulu native Liberty Helenihi, who had made the unconventional move of leaving Hawaii for Alaska, and in April 1953 announced the debut of her Lei Momi Hula Studio where she taught hula dance. On August 8, the *News-Miner* noted that Helenihi was overseeing a "Hawaiian Party" for Moose Lodge ladies that evening.[413] With *Space Jockey* just wrapping on Thursday, Helenihi must have been juggling the movie, preparation for the Moose party, and her dance studio work for a period of near-sleeplessness of the kind that Tucker described. Helenihi made the front page of

The POLARIS LOUNGE
ANNOUNCES WITH PLEASURE
THE RETURN OF: Liberty Helenihi

APPEARING TONIGHT
SATURDAY, APRIL 2
AT 8:30 P.M.

BACK AGAIN, ALASKA'S OWN — LIBERTY HELENIHI. IT'S A REAL TREAT TO WELCOME BACK LIBERTY, ONE OF FAIRBANKS' MOST BELOVED ENTERTAINERS.

Everyone's Invited

the *News-Miner* on September 24, 1959, when she, *Space Jockey* star Jeff Noble, and a third passenger required hospitalization after a single-car accident. Her injuries were the most serious, and a benefit concert was scheduled in October. By March 1960, the *News-Miner* reported that she had received surgery in nearby Vancouver (British Columbia), but that well-wishers had had difficulty in reaching her due to a name change; she and Noble had been married "a month ago."[414] But that union could not have lasted many years, as her 1965 song credit listed her as "Belfield," the name she carried to her 2003 obituary (survived by her husband, children, and many grandchildren and great-grandchildren).[415]

But of greatest interest in the crew is the only listed producer, Sam Leacock. Going back to the June 24 *Reporter* announcement of *Space Jockey* under the title *Return to Earth,* Leacock was listed as executive producer of American Artists. Anyone in Fairbanks who had actually been reading the *Hollywood Reporter* would have known immediately that Leacock was one of the anonymous investors in the new film company, and the news would have been unsurprising. But his connection to Tucker extends as far back as August 1952, when they were partners in Lea-Tuck Telefilms, Inc. and were planning a series called *How Julius Becomes Caesar*. Like Pruhs, Leacock was a club owner and local big shot whose name often popped up in the *News-Miner*. In July 1951, he played the left field position for the victorious Bar Owners baseball team, routing the Bartenders 14 to 4 in a win that avenged their loss of the previous year. In January 1953, he co-represented a group of club owners petitioning the city council to allow later closing times, and was committee chairman of the Moose Christmas Benefit that December. Leacock's Squadron Club burned to the ground in October 1956, and in May 1958 was listed as one of the area's "five biggest tax delinquents" in relation to property claimed by the local school district. Leacock in mid-1960 lost an estimated $60,000 in the fire that claimed his Casbah nightclub.[416] He made the news in happier circumstances that year and the following year for his involvement in Fairbanks' summer boat racing competition.[417]

Finally, there were two familiar names listed in the crew. Merle Connell, mentioned nowhere else in connection with the project, was listed as editor but, more fancifully, Elmer Bernstein was thrown in as composer. As Tucker admitted, Bernstein only composed for *Robot Monster* because of Zimbalist and was involved in more than one of his projects. Tucker might have listed Bernstein merely to fatten the crew list, but he might have sincerely wished to get his services for his next film. An informal, verbal agreement could even have been made with the composer who was years away from the Hollywood mainstream. But amongst Bernstein's papers, no score or other piece of music exists with the name *Space Jockey*.[418]

No subsequent mention of the film appeared in the *News-Miner*, and there is no evidence that the film was released or even survived. In a 2004 installment of *Film Threat*'s series on great lost films, Phil Hall made a common-sense guess that *Space Jockey* had never been completed.[419] As he noted, nothing on the film was available beyond its brief mention in *The Golden Turkey Awards*. But considering Tucker's intense drive and the detailed record of the film's production, there is no longer room for reasonable doubt of its completion. The truth is that its loss must have had something to do with Tucker's recollection of it as "the worst picture that's ever been made by anyone, anywhere." As *Robot Monster* and his later work demonstrate, Tucker was not afraid to put his name on a bad film and release it if possible.

Space Jockey must have therefore been simply *unwatchable*, which leads to a further conclusion. While lovers of bad cinema have pictured Tucker's lost film as rib-tickling in the extreme, the reality was probably far more mundane. Hilariously bad films at least have the virtue of not putting the audience to sleep, and are less likely to be un-releasable than dull films. But given the lack of fantastical elements described in the *News-Miner* accounts, and with a story centering on relationships and no monsters, Tucker's film may have contained nothing exciting and little exploitable. The truth is that *Space Jockey* was probably just plain boring.

With the film apparently lost forever, there are still remaining clues to what it was like, and even reason to believe that it was not entirely based on *Rocketship X-M* and *Lost Continent.* A fascinating item crept into the Los Angeles area radio schedule in early 1953. On Monday, January 19, the *Long Beach Press-Telegram* reported on "three new daily shows" added that day to the schedule of AM radio station KFOX (1280 on the dial). Along with the corny comedy of Judy Canova and a music quiz show, the country & Western station was adding to its 9:30 PM slot a program called "Space Jockey." There was no description provided and no one credited, but the same page listed it on that day's schedule of programs, and it continued to be listed on the *Press-Telegram*'s daily radio schedules twelve more times until its final appearance on February 20.[420] It was consistently listed at 9:30 PM, and in that slot was interestingly competing with a show called "John Brown" on station KGER. (Was this a show centered on the incredibly prolific radio actor John Brown, who would soon be providing the Ro-Man voices for *Robot Monster*? And if so, did the presence of Brown's show have any bearing on his working in Tucker's film?)

Although there is no proof that the un-credited "Space Jockey" radio show was the work of Tucker, the circumstantial evidence is compelling. The Fairbanks press write-ups of later that year mention his radio and television experience, and he recalled a background in St. Louis radio. Tucker Jr. described his father as someone who wanted to work in entertainment at some level, no matter what, and there is Tucker's own description of himself in his early Hollywood days as juggling a number of different projects, "screwing around with several different things" in that era. He did not recognize a division between film and television, and it is no suspension of disbelief

RADIO
KLAC-570 KECA-790 KFOX-1280
KFI-640 KHJ-930 KFAC-1330
KMPC-710 KFWB-980 KGER-1390
KBIG-740 KNX-1070 KVOE-1480
FM KLON-88.1 KFOX-102.3 KNOB-103.1

MONDAY, JANUARY 19, 1953

4:00 P. M.
KLAC—Gene Norman
KFI—Life Beautiful
KMPC—Johnny Grant
KECA—Mary M. McBride
KHJ—Fulton Lewis Jr.
KFWB—Red Rowe Rancho
KNX—News; Jimmy Wakely
KVOE—News
KFAC—Masterpieces
KGER—Commuter Carnival
4:15
KFI—News; Burritt Wheeler
KHJ—Frank Hemingway
KFOX—Music
4:30
KMPC—Bolero Time
KECA—Nancy Holme
KHJ—Curt Massey Time
KNX—Untold Story; Hawk [illegible]

John Hodiak
KFOX—Ray Heatherton
KGER—Dr. Vernon McGee
9:15
KHJ—Fulton Lewis Jr.
9:30
KFI—KFI Calling
KMPC—Dance Time in 12
KECA—Footnotes & Music
KHJ—Catch [illegible]
KNX—Jo Stafford Show, with Frankie Laine
KFOX—Space Jockey
KGER—John Brown
9:45
KECA—Inauguration Preview
KNX—Junior Miss
KHJ—Titus Moody (9:55)
10:00 P. M.
KFI—Hartfield Reporter
KECA—News; E. C. Hill
KHJ—Answer Man

KNX—Road of Life
KFOX—News; Assembly
KFAC—Composer's Corner
KGER—News; Earl Lee
10:15
KHJ—Tello-Test
KNX—Ma Perkins
KGER—Tommy Baird
10:30
KHJ—Answer Man
KNX—Young Dr. Malone
KFOX—News; Kuscale
KFAC—Song Recital
KGER—Helen Markham
10:45
KHJ—Inaugural Parade
KNX—Guiding Light
KGER—Rev. Leilov Koop
11:00 A. M.
KFI—Double or Nothing

KFOX adds three new daily shows today: Judy Canova, Country Style, at noon; Name a Tune at 4:30, and Space Jockey at 9:30 p. m. They also move "Long Beach Town Forum" to 7 p. m. and air the L. B. Hotels Jamboree at 7:30 p. m.

In early 1953, a *Space Jockey* radio drama played over the Los Angeles airwaves. This was likely the work of Phil Tucker.

to guess that he would take a radio gig if it came his way. The fact that the radio "Space Jockey" ended about two weeks before *Robot Monster* was announced is eerie. Tucker might have been doing the show live each time, or perhaps recorded a number of episodes with an initial deal of one month. The ratings might not have justified KFOX getting him to produce more "Space Jockey" adventures or perhaps they did, and he was the uninterested party with the production of *Robot Monster* imminent.

What is certain is that if the show was Tucker's, it has some connection to the film he made months later. The movie's basic premise—a space pilot's dangerous job and its complications at home—would have worked well in a half-hour radio drama. Many conflicts could be imagined around the scenario and, with the magic of sound effects, space travel would have been easy to accomplish in radio. If Tucker was recycling a radio idea when he made *Space Jockey* in Fairbanks, then some of that lost film's problems are clearer.

Tucker would have been taking an idea that worked well in one medium and shoehorning it into another where it did not translate. As well as he understood that *Robot Monster* had to have a monster (a gorilla wearing a diving helmet was better than nothing), it seems to have been lost on him that a movie about space pilots had to have some space piloting. He had created a cheap spaceship interior but there is no indication that he had thought out how to get the audience "screamingly transported" with actual depictions of space flight. For that matter, the story as described is only about the perils of space exploration without a hint of other exciting elements like aliens or enemy Soviet space jockeys. Tucker may have desperately fallen back on an old idea when he made the *Space Jockey* movie and, disgusted and energized from his treatment by Zimbalist, his better judgment may have been short-circuited. The pitfalls of turning this radio show into a film were invisible until the project was completed, perhaps because Tucker had already made more than one TV pilot on what was likely one set. (*Rocketship X-M* may have also been a bad influence on this point, as roughly half of it is set in a cramped spaceship.)

When one considers that Tucker had a leisurely schedule for *Space Jockey* (twelve days, probably three times his *Robot*

Monster schedule), it is amazing that he made an apparently unreleasable film—even if one accounts for the amateur cast and crew. But as Wade Williams notes, Mikel Conrad's dull *The Flying Saucer* was picked up by Film Classics (Zimbalist's old employer) for a two-year deal that began with explosive profits in 1950 that plummeted by the end of 1951. Writes Williams, "The general public was becoming less enamored with the somewhat dated film because it lacked traditional robots, monsters, and special effects now expected of the science fiction genre." And while 1952 was a dull year for science fiction, "1953 was a different story."[421] In the explosive wake of *The War of the Worlds, It Came from Outer Space, Invaders from Mars,* and many others, a no-budget independent had to reach a much higher bar than *The Flying Saucer.* But *Space Jockey* unfortunately was a 1950-style movie made in 1953 and, for science fiction films, the difference in those few years was epic.

Tucker's lost film is seen with even more clarity by exploring the origins and usage of the term "space jockey." In the available old newspapers there is no record of its use prior to 1951, when it began to show up as the reality of space exploration edged nearer. But a few years previously, in its April 26, 1947, issue, *The Saturday Evening Post* published a science fiction short story called "Space Jockey" by Robert A. Heinlein. As Bill Warren noted in *Keep Watching the Skies!,* Ray Bradbury was the mainstream face of early fifties science fiction.[422] It was perhaps because no one else in the science fiction pulps wrote with Bradbury's richly poetic style and feeling of wonder that few others graduated into the mainstream. But Heinlein, with his rugged individuality and sense of stoic heroism, was second to Bradbury, with "Space Jockey" and other stories published in *The Saturday Evening Post* rather than *Thrilling Wonder Stories.* Tucker might have picked up that issue of the *Post* in 1947 or thereafter, but he could have more easily been exposed to the story when it appeared in Heinlein's 1951 collection *The Green Hills of Earth.* As Tucker Jr. recalled, his father was a "fan of the [science fiction] genre" and was in general a "voracious reader," consuming two or more books in a week, fiction or non-fiction. Tucker even claimed, as discussed in Chapter 3, to have been a pulp science fiction writer. Whatever the truth of that claim, he was familiar with science fiction and Heinlein's tough, individualistic sensibility was a close match to his own.

Heinlein's story begins as a space pilot and his wife are about to enjoy an evening out. Their plans suddenly ruined by an incoming job, Jake Pemberton parts with his wife Phyllis on strained terms, their future uncertain. After rocketing to an orbiting space station, Pemberton goes through the mundane details of his career, such as chatting with navigator and computer operator Shorty Weinstein. The trip underway, the story's main dramatic moment comes as the ship is put in danger by a foolish, big-shot passenger and his bratty son. After getting the ship safely to its lunar destination, Pemberton gets an offer to be a moon pilot, ending his interplanetary missions and allowing Phyllis to join him in domestic bliss on the moon. As this summary shows, Heinlein's story was also an ideal property for a low-budget filmmaker. Adapted straightforwardly, it would be easy to film in a cheap studio with a minimum of set decorations. Even special effects shots are implied only occasionally and, if he could afford the rights, a Phil Tucker or Ed

Wood could easily film the story with some additional scenes to pad it out.

While few details remain of the Tucker film, there is an obvious connection to Heinlein's story beyond the title. As the *News-Miner* described, Tucker's film focused on a pilot with an anxious wife on Earth (pregnant in the Tucker version, while apparently not pregnant in the Heinlein story), so there is little chance that Tucker was not borrowing from Heinlein. And fascinatingly, Heinlein wrote a script of the story in 1952 or '53, intended for television but never filmed. With screenwriter Jack Seaman, Heinlein adapted many of his stories along with "Space Jockey" for a proposed TV series that never materialized, but which led to the 1953 Lippert movie *Project Moon Base.* Collected in a 2008 hardcover, *Project Moonbase* [sic] *and Others,* the unproduced *Space Jockey* script sticks very closely to the story, its only changes being additional scenes that dramatize some of the concepts that Heinlein described in his original.[423] (Heinlein's space pilots, for example, are the supreme authority on how the ship flies, even above the captain. Heinlein compares this to Mark Twain's description of riverboat crews, and this information is converted into a conversation in the screenplay version.)

But while Tucker borrowed from Heinlein, he was likely not working from the teleplay written by Heinlein and Seaman (even if Tucker did not recognize any distinction between TV and the movies). Between Tucker's memories and the *News-Miner* report, the film included elements that had nothing to do with the story, such as the comic relief character Mamie Dazell, the ending borrowed from *Rocketship X-M,* and the trips to Mars and Venus. The original title *Return to Earth* further implies that Tucker's film was a hodgepodge of influences. British science fiction writer Bryan Berry's 1951 novel *Return to Earth* was the story of a Venus colony's descendants' decision to leave for Earth. (There is also a 1937 short story by Willis Knapp Jones named "Return to Earth," which appeared once in the horror fantasy pulp *Weird Tales,* making it a less likely influence. There was no story or novel entitled *Return from Mars.*)

Tucker also would have played up the respectability of adapting a *Saturday Evening Post* story, and buying the rights from Heinlein would have eaten up his budget. But while there is no good reason to believe that Tucker had any involvement with Heinlein, Tucker could have counted on facing legal action if the film had been released. Heinlein later secured an out-of-court settlement over the very cheap *The Brain Eaters* (1958), due to similarities to his 1951 novel *The Puppet Masters.*[424] But closer to the time and concept of Tucker's *Space Jockey* was the radio and television series *Tom Corbett, Space Cadet,* which began on radio in January 1952 and continued on television through June 1955.[425] Widely recognized as partially inspired by Heinlein's novel *Space Cadet* (1948), the series was developed from writer Joseph Greene's 1946 radio script but with a fee reportedly paid to Heinlein for the use of the *Space Cadet* title.[426] Even if Tucker changed his movie's title from *Space Jockey* back to the less marketable *Return to Earth,* the prickly Heinlein would not have tolerated the borrowing of his story. Tucker's naming the film *Space Jockey* when producing it in Alaska suggests that he was blissfully unaware of the trouble he could find, and may indicate that he used the catchy title to lure in investors and talent for the production. Or perhaps he planned for the project to remain *Return to Earth* down in Hollywood.

It is hard to know if a lawsuit would have been better or worse for Tucker. He could not have afforded it, but any publicity is good to an unknown. And based on the available newspaper accounts, Tucker was directly tuned in to the zeitgeist by using the title of Heinlein's story. Just as the phrase "space jockey" is conspicuously missing from news reports before 1951, its usage ballooned from that point on, making it clear

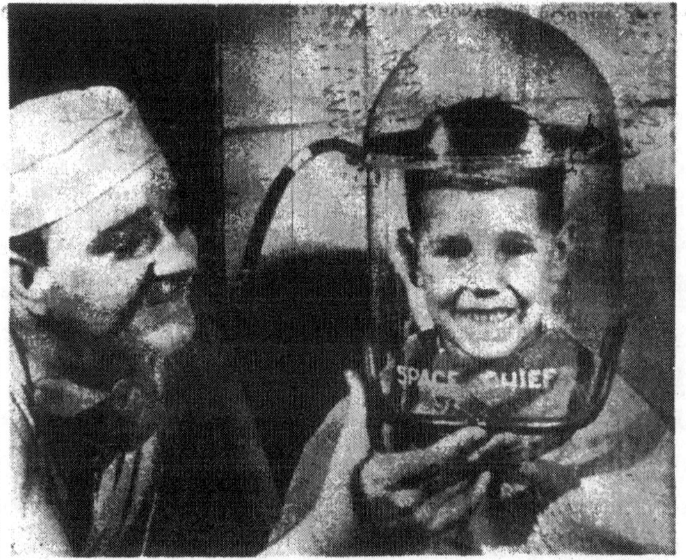

'SPACE HELMET' FOR JOURNEY INTO ETHER

Face mask modeled after a "space helmet" and designed to allay children's fears of anesthesia is modeled by Jimmy Bowden, 4, just before he undergoes tonsillectomy in Naval Medical Center at Bethesda, Md. Giving the anesthetic is Lt. J. G. Morrow, codeveloper of the mask, which Jimmy called a "pretty sharp trick."

The "Space Chief" title on the helmet in this early 1954 clipping demonstrates the popularity of the "space jockey" archetype.

that Heinlein must have connected with the broader culture.[427] Throughout the 1950s, many reports by various writers in different publications used the term, from Jack Burroughs of the *Oakland Tribune* in January 1953[428] to the editorial board of the *Kokomo Tribune* in February 1959.[429] Meanwhile, a *Parade* feature on space launch monkey Miss Patience from April of the same year noted, "Her 15-pound weight disqualifies her as a space jockey."[430] Back in September 1951, a press agent for the Gary Cooper film *High Noon* lamented to reporter Bob Thomas, "How can a guy on a pinto compete with a space ship jockey?"[431] But in December 1954, cowboy star Gene Autry would not tolerate the doom and gloom, according to AP reporter Wayne Oliver, who noted that the "millionaire cowpoke is unworried about being superseded by the space jockey."[432] Likely few realized or cared that the term wound its way back to a science fiction writer named Robert A. Heinlein, but anyone tuned into popular culture was recognizing the space jockey archetype in such forms as TV's *Tom Corbett, Space Cadet* and *Rocky Jones, Space Ranger.* (On that note, Johnny's shirt at the end of *Robot Monster* says "Rocket Ranger.")

Hall's assumption that *Space Jockey* was never completed illustrates another aspect of Tucker little appreciated until now. He not only had the relentless drive needed to finish a project, but the detachment to let one go if it could not be salvaged. The un-releasable movie could be gathering dust in some vault, but Tucker might have simply pitched it into the nearest Dumpster and moved on with his life.

There is one last piece of evidence regarding the mysterious fate of *Space Jockey.* Interviewed by Mark Thomas McGee,

American International chief Samuel Arkoff looked back to the early fifties roots of his company, a time when he and partner James H. Nicholson were uncertain if they could get it off the ground. By early 1954, a young former engineer named Roger Corman had completed a competent but routine effort that was soon released by Lippert as *Monster from the Ocean Floor,* directed by the man credited for writing *Robot Monster,* Wyott Ordung. Corman produced and soon followed it with the crime melodrama *The Fast and the Furious,* the beginning of his partnership with American International. But before Nicholson and Arkoff had their highly profitable arrangement with Corman, the situation at American International was utterly desperate. Arkoff summed up that time with this anecdote:

> You wouldn't believe some of the pictures Jim and I sat through before Roger brought us his picture. There was this one—I don't remember the title—that was filmed entirely in a warehouse somewhere, possibly Canada. They'd built this set inside of this warehouse which was supposed to be the cockpit of a spaceship. For the first half of the picture, these astronauts talked about what they expected to find on whatever planet it was they were headed for. When they landed the camera shook a little to give the impression that they'd landed. You never saw the outside of the ship. The astronauts walked out of [the] door and the film faded to black. When it faded in again the astronauts returned and spent the second half of the film talking about what they'd seen. You never got out of that cockpit.[433]

That film might not have been *Space Jockey*. But given the time frame, location ("possibly Canada"), storyline, and description of the set, it is unlikely that it could have been anything else.

While *Space Jockey* was stillborn, *Robot Monster* might have already become a pop culture influence as early as the year it was released, with a December 1953 Looney Tunes short carrying the title *Robot Rabbit*. But as for how Tucker was getting on with his life, he again got his name in the press and not in the trades or a small newspaper, but in *The Mirror*, a tabloid offshoot of the *Los Angeles Times*. Hopefully Tucker did believe that all publicity is good publicity, because the cover headline of the December 15, 1953 issue was not triumphant: "Mirror Halts Filmland Suicide." The story began on page three with news that reporter Gerry McCarthy and detectives H.T. Weil and A.W. Hubka had that day descended on the Hollywood Knickerbocker Hotel and "broke into" a room where Tucker was found unconscious in bed.[434] According to the report, "A packet of sleeping powders was found on his night stand beside a pulp copy of *Fantastic Tales*." The trio had moved in response to a letter from Tucker to *Mirror* publisher Virgil Pinkley that was postmarked on the 14th at noon, and received the next morning. Reproduced in the *Mirror* story (and apparently with some edits), this is Tucker's letter:

> As you read this I am quite dead in a room at the Hollywood Knickerbocker Hotel. Since I am writing this before I check in, I don't know which room it is but I am registered under my own name.

You may wonder why I write to you at a time like this—I will explain.

I want everyone to know why I'm doing as I am but I want that information given in a dignified way. I am only 26 but I feel that even self-inflicted death must be treated with dignity.

I was not a good businessman. Had I been, I would be alive now. I produced and directed at the very height of the 3-D craze, a 3-D picture.

It was good enough to open at the Hollywood Paramount Theater. I admit it was not a masterpiece but it takes a little ability—a little something on the ball—to shoot a picture that opens at a first-run theater.

I have never even received my wages as a director for that picture.

In spite of what I have done in the recent past I cannot find a job.

When I was refused a job as even an usher I finally realized that my future in the industry was bleak.

If I can't go on working there is no reason to continue to breathe . . . to sleep . . . to eat . . . for this is not living.

Had I been able to find a job . . . any kind of a job in the film industry, I would not have taken this way out!

> Who knows . . . in 15 or 20 years I might have been able to make many worthwhile contributions in the work I loved so much.
>
> Au revoir . . .
> Phillip Jay (Phil) Tucker

Tucker's address was printed as 1202 S. Bronson Avenue, and the detectives were trying to find his (unnamed) wife. "Tucker's letter was filled with recriminations for successful film producers who, he said, wouldn't give him a job," the *Mirror* noted, those "named said they never heard of Tucker." A day later on December 16, the *Los Angeles Times* ran a shorter, summarized version of the story that contained a few variations and additional details.[435] Tucker's pocket now contained "a pass from the psychopathic ward" of the West Los Angeles VA Hospital, where he was returned (in "fair" condition) after treatment at the Hollywood Emergency Hospital. The *Times* also noted that it was at CBS where Tucker worked as an usher, and that he had even been barred from seeing *Robot Monster* without paying by his partners in the film. The report closed with this detail:

> Although he subsequently gave a home address here, inquiries revealed he never lived there. When he signed into the hotel Monday, paying in advance, he registered as being from Fairbanks, Alaska.

7¢ THE MIRROR N.Y. STOCKS

Vol. VI—No. 56 64 Pages TUESDAY, DECEMBER 15, 1953 MA 2311—145 S. Spring, Los Angeles 53

Mirror Halts Filmland Suicide

(STORY, PAGE 3)

9

Santa Monica Jungle

Phil Tucker's suicide attempt of December 1953 is one of the few aspects of his life that survived through the years and formed his public persona. As Bill Warren put it in the original edition of *Keep Watching the Skies!*, "*Robot Monster* may be the only film so bad it drove its director to attempt suicide."[436] But Tucker's filming *Space Jockey* soon after the release of *Robot Monster* proves that he could not have been despondent to the point of self-destruction over his robot-gorilla movie. If the suicide attempt of an orphan and Marine sergeant who had spent his life taking on one challenge after another was genuine, it was not a reaction to one film but to a stalled career. While Phil Tucker Jr. allows that his father may have "believed in *Robot Monster* more than he let on in the Medved interview,"[437] playing it down later in the context of looking backward, he doubts that the suicide attempt was anything other than a publicity stunt. Suicide contradicts his father's very personality:

> To think of him trying to do such a thing would run against everything I have ever known about him. He was always very upbeat and optimistic, even in the face of extreme adversity. He was the ultimate example of someone picking himself up, dusting himself off, and starting all over again. There is no way that he would let one failed attempt at something get to him like that.[438]

Tucker's resilience in spite of a troubled childhood, his eager personality, and his knack for grabbing opportunities do not suggest a suicidal bent. He was not a moody artist. There is also a mutating, urban legend quality to the Tucker suicide attempt that calls it into question. This item was formerly on the IMDb and, as of this writing, still floats around elsewhere on the Internet: "Depressed and dejected, and believing that his acrimonious relationship with the film's producers resulted in their blackballing him in the industry, he attempted suicide by shooting himself. He missed."[439] (Even if he had lacked Marine Corps rifle training, Tucker could not have missed himself at point blank range.) Likewise, Conrad Brooks remembered the subject in contrasting detail:

> I remember one time, he wanted to commit suicide. He had a film can in his hand, and he was in the car, and I think he was trying to commit suicide. I guess he wasn't making any money, there must have been some reason. And I remember it hit the newspapers, like front-page news. He got some good publicity out of it. Maybe he did it on purpose?[440]

Brooks is astute in guessing Tucker's motivations, while the fleeting details he remembers ("in the car") do not relate to the incident reported in the *Los Angeles Times* and *The Mirror*. But how much useful publicity Tucker got is impossible to guess, if only for his suicide story being sandwiched between two others. Right on the front page of the *Times* was the news of a 27-year-old engineer who had hung himself, dressed in women's swimwear and chains. Tucker's write-up was on page 18, while farther back on page 32 was the story of a sad, isolated, elderly man who shot himself.[441]

But there is another great difficulty in accepting the suicide attempt as genuine: Neither the *Los Angeles Times* or *Mirror* stories mention *Space Jockey*. Tucker just spent months on the project, and wanted it to launch his own Alaskan mini-Hollywood. These plans were so far from reality that *Space Jockey* could not even be released. If Tucker was suicidal and was pouring his heart out in his letter, he could not have left unmentioned the life-consuming project that had just ended in disaster. It is no more likely that the *Times* or *Mirror* would have failed to mention it if he had. These stories referenced the Lucky Luciano stunt from the fall of 1952, but did not connect his listing Fairbanks as home with *Space Jockey* or any aspect of his career. They connect him primarily with *Robot Monster* and, from the viewpoint of the suicide attempt as a hoax, this makes perfect sense. Tucker was trying to get employed and, just as an applicant omits a brief grunt job from a résumé, he structured his suicide hoax to maximum advantage. This meant connecting him to his greatest success, and absolutely dissociating himself from his greatest failure. The suicide attempt was therefore *completely* about *Robot Monster,* and not at all about the fortunately unknown *Space Jockey.* Because Tucker's early career outside of *Robot Monster* was subterranean and undocumented, his suicide attempt was easy to take seriously, but a close appraisal now renders that impossible. As Tucker Jr. put it, "He was probably at his wit's end over the *Robot Monster* dispute and saw no other recourse at the time. But later in life I know he looked back and realized how foolish it was to do those things."[442]

And, according to Ray Zone, Wyott Ordung saw it much the same way:

> There was a picture of him in the Los Angeles *Mirror* on the front page. He was lying there clutching the cans of film. Was it because of the film? I think he wanted publicity. That's what I think. Young genius thinks he made a great picture for $45,000. People are not going to the movie and so on and he ended up in Camarillo.[443]

While Ordung's photo memory does not quite add up (there is no such picture throughout December 1953 and January 1954 of *The Mirror*), he understood Tucker's motives well. Also understanding the reality behind attention-grabbing suicide schemes was *Mirror* columnist Paul V. Coates. On January 8, 1954, *The Mirror* printed Coates' revealing depiction of another Los Angeles citizen alleging suicidal desires while unambiguously seeking attention:

> The call came in at 3:30 yesterday afternoon.
>
> "Suppose I told you a man was gonna die today?" a voice asked. "Suppose I told you the time and the place?"
>
> It's the kind of a call that comes in very often. You get them from drunks, from cranks and from the countless psychopaths who walk the streets of Los Angeles.
>
> But it's the kind of a call you can't ignore.
>
> "Who's going to die?" I asked.
>
> "Me," the voice replied. "I'm gonna kill myself today."[444]

According to the story, Coates talked down a desperate Army deserter from the top of a building while his despondent wife held their baby. And while the man in the story appeared genuinely distraught, the fact remains that if he truly wished himself dead he would likely have just gone ahead and jumped. But in relation to Tucker's stunt, it is noteworthy that Coates describes tips on impending death as a repetitive, and possibly obnoxious part of his job. Tucker was clearly not the first or last to pull a suicide stunt, and it is interesting to ponder just what went through the minds of the trio that found him in his hotel room. Perhaps they had seen enough similar situations to feel skeptical about the whole thing before they arrived.

One more aspect of Tucker's scheme is noteworthy. The text of his letter provides a rare opportunity to read his voice as a writer, and reading it draws forth an interesting parallel to *Robot Monster*. Tucker wrote:

> If I can't go on working there is no reason to continue to breathe . . . to sleep . . . to eat . . . for this is not living.

This series of verbs in a row that carry an existential plea has a famous analogue in Ro-Man's dialogue:

> To be like the hu-man! To laugh! Feel! Want! Why are these things not in the plan?

Tucker's suicide letter works less well as a cry for help than as evidence that it was he who wrote Ro-Man's words of self-doubt, added in post-production. The underlying desperation is similar, and the grammatical resemblance is striking. While Tucker was not suicidal, he was fictionalizing an exaggerated view of his frustrated career, a situation very much like what Ro-Man expressed in his soliloquy:

> I cannot, yet I must. How do you calculate that? At what point on the graph do "must" and "cannot" meet? Yet I must—but I cannot!

Did the suicide attempt pay off? Tucker was credited as director for at least six completed feature films in addition to *Robot Monster,* all made afterwards. But they were less prestigious and the issue of whether he got to make them out of suicide sympathy, or by virtue of completing a reasonably successful feature is not clear. Whatever the truth of these details, Tucker returned to filmmaking in 1954 but without publicity, glamour, or creativity. He settled into a holding pattern, making movies for hire that could have given him only temporary relief from subsisting on odd jobs. He re-entered the world of exploitation film that he later credited for apprenticing him in the basics of moviemaking, specifically back in the employ of George Weiss and Merle Connell.

Tucker made at least five movies within the space of two years: *Dance Hall Racket, Dream Follies, Tijuana After Midnight, Bagdad After Midnight,* and *Broadway Jungle.*[445] *Dance Hall Racket* fit the exploitation category of the vice film, sordid and sometimes supposedly true stories of the criminal underworld. *Dream Follies* and the *After Midnight* series were burlesque films, a separate and more escapist species of exploitation. And *Broadway Jungle* was a strange and extremely cheap effort that was probably not made for Weiss or any other producer, and was perhaps the one time that Tucker personally expressed himself on film.

Within the year of Tucker's absence from exploitation, an eccentric would-be director named Ed Wood convinced the cost-obsessive Weiss that he was the right man to make a film about a man who did not want to be a man. Transsexuality was topical in the early fifties thanks to Christine Jorgensen, the Army veteran who underwent a sex-change, and Weiss was ready to cash in. The charming, talkative transvestite Wood convinced Weiss to let him direct, shoehorning in a performance by the sickly, drug-addled Bela Lugosi. Universally referred to now as *Glen or Glenda,* the film profited less well than Weiss hoped but was earthshaking in the history of trash cinema. Wood went on to his other strange and terrible films, including the infamous *Plan 9 from Outer Space,* building the legend that lead to posthumous fame. And in terms of Tucker's career, Wood's involvement with Weiss provides some clarity.

Wood and Tucker are often mentioned in the same breath. While Wood has become the gold standard for a bad cult film director, Tucker has ranked a respectable second with a group of features that, while few and seldom seen, includes the legendary *Robot Monster.* As the preceding chapters demonstrate, the two directors were not that similar. Wood's defining quality was his delusion that his movies were good, while Tucker knew his were bad and only made them because no one would give him the money to make bigger ones. But both of them served in the Marines during the war, both had made unsuccessful TV pilots, both toiled in the same exploitation cinematic sub-basement, and both did so for Weiss. They had to have known each other reasonably well, and there is just enough surviving evidence to not only establish that fact but roughly sketch how they saw one another. Timothy Farrell, who worked with both, told Rudolph Grey, "Ed knew Phil, and I don't think they liked each other."[446] That view was confirmed to this author by Grey, who recounted Kathy Wood's observation that her late husband and Tucker were "friendly enemies." Further, Grey stated, his friend Don Fellman remembered talking to Wood in his later years when the subject of Tucker came up. Wood replied, "Phil Tucker is the greatest shitbird who ever walked the face of the Earth!"[447] Three accounts give the same impression, although there is ambiguity in the tension of being "friendly enemies." For that matter, Brooks stated that he "never heard anything bad" about Tucker and Wood.

Also according to Grey's book, Weiss recalled an obscure detail about Wood's cross-dressing feature that points to the intersection of a famous collaborator in Tucker's life and career:

"The Devil" in *Glen or Glenda,* his name is Captain De Zita. He was my booking agent. De Zita booked strippers. In fact he booked in where Lenny Bruce worked a strip joint. So De Zita was living next door to where I had an office called the Harvey Hotel.[448]

Captain De Zita was yet another of the colorful fringe characters who surfaced in the dingy Quality Studios universe, by Weiss' description living right next door. At least as far back as 1936, the supposed "ex-officer of the French Foreign Legion"[449] was wowing rural audiences in the southwest with his blindfolded driving stunts in his three-wheeled automobile,[450] as his Frank Zappa-like visage appeared in newspapers with plugs for an array of locally available products. An ad from California's *Woodland Daily Democrat* promised that one could "see the captain serve and draw beer blindfolded at the Del Mar Rendezvous,"[451] but the issue of whether or not he "booked strippers" while blindfolded years later was not addressed by Weiss. But Weiss mentioned the captain's connection to comedian Lenny Bruce, and Bruce had an undeniable connection with Tucker.

By the early sixties Bruce was embroiled in a legal firestorm for his uncharted forays into obscene language and taboo smashing, and was after his drug-related 1966 death a countercultural icon and posthumous martyr for freedom of expression. His legend lived on from such stunts as starting a show by addressing the audience as offensively as possible, until its members could not help laughing as Bruce hurled one slur after another at them. But in the early fifties, he was only one of many largely unknown and struggling performers. According to Albert Goldman's controversial biography, it was spring 1953 when Bruce and his stripper wife Honey Harlow arrived in Los Angeles, placing their arrival just as *Robot Monster* was

Lenny Bruce featured in a late 1953 Strip City ad.

in post-production and about to be released.[452] Bruce took on odd jobs but soon had the good fortune of securing standup comedian work at Strip City, one of the area's more respectable clubs, and stayed there for 18 months. Movie stars and other celebrities were often seen slumming at the nightspot described by Goldman as "Purple walls and purple ceiling. Purple bar and purple floor."[453] Given the early fifties time frame of his work with Tucker, Bruce could not have been in Los Angeles for long before they met. Unfortunately, while Tucker remembered meeting Bruce, his recollections cannot be completely accurate.

The subject of Bruce did not come up in Tucker's interview until he was asked about his 1960 science fiction film *The Cape Canaveral Monsters.* Harry Medved summarized:

> In order to earn a living, he had been washing dishes at this period of time. He met the mother of nightclub comic Lenny Bruce, who later introduced him to her son. Bruce and Tucker became as close to each other as two brothers. Oftentimes, when Tucker became tired of washing dishes, he would stage, along with Bruce, a mock suicide. Tucker would take a few sleeping pills, but not enough to be harmful. He would then go to a hotel, and lie down in his bed. Then Bruce would make an anonymous phone call to the newspapers and report an attempted suicide. Reporters would rush over to Tucker's hotel room, and he would then be taken to the Veteran's Administration Hospital. (He was a veteran of World War II.)

> Mr. Tucker dismissed these suicide attempts as mere gimmicks in order to procure free room and board.[454]

Because *The Cape Canaveral Monsters* (which will be discussed later in more detail) was filmed around early 1960, Tucker was wrong on at least one point. He and Bruce completed two movies together, *Dance Hall Racket* and *Dream Follies,* and they were both shot and released within a year of 1954. Unless Tucker had used his science fiction knowledge to unravel the secret of time travel, he did not meet Bruce at around the time of *The Cape Canaveral Monsters.* Tucker might have in his unrecorded words made a distinction between the earlier days with Bruce and that later film, but there is no way to know. As there is reason to believe that Tucker resorted to the same kind of attention-grabbing suicide scheme when he was trying to make his later film, it is logical that he could have had a mental lapse and associated his meeting Lenny Bruce with a later time.

But since Tucker recalled a number of details throughout the interview that have been verified (such as the aftermath of *Robot Monster* and the production of *Space Jockey*), there is no reason to doubt the details that he remembered, only the time frame in which he mislaid them. He was likely doing something like dishwashing in the months surrounding *Robot Monster* and *Space Jockey,* and probably met Bruce as described. According to Goldman, Bruce stayed financially afloat by running schemes similar to the sleeping pill suicide attempt and, in conjunction with actor pal Richard Shackleton, even financed *Dream Follies* this way:

> He put an ad in the *Los Angeles Times*: "Lenny, The Gardener, will clean, mow and edge your lawn for $6.00." At that time the standard price for the same job was $15.00, so, naturally, he had every moocher in the city calling the number in the ad. . . . When the people came across with the six bucks, Lenny, The Gardener, would split. According to Lenny, "I could do ten a day."[455]

If Tucker and Bruce were "as close to each other as two brothers," then they likely worked the suicide scheme exactly as Tucker described. Tucker might have even gotten the idea from Bruce, or at least the encouragement to go through with it. Back from Alaska with *Space Jockey* in hand, Tucker could have already been dishwashing as the film was cut and then been scrubbing longer hours after reactions such as that of Sam Arkoff. Tucker could have easily met Bruce in the fall of 1953 with the December suicide scam following.

Tucker would have directed any movie that came his way, so it is not surprising that he got to direct the two he made with his friend. Bruce's involvement in the two films seems to have been primary, so Tucker's prior experience would have made him the best available choice. Ironically, the Goldman biography claims that these movies were made in the shadow of Bruce's own brush with the Hollywood mainstream. Like Tucker he found an avenue into the movie world and saw it go up in smoke. Thanks to his friend Buddy Hackett, in Hollywood in 1953 for a role at Twentieth Century-Fox, Bruce was introduced to executive Leonard Goldstein, who needed a writer for revisions on a project already cast. Astonished by Bruce's quick-witted scripting, Goldstein put him on a weekly salary.[456] Then called *McCluskey Strikes a Blow,* the re-written film was eventually released in April 1954 as *The Rocket Man,* which the *Hollywood Reporter* called "Ideal Family Trade Fare."[457] But Goldstein died in July and, in a development that was perhaps related, Bruce lost his employment at Fox. Also worth noting is a November 1953 *Reporter* item that "Bruce, currently emceeing at the Strip City nitery," was working for Goldstein but had "previously wrote sketches for the *Broadway Open House* TV show in New York three years ago."[458] Like Tucker, he had dabbled in television, trying different show business angles for years.

Bruce aspired to be taken seriously as a writer but had yet to develop the comedic material that would make him infamous, and he kept plugging away. Like Tucker and Wood, he had even been working on a television pilot, the unproduced *Honeytime* that was intended to showcase his wife's dancing.[459] But whether Bruce got connected to the world of Weiss and Quality Studios through meeting Tucker through his mother, or whether Captain De Zita's job at Strip City was the conduit, Bruce would soon write and star in *Dance Hall Racket* for Weiss and Strip City's owner Joseph Abrahams, credited as associate producer.

Dream Follies was apparently made earlier, about mid-1954, which makes sense. It was not much different from other burlesque movies, which were easy to make quickly for little money. Abrahams was also associate producer on *Dream Follies* (Weiss was not involved, but Connell did camerawork), and its successful completion perhaps gave him the confidence to produce *Dance Hall Racket* later in the year. According to Goldman, *Dream Follies* "led straight on" into *Dance Hall Racket* and, regarding the director of both pictures, "Tucker understood about camera angles and cutting, but was pretty naïve about everything beyond the most basic mechanical processes."[460] This assessment squares with Claudia Barrett's assertion that Tucker "was not familiar with camera techniques,"[461] and his appraisal of himself in those years as "a third or fourth-rate director." In Goldman's cynical estimation, Bruce frequently and coldly used slapdash assistants in many areas of his life, in the belief that they were malleable extensions of his personal genius. "In any case," they continue, "Tucker proved useful as they ground through day after day of shooting in a chintzy little studio on Santa Monica Boulevard behind the Harvey Hotel."[462] (Quality Pictures, geographically described identically to the Weiss quote about De Zita.)

Dance Hall Racket is Tucker's second most important film, as it is widely available and fairly often seen and reviewed. It also was at least completed and had enough potential to be distributed. Its major appeal today is Bruce's involvement as writer and actor, both also true of *Dream Follies,* but for the purpose of exploring Tucker as a filmmaker, *Dance Hall Racket* is an essential point of reference. What are its similarities and differences to *Robot Monster,* in what ways is it better or worse, and how does Tucker handle material outside the science fiction milieu of *Robot Monster* and *Space Jockey?*

There is a slight storyline in *Dance Hall Racket* and a smidgen of character development, but mostly a collection of isolated incidents centered on the shady proprietor of a seaside nightclub,

Timothy Farrell as Umberto Scalli in *Dance Hall Racket*.

Umberto Scalli (Timothy Farrell), whose last name could suggest scaly-ness of the reptilian variety, were it not mostly pronounced SKAAH-lee. Bruce plays Scalli's violently unbalanced henchman Vincent, and the film tells in flashback their business in running contraband through the club, via merchant sailor patrons (referred to six times as "seamen," apparently to draw idiot laughter). Interspersed with their scenes are an endless parade of unrelated incidents: couples dance, couples talk and smooch at tables, eccentric customers provide comic relief, the management roughs up troublemakers, the dancers change costumes backstage, until finally Vincent kills Scalli, only to be taken down by an undercover cop. The film ends as it begins, with a police inspector in conversation with a reporter, providing the obligatory respectability brackets of exploitation. The dockside dance hall continues, the inspector informs us, under the management of the brooding Burt, one of Scalli's more stable men. In time they will only have to raid it again. Cut to the same shot of dancers that introduces Scalli's Dance Emporium at the beginning, and the incredibly static film ends, feeling like a Mobius strip that will repeat eternally.

But *Dance Hall Racket* is imbued with stasis in virtually every frame, with unimaginative compositions and few camera movements throughout, the boredom intermittently relieved by its bizarre qualities. A thick-jawed comic relief drunk named Punchy wears an ill-fitting fedora and speaks in an exaggerated Scandinavian accent, later entertaining Scalli and his friends for thirty extremely long seconds with the "Tahitian love dance." At various points, customers enjoy the privilege of getting to "go to Hawaii." In this absurd variation on a table make-out session, a large plant is placed on the table for exotic atmosphere. (The cheap, rip-off quality of going to Hawaii is an excellent metaphor for all of exploitation film.) A shy, eccentric patron who is saving up his hundreds of dance tickets for one night of monopolizing all the girls finds a little romance backstage, as well as the respect of Jack the bartender: "What a beautiful thought, kind of poetic somehow. You know they can say what they want to, but I like you. You think big." Also worth noting is Bruce's wife Honey as his onscreen girlfriend Rose and his mother, Sally Marr, as Maxine, an aging and discarded paramour of Scalli. Marr much resembled her famous son, and her character essays a hardboiled diatribe to a young colleague on the subject of men.

Variations in surviving copies of *Dance Hall Racket* also illustrate the distribution practices common to exploitation. One copy that has floated around home video contains abrupt jump cuts in scenes of the dancers backstage. Unedited, there would be brief flashes of nudity, but the source print was one used for cold territories that would not allow it. One version of this cold print that has appeared on VHS seems to enter a rift in the space-time continuum halfway through the brief running time. An early scene where Rose is sadistically attacked by a guy who sold stolen diamonds to Scalli is repeated out of nowhere; even though the attacker was killed by Vincent earlier, the entire scene, killing included, is replayed. Stranger still, this replay cuts to another scene not yet established. Scalli roughs up a scheming blonde with little sense of why, the scene reappearing later—and making more sense this time—after the blonde is shown manipulating a customer for his savings and keeping it all to herself. While nonsensical, this time-warping repeat and premonition of violent sequences had a purpose. Exploitation movies were not supposed to be good, merely not boring. To that end, spectacle was their mainstay, according to Eric Schaefer's *Bold! Daring! Shocking! True!*[463] Critical opinion of such movies did not matter to those who paid money to see them, and few critics reviewed them anyway. The only thing that mattered was that some degree of sensation was offered. Some of these changes may have been made in the home video process (the time-warp edits look very awkward and not necessarily like film editing), but they nonetheless illustrate the exploitation mentality.[464]

Dance Hall Racket demonstrated another exploitation pattern, that of using a repeated character with no regard to his previous history. Umberto Scalli had been the villain of two earlier Weiss productions, *The Devil's Sleep* (1949, directed by Connell) and *Racket Girls* (1951, directed by Robert C. Dertano, another regular member of the Quality crew). Scalli was dead at the end of the latter film, but is alive and well in *Dance Hall Racket* and then killed off yet again, it being anyone's guess if it is permanent this time. Farrell noted that Weiss and company "just liked the name" and therefore recycled it,[465] but the practice of reusing characters in defiance of continuity had an economic value to the exploitation filmmaker. According to Schaefer, there was some potential for name recognition in a familiar character (although there were probably no legions of

"I think big."

Umberto Scalli fans longing in vain for a fourth installment), and a familiar character reduced the need for preparation.[466] Rehearsal time was non-existent to minimal in exploitation; as Dan Sonney commented to Schaefer, scenes were shot "never over three times. Never."[467] As Farrell remembered in an interview with Grey, he was the Spencer Tracy to Weiss' Louis B. Mayer because he could regularly get through lines without blowing them and could, at worst, just improvise.[468] (But Farrell was a good actor, had a great voice, and was better than everyone else in these films. As bad as some of the acting is in *Robot Monster,* it is mostly a couple of notches worse in *Dance Hall Racket.*)

The finished product of Bruce and Tucker's efforts was of course very bad, though the logical result of its script, budget, and intentions. Goldman called it "well up front in the competition for Worst Movie Ever Made."[469] It is to Warren "about as bad as *Robot Monster.*"[470] One IMDb poster gave the movie an amusing review from a sarcastic "art film" viewpoint, calling it "Phil Tucker does Robert Altman," and noting "spare, washed-out cinematography only rivaled by Dreyer" and continuity "as confounding as anything by Alain Resnais."[471] (If *Dance Hall Racket* had been shot in color and widescreen with a mercilessly compressing telephoto lens, its huge cast and meandering narrative would approximate an Altman film.) It is tempting to imagine Tucker as a mad auteur, exuberantly injecting as much lunacy into the movie as possible. But of course the mundane truth is that all of *Dance Hall Racket*'s bizarre touches are typical of Weiss productions made with the help of Connell, and the film demonstrates other common exploitation tendencies.

The lifeless visuals were more a consequence of budget than an intended style or the result of incompetence. As actor Henry Bederski recalled to Grey, on the set of *Glen or Glenda* William C. Thompson was so obsessed with getting the light just right and not wasting film that even Wood thought he was making scenes too static. And yet actress Evelyn Wood (no relation) remembered that Ed Wood's personal goal was "two takes or less."[472] In such circumstances, directors were doing well just to get their scenes captured on film even if, as Goldman put it, the camera was "stuck in cement."[473] Visual finesse was not a luxury they could afford. Therefore, *Dance Hall Racket* lacks any overall sense of geography and the camera does not pan from one room to another. Significant spatial transitions are always achieved with straight cuts and dissolves, possibly because complicated camera movements were too much trouble, or because there was literally no more than one set standing at any time. Given the cramped nature of Quality Studios, every set was probably constructed on the same spot. Similarly, even if *Dance Hall Racket*'s uninvolving plot and revolving cast of characters were meant in Bruce's script as an experiment, it would not have mattered to Weiss or to the audience. Because the genre's emphasis was on the spectacle of some forbidden subject, story coherence was the last priority of the exploitation filmmaker. Coherence could be detrimental to getting as much spectacle on screen as possible, and such films' intended viewers only needed to be distracted in the hope of forbidden thrills unfolding before them.

Along with exploitation qualities in *Dance Hall Racket* that seem merely strange today, there are noticeable flaws that were the result of its low budget and standards of quality (or Quality). The somnambulistic police inspector can be seen gazing into the camera in the opening shot, establishing out of the gate just how bad a movie *Dance Hall Racket* is going to be (but with the reporter talking during this part, the shot could not have been easily shortened). But even the opening credits that precede that first shot are lacking. There are two fonts in the credits, a sans-serif font (probably Futura) used for big, solo credits and a serif font (vaguely like Times New Roman) used in smaller form for list credits, and even here there are problems. Weiss' name appears in title case, while Bruce's appears all caps as LENNY BRUCE. Both are at least in the sans-serif font, whereas Tucker gets his director's credit large in the serif font. The three credits following one upon the other, the result

***Dance Hall Racket* breaks the fourth wall.**

is a sense of shoddiness, even if one does not consciously recognize the reason why. Likewise, the urgent orchestral cue that runs over the credits is repeated twice throughout the main body of the film, and once more near the end, not developed or expanded, but just needle-dropped repeatedly. Subtler is an audible echo on all dialogue that takes place in the dressing room set. Whether the occupants are dancers, Vincent, or others, dialogue always echoes here and is sometimes distracting. This means that probably all dialogue in *Dance Hall Racket* was recorded live and, as Tucker indicated was the case with *Robot Monster*, dialogue would not have been re-dubbed because of expense. One surprise in *Dance Hall Racket* is that the recognizable IATSE union "bug" can be seen in the credits. As Farrell told Grey, "I think [Tucker] and Ed [Wood] were both on the unions' 'don't work for' list."[474] But not every movie carrying the symbol was sanctioned; as Bri Murphy told Tom Weaver, title houses could sometimes be persuaded to slip the bug on the credits for a few hundred dollars.[475] (Farrell also noted that while he typically made "the magnificent sum of $300" for "three days of the five" it took to make Weiss productions, the pay was "a little over SAG minimum."[476])

It is in the gulf between the low intentions of exploitation makers and the assumptions of modern audiences—raised on the idea of directors as *auteurs*—where exploitation movies take on their bizarre and occasionally surrealistic quality. As Schaefer put it:

> The spectacle in exploitation films . . . works to produce confused or excited reactions in the spectator . . .. Delirium is perhaps the best way to characterize the

> experience of viewing exploitation . . .. Thus audiences had, and continue to have, a good deal of interpretive leeway as they approach these movies.[477]

Viewers naturally now scratch their heads and chuckle at exploitation. Since the widespread acceptance of television, Hollywood product increasingly followed a formula that, while having the virtue of professionalism, is homogenized and devoid of rough edges. Everything in more recent and mainstream films seems there intentionally, and accidental elements are only retained if they fit a smooth viewing experience. Therefore, the way that exploitation films pause for spectacle makes no sense to modern audiences. Every major character, and many a minor one, in *Dance Hall Racket* gets to have a passionate kissing scene, and in a time where Hollywood kisses were brief and not steamy, importing a lot of kissing into a film was a logical way of mildly crossing the line. This continually teased viewers with the hope that something hotter—forever just out of reach—was about to be seen. Similarly, modern viewers may not even notice that the shot of dancers which opens and closes the film begins in a close-up of the female partner's backside moving up and down rhythmically in her partner's arms. There is nothing dirty going on, just a dance, but for a couple of seconds the audience is teased by the suggestive, like another shot that begins on Honey Harlow's bust before pulling back. Audiences today would be unimpressed by double-meaning lines like "he almost passed right out on the stool," or "I met a casting director—he had his own couch," but they provided a small thrill of naughtiness in their time. Modern viewers cannot help but see these movies in a different context than when originally seen, but this leads to an unfortunate misinterpretation when competent exploitation filmmakers are assumed to have been incompetent artists.

With the idea of understanding Tucker's intentions in filmmaking in mind, what similarities could there be between Tucker's two best-known films? Beyond the most rudimentary qualities—black-and-white, cheap, crudely made, and short—little suggests they were by the same man, but those few similarities are worth exploring in detail. When Scalli and Vincent get Lois the scheming blond to cough up her withheld income, Vincent slices open the front of her dress in a move reminiscent of Ro-Man ripping the straps off Alice's dress. Like Ro-Man, Vincent is an irrational destroyer, infatuated with a woman while suffering an uneasy relationship with his superior. In contrast to Ro-Man, he enjoys the requiting of his affection, but stained with teasing dissatisfaction. Rose pretends she would like to be free of him, admits she cares for him, but does not want to end up stuck at the Emporium, past her prime and struggling. The congruence of Vincent's twin problems destroys him when Scalli has Rose doll up for his returning crime-lord pal Victor Pappas. Scalli tries to reason with Vincent that he cannot get the gold bullion they planned to take from Pappas if he kills either of them, but the jealous Vincent does not care. Like Ro-Man in the depths of infatuation with Alice, Vincent is blinded by jealous passion and is beyond being rational. He kills Scalli, drags Pappas out of the Emporium for a protracted revenge, but is gunned down by Edson the undercover cop.

In each case, the boss treated his underling's infatuation as insignificant, habitually thinking coolly and unable to understand the grunt's perspective, leading to mass destruction. It is the mistake of the competent misinterpreting and not recognizing the glaring weaknesses inherent in another. And while it should not be assumed that Tucker meant for this similarity of character and theme to connect the two films, the idea should not be discounted either. Although Tucker was not going for "art," he may have unconsciously had this theme rolling around in his mind, and contributed it to the script of each (despite the official writing credits). Perhaps Tucker had his own struggle with the green-eyed monster, or perhaps this was his perspective on what he had witnessed in others. Tucker was competent and unflappable, and he may have looked on with sympathetic disdain at the self-destruction of others who were blinded by emotion, or simply not good enough to get their jobs done. From this perspective, perhaps Tucker felt a degree of identification with Scalli and Great Guidance.

A minor, and more puzzling, similarity between *Robot Monster* and *Dance Hall Racket* is the motif of disfigurement. Roy's ear in the first film is shown with blood trailing out, and there is another temporarily damaged ear in the second film. The thief who attacks Rose, and is killed by Vincent, brought in diamonds to Scalli with them glued to the inner flap of a dog's ear. The ear theme does not seem to have much resonance, except that it may connect victims of jealous violence. Roy is savagely attacked by Ro-Man, and the sailor with the dog is killed. But the motif extends somewhat into a larger theme of bodily abnormality. Pappas, the aged ex-con who causes Vincent's fatal blast of rage, is a mute because of a severed tongue (making the damaging of the ears of others unnecessary). As will be discussed later, mutism and deformity will continue to run through Tucker's films.

With the similarities between Tucker's two best-known movies considered, there are two clear points in *Dance Hall Racket* in which Tucker was perhaps expressing himself. One truly Phil Tucker moment occurs courtesy of Vincent, as he reads a pulp science fiction magazine and enthuses to Scalli, "This is the most crazy story! It's about a space guy, comes down on a beam . . . ." More subtle, but more telling, is a quick subplot involving Icepick, a mellower bouncer with a comically obnoxious voice and a reserved manner, who asks Scalli's permission to leave organized crime to marry and work in a legitimate capacity. Scalli agrees, even when the insecure Icepick asks him a second time to make sure. Scalli hesitates as if he has changed his mind, but is fine with Icepick being done immediately, noting "I guess you're anxious to get things started with the . . . factory." Farrell drags out the line with the last word delayed, putting contempt into it, as if choosing the word "factory" is the least offensive way he can refer to the straight work that viscerally disgusts him. For Tucker, the hardnosed individualist, this was probably not far from his and Bruce's own perspective.

But even while pondering these elements, *Dance Hall Racket* very much exemplifies the exploitation film, could have been made by just about anyone, and there is little that distinguishes it from others. *Robot Monster* is, while recognizably part of its genre, an utterly unique example of it, and is not easily mistaken for another film. Even if viewers cannot remember the title, they do not forget the robot-gorilla movie. Consider further the whacked-out soliloquies of Ro-Man (just as unforgettable as the costume), and compare them to the average and pedestrian dialogue of *Dance Hall Racket.* There is also, despite the bizarre continuity gaffes in some copies, nothing in *Dance Hall Racket* that approaches the epic and apocalyptic level of surrealist lunacy found in *Robot Monster.* There is simply the "delirium of exploitation" to be found in *Dance Hall Racket,* created by the absurdity of character and acting, as well as the repetition of sequences.

Finally, consider that *Robot Monster* tightly follows a single group of characters while *Dance Hall Racket* meanders around a few main characters through a larger constellation of anonymous bit players. Each approach to storytelling fits the needs of its respective film, one creating sympathy for the fate of a tiny group of survivors and the other allowing the audience successive views of many sordid lives. And what that fact illustrates is that Tucker was a malleable director, serving the needs of the particular story. An artist is someone with a vision, and whatever material at hand will be pushed, pulled, bent, and shaped to fit that vision. If Stanley Kubrick or Federico Fellini had made both *Robot Monster* and *Dance Hall Racket,* they would be recognizably the work of the same man, through similarities in story structure, set design, casting, editing, music, and other factors. But Tucker, like a respectable Hollywood craftsman who got stuck with an impossibly tiny budget, filmed each project as straightforwardly as possible.

If Tucker had structured *Dance Hall Racket*'s story to center on a small group of characters trying to survive the sleazy world of the Emporium, if one of the characters had dream sequences or imagined the entire story, or if the film cut to unrelated

***Dance Hall Racket*'s resident drunk and undercover cop.**

footage from another movie, then there could be more tangible similarity between *Dance Hall Racket* and *Robot Monster.* But there are few such similarities, and this is because Tucker was by his own admission not an artist, and just wanted to work in movies. The delusional Wood also made terrible movies, but movies that repeatedly used pretentious and abstract narration, similar and repeated characters, and the constant fetishization of angora sweaters. Wood contained, in his own skewed way, something of the artist's obsession, even if he lacked much talent. His *Glen or Glenda,* despite being a Weiss production, seems nothing like *Dance Hall Racket* or any of the Umberto Scalli films. For that matter, it is difficult to pick out any stylistic quirks that differentiate the Scalli movies. Tucker, Connell, and Dertano were all essentially transparent directors.

Conrad Brooks told me that he worked on *Dance Hall Racket* uncredited for a day, and his comments reinforce the faceless quality of the direction:

> I was on the set when they were doing that picture with Lenny Bruce. I didn't see Phil. Lenny Bruce was directing the scene. You know [how] when you do those low-budget movies, Phil probably was directing the picture, and they were probably doing some pick-up shots and probably didn't need him there. I didn't even know Lenny Bruce at the time. I was just walking by the studio [to] drop in and see George Weiss. And I walked over and I see they were shooting a movie and I see Lenny giving some instructions to the actors, what they do and all that. Then I called Weiss and Weiss asked me if I wanted to go to work, and I said, "Yeah." So I was like an assistant to George Weiss [on] *Dance Hall Racket*. In other words I helped George out with the actors. The girls, I remember, were doing some readings and I was kind of coaching them. I actually worked one day on it, without any screen credit.[478]

In Brooks' recollection, Bruce actually directed some bits of the film, and Tucker was not around. Brooks is quick to point out that Tucker was probably elsewhere working on some part of the film, but his memory still reinforces the fact that Tucker was not the author of *Dance Hall Racket* just by virtue of being its director. He not only did not write the film, but was apparently fine with doling out bits of the directing work. Tucker did the best he could and wanted it to succeed, but it was not a personal matter beyond that. Furthermore, Weiss' decision to hire Brooks on the spot is a reminder that, as producer, he was financing the film and obviously calling the shots. There was no deference to Tucker on the matter of hiring Brooks; if Weiss had felt compelled to clear it with his director, then Brooks would have remembered seeing him around. Farrell's memories of his Weiss work reinforce the point, noting that "very little direction was given by the director on these pictures, and that mostly consisted of moves. If you were going to move, he would want you to move from A to B, and that would be set up so the camera could follow you."[479]

Photographer William Karl Thomas, Bruce's friend and collaborator from about 1956 on, stated in his memoir that, having later watched *Dance Hall Racket,* "I suspect[ed] there never was a script and the accusation I heard was true that it was largely a scam to get money from a backer who was primarily interested in scoring with girls in the cast."[480] But while the sentiment rings true and could be the reaction of many viewers, the movie could not have come together without a script, and that fact illustrates that it was not an accidental side effect of laziness. All movies are hard to make and every completion of even a terrible one is an amazing thing. There is a minimal story in *Dance Hall Racket* and events are referenced throughout with some consistency, especially the impending party for Scalli's recently released associate ("Victor Pappas, Public Enemy Number Three") that climaxes the film. And if the film's dialogue had not been written, the mostly amateurish cast would have come across even worse than they did. Within the constraints they were faced with, Tucker, Bruce, and Weiss went to a great deal of trouble on the film, and the little that Tucker recalled confirms the point:

> *This was, what, '55?*
>
> And then they sent me across the country to sell it, because I knew all the distributors. We ended up making around $2,000 on the picture, not enough money to do well.
>
> *What was the original budget on Dance Hall Racket?*
>
> I think the original budget was supposed to be around five [thousand]. But there was some re-shooting, additional scenes, and this and that and the other, and we

Vincent (Lenny Bruce) gets roughed up.

> made a deal with a film editor to cut it, and he wouldn't [work out], so Merle Connell cut it, who automatically charges a thousand dollars for cutting anything. It went up to around eight.

If Tucker's memory was accurate, *Dance Hall Racket*'s budget was literally *half* that of *Robot Monster*'s. As exploitation movies typically hovered around $10,000 and hit a ceiling of around $20,000 (a few are documented to have gone higher),[481] the money spent on *Dance Hall Racket* was average for what it was. What is more instructive about Tucker's memory of making *Dance Hall Racket* is what it indicates about his ambition. Tucker frequently did editing work from the sixties onward, but has no editing credits prior to the late fifties. It is therefore no coincidence that he hired an outside editor to cut the film, and then had to pay Connell a thousand dollars after the first editor fell through. However much knowledge he had imbibed in his early days with Weiss and Connell, he did not yet have the skill to edit a film. And from his impersonal and off-hand reference to Connell—the only time Tucker mentioned him—it is clear that he did not remember him as a close friend, despite their sharing credits on so many films. (And Connell apparently did no favors for Weiss, receiving his standard $1,000 fee for editing *Dance Hall Racket,* above and beyond the film's budget.) But Tucker had a good working knowledge of the state's-rights distributors (which is reinforced by his comments from the *Alaska News-Miner* on his distribution plans for *Space Jockey*), and he must have struggled for the best for *Dance Hall Racket,* going to the trouble of "re-shooting" and "additional scenes."

The film showed up in print ads by 1955, the earliest found being an August ad for a San Antonio drive-in, where a tall, narrow ad showcased the legs of a dancer (paralleling a statuesque Marilyn Monroe from another ad on the same page) and enjoined viewers to "buy a ticket and take a chance with Satan's sister."[482] A competing drive-in was showing *Tijuana After Midnight* ("In English," the ad noted), meaning that two Phil Tucker films were showing at the same time in the same market. (On the same page of movie ads, yet another drive-in was using Wood's non-risqué crime drama *Jail Bait* as the bottom end of a double feature, and Wyott Ordung's *Monster from the Ocean Floor* was showing at a fourth drive-in.) As Weiss was uncredited on *Tijuana After Midnight,* it is a logical guess that Tucker did the distribution work for both films (and perhaps for *Jail Bait* as well). By December, *Dance Hall Racket* was used in a Waco drive-in as the bonus feature for another vice film, Mack Enterprises' *Honky Tonk Girl,* a re-titled re-issue of 1937's *Hitchhike to Hell.*[483] Pat Carlyle, director of what was at that moment being called *Honky Tonk Girl,* had directed the exploitation classic *Marihuana* (1936) (aka *Marihuana, the Weed with Roots in Hell!*) and also co-directed with William C. Thompson *The Irish Gringo* (1935) (mentioned in Chapter Two). For *Dance Hall Racket* to get booted to the bottom end of a double bill in favor of a rehashed 1937 cheapie speaks volumes about its quality, and about how much faith distributors had in it. Most tellingly, it was again used as the B picture in Ada, Oklahoma in April 1956 when the A picture was none other than *Tijuana After Midnight.*[484] And in September in Burlington, North Carolina,

SAN ANTONIO LIGHT 31
Tuesday, August 30, 1955

SEE A SHOW TODAY
Movies are your Best Entertainment

OLMOS
"Land of the Pharoahs"

AZTEC ... Now!
HOLDEN · JONES
Love is a Many-Splendored Thing

TRAIL DRIVE IN THEATRE S.E. Military At Roosevelt Tonite
THIS IS IT! CAN YOU TAKE IT!
The Most Thrill Defying Program Ever Assembled
TERROR! HORROR! EXCITEMENT! MYSTERY!
THEM!
"THE MONSTER FROM THE OCEAN FLOOR"
IT CAME FROM OUTER SPACE
PLUS 4—YES 4 COLOR CARTOONS
Bring Your Own Sedatives, We Don't Have Enough to go Around

BROADWAY
LAUREL
John Wayne, Claire Trevor
"The High and The Mighty"
—Plus—
John Wayne, Geraldine Page
"HONDO"

★ TONITE ★
RIGSBY and SO. LOOP
DRIVE-IN THEATRES
REGULAR PRICES

SAN PEDRO
Doris DAY · James CAGNEY
LOVE ME OR LEAVE ME
LANA TURNER — PIER ANGELI
"FLAME AND THE FLESH"

THE DANCING LEGS OF A HONKYTONK HOSTESS!
BUY A TICKET and TAKE A CHANCE with SATAN'S SISTER

TEXAS HELD OVER!
YEAR'S MOST DARING FILM!
NOT AS A STRANGER

MAJESTIC • NOW!
TO HELL and BACK
AUDIE MURPHY

EL CAPITAN DRIVE-IN
TODAY and WEDNESDAY
ADULTS ONLY! BUCK NITE $1 CARLOAD
BURLESQUE SOUTH OF THE BORDER!
TIA JUANA after MIDNITE
RITA RAVEL
MISTY AYRES
See Drive-In Ad for Second Feature

JOSEPHINE
"A FINE FILM... A GEM!"
MARTY

ARTS
Now Showing!
Too Young for Love

WOODLAWN
JAMES STEWART
THE MAN FROM LARAMIE

HIGHLAND

FRANCIS

VARSITY DRIVE-IN THEATRE
TWO SUPER SHOCK SHOWS!
THE BIG COMBO
JAIL BAIT

CHARLES K. FELDMAN
the seven year itch
Directed by BILLY WILDER
MARILYN MONROE
TOM EWELL
CINEMASCOPE
BILLY WILDER and GEORGE AXELROD
MAJESTIC STARTS WEDNESDAY

DRIVE IN THEATRES
ALAMO
CAPITAN
FIESTA
FRED RD.
KELLY
LACKLAND
MISSION
PARKAIR
RIGSBY
ROXY
SAN PEDRO
SO. LOOP 13
TRAIL
VARSITY

LACKLAND
ONE OF THE SOUTHWEST'S FINEST

VISIT OUR SNACK BAR
JACK WEBB
Dragnet

NON-STOP LAUGH SENSATION!
Stop You're Killing Me

An ADULT PICTURE of EASY-MONEY GIRLS and HOODLUM BEASTS of the Underworld JUNGLE
See Dance Hall Racket

THIS IS GWEN... AND YOU CAN HAVE HER!
Good Time Girl
JEAN KENT

Dance Hall Racket was tacked on the end of a "late show double feature" in favor of something called *Rock and Roll Follies.*[485]

To judge by these ads, *Dance Hall Racket* fell very quickly from its initial debut as a main exploitation feature, and no wonder that Tucker remembered it netting little money in the end. And according to Goldman, the film's reception was mediocre, for reasons unclear largely shut out of Los Angeles theaters, with the exception of "a dirty dive down on Main Street" (reinforcing Tucker's use of the term "main street pictures"). *Dance Hall Racket* debuted "in this itchy joint about three one morning," with Bruce, Harlow, and a few others in attendance, "while all around them snored the bums and the winos"—a fitting omen for how the film would play across the state's-rights circuit. For Bruce's part, he left Strip City at about the time the movie was made in late 1954, and began working in nastier joints on the outskirts of the city.[486] Irritated by his surroundings into a torrent of uncensored creativity, he also delved increasingly into the drug abuse that eventually took his life in 1966 after achieving notoriety. In the final analysis, *Dance Hall Racket* best demonstrates that the jaw-dropping lunacy of Tucker's best-known film does not reappear in its next-of-kin. As Warren allows, it does not have "*Robot Monster*'s overweening pretension," and is "simple and direct."[487] Both films are awful but they are not of a kind, and the rest of Tucker's work as director is much more *Racket* than *Robot.*

As shoddy as *Dance Hall Racket* was, it was at least a narrative film with characters, dialogue, and a story. But Tucker's remaining work in exploitation was mostly in burlesque film, which was the canned, celluloid equivalent of live burlesque shows. A distant cousin of vice, and the last form of exploitation to evolve before it died out in the more permissive 1960s, burlesque often had baggy-pants comedian acts interspersed with striptease sequences in a variety show format. Burlesque could have never existed in the early years of exploitation, where sexual content was only barely permissible on some flimsy pretext of educational value. But social mores loosened just enough in the post-World War II era that burlesque entertainment, a stage attraction up to that point, could make a comeback on film. One significant factor in that change was the acceptability of cheesecake photos and paintings of pin-up girls, treasured by servicemen as a morale booster during the war.

But the burlesque movie did not make a clean break with the exploitation tradition of presenting itself in a marginally higher light than that of crude titillation. Just as most exploitation movies claimed to be exposés presenting shocking truths, it being unpleasant but necessary to reveal them, burlesque clutched at respectability by an appeal to historical value. Often billed as old-fashioned entertainment, a nostalgic and supposedly classy look at a vanished era of live entertainment,[488] they were extremely cheap and easy to make. According to an in-depth 1952 *Variety* piece on the burlesque movie trend, "One was made recently for $12,500" while the average was "around $15,000" with sometimes an additional $5,000 if "a name stripper is used." *Variety* noted, "Half a dozen people have turned them out; most have been produced by Merle Connell . . .. He, incidentally, is the father of James Connell, who'll head production for Candl Films." Candl was "incorporated in L.A. to make a minimum of six such pictures during its first year, and even more if the demand is there." Candl and its backer Bernard Lust were "trying to put on a systematic, business-like basis something which has existed in a sketchy, haphazard manner for the past six or seven years."[489] But however risqué burlesque continued to seem in the fifties, its shelf life was brief, and it would be dead by the early sixties. Russ Meyer's nudie-cutie comedies, magazines such as *Playboy*, and the overall sexual revolution of the era launched a tidal wave of far more explicit smut that today makes burlesque seem almost quaint.

Tucker made a number of these movies with the involvement of Weiss and Connell, and was of course not in it for art. And there was even less opportunity for a filmmaker's personal expression in burlesque film than in other species of exploitation. As Schaefer makes clear, there is very little sense of a distinct personality behind burlesque films because they were often made in the same city by the same people.[490] Whether directed by Tucker, Dertano, Merle Connell, James R. Connell, or Lillian Hunt, the end result was the same. But to go beyond Schaefer's point, even if these movies had not been assembled by the same small group of people, they would be just as faceless. Few directors could imprint much personality on a ten-minute reel of a stripper doing her act.

When Tucker spoke of his days of making "main street pictures," he went on in detail:

> Then I met a guy named George Weiss who made main street pictures.

Do you want to explain what main street pictures are?

Pictures that are intended to play on the main streets where the twenty-cent theaters were in those days, now I guess it's five bucks or whatever it was all throughout the country. And they had—[Very brief recording break.] I did what they called the *After Midnight* series, which was about twenty-five or thirty pictures: *Tijuana After Midnight, Hollywood After Midnight, Paris After Midnight—*

Did you work on these?

I directed and produced all of them.

I see, so what was your first one, do you remember exactly?

I have a hunch that *Tijuana After Midnight* was, but I couldn't be sure. They were remarkably similar, each to the other.

To take his words at face value, Tucker would have made all of these films within a short span of time that preceded the 1953 making of *Robot Monster.* But his credits prove otherwise, as his surviving burlesque films were all made from 1954 to 1955. *Paris After Midnight* was released in 1951, but Tucker did not direct it (Dertano did) and there is no burlesque film called *Hollywood After Midnight.* (It perhaps vanished into the same netherworld that contains Lon Chaney's lamented and lost silent horror *London After Midnight.*) *Tijuana After Midnight* was directed by Tucker, as was *Bagdad After Midnight.* Schaefer's exploitation bibliography also lists a short called *Cairo After Midnight* (1954) that was filmed at the same time as *Bagdad After Midnight* and of which Tucker was presumably director.[491]

Along with *Dream Follies,* Tucker is credited as director on a 1955 release called *Strips Around the World,* which its title and cast indicate is *Bagdad After Midnight* under a different title (and possibly re-edited). Tucker could have worked on the 1951 *Paris After Midnight* in some un-credited capacity, even as co-director, just as Brooks received no credit on *Dance Hall Racket. Paris After Midnight* fits the pre-*Robot Monster* era of Tucker's formative work for Weiss and, given Tucker's frequent confusion of the sequence of events in his life, this is not unlikely.

But while Tucker probably did make a respectable number of these films, his count of "twenty-five or thirty" must be exaggerated. The basic formula of the exploitation business was producing a film for virtually nothing and squeezing the maximum profit from it and, even accounting for some films being lost, Tucker could not have done so many jobs for hire as a burlesque director (he has no credits for producing burlesque). But in fairness, it may have really seemed to Tucker that he had made twenty-five or thirty films within the confines of the few that survived. Each burlesque performer was filmed in a segmented manner, dancing in front of a static camera and directly making fourth-wall eye contact, then disappearing behind the curtain. With each re-appearance the dancer would be less clothed than before, often near nude in the final number. As Tucker remembered:

> Basically, there was a burlesque theme and four or five burlesque girls. And you would use all the standard bits of [inaudible], plus they usually had their own standard scenes that they did. We would have them do the whole

> routine and then the parts that we liked, things that we thought worked, we would cull. We had not so much a shooting script as about a tenth-of-a-page, guiding outline. We would then set up two cameras and let them do their stuff, edit out the slates, and away it went.

The retreat of dancers behind the curtain allowed flexibility in assembling the final product. With minor editing, the illusion of a continuous performance was achieved and, with enough of them together, they instantly formed a feature-length film. Alternatively, discrete chunks of any performance were sometimes combined into further compilations, or released separately as shorts. Likewise, the hottest parts of any dance could be neatly removed for showings in cold areas. Burlesque was filmed in such an assembly line manner that it would be difficult for anyone to remember details of what could have made one movie marginally different from another, or which routines were cut into which feature. Tucker's note about using two cameras, and only printing the needed material, resonates with his cost-cutting ideas for the filming of *Robot Monster*, but requires some exploration, and carries a fascinating implication. As cheaply as they were made, some burlesque films were probably shot with one camera simply to use less film, although Schaefer states that the use of two cameras was also common.[492] As mentioned in Chapter 4, Sonney had dabbled in 3-D in the early 1950s, and Sid Pink blended new 3-D sequences into the 1947 Poverty Row melodrama *Linda Be Good* to create the 1953 *I Was a Burlesque Queen*.[493] While none of Tucker's credited burlesque films were shot in 3-D, with Sonney's connections to

Connell, Tucker could easily have been an un-credited assistant on Sonney's 3-D work. Tucker may have wished for *Robot Monster* to have been shot 3-D back when it was *Robot Killer,* but could not have afforded the added expense of using two cameras full of film, and then was able to use the format once Zimbalist was involved. Perhaps it was Zimbalist's idea, even with no previous 3-D track record, but Tucker could have sold his project to Zimbalist on the promise that he knew how to make 3-D work. It seems more and more likely in light of how Tucker remembered his burlesque films that he brought in the "Sonney cam" when it was time to make *Robot Monster,* or at least knew enough to duplicate it. According to the November 3, 1952 *Reporter,* Sonney's *A Virgin in Hollywood,* which contained 3-D sequences, was then "just finished."[494] If Tucker had worked on that particular 3-D project, he would have been ideally ready to use 3-D on his own film in March.

Of Tucker's three-or-so burlesque features, *Dream Follies* is unique because it was his other collaboration with Bruce, who played a pair of comedy roles onscreen. But most interestingly, all three films include a thin story as a framing device, whereas the variety show format of burlesque film often dispensed with story altogether. *Dream Follies* uses the story of a brow-beat husband who escapes to the dancing girls and doofus comedy of the local club; *Bagdad After Midnight* centers around a vaudeville entertainer visiting the Middle East; and *Tijuana After Midnight* is padded with the exploits of a pair of losers who scheme their way into a burlesque house south of the Rio Grande. According to Schaefer, such use of narrative in burlesque was uncommon, and he notably lists *Paris After Midnight* as one such exception.[495]

It seems that between Weiss, Connell, and perhaps Tucker, there was a preference for doing burlesque movies with a story.

As Tucker confirmed, burlesque advertisements were typical of exploitation, promising audiences the moon while the films themselves were always a letdown. In a different sense, they really did give paying customers the moon:

> *Was there any sex in these pictures?*
> There [were] always suggestions of sex and double entendre lines, [but] no way—because you had to be less sexy than a regular picture in order to get it cleared. But the lobbies were wild!
>
> *Tell me something about the lobbies, describe how they were.*
> All the stills were made so that you assumed the very next frame you would see in the picture was going to be something really bad. You would see somebody's hand reaching to tear somebody's dress. But of course in the picture what it is [is] that they were putting [back] a pen knife. But the right still, properly conceived and executed, gave the audience [the impression that they would see something] dirty. All the headlines and captions indicated "My God, you're only seeing a tenth of it—inside it's really wild!"

It is of course not literally true that burlesque movies were "less sexy than a regular picture," as the very subjects of exploitation films were things that Hollywood could not handle but, taken as an exaggeration, it is true enough. Blatant pornography

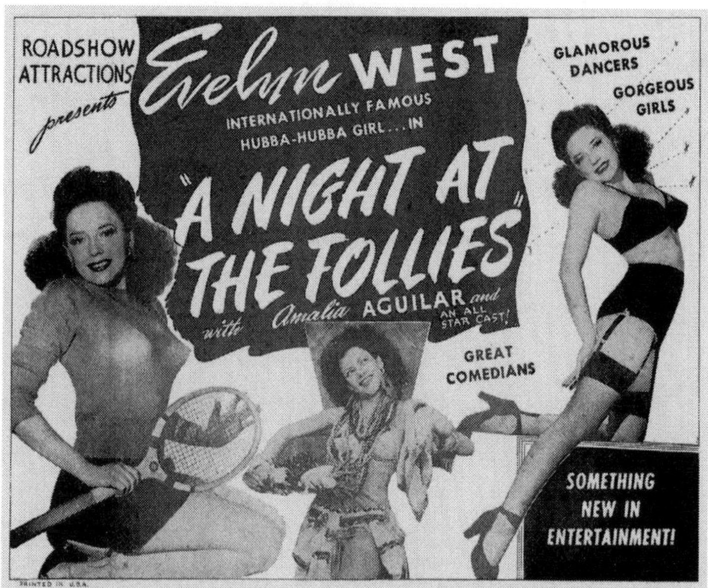

Merle Connell and Dan Sonney's 1947 *A Night at the Follies*, an early burlesque film.

was still unacceptable in the era of the burlesque film, and authorities would arrest those in possession of anonymously produced "stag movies." But burlesque dancers at least performed dances, had costume changes, and only became almost nude at the end of the acts in which they dominated the stage and the film frame. Therefore burlesque managed to be borderline acceptable with its thin degree of respect for the performers that did not completely depersonalize them into objects.

This ambiguity about whether or not burlesque was genuine smut ran through the center of the supposedly straitlaced fifties. The New Year's Eve, 1954, *Reporter* noted that stripper Tempest Storm had applied "for a $1,000,000 Body Policy from

Lloyds of London" at a publicity event "amid a pile of money bags."[496] Probably even better known, Lili St. Cyr (whose 1952 film debut, *Love Moods,* was a Sonney production) made the pages of *Variety* in January 1953, when producer Al Zugsmith cast her in something called *Space Girls,* along with the son of Charlie Chaplin.[497] The same issue reported that St. Cyr had also been hired by Sol Lesser to dance in a short, modern dance interpretation of *Carmen.* Alas, on January 13 *Variety* reported that St. Cyr was out of *Space Girls* (though Zugsmith had been able to add the son of Edward G. Robinson), while the next day they ran a half-page burlesque ad split between her and Zabouda, the "terrific Turkish torso twister."[498] *Variety* also reported multiple times on the film and nightclub career of Christine Jorgensen, the man who had undergone a sex change (and inspired Weiss to finance Wood's *Glen or Glenda*), with occasional barbs like "Christine is facing more changes."[499] The Hollywood establishment, in sum, took an interest in the entertainment fringe when there were attractions to be ogled or mocked, but were seldom friends to the little guys.

Meanwhile, less swanky locales than Los Angeles sometimes refused to allow burlesque. In August 1953, a Minneapolis theater had been raided by police who "confiscated the burlesque type film," according to *Variety,*[500] and the 1959 *Reporter* noted that two such films had been banned in Glasgow, Scotland where "the city constabulary would refuse to have burlesque films shown in this city."[501] The highlight of community response to burlesque may be the 1957 prosecution of two theater owners in Reading, Pennsylvania for showing *Paris After Midnight.* After the film was seized in March, a judge ultimately dismissed obscenity charges against the owners after a screening and the district attorney's motion for dismissal, but required that the owners pay court costs. The judge stated that while it would be difficult to prove *Paris After Midnight* legally obscene, "It was trash that shouldn't be shown in our theaters and I hope such things are never shown here again. It was suggestive, putrid, and had poor acting." Interestingly, some viewers wondered if the film had been edited since its seizure as "Scenes seemed to be cut and certain passages lacked continuity . . .."[502]

Dream Follies, again, was apparently made before *Dance Hall Racket,* in 1954, and there is reason to believe that both of Tucker's *After Midnight* features were made prior to *Dance Hall Racket* as well. On July 31, 1954, *The Billboard* reported:

> Harry Wald, operator of the World pix theater in St. Louis, returned last week from the Quality Pictures studio in Hollywood where he completed shooting a feature length burly pic, *Tijuana After Midnight,* produced in Mexico and Hollywood and starring Rita Ravell and Misty Ayers. Other talent includes an eight-girl line, several old-time favorites and a few acts entirely new to films. Assisting in the direction were Marle [sic] Connell and Phil Tucker.[503]

Tijuana After Midnight was made at a time that could have been within weeks, or even days, of *Dream Follies* and given *Bagdad After Midnight*'s release year of 1954, all three could have been filmed in close succession. They were all likely made prior to *Dance Hall Racket,* no doubt giving Weiss confidence that between having made them and *Robot Monster,* Tucker could handle the relatively ambitious *Dance Hall Racket.* But what the *Billboard* report makes clearer than anything else is how utterly meaningless directorial credits are on such films. Tucker, credited as director on *Tijuana After Midnight* is described in this account as only "assisting in the direction," and even there in a capacity divided between he and Connell. Little wonder then that Brooks remembered Bruce directing parts of *Dance Hall Racket;* un-credited work was standard practice in exploitation. From this write-up it would seem that Harry Wald of St. Louis had directed the film and, so far as Connell was concerned that would have been fine so long as the money came through. (Raised in the Bronx, Wald got into the local burlesque theater business, traveled, and finally owned St. Louis theaters and distributed films in the Midwest.[504]) Tucker may have worked harder on securing the funding and distribution of the film whose main backer was a theater owner in his home town than he ever did on the film itself.

To judge by his filmography, Tucker left this era with one last film, more or less exploitation, not burlesque and almost vice, yet something stranger and harder to define. *Broadway Jungle* (1955) received no mention in *The Golden Turkey Awards,* Schaefer does not list it in his exploitation bibliography, and Tucker did not mention it when interviewed. It was in fact apparently lost for many years until it was released on VHS in the nineties and more recently on DVD-R.[505] Extremely obscure even to the present, it is an awful film but deserves the attention of anyone who wishes to understand Tucker. As the few who have commented on it all point out, its story and characters carry fascinating autobiographical overtones. On that point, note first that the film was originally called *Hollywood Jungle*, and it has nothing to do with the stage world of Broadway. Tucker's *Jungle* begins with a shot of a street sign for Hollywood Boulevard, from which the camera pans to the right and then jarringly cuts. The music abruptly changes and onscreen appears an obviously unrelated card for the title *Broadway Jungle*. Then the real world footage and initial musical score resumes, showing handheld shots of various studio locations around sunny Hollywood beneath the credits. And if it is not already obvious enough, the film's unbilled narrator uses—and closes the film with—the phrase "Hollywood jungle."

It is bitterly ironic that Tucker's *Hollywood Jungle* only survives under an East Coast distributor's re-title, and also appropriate. The film is a microcosm of Tucker's mangled early career, arguably a fictionalization of his own perspective on the movie business. The film's minimalist story concerns a low-rent movie director, Fletcher Mathering, trying to assemble cast and crew for a movie, while dodging his landlord and arranging financing from local mobster Georgie Boy Gomez, who wants to date the film's leading lady, Lena Little. Behind the scenes, an even rougher gangland character (never named but sometimes called "Boss") wants to rub out both Mathering and his backer because of money owed. Eventually, after a comically bad audition sequence and twenty padded minutes of characters wandering the streets of L.A., cast and crew assemble in a rancid little (Quality?) studio where Mathering ruins a rehearsal with his pointless and baffling directions. Running an errand later, Little is almost killed by Boss, while Mathering indifferently continues his existence of scamming others for money. In the film's unexpected closing sequence, a previously unseen black janitor enters Mathering's office, puts down his mop and does a mocking imitation of a director on set, repeating Mathering's frequently spoken favorite phrase, "Quiet on the set." The narrator warns of the "slimy animals that prey on you, and me, and anyone else that dares to trespass on the byways in the Hollywood jungle," and the film closes with a jittery shot of a busy Hollywood street (probably captured in a moving car).

The question that fascinates anyone who makes it through to the end of *Broadway Jungle* with some knowledge of its writer-director is whether or not it is autobiography. Fletcher Mathering—scheming, amoral, untalented but filled with artistic pretensions—is not much like Tucker, who admitted his abilities were questionable and could not have been any clearer that he did not see himself as an artist. But Mathering frequently speaks in a pompous manner and makes bold pronouncements about the greatness of his movie, while all the while he seems extremely lazy, an even greater divergence between him and the energetic Tucker. There is no sense that Mathering loves film or show business, and he comes across as an all-around incompetent. After hiring an assistant director he has to ask her how to begin the production, and later has to be reminded that actors have to rehearse. Mathering does not have the first clue how movies are made, still sees himself as a director, and yet is more than slightly attached to money. He dodges the rent, lets others get stuck with his bar tab, and is eager to ply money from Georgie Boy. Mathering is the type of person who wants the acclaim of an artist but lacks the talent and work ethic to earn it, while he also craves the comfort of money but is unwilling to earn that either.

There can be no serious doubt that the bitter, acerbic tone of the film was influenced by Tucker's inability to get off the bottom of the Hollywood fringe, and the film therefore contains some essence of his life. But since Mathering's character diverges from Tucker's, the logical question is if Mathering is either a composite portrait of the lazy wannabe type or a satire on a specific person. At least one individual in Tucker's orbit was a serious candidate for such treatment. In addition to his delusions of artistic ability, Ed Wood schemed money out of backers with equal charm and lack of concern for return on investment, most famously so on *Plan 9 from Outer Space.*[506] And as Ronnie Ashcroft recalled to Grey, Wood lost time and budget with friends at a nightspot when he was supposed to be filming *Night of the Ghouls* in the late fifties.[507] But Wood's mismanagement of the Western *The Outlaw Marshal* (*The Lawless Rider*) was already history in the mid-fifties, and Wood likely displayed the same behavior multiple times. Mathering is arguably a much more realistic depiction of Wood than the sanitized one created by Tim Burton.

The memories of Farrell, Fellman, and Kathy Wood of the two directors as "friendly enemies" or worse make it only more possible that Mathering was an attack on Wood. Tucker's dislike of him may have gone beyond the old truism that two of the same trade do not agree, and into the fact that Wood had abruptly swooped into the Weiss circle when he made *Glen or Glenda.* Wood did not participate in the *After Midnight* series as Tucker did, and he was more consistent in his repetition of the same themes and motifs. Tucker may have resented Wood as an interloper who had not paid his dues with Weiss, and Wood's obnoxious self-confidence in recruiting backers was perhaps another sore point. Finally, Wood was known to tell outlandish stories about his Marine Corps days (such as his claim that he stormed a beach wearing women's underwear under his uniform), while Tucker was, at least to his son, very taciturn about his time in the war.

It is therefore fascinating that an unbilled Weiss appears onscreen in *Broadway Jungle*, at around 43 minutes into the film, when Mathering with cast and crew arrives at the studio for rehearsals. Without dialogue and onscreen only briefly, Weiss can be seen pantomiming confusion with other crew members while Mathering gives orders. Although Weiss decades later

Norman Wright as Fletcher Mathering.

spoke with affection for the deceased Wood, he also recounted that *Glen or Glenda* underperformed and it seems that he did not often re-team with Wood. Weiss, who also did a silent cameo in *Glen or Glenda,* might not have minded joining Tucker in poking fun at Wood. Finally, there is a notable aside snuck into the dialogue, in a near-end scene where Mathering sits drinking alone when an assistant rushes in and demands to know why he is lounging. Mathering replies, "What does it look like I'm doing, taking a Turkish bath?" Though Wood was heterosexual, his open transvestitism was known in the movie fringe, and the "Turkish bath" line could have been a swipe at him.[508]

What is certain is that Tucker must have poured his frustration into *Broadway Jungle.* In relation to his career, it is almost as weirdly fascinating as the parallel "thematic autobiography," *Glen or Glenda,* is to Wood's life. The film world is depicted as hopelessly venal, false, and sleazy, the audience denied even an idealistically doomed artist to care about. With no exception, the characters exploit one another, and even the victimized Lena Little is morally compromised by her willingness to sell herself to a backer. One senses that if the minor characters were fleshed out, they too would be corrupt. When Mathering has a casting call, all of the applicants are absurd grotesques: a vaguely European airhead blonde with a bad accent, a flirtatious brunette pushing her charms with zero subtlety, a hick from Tennessee, and a pushy old bat. Ostensibly classier is supposed leading man of stage and screen John Humberstone, who describes with perfect seriousness the starring roles he has performed in theater and for major studios. Tucker could not have possibly expected the audience to believe that someone with those credits would be trying to get into Mathering's film (*Death Takes a Spree*), and so Humberstone is just a subtler weirdo. When he reacts in outrage that Mathering will not even pay him scale, the fleabag auteur informs him that he will be working for "Art, Mr. Humberstone, art." Tucker was there putting into fiction the view of film as art that he had expressed during the production of *Space Jockey*. Perhaps he admired great films, but he unquestionably knew that the intangible mantle of art was a convenient cloak for hacks and flakes. And the most fascinating point is that Mathering is such a joke that a black janitor working within the white world of the mid-fifties ridicules him.

But although Tucker must have expressed himself in this film, that fact leads to further complications. *Broadway Jungle* is an unbelievably cheap and shoddy film, about one notch above home movie footage, and makes *Dance Hall Racket* seem like an RKO film noir in comparison. Whatever the very low budget of *Broadway Jungle* was, it looks like it must have been in the neighborhood of half of what was already a ludicrously low budget on *Dance Hall Racket.* All exploitation films lived and died on their advertising, but the gulf between promise and product is so wide in *Broadway Jungle* that distributors may have balked at picking it up, and perhaps only did so when it was tossed into a package as added value. (Schaefer does not list it in his extensive exploitation bibliography.) And although Weiss appears briefly onscreen, his name is not on the credits and neither is Connell's (and Tucker is the only producer listed in the credits). Given *Dance Hall Racket*'s disappointing performance, it is difficult to believe that anyone gave *Broadway Jungle* any serious financing, but the more puzzling idea is that Tucker apparently spent a few thousand dollars to vent his frustrations. This goes back to the popular urban legend of Tucker as a self-destructive flake, not so far gone as suicide but far enough to make a movie that could not succeed.

But while *Broadway Jungle* is so cheap that it begs the question of why it was made, that question does not hang on the notion that Tucker was expressing himself. He had a plausible, practical reason for making the film. Tucker often did editing and other post-production work in later years, and had great facility for operating complicated editing equipment. But Tucker had no editing credits until the 1957 burlesque film *Kiss Me Baby* (directed by Lillian Hunt, and featuring Lili St. Cyr), and his post-production work did not begin until the mid-sixties.

The character known as Boss.

His work before that film was entirely credited as director, producer, or writer. This is significant, as is the fact that he hired Connell to edit *Dance Hall Racket* for $1,000. In other words, Tucker could not have edited *Dance Hall Racket* himself in 1954 or '55. If he could have, he would have done the job himself and saved Weiss money on post-production. But by 1957, he had learned to edit well enough that he got a credit for it. Where did he pick up the experience?

Broadway Jungle is the missing link in Tucker's gaining experience as a competent editor, experience that enabled him to handle post-production across the board. Credited on the film is Jack Housch, an editor with no other credits in any capacity. This is uncommon for someone with editing skills; fly-by-night filmmakers may have one credit for acting, producing, or writing a script, but editing is a labor-intensive ability that cannot be winged. Also noteworthy is the fact that Jack Housch shared his last name with George Housch, one of the listed officers of "the newly formed American Artists Film Corp." According to the May 26, 1953 *Reporter*, American Artists had purchased the script *Return from Mars*, initiating the project that eventually became *Space Jockey*. But as George Housch was uncredited on anything, it seems clear that, for whatever reason, Tucker was drawn to using the name Housch when creating imaginary collaborators.[509]

As Tucker was already crediting himself on the film as writer, producer, and director, it would be logical to disguise his own editing under a pseudonym. (Artificially swelling a crew list with fictitious workers was a common practice on cheap productions; Coleman Francis and Jerry Warren were two flagrant practitioners.) The very nature of the film's editing lends credence to this theory. The movie's only reviewer on the IMDb (as of this writing—and after a decade since being posted) noted the use of "weird, primitive lap dissolves" in the film, and the editing is frequently strange indeed. On several occasions, transitions occur with a variety of black shapes filling up the screen, and they go far beyond the common pattern of the picture disappearing in a contracting circle. There are such patterns as a swirling vortex, finger-like protrusions intersecting with one another, and unfolding triangle shapes, as well as the use of a good old-fashioned, straight horizontal wipe. There are also traditional edits as the film goes along, with simple fades in and out with black, a dissolve, cutaway shots in the middle of dialogue, and some contrasting back-and-forth between Boss attacking Lena while Mathering sits nursing a drink.

This patchwork of editing techniques demonstrates not incompetence or sloppiness, but that Tucker was teaching himself how to edit. Connell's editing on *Dance Hall Racket* was simple and practical, but Tucker took the opportunity to try every editing trick he knew of on *Broadway Jungle*. Practical as he was, he knew that he needed more options than trying to create entire movies from scratch with no guarantee that they would pay off. By spending (after perhaps raising from who knows where) a little money for an extremely cheap movie that he could completely control, he was finally getting the experience to make himself valuable to others. If the movie bombed, he was not out much because he had already achieved what he had set out to do; the movie's budget was really the cost of his "tuition." Along the way he got to channel his Hollywood experiences; since the eventual fate of the movie did not matter, he might as well have fun with it.

And though *Broadway Jungle* plays as a forgotten exercise in amateur filmmaking that served its maker's purpose long ago, close examination reveals many details fascinating in themselves that connect it to Tucker's other films. Once again, the themes of competence and employment figure largely in a Tucker movie, as Mathering is the most incompetent of all his protagonists. Georgie Boy shows him contempt and does not care about the movie he is funding, just his proximity to the star. As a boss, Mathering is even worse with his reliance on his assistant director, disastrous attempts at directing, and indifference to Lena's suffering. Also incompetent is the assassin Bruno, sent by Boss to kill Georgie Boy but only wounding him. When Bruno returns and lies, Boss has him taken away and then—wanting to get the job done right—proceeds to take Bruno's job himself.

Fascinatingly, Bruno is another mute, along with the old crime lord from *Dance Hall Racket.* Tucker's fascination with competence is easy to draw out of his very self-made life, while the repeated linkage of quiet with doom is more puzzling. Chatterboxes like Mathering would seem to be an annoyance to a tough stoic like himself, and his nemesis Wood was known for his outgoing personality. But in another linkage to this theme, the talkative Johnny in *Robot Monster* speaks too much to the enemy and abruptly covers his mouth. Johnny dooms his family, though only in a dream, the ex-con in *Dance Hall Racket* seems to survive, and Bruno is presumably murdered. Perhaps Tucker was expressing a belief that keeping quiet and staying in the corner will not save anyone from life's troubles, and it is better to aggressively get in the thick of things. In any case, one more familiar motif was snuck into *Broadway Jungle.* When Boss attacks Lena in the studio near the end, he grabs her blouse and removes a strap before she escapes.

In the anti-perfect fashion of Tucker's films as director, the very form of *Broadway Jungle* goes beyond its destitute feel by adding layers of accidental surrealism. There has likely never been a more strangely botched soundtrack; music comes and goes at arbitrary moments, voices are sometimes ludicrously dubbed, and music blares overdramatically during a love scene. Most amazingly, dull outdoor scenes are scored with the sound effect of relentless nearby honking, the same three honking patterns repeat over and over, like a repeated musical theme. The cars onscreen move leisurely, are un-crowded, and seem to have nothing to be impatient about. No one ever sees these angry phantom cars of the soundtrack realm; they remain forever on the periphery of vision, commenting like a screaming, schizophrenic Greek chorus. The soundtrack even sneaks in one use of the endlessly re-used main theme from *Dance Hall Racket,* here not a repeated motif but only one scrap of a mismatched sonic quilt.

In visual terms, *Broadway Jungle* is also Tucker's most chaotic film. His previous exploitation work had the plain minimalism common to conditions of little film and no time, while *Broadway Jungle* looks comparatively unhinged. There is the familiar Merle Connell-esque motif of Venetian blind lighting on cheap set walls, but much of the movie was filmed on location, following characters around in documentary fashion through some of L.A.'s grimier areas. At least one interior takes place in an actual home, and the exterior of a real boarding house is featured (Tucker might have stayed in this establishment on a few occasions). There are also glimpses of a hospital, various businesses, and a theater showing some exploitation titles ("Spicy Adult Films"). As all of these elements attest, this is a movie filled with a sense of that old favorite of film scholars, voyeurism. These boring padded scenes are fascinating if watched as a window into Tucker's real world.

The easiest to miss of all of *Broadway Jungle*'s strange points is the fact that at least one legitimate actress appears under a pseudonym. The first female credited in the cast is June Gilmore, who had no other credits, and would have been the actress to play Lena Little. But a good look at Gilmore will strike a familiar chord in anyone who remembers Roger Corman's *The Undead* and *Attack of the Crab Monsters* (both 1957), the best-remembered roles of Pamela Duncan. It is Duncan who plays Lena, and neither her presence in the movie or her using another name is unusual. According to Weaver, Duncan did many low-budget film and TV parts (along with Army training films) before leaving the business in the mid-sixties[510] and, for whatever amount Tucker managed, she would have taken his low-paying gig. That she went under another name makes sense; *Broadway Jungle* would not have enhanced her résumé, and she would not have wanted her name on a film destined for raunchy dives.

Also listed in the opening credits is Eve Miller, an actress who briefly hit the mainstream from around 1952 to '53, as exemplified by her lead role opposite Kirk Douglas in *The Big*

Trees. She had a troubled personal life, including a July 1955 suicide attempt when she stabbed herself after her boyfriend hesitated to marry her. At around the same time, her brief fame dried up and her credits show an immediate nosedive from studio films to guest parts on television. Whether this was a precondition or a consequence of her suicide attempt is not clear. Her career ended after 1961, and she eventually killed herself in 1973. But although her career quickly declined, it is hard to believe that she fell so far that she appeared somewhere down the cast list in *Broadway Jungle,* even if she could be tenuously connected to Tucker by way of Norman Dawn's *Arctic Fury* (1949). She cannot be spotted onscreen and, if Tucker had been able to use her, he would have given her the Lena role or written her a bigger one. So perhaps some other Eve Miller appeared in the cast, or perhaps the use of her name was similar to that of mysterious editor Jack Housch. Her mid-1955 suicide attempt was big news at the time, and Tucker could have thrown her name on the credits because viewers would recognize it. (They might have guffawed and thought she had really fallen far, or perhaps it was just a sick joke to suggest that exploitation was where she was headed.) Tucker would not likely have been sued given how few people would see the picture, and any female onscreen other than Duncan/Gilmore could have also had the name Eve Miller. Tucker might have even related to Miller's failed suicide attempt, and saw it as another attempt at getting publicity out of unsuccessful self-destruction. And Miller was not unlike Lena, as *Broadway Jungle*'s unidentified narrator introduces her:

> Meet Lena Little. She was once a star. Now, still trying.

Like so much in the film, the meaning is clear but the form is puzzling; the grammar here is as unconventional as any of the editing. It makes sense, more or less, to have "once" been a star and be "still trying," although it just sounds bad.

Two others in the cast had notable connections. Bruno Metsa played Bruno, oddly enough, and Norman Wright played Mathering, both of them with one other exploitation film to their credits. Metsa appeared in the Wood-scripted girl-delinquent film *The Violent Years* (1956), and even got to speak on-screen, but had no other film credits. He apparently found the movie world unrewarding and was a few years later showing up in theater. In 1957-58 he was "technical assistant" on Norman Corwin's *The Rivalry,*[511] and in 1959 was "assistant stage manager and driver" for touring actress Katharine Cornell.[512] He comes across as well as anyone in *Broadway Jungle,* and his rapidly darting eyes make for an interesting performance. The raccoon-eyed and goateed Wright had a lengthier career than Metsa, though it was sporadic. He appeared in Connell's *The Flesh Merchant* (1956), in which his character is not a buffoon and he is a far more sinister beatnik. But Wright was not the only element shared between the two films. Plainly visible in many shots, a framed picture of a horse on Mathering's office wall can also be seen as a decoration in *The Flesh Merchant.* One of many others in Connell's film, it stands out alone on the bare walls of the *Broadway Jungle* set, its view of the front end of its subject perhaps intended as the completion of that which Mathering only provides the back end.

But the most surprising element of all is how *Broadway Jungle* tries and succeeds in being funny. If stripped of the padding

Pamela Duncan (billed as June Gilmore) with Norman Wright.

that takes up a third of the running time, it would make a good, albeit weird, comedy. Many of the actors in small parts are convincing and play up the absurdity of their roles very well. And as Mathering, Wright is wonderfully full of himself, pompous, false, and always getting caught in his own buffoonery, such as a scene that begins with him cutting out paper dolls. In the botched rehearsal scene, Tucker used his own deficiencies as a strength, wringing humor out of minimalist repetition as Mathering explains over and over to the actor that the scene is about him "making *love*" to his co-star. Each take lasts about a nano-second before Mathering interrupts with over-dramatic dismay. Likewise, the many repetitions of the line "quiet on the set" are funny because of their absurd context (the set is only un-quiet when Mathering bellows out directions). Within this sequence, a crewmember saunters through to the annoyance of the director:

MATHERING

Just a moment. Who are you?

CREWMEMBER

I'm a working man. What are *you*?

MATHERING

Uh, make a note. No more working men on my pictures.

For all his shortcomings as a writer, Tucker managed to sneak in more such effective dialogue, sometimes with the fun, off-kilter quality of the best bad movies. Describing the ineffectual assassin, the narrator intones: "Meet Bruno. Mute. Can't talk. But he can hear. And kill." One could almost believe that Coleman Francis watched *Broadway Jungle* just before recording the narration for *The Beast of Yucca Flats.*

When Georgie Boy arrives to discuss financing with Mathering, he cagily grills him on how well he knows Lena. Twisting his first two fingers together, Mathering assures him, "Lena and I are just like that." Georgie Boy replies, "Which one are you?"[513] This brief implication of the naughty finger is borderline witty, far funnier than *Dance Hall Racket*'s sledgehammer attempts at innuendo, all the more so because it relates to Mathering's character. Tucker also snuck in a subtle in-joke, when an aged floozy auditions for Mathering. In summing up her career she says, "I've done everything from *The Ten Commandments* **to** *The Ten Commandments.* I have broken all twenty of them." One of Wright's few other roles was as the

Assyrian ambassador in Cecil B. DeMille's 1956 remake of *The Ten Commandments.* Its studio portions filming in 1955, it is no coincidence that Tucker made this reference.

With its combination of a downbeat look at the ugly underbelly of Hollywood, bizarre sonic and visual qualities, and its incongruous and weird sense of humor, *Broadway Jungle* almost feels like it was intended as an absurdist stunt. Next to *Robot Monster,* it is Tucker's most delirious and strange offering, and almost makes one believe for a spell that the surrealism of both movies is related, an extension not just of low budgets but of a creator's personality. It is not a good movie but it is a fascinating document of Tucker's life and ambition and, given the five-year gulf between it and his *The Cape Canaveral Monsters,* it echoes with a sense of reality.

At some point in 1955 Tucker returned to the scene of his greatest failure, Fairbanks, Alaska. Why he went, how long he remained, and how well he was received after the failure of *Space Jockey* are a mystery, but the *Fairbanks Daily News-Miner* made clear what he had been up to in the Wednesday, May 11, issue:

> **Taken to Hospital**
>
> Phillip Tucker was brought to St. Joseph's hospital Monday afternoon by city ambulance after he was found ill in his room at the Gilcher rooms, 523 Third avenue. He was suffering from the effects of an overdose of sleeping medicine. Tucker has recovered from the effects of the medicine.[514]

Nearly a year-and-a-half after the December 1953 suicide attempt in Los Angeles, supposedly caused by the aftermath of *Robot Monster*, Tucker again overdosed on sleeping pills in a hotel room, was hospitalized, and had the affair written up in the local press. On the assumption that he was actually trying to kill himself with pills, the odds are extremely low that he could try and fail twice. Just how non-existent then were his Hollywood prospects that he went back to the town where he made *Space Jockey*? Lest there be any more doubt about his motivations, the *News-Miner* printed the following classified ad the Saturday after the suicide attempt, May 14:

Situations Wanted

> WRITING—Producing, directing, programming announcing, acting, either radio or TV or any line of entertainment. Write Phil Tucker, P.O. Box 662, Fairbanks.[515]

Tucker may have gotten "some good publicity" out of such stunts, as Brooks surmised, and he may have sometimes felt "depressed" and needing "attention," as he later explained. But there is one point that is absolutely clear: he was not suicidal.

From the mid-fifties production of his burlesque movies and the nearly forgotten *Broadway Jungle,* Tucker's life entered a mysterious phase, where few references to him have survived. Like a space probe rounding the dark side of the moon to return and leave radio silence behind, he returned full force to science fiction film with *The Cape Canaveral Monsters* in 1960. But in the meantime his two best-known *Robot Monster* collaborators were busy.

10

"I like 'em stupid."

From the time of *Robot Monster*'s release, Al Zimbalist maintained a relentless pace that lasted into the next decade. The films he produced were mostly monster or jungle adventures, but two common denominators were almost always present: extreme cheapness and abundant stock footage. Through these films, producer Zimbalist made less of a personal impression than Phil Tucker did in his mostly faceless directing work. But the degree to which these films dovetail with *Robot Monster* is essential to understanding it. Although Zimbalist had no artistic sense, he was responsible for much of the shape of the final film. If the question can ever be resolved of who authored its strange and surreal dream world, it must account for Zimbalist's career. Furthermore, what does it indicate about his treatment of collaborators? Does it corroborate Tucker's claims of being swindled?

Two weeks almost to the day before the *Robot Monster* production was deployed, the March 6, 1953 *Hollywood Reporter* reviewed Zimbalist's completed *Miss Robinson Crusoe,* finding it "a fine example of what can be achieved at low cost when every penny is made to count."[516] The anonymous reviewer praised the acting of Amanda Blake and George Nader, the use of jungle flora and fauna, Elmer Bernstein's "imaginative" score, and noted the "excellent" color cinematography, that "occasionally even [gives] a 3-dimensional effect." The *Reporter*'s reviewer in, fact, really found nothing to dislike about the film, giving Tucker one more reason to believe he was in good hands. But fittingly, when *Harrison's Reports* reviewed *Miss* ***Robin*** *Crusoe*—its final released title—on October 31, the view expressed was almost as far opposite of the *Reporter*'s as Tucker's career was now opposite that happier month of March. Calling the film's color visuals "so-so" and the editing "poor," this unknown reviewer described it as a "mildly interesting melodrama" that "has been produced without much skill or imagination."[517] And unmentioned by the *Reporter*, the *Harrison's* review noted "library shots of different animals" in the film. Whether Zimbalist was important enough yet to dictate that aspect of the film or he was just schooling in the art of stock footage saturation, the pattern predated *Robot Monster* at least as far as this production.

Al Zimbalist promoted *Miss Robin Crusoe* with a short-lived comic strip.

Zimbalist's twin penchants for exploiting name confusion and juggling a number of projects were on display in the aftermath of *Robot Monster*. The March 31 *Reporter* noted that Nader was already cast in Zimbalist's *Miss Robin Hood*,[518] the project announced in January as rolling in February with Maurice Geraghty and Shamrock Productions. Zimbalist was now making the film solo in color and, hot off the heels of *Robot Monster*, in 3-D. But of greater interest was the May 5 *Reporter*'s news that MGM's Sam Zimbalist was producing an already scripted, upcoming Robinson Crusoe film with Stewart Granger.[519] The June 22 issue noted that Sam was moving on to *Robinson Crusoe* and *Beau Brummel* for MGM, now that the Clark Gable adventure *Mogambo* was edited.[520] Al must have known about this script, which would have been in the studio pipeline for some time, and made his own version accordingly. But in a complication that likely nettled him, a Mexican version of *Robinson Crusoe* (directed by Luis Buñuel) was being shopped around for distribution in early July and, as noted in the July 6 *Reporter*, producer Henry Ehrlich refused to back down from using the public domain title for his film.[521] Though faced with taking his own medicine, Al was probably not that put out; his version had not long before been picked up by Twentieth Century-Fox. Finally, the next day's *Reporter* noted that Lippert was cashing in with yet another version, this one a reissue of 1932's *Mr. Robinson Crusoe* with Douglas Fairbanks in his last starring role.[522]

Along the way, Zimbalist stayed visible in the press with a bevy of proposed projects. The *Reporter* noted on April 15 that he wanted "to smoke out Mickey Rooney to star and co-direct

Baby Face Nelson in 3-D,"[523] and then on June 2 brought the news that Zimbalist's 3-D process, Tru-Stereo, was purchased for $5,000 plus a profit percentage by producer Robert Stillman for his *The Americano.*[524] Then on June 23, Zimbalist's most reliable collaborator made the pages of the *Reporter* with the note that Zimbalist "has bought a Guy Reed Ritchie original, *King Dinosaur,* which will be placed on the independent producer's schedule for fall."[525] Meanwhile, Zimbalist had the following line-up already planned: "*Pirate Women, Conquest of the Moon,* and *Baby Face Nelson.*" And Eugene Frenke, director of *Miss Robin Crusoe,* was also getting into the act. The July 1 *Reporter* stated that he would soon be directing *Women of Venus,* "a 3-D science fiction story for United Artists release" with the use of Tru-Stereo.[526]

But through this maelstrom, Zimbalist's much-publicized career finally found a recognizable focus. July 17's *Reporter* listed an item for Zimbalist that was the most fanciful yet, noting a deal with Jules Weill of Explorers Pictures Corporation "for production of three features to be partly photographed in Africa in 3-D."[527] The first, *African Lost World,* got another mention on August 7, when it was noted that Zimbalist was working on it and another feature, *Cat-Women of the Moon.*[528] No mention was made of Mr. Weill and his company, but Zimbalist had been "in New York for financing" and was now back to "his Samuel Goldwyn offices," preparing for a "late September" start on *Cat-Women of the Moon,* which would be in "Tru-Stereo 3-D." The August 17 Reporter said that he was soon in New York "to close final bank details for financing of **Catwomen on** *the Moon,*" with Savini "associated with him in the production," and *Robot*

Monster recently "bought by the RKO circuit."[529] No mention was made of when the ambitious *African Lost World* was supposed to begin, nor did it reappear on September 4, when the *Reporter* announced a "joint production agreement between Astor Pictures and Al Zimbalist," with *Cat* ***Woman on*** *the Moon* "starting about September 15."[530] As mentioned in Chapter 6, the July 28 *Reporter* stated that Astor had obtained an "option" on *Cat Woman/Women* when they arranged *Robot Monster*'s distribution. That fact would make it seem that *Cat-Women of the Moon* had always been Zimbalist's most likely project during this time; he may also have had serious interest in more ambitious projects like *African Lost World* and *Baby Face Nelson,* or have been using them only to keep his name in the public eye. Meanwhile, *Variety* took a moment on September 2 to dub Zimbalist "the poor man's Sam Katzman."[531]

There seem to have been no speed bumps en route to the completion of *Cat-Women of the Moon.* The September 21 *Reporter* noted that Zimbalist bought yet another script, *Spirit of Annapolis,* from the prolific Guy Reed Ritchie, with *Cat-Women of the Moon* ready "to roll early next month."[532] A director was signed by the 28th, the *Reporter* announced that day, with editor and recent "TV director" Arthur Hilton "signed over the weekend" to helm the production.[533] The report also specified that it would be shot in widescreen, which, filming after mid-1953, was inevitable. Unlike *Robot Monster,* shot right as Hollywood swirled in uncertainty over aspect ratio, *Cat-Women of the Moon* is an unambiguously wide film, shot flat for projection somewhere from 1.66:1 to 1.85:1. The *Reporter* also now credited the script to Roy Hamilton (of *Conquest of the Moon* fame), whose name would make it to the credits and whose brief screenwriting career ended soon after. Zimbalist's co-producer was also first mentioned here, special effects man Jack Rabin who did *Robot Monster* effects and perhaps met Zimbalist then. Co-credited with Zimbalist for their "original story idea," Rabin remembered that the film had surprisingly thoughtful origins, at least for his part:

> My basic idea on *Cat-Women* didn't come through. My original thought was that Einstein, Galileo, Copernicus, or whoever, weren't that brilliant-minded. These Cat-Women had lost all their energy resources and they began to telepathically develop Einstein's and Galileo's minds—knowing that this takes time—to get them to the point that they would've worked out the formula for the development of atomic energy. Then they'd come to the Earth and perpetuate themselves. So Man hadn't his own real destiny, wasn't figuring out his own thing; he was being monitored by thoughts.[534]

On September 30, the *Reporter* noted that Zimbalist made a film processing arrangement with General Film Laboratories for five movies with the specification that all of his 3-D projects "in the next 12 months" be developed there.[535] Then the October 2 *Reporter* announced that Douglas Fowley, added to the *Cat-Women of the Moon* cast, was also assistant to Zimbalist and Rabin, with filming beginning October 12 (the start date was reinforced in the same issue's "Pictures in Preparation" section).[536] Then on Tuesday the 6th, Victor Jory was added as "star" of the film,[537] with the remaining cast fleshed out in the "Pictures Now Shooting" list in Friday's issue.[538] That listing repeated on the 16th, following a noteworthy item from the previous day. The October 15 *Reporter* announced that Zimbalist and Rabin were already planning a sequel, *Return of the Cat-Women,* for February production with the first film "currently filming."[539] On the 19th, filming was wrapped on Friday and the project headed "to the lab for six weeks of special effects by co-producer Jack Rabin."[540] On the 28th he and Zimbalist had formed a new firm, "Z-M Productions with attorney Edward Mosk to co-produce *Miss Robin Hood,* from their own original."[541] This project, credited to the Z-M Productions triumvirate, was before attributed to "[Maurice] Geraghty from his published story." (Perhaps the trio had just concocted their own original story, keeping the same title as Geraghty's work, or perhaps there had never been a Geraghty script.) Also noteworthy is Ed Mosk, not listed in the *Robot Monster* credits but whom Tucker remembered present in planning its release.

According to the November 13 *Reporter,* contract composer Elmer Bernstein would on the 20th "conduct his original musical score" at Samuel Goldwyn Studios, the film currently in "final editing."[542] The November 24 issue noted that Zimbalist and Rabin intended the use of Eastman Color for all future projects,[543] while on December 3 the intrepid pair was planning an "original idea," *The Blond Musketeer,* for TV series production.[544] Rabin was sufficiently close to Zimbalist that they would leave soon "for a week of finance conferences in New York." Then, on December 8 the *Reporter* previewed *Cat-Women of the Moon,* giving it the singularly glass-half-full treatment that it seemed to reliably dish out for Zimbalist.[545] On the same page where reports trickled in on George Pal's upcoming *Conquest of Space* (Zimbalist's film of the same title from May never appeared), the anonymous review called *Cat-Women of the Moon* "well-made," "well-acted," "capably directed," with "intriguing special effects" and "solid exploitation potential." In closing, the film's aspect ratio of 1.85 to 1 was spelled out, along with its availability as both a 2-D and 3-D presentation.

Only a day after, the *Reporter* gave *Cat-Women of the Moon* a completely new form of publicity. Z-M Productions, represented by Mosk with Irwin Gostin, the previous day filed a $1,200,000 suit in Superior Court against the network, sponsor, production company, two writers, "and others" involved with the radio comedy *My Little Margie.*[546] "The unusual suit," as the *Reporter* put it, alleged that writer Lee Carson had been on the *Cat-Women of the Moon* set during filming and used his inside knowledge to craft the show's October 13 script, incorporating a spoof title: *Cat Women from Outer Space.* Amongst the "twelve causes of action" were "disparaging, ridiculing and libeling the film," and "plagiarism."

The moronic lawsuit (Carson could not mock the title without visiting the set?) went further unmentioned by the *Reporter,* and may have been settled out of court. There seem to have been zero references to it in newspapers. In *Keep Watching the Skies!,* Bill Warren charitably summed up the legal action as misguided "guilelessness" and "lack of awareness" on the part of "naïve" filmmakers,[547] but that does not wash. As Zimbalist's career proves, there was nothing charmingly goofy about his actions as producer. He was probably tasteless but he was not

WADE WILLIAMS DIST.

a fool, and probably did not have to wait for Mosk to explain to him how pointless it was to pursue the "libel" of a film by parody. (The mind reels at the thought of Zimbalist living to see the 1987 spoof *Amazon Women on the Moon.*) Either he was angry about the *My Little Margie* parody and had to express it, even if the suit could not go anywhere, or the suit was just one more means of stirring up publicity.

On that note, it may or may not be coincidence that Hal Roach Jr. was listed in the June 8 *Daily Variety* as co-producer with Roland Reed on that fall's new season of the television version of *Margie.*[548] According to the August 18 *Reporter,* the show was "the first situation comedy specifically developed for TV" to be adapted for radio and continue on in both versions, and the radio version was as well a Roach-Reed production.[549]

Zimbalist knew the Roach outfit well, as they had licensed the *One Million B.C.* stock footage for *Robot Monster* (and Reed's production *The Sickle or the Cross* had been acquired by Astor in April 1952).[550] And mere days later in the very week that the *Robot Monster* shoot wrapped, the March 27 *Reporter* announced that "George Nader had been signed for a leading role in a *My Little Margie* TV film which Roland Reed started shooting yesterday."[551] Nader likely went straight from Zimbalist to Roach precisely because the two producers knew each another. Roach might have been giving Zimbalist free publicity on his radio show, and Zimbalist might have returned the favor with his incredible vanishing lawsuit, the whole situation premeditated mutual back-scratching.

Similarly, the bizarre title *Cat-Women of the Moon* was probably more a means of publicity-stirring than modern viewers realize. While the film was designed to cash in on the ongoing monster movie craze with emphasis on the still viable 3-D trend, its title tied in to an ongoing Hollywood controversy. Amidst the technological furor of 1953, the biggest movie buzz was Otto Preminger's adaptation of the stage hit *The Moon Is Blue.* Facing Production Code Administration disapproval, United Artists released the marginally witty sex comedy anyway, as *Variety* reported on May 27.[552] The events surrounding the film not only dominated the trades but were frequently reported in the mainstream press, along with a slew of advertising.

Tucker's concept for *Robot Monster* was to exploit the real-life ruins of Chavez Ravine, and the inspiration for *Cat-Women of the Moon* was probably similarly exploitative. The *Cat-Women* project appeared in embryonic form in May, when Zimbalist would produce *Conquest of the Moon* from a story by Hamilton. Whatever the nature of his story, it might as well have been based around a catchy title and not a story proper, because Zimbalist's instinct was to mold it that way. Viewers now wonder at the film's many inanities but they were just as secondary to Zimbalist as those in *Robot Monster.* What probably mattered to Zimbalist was that he had a monster movie property with the word "moon" in the title, which gave him another exploitation angle. Playing off the *Moon Is Blue* controversy, it made sense to ditch *Conquest of the Moon* for something spicier, and the vague sensuality of "cat-women" fit the bill. Hamilton's final script would accommodate whatever the term implied; throw in 3-D, and a low budget would make it a certain hit.

And little wonder that the film makes no sense. *Cat-Women of the Moon* is very much *Robot Monster*'s sister film and while its lunar lunacy is less surreal, it is just as insane. After a bombastic opening where credits slam onto the screen with 3-D in mind (certainly slicker than the *Robot Monster* credits), the film starts promisingly, if pretentiously, with a voice-over accompanying a static field of stars:

> The eternal wonders of space and time. The far away dreams and mysteries of other worlds, other life, the stars, the planets. Man has been face to face with them for centuries, yet is barely able to penetrate their unknown secrets. Some time, some day, the barrier will be pierced. Why must we wait? Why not, now?

If Hamilton wrote something more plausible when the project was *Conquest of the Moon,* this introduction could have been part of it. It does not seem suggested by the *Cat-Women of the Moon* title, and the rest of film is a sad excuse for discovering the "unknown secrets" of the cosmos. It cuts from the voice-over to a sudden rocket blast and the ship's interior; from this point, all credibility is jettisoned. The moon mission crew of four men and one woman sit in a questionable control room set, with corrugated plastic walls, desk drawer, and rolling office chairs. (Warren was in amazement over a film reel hanging on the wall that the filmmakers presumably thought would seem like exotic technology, rather than a familiar sight from high school biology class.) They all try admirably to press themselves down in the chairs and loungers to suggest gravity pummeling them, but the effect is ridiculous.

Marie Windsor, as Helen the navigator, spends a lot of time primping her hair and so forth while guiding the ship accurately. In addition to Fowley as a lower crewmember and the grumpy Victor Jory as the first officer, young William Phipps played the radio man[553] and the often maligned Sonny Tufts played the captain. Tufts was a beefy, likable actor but a laughingstock in the press thanks to his name and drinking problem. As Warren pointed out, it is bizarre that the tall and handsome Tufts was cast as the boring commanding officer while the perpetually grouchy Jory plays what is supposed to be the dynamic first officer who owns the heart of the navigator. Tufts is not bad in his role but he characteristically lacked subtlety, and causes unintended humor when bellowing into the radio communicator or sounding like a tired fuddy-duddy when giving the crew a stern lecture. Even better is the sequence where Jory dons a spacesuit to climb to a lower level and fix a radiation leak. Hysterically, the hatch is opened and seconds of poisonous fumes drift in before Jory even has his suit on and fumbles over. He waves an extinguisher all around the smoke-filled lower level, putting something out and somehow fixing the problem.

The crew arrives on the moon and enters an underground cavern where there is oxygen, and a ridiculous fight with giant spiders ensues.[554] The first lunar arachnid is genuinely creepy when introduced as a silhouette of dangling monster legs descending into our view of the unsuspecting explorers, but the film unfortunately cuts to a full reverse-angle view of its silliness. The spider attacks three of the guys, meaning that they bumble around with the obviously wire-hung monster, like Bela Lugosi's rubber octopus fight in Ed Wood's *Bride of the Monster*. According to Tom Weaver, Phipps recalled that the film was as ridiculous to the cast as it was to the audience[555] (". . . I thought I was workin' for Soupy Sales!"), while Windsor said it took a whole "Five minutes!" to know she was up the creek.[556]

As the crew enters an underground city and a series of palatial rooms—decorated in a randomly ancient motif—the menace of the Cat-Women is finally introduced with surprising subtlety.[557] There is a Val Lewton wall shadow, feet and legs slinking into view, leading to a Cat-Woman performing weird hand motions over Helen—culminating in a strange effects shot of a pale, out-of-focus spot on her hand. Helen is thereafter possessed by the Cat-Women (who wear black leotards and exaggerated eyebrows but seem human) and unwittingly supports their plan; they profess benevolence to the crew with only Jory the grouch correctly seeing their ulterior motives. Led by the trio of Alpha, Beta, and Lambda, they intend to use the visiting spacecraft to conquer the Earth. But thanks to the lonely Lambda's budding romance with the radio operator, the plot is foiled and Helen restored to normal. The story culminates in a note of odd pathos, Lambda dying in her Earthman's arms (making her a sacrificial Lambda) and the film abruptly ending with the sinister Alpha and Beta shot off-screen. In a movie generously gifted with inanities, this sudden stop stands out, and it only seems like it was done to wrap the shoot early because that is exactly what happened. According to Windsor and Phipps, those in charge "just pulled about six pages out of the script" because "they didn't have any more money and couldn't go another day."[558] According to Rabin, the shoot took five days.[559]

Cat-Women of the Moon is *Robot Monster*'s closest relative, despite the lack of Tucker's involvement, and comparisons between the two are just as instructive as comparisons between *Robot Monster* and *Dance Hall Racket*. *Cat-Women of the Moon* shared the same producer, distributor, composer, special effects artist, 3-D process, year, and genre with *Robot Monster*, and it was not until 1960 that Tucker again directed in that genre. Windsor also stated that Hilton did little directing,[560] and all of these similarities raise the possibility that *Robot Monster*'s uniqueness was more the result of Zimbalist than Tucker. But there are also contrasts. *Cat-Women of the Moon* is a far slicker film than *Robot Monster*, cheap enough but comparatively bringing out the earlier film's grunginess. The dearth of location shooting worked to its advantage, as its high-contrast black-and-white, set-bound world has a cleanness and smoothness alien to *Robot Monster*. But *Cat-Women of the Moon* is separated from *Robot Monster* and most Zimbalist productions by containing little, if any, stock footage. With Rabin co-producing, it may have been a matter of some pride for him to do the effects as originally as possible and, while they are never extraordinary, they are mostly serviceable. (Exceptions include a sparkler-like effect that would have been at home in *Robot Monster*, and an extremely cheesy shot of the ship spinning around. One of the best effects ideas in the film is also one of the simplest: the use of camera movements over still lunar pictures.)

The subtle but definite improvement in production quality from *Robot Monster* to *Cat-Women of the Moon* is also noticeable by comparison of Bernstein's musical scores. The *Cat-Women*

WADE WILLIAMS DIST.

main title is appropriately like a cousin to *Robot Monster's* theme, with a prominent low brass melody. But while instrumentation was similar, Bernstein's new melody was completely different, and there are bell-like ornaments, perhaps glockenspiel, prominently laid over the top. Bells were noticeably part of the *Robot Monster* score but only an occasional counterpoint, filling in quiet respites from menacing brass. Although they occasionally take the form of insistent quarter notes in *Cat-Women of the Moon,* they frequently dominate the newer score, much as the title characters dominate the male explorers. This musically reinforces the move away from the threat of Ro-Man's aggressive masculinity to the indirect, feminine threat of the Cat-Women. Bernstein's score is in every way an evolution from the single-mindedness of *Robot Monster,* with a greater variety of instrumentation and moods, and even briefly heard grating, honking discord during the spider battle. (Bernstein's name was misspelled in the *Cat-Women of the Moon* credits as "Bernstien," just as Selena Royle became "Royale" in the *Robot Monster* credits. This could have been done intentionally to give the filmmakers an escape if they got into any controversy for using politically tainted talent.)

But the estimable improvements from *Robot Monster* to *Cat-Women of the Moon* are still minor, and diminish next to the many inane qualities that connect the two movies. Much of the dialogue is ludicrous, and could be reinforcement for Wyott Ordung's claim that Zimbalist had a relative doing rewrites. No one says, "I cannot, yet I must," but Lambda says, "Two million years of civilization: Does one gamble that on . . . on a promise?" Also pretentious: "They didn't want to, for one thing. They couldn't, for another." The dialogue features a slew of pseudoscientific malarkey (particularly in a speech by Alpha) that would have fit right into *Robot Monster,* including a reference to a "speed control retarder" and the assurance on board the ship that the "nitrate-pictate acid [is] secure." None of that is outdone by Fowley's immortal line, delivered while giving Beta a guided tour of the rocket: "You're too smart for me, baby. I like 'em stupid." Zimbalist was partially responsible for the most iconic image of this genre, Ro-Man, and also a line of dialogue that sums that genre up.

Beyond dialogue, the film piles on more inanities and—like *Robot Monster*—many are humorous while a few have a disquieting, surreal quality. Just as *Robot Monster* was edited with not much more dubbed in than music, sound effects, and John Brown's voice, the *Cat-Women of the Moon* soundtrack occasionally reveals lack of care for believable audio. The sounds of crackers being munched, drinks being poured, and a wrapper being folded up are nice and loud—louder than they really need to be and probably that way because recorded live and left in. The underground world of the Cat-Women comes complete with a cumulus cloud-rich sky, incredibly jarring even if it was not scientifically ludicrous. Also inexcusable is a two shot of Doug the radioman and Lambda that cuts to close-ups where their eye-lines point in the wrong direction, then back to the original two shot. This could have been easily avoided by flipping the film over for the close-up shots, but no one noticed (or cared). And the Cat-Women perform an extended dance number; the importance of it to their two million year-old culture is never explained, but it pads the movie out slightly.

As alluded to earlier, the Cat-Women are sometimes treated with an eerie indirectness that almost rises above the silliness. The moon minxes teleport by jump-cutting out of the film, an especially effective trick when Lambda disappears in the midst of a chase, the music on the soundtrack abruptly disappearing with her. (Again, the kind of effects that David Lynch is critically acclaimed for were often done before without "art film" respectability.) There are also mysterious cuts of Cat-Women eyes to imply the increasing possession of Helen, and an unexplained insert shot of one Cat-Woman waving her hands through a fire before it extinguishes.

Most interesting of all is a feminine thematic connection to *Robot Monster*. Alice is not only a brilliant scientist but willing to do anything for survival, even compromise herself by seducing a monster. Helen is the navigator of a spaceship and only becomes a liability to her crew because she falls under the mind control of hostile aliens. Neither she nor Alice are helpless females, but there is a contrast apparent here. The subtle, feminine attack that Alice uses is the very tactic of the Cat-Women for gaining control of the crewmen. *Cat-Women of the Moon* could be interpreted as a moral condemnation of Alice's decision in *Robot Monster*. Feminine deception is something that only the bad guys practice, in this point of view; perhaps Johnny would express shame that his sister could be a Cat-Woman.

Another parallel connects Lambda to Ro-Man. She tells Alpha that she does not want to be part of the Cat-Woman "plan" to take over the Earth, much as Ro-Man told Guidance that he cannot destroy Alice. In both films, it is because the alien falls in love with an Earthling (sex roles opposite in the two films) and cannot carry out orders that violate that love. Lambda tells them that she loves Doug, and they do not care as they tell her that even her reproduction will be planned. Lambda cannot go along with her plan any more than Ro-Man can fulfill his, and she is likewise killed by her superior (very brutally with a stone smashed into her head). Do these comparable and contrasting points between the two films tell us anything about who really authored *Robot Monster*? The thematic similarities may have been imitation, coincidence, or an uncredited rewrite from Zimbalist's shadowy relative (or Frederic I. Rinaldo), but what will be clear is that Zimbalist probably did not intend any resonances between the two films.

A look at Zimbalist's next project, *King Dinosaur* (1955), makes this point obvious. The project was mentioned in the *Reporter* in June 1953, "a Guy Reed Ritchie original" that was in the stew that Zimbalist had simmering in the wake of *Robot Monster*.[561] *King Dinosaur* reappeared in the *Reporter* later in the year as *Cat-Women of the Moon* was assembling, with Rabin still closely involved. The two "returned to Hollywood over the weekend," the December 21 issue noted, and would "start production of *King Dinosaur* on January 15 using Carl Dudley's Vistarama lens for the anamorphic type production."[562] That final detail would have been impressive if true, as *Cat-Women of the Moon* was not shot in an anamorphic process.

As the New Year got underway, the January 8 *Reporter* announced that Zimbalist and Rabin would reuse Fowley and Tufts in a TV film called *Oui! Oui! Paree*, with *Pirate Women* in pre-production alongside *King Dinosaur*.[563] According to *Variety* on January 13, Bela Lugosi had signed the day before to co-star in *Oui! Oui! Paree,* and would film it after a week of appearing in *Arsenic and Old Lace* on the St. Louis stage. Lugosi and Tufts were also scheduled to star in a TV series called *Robinson Crusoe on Mars*—continuing Zimbalist's string of *Crusoe* projects—but neither it nor *Paree* ever appeared.[564] Rabin's place in this arrangement seemed secure, as evidenced by the January 29 *Reporter* ad placed by his former partners at Complete Film Service, wishing him luck in his "new career as a motion picture producer."[565] But his part in Zimbalist's scheme soon dissipated as it was reported on February 11 that he and Louis DeWitt partnered on a new effects house, Technifilm, under the umbrella of "American National, telefilm company, which has taken over Eagle-Lion."[566] Rabin was mentioned in connection with Zimbalist in a March 11 report on a Pennsylvania *Cat-Women of the Moon* premiere[567] (headlined by someone at the *Reporter* as "'Cat Woman' Gets P.A. Plugging"), and on March 24 with DeWitt as effects providers for a "new" Zimbalist TV series: *The Adventures of Robinson Crusoe,* starring Tufts.[568] But Rabin was absent from a June 7 *Reporter* note that Zimbalist had been in New York for deal-making on a new program, *Chicago Vice Squad,*[569] nor was he mentioned in a July 7 note that Zimbalist had acquired 52 films from "the late Thomas H. Ince."[570] It may be significant that, when interviewed by Robert and Dennis Skotak, Rabin remembered a slew of *Cat-Women of the Moon* details but never mentioned Zimbalist. Comparing himself to "a punch-drunk guy" as he dusted himself off from one disappointing project in readiness to begin anew on another, Rabin admitted, "I've never seen *Cat-Women of the Moon.* Why were these films made?"[571]

On September 14 *King Dinosaur* reappeared, this time with no trace of Rabin.[572] With a new partner, Bert I. Gordon, Zimbalist acquired the services of "Ralph Helfer, animal trainer and explorer," and the next day the film was "currently shooting," with future project *White Slave Ring* to follow.[573] In the December 7 *Reporter* came the news that Zimbalist and Rabin "returned from Mexico City early this week following initial tie-ups for co-production of their property, *Indian Story*. Pair are also in the final stages of editing their latest film, *King Dinosaur*."[574] Then on December 16 Zimbalist and Gordon would "start dubbing tomorrow" on the film, to be released in "Sepia color" with "two major studios" potentially interested in releasing it.[575] There was no further report of Zimbalist's reported intention of using an anamorphic process for the film, and it would be issued as one of Lippert's final releases.

Gordon is a familiar name to monster film fans for the many size-focused, low-budget features he cranked out with little money and his own sweat, such as *Attack of the Puppet People* and *The Amazing Colossal Man*. *King Dinosaur* was his first credit as producer, and he was perhaps hired to replace an uninterested Rabin. Lesser known was one obscure feature made right before *King Dinosaur*, 1954's *Serpent Island*. The directing debut of Tom Gries (*Will Penny*, *Breakheart Pass*), who also wrote *King Dinosaur*, the cheap little movie starred Tufts, fresh from *Cat-Women of the Moon*. Zimbalist was not officially credited on the movie, but his connections to it are apparent. Bernstein's opening music from *Cat-Women* was edited down and played over the *Serpent Island* opening credits, which were set in the same font as *Robot Monster*.[576] Gordon told me,

> [I] didn't know Phil Tucker but I share his ". . . [quoting my words] claimed that [Zimbalist] froze him out of any profits from the movie" . . . and it wasn't just one movie for me. . . . I co-produced *King Dinosaur* with him in addition to directing it, writer, editor, and creating the visual effects. On *Serpent Island* I was the cinematographer, editor, and created the visual effects. I had a 50 percent profit deal with him on both films, and received nothing. It was my introduction into the business.[577]

It is too bad that Zimbalist did not instead focus his energies on a *Cat-Women vs. Ro-Man* sequel, perhaps with Ed Wood as writer-director this time; it would at least have been entertaining. *King Dinosaur* is a dull film, "dreary, phony, exploitative,"[578] according to Warren, and it "represents," according to Mark F. Berry's *The Dinosaur Filmography,* "the very nadir of the dino-movie genre."[579] Zimbalist returned to his stock footage roots in the opening sequence, a well-edited montage of science stuff narrated by Marvin Miller (the voice of *Forbidden Planet*'s Robby the Robot) that is far better than anything that follows. (Zimbalist was so adept at recycling stock footage that he could make it the best part of a movie.) From that point, the film concentrates for the better part of an hour on an extremely tiresome and whiny crew of two men and two women as they explore a newly discovered jungle planet, populated by very normal Earth creatures, sometimes superimposed to look large and menacing. At the end of it all they detonate a nuclear weapon, an action with no apparent purpose since they have escaped from the "dinosaurs" in pursuit. (The purpose was probably just to give Zimbalist an excuse to throw in some nuke test stock footage.)

There is no point in covering the film's inanities further; what is already visible here is a lack of meaningful continuation of the tendencies that linked *Robot Monster* and *Cat-Women of the Moon. King Dinosaur* has none of the fun absurdity of the earlier two films, nor does it ever approach their surreal, dreamlike qualities. There is little hilarious dialogue in *King Dinosaur,* and lizards photographed as pretend dinosaurs cannot compete with a gorilla in a diving helmet, or even with telepathic leotard-wearing Cat-Women. *King Dinosaur* is even dingier and cheaper-looking than *Robot Monster* and relentlessly boring in a way that it never could have been. (For what it may be worth, Berry states that the version of *Robot Monster* with a pointless dinosaur fight introduction borrowed the footage "from *King Dinosaur*".[580])

The pattern that connects Zimbalist's productions now becomes increasingly clear. He made his films as cheaply and exploitatively as he could manage, and any memorable qualities were likely unintended silver lining that he may have been oblivious to. As if to prove the point, he soon made a film that was not as bad as *King Dinosaur* but far better than anything he had attempted. With a more talented and experienced collaborator hired to bring a project to life, Zimbalist was actually responsible for a good movie. That collaborator was director Don Siegel, and the film was *Baby Face Nelson.*

Finally released in 1957, the project was part of Zimbalist's stable of loosely in-production titles at least as far back as an April 1953 *Reporter. Daily Variety* claimed in December 1954 that Gordon would direct the film, but announced Siegel as director in June 1957.[581] According to Siegel's autobiography,[582] once screenwriter Daniel Mainwaring was hammering out a script, Zimbalist soon informed Siegel that he had "got lucky" in obtaining some 1940s cars for the film. When Siegel refused to use cars that were clearly anachronistic for a story set in the early thirties, Zimbalist exclaimed, "Do you know what 1930s cars cost?" Siegel was later forced to complete "fifty-five tough set-ups" within the space of what became the last day of filming. With three days remaining on the schedule Siegel was told by Zimbalist, "You've no choice. I've run out of money." Siegel blazed through the final day with absolutely no time wasted: "Every foot of film I shot, I used." But unlike the unfortunate

Hilton on *Cat-Women of the Moon,* Siegel at least got everything shot.

He was especially motivated by a last-minute betrayal. Siegel overheard his star, Mickey Rooney, offering Zimbalist his own directing services if Siegel could not get the film wrapped on the abruptly altered schedule. Something similar happened to

Mickey Rooney as *Baby Face Nelson.*

Mainwaring when Irving Shulman, author of an earlier and rejected *Baby Face Nelson,* copied his script and dated it to make it look as if Mainwaring had copied him. Siegel was able to disprove this attempt at reverse plagiarism by pointing out a name in the script that he and Mainwaring had chosen to name after Siegel's mother. Shulman's ploy fell apart, no thanks to Zimbalist, who conveniently told Mainwaring he had no memory of one script versus another. (Both writers were credited on the film.) Rooney later recalled "[feeling] really good about" the "25 percent of the profits" he received, until he had to unload it "a couple years later, when [he] really needed the money."[583]

The final result of the tangled production was a brutal crime melodrama that, according to Zimbalist, "show[ed] Nelson as he was—a lousy punk who knew what he was doing and who paid for it with his life."[584] In truth, the film depicted Nelson in mixed fashion, with sympathy for the odds stacked against him along with revulsion at his psychopathic tendencies. The best part of *Baby Face Nelson* was actually Sir Cedric Hardwicke as a lecherous, alcoholic underworld doctor. Looking back in context, the *Overlook Film Encyclopedia* credited it as "one of the most impressive entries in the late-fifties cycle of gangster biopics," noting its "bleak, flat grey" feel.[585] Zimbalist actually produced a good movie, although credit belongs to the director. But his involvement with a better film than usual shows that Zimbalist did not care if a movie was good or bad so long as it was cheap and exploitable.

Not surprisingly, his other projects seem like a return to form. *Monster from Green Hell* (1957), released just before *Baby Face Nelson,* was almost a re-tread of *King Dinosaur.* While earthbound and using different stock footage, it is also an incredibly boring and unwatchable exercise in padding. Reuniting partially with Rabin[586] who, along with DeWitt and Irving Block, provided effects, Zimbalist used extensive footage from Fox's *Stanley and Livingstone* (1939) to fashion a jungle excursion involving giant insects. Block remembered a conference with Rabin, Zimbalist, and a writer, where disagreement ensued on how large the bugs should be. When the writer suggested they be a foot long, Zimbalist replied, "Hell no! We gotta be realistic in this picture. They gotta be GIGANTIC! Big as an elephant!" And when Block warned Zimbalist about matching problems with footage of 19th century explorers, he was unworried: "For the close shots our actors will wear pith helmets too!"[587] This explains star Jim Davis' archaic fashion sense onscreen, and Warren's opinion that Zimbalist "doesn't seem to have cared about anything except exploitation." With bug monsters done in the same cheap style as *King Dinosaur,* he summed it up as "sleazy, tiresome, and forgettable."[588] But makeup artist Paul Blaisdell's account of providing "a series of production illustrations" for Zimbalist's pre-production of the film is of great interest. According to Blaisdell biographer Randy Palmer, the artist agreed to design and build the monsters but "days passed" without word from Zimbalist after Blaisdell submitted designs to him. Zimbalist proved inaccessible and weeks later could not be reached by Forrest J Ackerman, who was acting as Blaisdell's agent. According to Blaisdell he was "never paid" for his design work, which could nonetheless be seen on film.[589]

The rest of Zimbalist's filmography is more of the same, and there is no need to comment in great detail. Two jungle adventures minus any monster element were next, *Watusi* and *Tarzan, the Ape Man* (both 1959, and both for MGM[590]). According to Tarzan movie historian Gabe Essoe, the latter film was an attempt to cash in on Sy Weintraub and Harvey Hayutin's *Tarzan's Greatest Adventure* (1959).[591] The MGM Zimbalist knock-off was a remake of the original *Tarzan the Ape Man* (1932), and was so poor that it actually borrowed footage from the earlier film with Johnny Weissmuller's face obviously visible. (What makes this even more incredible is the fact that the newer version was filmed in color while the original was shot in black-and-white.) Author David Fury marveled at the remake's "kindergarten filmmaking techniques," exemplified by "two separate close-ups of the face of [a] stuffed animal, resplendent with its plastic fangs and button eyes."[592] Star Denny Miller, interviewed by Weaver, remembered the production with fond bemusement, and recalled that Zimbalist may have been fired from MGM after the film was completed.[593]

Zimbalist made one last foray into monster territory. As the October 28, 1960, *Reporter* noted, he and "associate Byron Roberts" were heading to New York in regard to financing for the Jules Verne property *Career of a Comet.*[594] Released in 1961 as *Valley of the Dragons,* the film not only used stock footage in the finest Zimbalist tradition, but went all the way back to the producer's roots by borrowing it from *One Million B.C.* According to a December 19 *Reporter* piece, the film was to be a Columbia release, with Edward Bernds hired to direct and with Zimbalist's son, Donald, in charge of "literary research" for his father's recently formed production company.[595] In a Weaver interview, Bernds revealed that the film originated because the younger Zimbalist had found a copy of an obscure Verne novel while vacationing, and showed the never-filmed public domain work to his dad (leading to Donald's story credit—which began and ended with finding the book). Al at this point "had an option to use any or all of the *One Million B.C.* film," and also kept the production cheap by making a deal with Columbia brass in New York City, rather than Los Angeles. This angered the Hollywood brains of Columbia, and may have ended his opportunities there.[596] Blaisdell claimed that Zimbalist was canned by Columbia, and from that knowledge gained "a great deal of satisfaction!"[597] The final film "was built around the *One Million B.C.* stock footage," according to Bernds and, according to Berry, "probably uses more [of it] than any other film . . . ."[598] *Valley of the Dragons* at least did not take itself seriously and is actually one of Zimbalist's more enjoyable monster mashes, with likable characters and the familiar stock material smoothly integrated into the rest of the film. This Zimbalist production was notches above *Missile to the Moon* (1958), a recent remake of *Cat-Women of the Moon* that Astor had cooked up. By wide-ranging consensus, it had none of the fun goofiness of the original and Zimbalist can at least be credited for being uninvolved.[599]

A young Mariette Hartley, then one of the last MGM contract players, suffered the indignity of being loaned out for Zimbalist's *Drums of Africa* (1963) soon after completing Sam Peckinpah's *Ride the High Country* (1962). In her autobiography, she states that she will "never forget" Zimbalist, with his "visored hat" and habit of "[carrying] hard candy, offering it to everybody, including the animals." In her estimation, the "one week" production probably amounted to "about eight minutes of new film. The rest was borrowed from *King Solomon's Mines.*"[600]

Variety reported in June 1964 that Allied Artists would release worldwide twelve films to be produced by "Al Zimbalist, former Metro producer" with a slew of titles listed. Along with "Edgar Allan Poe's *World of Horribles*" and such imaginative titles as *King Tyrannosaurus* and *Beast from Green Hell,* the report mentioned *Young Dillinger* (1965).[601] Possibly Zimbalist's final completed production,[602] the violent gangster melodrama starred Nick Adams and Robert Conrad and followed Hollywood's increasing trend for turning violent criminals into misunderstood rebels. One newspaper reviewer marveled that "you'd think [Dillinger] and his girlfriend were just juvenile delinquents . . .."[603] It is not clear if Zimbalist saw Dillinger as a "lousy punk who knew what he was doing" like Baby Face Nelson before him.

***Young Dillinger*, with Nick Adams and Mary Ann Mobley.**

But the production of *Young Dillinger* lit up the pages of *Variety* for a time, providing an entertaining view of Zimbalist butting heads with the IATSE union. In August, *Variety* noted that Zimbalist's extensive line-up of projects (now "12 features and a video series") with Allied Artists would no longer involve production in Canada, Germany, and Puerto Rico. Everything on the schedule would be made in the U.S., thanks to "concessions in numbers of workers that union 'tradition has more or less fixed without always stating in black and white,'" and without reduction of "contractual wage scales."[604] But something in this win-win scenario must have gone sour, as the *Young Dillinger* shoot was shut down in November by three IATSE reps because of Zimbalist hiring "a registered nurse rather than an IATSE first aid man on *Taffy*, film he shot largely on Thousand Oaks location prior to *Dillinger*." With Zimbalist absent, production resumed after "Nick Adams and associate producer Byron Roberts agreed to sign a pledge that the $150 would be paid." Zimbalist subsequently paid the fee (with "Paid in protest" written on the check's reverse) and planned to sue. Regarding the unused IATSE first aid man, Zimbalist described him as being "as much use as a brassiere on an ant."[605] Then, four days later, Zimbalist again relented to IATSE pressure and "hired a hairdresser from IA Makeup and Hairstylists Local 706." As he explained the film's lack of need for a hairdresser, "We only have one girl on the picture and she wants to do her own hair . . . besides she wears a wig."[606]

Zimbalist's career was about as simple as it seems on the surface. The fact that he unleashed his astonishing Ro-Man/Cat-Women one-two punch in the same year does not mean that he was responsible for much of the unique quality of those films, as most of his others only became shoddier and less imaginative. This steady decrease in quality was probably a result of success. He had zero artistic ambitions to balance his financial ones, and his career resembles that of an exploitation producer with better connections. With experience he learned how to reduce filmmaking to an ever more basic formula, with likely less control given to those hired to bring his projects to life. His continued extreme use of borrowed footage in later productions was a means of bringing frugality and control to near perfection.

One other element of Zimbalist's career needs consideration. As the dizzying number of his press reports attest, he had several projects brewing at any one time and some percentage of them were perhaps seriously intended if financing could be arranged. As his films became generally worse, he continued to make attention-getting announcements. Since at least 1956, Zimbalist had announced plans for various TV productions, but these projects seem to have all fizzled.[607] According to an August 1957 Louella Parsons column, he bought film rights for the lesbian novel *The Well of Loneliness*[608] and, according to Barbara Bladen in 1965, was working on a female James Bond knock-off called *Christy O'Hara.*[609] *Variety* even noted in 1965 that Zimbalist was working on a General George S. Patton biographical movie.[610] August 1969 news reports announced that he was capitalizing on the recent moon landing by registering the title *Sea of Tranquility*[611] (which is so poetic that it is fortunate that he never made it into a movie). One account of the project contains an unbelievable example of Zimbalist's ballyhoo, courtesy of entertainment columnist Florabel Muir: "Zimbalist has produced 30 pictures, all told, one of which actually dealt with a lunar landing and was released back in 1959. Its title was *Conquest of Space*, and it was made in 3-D by means of Zimbalist's own process. . . . He has made 17 science-fiction movies."[612] Zimbalist had even revived an old Tucker scheme, planning in 1962 to film the life of Lucky Luciano, who had recently died. The project was disavowed almost as quickly as Tucker's when Zimbalist could find nothing worthwhile about the gangster.[613]

An October 1959 Parsons column reported Zimbalist's audacious claim that he would soon be in discussions with Marilyn Monroe and husband Arthur Miller on the film adaptation of a play called *The Cherry Blonde*.[614] Nothing came of this production and I could find no record that there ever was such a "stage play." According to Parsons it was the work of Guy Reed Ritchie, the writer mentioned repeatedly over years of Zimbalist press reports. But Ritchie received no writing credit on *Cat-Women of the Moon*, the film that had perhaps evolved from his *Conquest of Space*. Nor did Ritchie receive credit on *King Dinosaur*, nor was a film made from his short story "Adam and Eve," or from his script *Spirit of Annapolis*. Guy Reed Ritchie has no writing credits whatsoever, in film or on stage, nor is anything copyrighted in his name. There is in fact no evidence that there was such a person as Guy Reed Ritchie.

The game was given up by Zimbalist himself, if anyone was paying attention. As late as August 1969, he was reportedly buying Guy Reed Ritchie material, such as *Laugh, Clown, Laugh*, one piece of an ambitious sixteen-project schedule described in

Variety. Also listed in the same article was "*The Skirts of Sergeant McHugh*, based on series of short stories by Donald Zimbalist recently published."[615] But in October 1962, "Zimbalist and Philip N. Krasne added *The Skirts of Sergeant McHugh*, tome by Guy Reed Ritchie, to their Metro production slate."[616] Between 1962 and 1969, the same project had completely different origins, the first with Ritchie and the second without but with another alleged Ritchie project in tow. But the best detail was reported by *Variety* in September 1969, a month after the other story from the same year: "Al Zimbalist has purchased *Planet of the Damned*, sci-fi novel by Donald Reed Higgins, from galley proofs for production by his new company, American Artists Associates."[617] The title *Planet of the Damned* had been used in science fiction in 1952 and 1962[618] but not in movies, and Donald Reed Higgins had no credits in literature or film. Perhaps it was boredom or amusement that caused Zimbalist to substitute a new fake name for the usual one, as Donald Reed Higgins, similar to Guy Reed Ritchie with identical middle names, was just as illusory and was a joke hiding in plain sight: Donald was the name of his son, and Higgins the maiden name of his wife.

Since it appears that Ritchie only existed as a convenience for appearing to expand the ranks of Zimbalist's production circle, it is fascinating that the name even once appeared in connection with *Robot Monster*. In notes compiled by the American Film Institute, available on the Turner Classic Movies website, there is this production note: "Although the SAB credits Guy Reed Ritchie as co-writer of the screenplay, notes on the AMPAS Awards card indicates that the production company refuted Ritchie's contribution."[619]

How was an imaginary person credited as co-writer of a screenplay? And how could this person be expected to respond to the production company's refutation (being imaginary, after all)? Heads or tails, Zimbalist came out ahead in this situation. Between his production company and his imaginary friend, writing credit would become his, along with the accompanying benefits. And as for Ritchie, he might as well be given a co-writing credit for the final film. Whoever Zimbalist's unknown "relative" was, perhaps the blacklisted Frederic I. Rinaldo, that anonymous script tinkerer could be labeled Guy Reed Ritchie.

According to Ray Zone, Wyott Ordung eventually spoke with Zimbalist on lack of payment for his script:

> I finally got to Al Zimbalist seven years after the picture opened. I got to him and he said, "We haven't made a dime on that picture." He said, "We still owe $6,000 on the picture." I said, "I own ten percent of the picture." He said, "I know, I've seen your contract. When we get the money we'll pay you." The next thing I see, it's on television.[620]

Given what Zimbalist did to the writing credits, and given the documented examples of how he played with credits and money on *Robot Monster* and other films, how did he treat Tucker? On that point, we at least have Tucker's account:

> Al personally made enough money off of that picture by stealing from me.

11

Walk the Dark Street

They cut me out like a boil.

Wyott Ordung's memory of the aftermath of *Robot Monster* paralleled that of Phil Tucker. After the "fish bowl" test shoot and rehearsal, he claimed to have had no involvement in the production, and was never paid even "a cent" either. No one "owes me anything because Al Zimbalist sold it away outright, supposedly free and clear. I don't know if Phil Tucker's been paid off, but I think that he got some money going in." Running into Ordung, Tucker told him, "You're lucky that you weren't there."[621] But Ordung was at the time lucky in comparison to Tucker all around. The years immediately following *Robot Monster* were ones of busy activity, tremendous promise, and some achievement, and he was present at a moment when others got their big break and launched to fame. Tucker would have been very lucky in those days to get as close to the mainstream as Ordung soon managed.

Ordung struck most people as unusual, and some comments he left behind suggested a questionable hold on reality. But the strangest thing about him is that he was not only a good actor and a competent writer, but a director of some ability. It is not quite true that most of his credits were "on the level of *Robot Monster*," as Tom Weaver once stated in an audio commentary.[622] Ordung racked up some respectable writing jobs, but he more importantly directed two low-budget films that while not extraordinary, displayed talent and intelligence. By the time he directed those films, Ordung's skills were honed by years of film acting and scriptwriting, as his name had been regularly popping up in the trade press since 1951.

But his first write-up went all the way back to October 1947, when *Daily Variety* reviewed an Actors' Lab production of the 1935 comedy *Three Men on a Horse.* With Sam Levene directing, producing, and starring, *Daily Variety* noted, "Levene's slick timing and comedy grabbed most of the guffaws, with Russ Conway and Wyott Ordung ably aiding and abetting."[623] A month later, Ordung's name was one of several signed on a full-page, *Daily Variety* ad that supported actor Larry Parks in his public criticism of the House Un-American Activities Committee. Placed by Progressive Citizens of America, the ad read, "We, the undersigned members of the acting profession, acclaim Larry Parks, one of the 'unfriendly nineteen' . . .."[624] While Ordung may have been sincere, it is notable that he appeared apolitical otherwise, and did not discuss the blacklist in interviews. As the list contains numerous other Actors' Lab names—Roman Bohnen, Lloyd Bridges, Jeff Corey, Howard Da Silva, Russell Johnson—it raises the possibility that signing was a matter of going with the flow for some Lab students. In August 1951, Ordung reappeared in the press in earnest, hired to adapt his own story "Sniper's Paradise" into a script, and in October got a part in a *Dick Tracy* episode.[625] By January 1952, he was cast in Brian Donlevy's *Dangerous Assignment* series, in February was hired to write a *Big Town* episode and then a teleplay called *Prowl Car* in March, and was cast in a series called *Fighting Man* that summer.[626]

While continuing to grab small acting and writing jobs, Ordung soon found grander opportunities. In quick succession, he established his two most important working relationships in 1953. On February 16, the *Hollywood Reporter* noted that he had

Wyott Ordung as early fifties actor. (*Clockwise from upper left*) **Opposite Brian Donlevy in *Dangerous Assignment*, another *Assignment*, and two views of Ordung as *Dick Tracy* villain B.B. Eyes.**

been signed to script *Steel Bayonets* for producers Jerry Thomas and Jack Broder, from Broder's "original story."[627] Ordung was hired by Broder to write a Western in May, and on June 5, with *Robot Monster* almost released, Ordung sold "his third original story" to Broder, *Merrill's Marauders,* a war story like its predecessors *Attack* and *Beyond Valor.*[628] Ordung's planned screenplay for *Marauders* would "be filmed by Broder Productions this summer." Then on July 13, the *Reporter* revealed that Broder was hiring Ordung to turn his own short story "If" into a script.[629] Two more brief items followed; on July 29 producer Herman Cohen had purchased a screenplay co-written by Ordung and James H. Nicholson, the deal brokered by Forrest J Ackerman.[630] (This project became *Target Earth* in 1954.) Then on August 12 came the news that Ordung scored a role in the upcoming "Guam" episode of *International Police.*[631]

The repeated mentions of Broder in these clippings were no fluke, and indicate an association that continued after Ordung's career eventually dried up. According to friend Ewing Miles "Lucky" Brown, "they became friends, [and Ordung] was very fond of him."[632] Originally from Detroit, Broder was a serious player in that city's exhibition business. *Variety* noted in 1938 that he was successfully using overnight radio promotion to get customers into "all-nighter" movie theaters.[633] By October 1940, he was "building up his chain," a recent acquisition giving him control of a total of four theaters.[634] Broder co-founded Realart Pictures in 1948, a small company specializing in such reissues as this one from the March 5, 1952 *Reporter,* where it was noted that they would "reissue the original *Dracula* and *Frankenstein* during the month of April . . .."[635] Realart's Universal horror reissues are what it is often remembered for but, as other *Reporter* items demonstrate, its program was broader. The March 10 issue noted that the company "acquire[d] 6 British films" while April 1 noted the purchase of five more from mostly British sources.[636]

Broder's company ground out a few original productions and even some of quality, such as the coming-of-age story *When I Grow Up* (1951) and the boxing drama *Kid Monk Baroni* (1952), with a very young Leonard Nimoy. But the Broder ethos is probably better represented by a project that began in the spring of 1952 as the *Reporter* announced the hiring of Cohen, later an important independent producer, as "vice-president of Jack Broder Productions."[637] Cohen would immediately work on *White Woman of the Lost Jungle*, to film May 14. Then on May 13, with the film "rolling tomorrow at General Service Studios," the *Reporter* announced that Realart had "signed Bela Lugosi to star."[638] There would seem to be little more to say about a film whose star was officially cast the day before filming, but the production was weirder yet. Broder had hired the legendarily efficient William "One Shot" Beaudine to direct, and signed the comedy duo of Duke Mitchell and Sammy Petrillo—a pair of flagrant Dean Martin and Jerry Lewis imitators—to appear in the film.

Released as *Bela Lugosi Meets a Brooklyn Gorilla* in the fall, it was as unbelievable as its title. According to Weaver's interview with Cohen, the title changed when he pointed out to Broder that Lugosi's name should be exploited, but just why Lugosi was added at the last moment to this lame-brained jungle comedy remained a mystery to Cohen. What he remembered was

Jerry Lewis imitator Sammy Petrillo sums up *Bela Lugosi Meets a Brooklyn Gorilla.*

the day when Jerry Lewis walked in to Realart to see Broder about the film starring his imitator, and the obscene screaming match that ensued.[639] According to a Louella Parsons column from June, producer Hal Wallis was waiting to possibly "take legal action" on seeing the film.[640] This situation was fine with Broder, as Cohen remembered, because he was happy to sell the film to Wallis and let it be unreleased if the payment was greater than the potential profits. The film was released.

As these twists and turns show, Broder's career was not so different from that of Al Zimbalist, with its relentless focus on the bottom line and exuberant embrace of bizarre publicity stunts. It is uncertain if Broder was serious about an item on the front of the May 20, 1952 *Reporter,* headlined "Broder Suing for *African Queen* Cut," but the article stated that he felt entitled to a percentage because of money he claimed to have "invested" in the film.[641] But Broder was on the receiving end of "an investigation into the disposal to television of four features released theatrically by [himself] in 1951," according to the August 21, 1953 *Reporter,* due to guild concern over residual payments.[642] The November 20 issue reported that a suit against Broder by actor-couple John Ireland and Joanne Dru had been dropped, but the November 23 issue had the suit back on, with "other remedies" now "available to plaintiffs."[643] But the similarities between Broder and Zimbalist extended to occasionally discovering new talent in need of a patron. As Cohen recalled, he introduced Elmer Bernstein to Broder, who was excited to hire him to cheaply score *Battles of Chief Pontiac* (1952), not long before Bernstein was contracted to Zimbalist.[644]

In the history of Broder and Realart, the genial Cohen is often mentioned due to his later success, but Ordung was not far away when American International Pictures (AIP) was born in Broder's office.[645] He was on the periphery of those events as they unfolded, as was the unfortunate Ed Wood. AIP was formed after Samuel Arkoff, working as a cheap lawyer for (his phrase) "one-lung producers"[646] like Wood, brought a complaint to Broder on behalf of producer Alex Gordon. The title *The Atomic Monster* had been used (perhaps coincidentally) by Broder, after it was already the title of a script co-written by Gordon and Wood. When the incredibly cheap Broder opted to pay Arkoff rather than go into a legal battle, the improbable event was noticed by James H. Nicholson, Broder's right-hand man after the departure of Cohen.[647] Having met thus, Arkoff and Nicholson soon formed AIP and became hugely successful at exploiting the tastes of teenagers, but they were at this early point lacking anything to release. Ordung played a significant role in solving their problem.

On October 6, 1953, right about when Tucker was pushing *Space Jockey* on AIP and anyone else who would look at it, the *Reporter* announced that Ordung would "direct his first film, Palo Alto's *The Sea Demon,* an original by William Banch [actually William Danch]."[648] With "Ann [sic] Kimball [sic] and Stuart Wade" already cast, filming would begin on October 17 in "Ensenada, Mexico." These production details were affirmed on October 16, when *The Sea Demon* appeared in the *Reporter*'s Friday "Pictures Now Shooting" section (right after *Cat-Women of the Moon*).[649] Added to the cast were Ordung, and "Jack Hayes," soon after prolific low-budget actor Jonathan Haze. But most important was the listing of "Robert Corman" as producer, of course a mangling of Roger Corman, whose uniquely profitable career took off with the Ordung-directed film.[650] According to Mark Thomas McGee's history of AIP, "Ordung was washing dishes and hauling garbage at Alfonso's Restaurant when Corman met him. After appearing in over 30 pictures, Ordung still couldn't earn a living as an actor."[651]

After an unsatisfying experience with his first script sale and co-production, a crime drama released as *Highway Dragnet,* Corman decided that he could take the reins and make films more efficiently. After reading a newspaper article about an experimental electric one-man submarine, he contacted the manufacturers about using it in a movie, and began raising a small budget. Around this time he met Ordung, an "acting

Shot soon after *Robot Monster,* Wyott Ordung and Roger Corman's *Monster from the Ocean Floor* actually showed a diving helmet onscreen, in contrast to the earlier film. (A gorilla suit, however, was nowhere to be seen.)

student" as he remembered him, with a few thousand dollars to contribute from a script sale.[652] Haze remembered Ordung from when he was new in L.A. and working at a gas station. "This little guy named Barney Ordung used to come in all of the time in a beat-up old car, talking about how he was going to make a movie with a guy named Roger Corman."[653] Ordung remembered putting up nearly all of the budget, while Corman claimed that there were other investors.[654] *The Sea Demon* hit a few snags toward the end, including badly recorded sound that had to be dubbed, and a rocky preview screening. According to the *Reporter,* the production wound on the weekend of October

31 and November 1.[655] And Ordung's morbid fear of birds, described at length in his *Fangoria* interview and which he claimed began in 1957 or later, actually dated at least as far back as his directorial debut. Not understanding Ordung's problem or just being kind, Haze recalled, "Barney was allergic to seagulls. Everytime one flew by he wanted to throw up."[656]

The film was sold to Lippert who released it as *Monster from the Ocean Floor*, and it proved profitable for everyone involved as it played widely and cost little (a final cost of $39,000 according to Ordung, much lower according to Corman). Although it is cheap and average it is not ludicrous, and is competently acted, and benefits from a reasonably effective title creature. And Ordung's performance in a supporting role is the best in the movie. He is far more animated, expressive, and interesting

Wyott Ordung (*left*) in *Monster from the Ocean Floor*.

than the rest of the cast. In a motif that would continue for Ordung as director, the film is impressively atmospheric, emphasizing the sounds of wind and ocean. Floyd Crosby's cinematography is rich with high contrasts and inky blacks, although he remembered the project dismissively as "the only picture I saw made without any direction at all."[657] Interviewed by Weaver, Corman remained diplomatic on the subject of Ordung's abilities as a director, but admitted agreeing with Crosby's assessment and indicated that Crosby guided Ordung through the short shoot.[658]

Corman very rapidly parlayed this success into his next project, *The Fast and the Furious* (1955), and from there was regularly selling his economically minded films to AIP. But while Corman became known for keeping a slew of associates along through his many projects, Ordung was not one of them. His eccentricities caught up with him early on, to judge by Corman's account:

> . . . I helped build a camera platform so we could shoot from out in the ocean—then lugged it out into the surf. My director didn't want to help me. "I can't carry that platform," he said, "because I'm the director." I couldn't believe this. "Barney," I said, "I'm the *producer.* Just grab the other side." Barney let me know how he felt. He dropped his side. It fell and hit me.[659]

Ordung appreciated decades of royalties from the film but claimed, according to McGee, that Corman played fast and loose with money. Corman claimed that Ordung had only invested $4,000, while Ordung claimed that he used an insurance policy and his home to raise money with Corman contributing merely $2,000. Ordung further claimed that Corman oversold the film to 120%, somehow came out owning 60% of it, and saw his own share altered from 20 down to 15%.[660] As McGee remembered, "'If you ever meet him hold onto your balls,' [Ordung] warned me. Being all of twelve at the time, I took his remark to mean that Corman was a homosexual."[661] But despite any setbacks, Ordung was not much delayed and would not have had any idea of how far Corman would rise without him. He was immediately in the press with more scattered announcements, such as a note from the February 9, 1954, *Reporter* that he was "preparing *Treasure of Rabaul,* being co-written with Lee Backman, for April production in Cuba."[662] Then on May 11, the *Reporter* announced an ambitious four-film plan for "Valor Pictures, headed by Wyott Ordung," with the Consolidated Film Industries lab, to be initiated with "*The Sporting Game,* rolling June 3 at Keywest Studios."[663]

Ordung was by June 2 already scouting locations, and the film's title had been changed by June 9.[664] The June 30 *Reporter* announced that "Chuck Connors is bicycling between *Police Story* at Allied Artists and Keywest Studios where he is starring in Valor's *Walk the Dark Street,*" with "his daily TV sports show" on the side.[665] Connors, famous for his incredible athleticism (professional baseball *and* basketball) and later beloved as TV's *The Rifleman,* was beginning to carve out an acting career, so far largely confined to small roles. A newspaper article that appeared on July 11 clarified that the TV show ("a baseball warm-up program") was filmed at night, with *Police Story* filming afterwards, and Ordung's movie filming during the day. Connors was able "to get his sleep only in catnaps,"[666] and was in fact a last-minute fill-in for actor Sean McClory, who *Daily Variety* reported on June 24 as having been replaced by Connors.[667] The new Ordung feature happened so rapidly that the July 7 *Reporter* had the film "just completed" at a head-spinning "two days under schedule," with Ordung planning another Valor production, *The Devil Has Nine Lives.*[668] By August 10, Ordung planned to follow it with *Gusher* "in early 1955," based on Ordung's "own story."[669] And on August 17, "Dick Bernstein and Tony Michaels," veterans of *Walk the Dark Street,* were added to the crew of *The Devil Has Nine Lives.*[670]

But for all of these details, there was no *Devil* in them as the film was never produced and there is no record of Ordung directing after the pair of movies he completed in one year. *Walk the Dark Street* was the only film he directed other than *Monster from the Ocean Floor,* and it is that much more important because he wrote and made it under his own banner, and with at least two actors he recently worked with on stage, Ewing Brown and Don Ross.[671] It was as much his as any film can be the personal expression of a director, judging by the control that this fiercely independent man momentarily enjoyed. It was even the occasion of a significant move into the Hollywood mainstream, which he handled in the classic Ordung manner. According to *Daily Variety*:

> Those who talk to themselves have nothing on Wyott Ordung, prexy of Valor Pictures.
>
> About to direct *Walk the Dark Street,* Ordung paid his dues to the Screen Directors Guild, but was informed by

the SDG that he needed a letter verifying his employment. Ordung dictated and forwarded this missive:

> "Dear Mr. Ordung: Valor Pictures employs you as director of *Walk the Dark Street,* in accordance with all SDG bylaws and ordinances. Sincerely, Wyott Ordung, president, Valor Pictures."[672]

While *Walk the Dark Street* is consistently listed as a 1956 release, it could have easily been squeaked out by the end of 1954. A taste of what caused this unenthusiastic and delayed debut is hinted at by the *Reporter*'s September 14 review, where the film was damned with faint praise and measured criticism as "just [a] programmer."[673] Reviewer Marvin Fisher acknowledged the "good exploitation possibilities" of Connors as star and "a unique story premise," but decried a lack of "logical reasoning, tempo, and other essential elements," surmising that Ordung had bitten off more than he could chew with an ambitious low-budget effort.

In Ordung's own account, it was his best film and "a damn good little mystery," done for "$100,000 in eight days," partially funded by his agent Ackerman. In the end "I didn't have the money to keep it going and I sold it out and everybody made money but me." Decades later, Ackerman told me what he remembered of his friend's career:

> I remember he wrote a script I think called *Down Three Dark Alleys,* and he needed money to produce it as a picture, and he made an offer that [if] anybody would lend him the money for it, he would I think give them the

> profits of the picture, and also would give a share of the profits of the next six films he planned to make.[674]

Ackerman may have been confusing *Walk the Dark Street* with the title of the 1954 film noir *Down Three Dark Streets.*[675] But the details that Ackerman recalled gel with *Reporter* accounts of Ordung's ambitious plans for Valor Pictures, and with his memory of Ackerman's investment. More importantly, Ackerman remembered something of the film's release:

> But his first film was a miserable flop. I think it played just three days locally and then was removed because word of mouth was killing it, and I don't believe he ever made any other films. He had a script, I think it was called *Hell in the Heavens,* but that was never made, and I haven't thought about it in years, but I think he made another, something like *The Last Boy on Earth?*

Ordung's "first film" here was clearly *Walk the Dark Street,* and not Corman's *Monster from the Ocean Floor,* which got a long-running and profitable release. With the film apparently only receiving an initial three-day run, its association with the year 1956 surely indicates that at that point it showed up as double-bill filler at drive-ins and cheaper theaters. (According to *Daily Variety,* it was picked up by Dominant Pictures in early 1956.[676]) With Connors' increased visibility via the success of *The Rifleman,* debuting in 1958, the film remained ever more exploitable and newspaper ads reflect that fact. An April 1959 newspaper TV schedule from Flagstaff, Arizona lists *Walk the Dark Street* as the 10:30 movie,[677] while an August 1960

Anniston, Alabama clipping advertised it as the second feature at a drive-in double bill.[678] Already on television in one market, it played outdoors in another over a year later. Connors' popularity gave the film longevity and it is too bad that Ordung did not get a trickle of the resulting income, but the film's intrinsic quality should not be underestimated.

Ordung's best film is in reality not bad at all, and on some levels is very impressive. When compared to D-minus efforts like *Dance Hall Racket* and *King Dinosaur,* it seems positively brilliant and so, whoever was responsible for making *Robot Monster* bizarre, the man credited for writing it seems less and less the culprit. *Walk the Dark Street* suffers from many shortcomings: Its cheapness frequently shows through, its plot relies on ridiculous coincidences, it gets lost in stretches of silence and inaction, and it contains serious gaps of logic. But it also displays great imagination with a unique concept, striking visual compositions, an unnerving sense of dread, and a relentless focus on the warped psyche of Connors' character. Ordung was no worse as a filmmaker than an underdeveloped talent, and it is a shame he lacked the opportunity (or the personality) to make other films. He was capable of more creativity than Tucker or Zimbalist, and it is a sorry reality that Zimbalist's garbage received so many glass-half-full appraisals from the *Reporter* (anonymously) while Ordung was not encouraged to keep trying.

Walk the Dark Street neatly divides into a three-act structure. The film begins with the striking of a match to reveal a wristwatch, and the feet of a man lumber along as the credits roll. Hearing a loud noise, he ducks, discovers that it was only the popped tire of a passing car, and continues as the film dissolves to stock footage explosions. A platoon is on patrol in Korea (looking much like a California park), and recently promoted Army Lieutenant Dan Lawton (the man from the credits, played by Don Ross) has drawn the ire of Sergeant Tommy Garrick (Eddie Kafafian), a former friend who wanted his promotion.[679] Tommy dies in combat after ignoring Dan's orders, but not before sending a letter of complaint to his brother in the States.

The first act proper begins with Dan, now discharged, visiting Tommy's brother Frank (Chuck Connors) back home. Frank was reading his brother's letter and, unbeknownst to Dan, has a motivation for revenge. Frank and Dan drink and chat about life and their shared love of hunting, with Frank taking the opportunity to show Dan his films of animals in the wild. Frank reveals he has a bad heart and can no longer hunt,

This early 1960 promo for actor Don Ross indicates that he was to appear in Alfred Hitchcock's *Psycho*.

but longs for the pursuit of the most dangerous game. He offers Dan the proposition that they could harmlessly hunt one another with "camera guns," rifles loaded with film negative that take a photo when fired. Being given the better part of ten-to-one odds in a bet, Dan accepts but does not realize that Frank's gun is loaded with a real bullet.

The second act consists of the pair stalking each other across the unidentified city, mostly in silence and with some tedium, until the third act brings in Helen (Regina Gleason), a woman Dan meets in a nightclub where Tommy was a singer. Once Tommy's fiancée, she discovers that Frank (who she always thought disturbed and controlling) has Dan set up for revenge and warns him. Dan finally runs Frank down and each accidentally takes the other's rifle. Having discovered the gun switch and knowing that Dan is coming after him with live ammo, Frank's weak heart fails and he dies. With Helen along, and a curious police officer trying to sort out Frank's death, Dan unloads the rifle, expecting to see a camera negative but finding a bullet instead. Dan and the policeman stare in bewilderment as the movie ends.

From the beginning, the seams of Ordung's film are visible. After a well-edited chunk of stock footage and an American-looking tour of Korea, Frank's home features an obviously stage-quality door (with no screen), as well as an even more unbelievable portrait of Tommy. It would be difficult to find an actor of the same race who resembles Chuck Connors less than Eddie Kafafian, whose dark eyes and curly hair do not suggest the straw-haired and blue-eyed giant of the (still Brooklyn) Dodgers. They could have been intended to be stepbrothers, but the script makes no such hint. Corresponding to that discrepancy, the title suggests the high-contrast lighting and inky cul-de-sacs of film noir, but they are inadequately represented onscreen. After the opening credits scene which looks suspiciously like an uncertain attempt at day-for-night shooting, there is an indoor scene at Frank's house at night, a few pursuit scenes in the same poor day-for-night style, and night scenes of Frank in a hotel room. Frank advises Dan before the hunt, "If you want to make it even, find places that are off the beaten path. Stick to the alleys. Walk the dark streets." That last piece of advice is as close as the film comes to matching its title. While the duo covers a lot of down-and-out territory, hardly any of it is dark.

The film's flawed logic is worse. Neither Frank nor Dan is fazed by strolling around with rifles in a contest that requires them to remove the cases, take aim, and fire in public. How they are supposed to avoid being stopped or gunned down by the police is a mystery. Even with one lengthy sequence in a marina by a field of oil derricks, the competitors spend most of their time on city streets. To Ordung's credit the extended pursuit of the film's middle act closes with Frank being hauled in by a cop. "It's not against the law to walk around with a weapon in plain sight," Frank snarls to an initially polite officer at headquarters. This story point adds verisimilitude, but anyone thinking about the plot will still wonder why they ever agreed to the contest.

Also highly suspect are the weird coincidences that drive the story. Frank follows Dan to the marina and both skulk around the premises, narrowly missing each other's presence repeatedly. More compact but no more believable is a gun shop scene where both are in the same store, missing each other by seconds and unwittingly switching guns in a twist that drives the film's conclusion. But other twists and turns are better, such as when Dan runs into Tommy's old flame at the Hat and Cane nightclub (which, judging by its neon sign, was a real place). Dan arrives there because he knew that it was where Tommy worked, and he could believably meet Helen. From there her pivotal role as the axis between the two opponents makes sense.

Frank's heart condition might smell of allowing a convenient resolution, but it is established early and fits the logic of Frank's obsession with hunting Dan. Told he cannot hunt, Frank lacks conventional outlets for his violent urges and is that much more motivated. The camera gun assures him that he is in no danger, and he perfectly rationalizes his desire to gun down another human being by the convenient, perfect target of the man who can be blamed for his brother's death. That Helen can see that Tommy scapegoated Dan for his shortcomings, while Frank cannot, perfect illustrates Frank's warped psyche. If this calm thought ever crossed his mind, it would be drowned in self-righteous anger. Tommy was constantly manipulated and controlled by Frank, and is still posthumously used by him for self-fulfilling ends.

Ordung's belief in psychic forces may have been a strong influence on the story. As Frank explains to Dan in the first act, "When he felt pain, I felt it. When he died, a little of me died too." Frank reminisces about his singing at the Hat and Cane: "I used to listen to him all the time. Even now I go there. I get the feeling Tommy's still around." While nothing is spelled out, Tommy may be guiding the odd turns of fate that protect

Dan. The first scene at the Hat and Cane curiously starts with a close-up of a singer, dark and similar to Tommy's looks (much closer than Frank), and he belts out a song called "Show Me the Way," with lyrics almost sounding like they are from Frank to Tommy. Perhaps Tommy wants to lure Frank into the next life, or perhaps Dan will be in trouble after the policeman sees him unwittingly unload a bullet from Frank's rifle. And there is an awesome moment near the end when Dan walks toward Frank's apartment as he pears from his window, the two recognizing one another from a distance and their final conflict initiated. This adrenalizing sequence plays like the prototype of confrontations in crime films like *Manhunter* or *Heat,* as opponents crash together with an understated sense of fate at work.

But Ordung showed great ability in every aspect of *Walk the Dark Street,* and its deficiencies are easy to forgive. The film has amazing visual dynamism for such a lowly effort. The second act kicks off with a fade in from black as Dan walks out of the camera and, a short while later, walks into the camera as the film dissolves to Frank poring through a phone book. Similar effects occur later in the final chase, as both run into the camera, legs getting huge and flying over. And in the climax Dan walks into the camera in anger, his face filling the screen with rage and darkness. Ordung used the camera to track action, particularly in this final sequence, with a succession of dynamic views of running and driving—Frank wrecks a car, Dan chases him—the film coming alive in the edited flow of these shots.

He also showed tremendous intelligence in compositions, in how action plays out within them, and in such editing choices as an insert of Dan's hand knocking on Frank's door. Many

Chuck Connors in *Walk the Dark Street.*

films would have only dubbed in a sound but this simple shot breaks up monotony, and is the kind of small detail lacking in *Robot Monster.* Frank is stopped by the flashlight of a cop who silently displays his badge, and the film cuts to the loud vocals of the Hat and Cane singer in close-up. Similarly, Ordung knew when not to cut. In one sequence Frank looks up phone numbers while the camera lingers on the phone book and Frank's scribbling within it, his disembodied voice mixing with a tinny telephone sound hanging invisibly above and beyond. In a brief café scene, a waitress silently stands in Dan's presence and gazes at him, this action making the viewer uncomfortable as the unaware Dan takes time to realize he is being observed. Ordung also used composition in fascinating ways, such as the nightclub scene where Dan and Helen sit in the background between another couple framing them in the foreground. A similar effect occurs in a muddy day-for-night sequence where another couple kisses in a park, separating to reveal Frank hulking in the background.

One quick scene played out in a single shot depicts Frank quickly buying a used car because he cannot get a cab, the interactions between the salesman and Frank all pantomimed. (More than one part of *Walk the Dark Street* suggests that Ordung's visual sense was honed on the storytelling style of silent films.) Frank's realization that the rifles are switched is emphasized by the camera closing in on his face, a motion used casually in other films that stands out here in contrast to the restraint shown otherwise. Ordung put all of his visual tricks together best in the marina sequence, featuring such elements as a rotating 360-degree pan starting on Frank, intercutting with other shots, and finally panning back to him. Best of all is a stunning composition with two levels of a ship in the same shot; Dan and Frank move in different directions on separate levels, sensing each other's presence but never making contact. This sequence plays without dialogue but with fascinating use of sound; sea birds call and metal atmospherically clangs in the breeze, as a field of quiet oil derricks pump endlessly in the land beyond. There is no budgetary reason that cheap movies cannot be visually arresting; it only takes imagination and preparation, and Ordung was one of the rare low-budget directors to make the effort.

It could be argued that this visual dynamism should be attributed to cinematographer Brydon Baker. As Corman indicated, Crosby assisted Ordung in directing *Monster from the*

Ocean Floor, and perhaps that scenario repeated itself. But *Walk the Dark Street* was a different project in many respects. It was made from Ordung's script after he completed his first directing job, and there is most importantly little in Baker's work to suggest that he created the film's look. While Crosby began the 1930s winning an Oscar for shooting F.W. Murnau's *Tabu*, Baker spent much of the decade working with both of the era's notorious B Western bottom-feeders, Victor Adamson and Robert J. Horner. He had more recently worked on such incredibly gray projects as *The Phantom from 10,000 Leagues* (1955) (a film that Ordung remembered working on). This is not to disparage Baker, who undoubtedly brought his best to a project as much as William C. Thompson, but his work seems only as good as his director wanted it to be.

And not surprisingly, Ordung the actor-director also brought a sure hand to his treatment of the cast. Ross, looking like a black-haired Spencer Tracy, is just right as Dan, an average Joe exceptional enough to be the enlisted man who got promoted. He can only be criticized for being a little bland. Gleason and Kafafian are likewise good, if similarly average and sometimes overdramatic. Also noteworthy is a recurring cameo by Ordung as a hotel desk clerk; both his features and his tough guy voice resemble Harvey Keitel. But truly outstanding and really flawless is Connors. He later developed a heroic persona on television, and this early role shows a darker version of that same charisma. Connors' personification of the demented Frank is so total—running the gamut from intense hatred, cold manipulation, to crumbling cowardice—that it is as integral to the film's quality as its visuals.

Wyott Ordung directs and makes an onscreen cameo.

Connors' performance comes particularly to the fore in an astonishing two-and-a-half minute sequence from the first act. Frank shows Dan his wildlife films, innocuous enough but disturbing in context. Paul Dunlap's unsettled modernist musical score, with an uneasy flute melody moving against churning woodwinds, resumes here after minutes of silence and makes plain what is implied. Dan watches the film while Frank watches him watching it, as attentively as when he listened to Dan talk about civilian life, massive chin immobile and eyes prodding Dan with unfathomable malice. Frank is effectively shot in profile, staring at Dan as he watches the movie (which Frank never watches—he knows it by heart and prefers seeing it affect someone else), the reels roll along with their shadows on the wall, suggesting the dark mechanics of Frank's mind. There is a change of perspective when a chimp is threatened by a tiger—we see Dan straight on, and then Frank straight on, his eyes fixated on Dan's reaction. Then a rhinoceros runs in eerie slow motion, the same animal is dead, and the film-within-a-film builds to a crescendo as an angry snake lunges at the camera right before the end. The film's climax foreshadows the threat that Dan, staring into the serpent's rage, soon faces from Frank.

A half-decade before *Psycho* and *Peeping Tom* established the cinema's obsession with psychopathic voyeurism, Ordung's film put it there in detail. Even Hitchcock's other voyeuristic masterpiece *Rear Window* premiered on August 1, 1954, mere weeks after the filming of *Walk the Dark Street* wrapped. Ordung beat them all, and did them one better. The creepy hunting movie sequence establishes that Frank is not only disturbed and hunts for love of violence, but actually associates the act of seeing with killing. The camera gun, erasing the line between different kinds of shooting, is the logical invention of this bent personality. It can significantly be loaded with bullets and used as a real gun, which drives the film's conclusion. Knowing that the camera gun Dan carries is loaded with a bullet, Frank dies in fear as Dan approaches, his glare filling the screen. Living by the malignant stare, Frank dies by it.

Imposing and believable as he was, the sleep-deprived Connors may have been a burden on his director. There is some evidence from outside the *Walk the Dark Street* production that Connors could be difficult. Assistant director Paul Wurtzel told Weaver his vivid memory of Connors from the production of 1957's *Tomahawk Trail*:

> He was crazy—literally. I don't know what was wrong with him. He was a nice enough guy to work with, but get a few drinks in him and he'd want to pick fights with everybody and stuff like that. He'd get wild-eyed—it was really strange! He got in a big scrape in the dining room one night, at dinner. There were other people eating there, tourists and stuff, so one great big Teamster driver grabbed Connors and kinda shuffled him out of the room before he could start breaking up the furniture.[680]

There is also evidence that Connors' dark side manifested itself on the *Walk the Dark Street* set. According to Ewing Brown, who played the gun shop clerk:

> It was such a little bit of money, [Ordung] was living on aspirin tablets! He was just trying to get it done on no money and one of the leads, who later did *The Rifleman*, was taking the whole thing kind of flippant. The scene where he does the heart attack, and I helped him back into the back room of the gun store, they were shooting him coming through the door. We were starting to do that. Now you realize, time is money and film is money? He grabbed me, and picked me up off the floor, and carried *me* in, and thought it was a big joke. And [Ordung] just about had a heart attack, cause he's running short on film and money. I think that was a couple more aspirin tablets. But I went back and I said, "Hey, this thing is running very low on money and time, we've got to get finished and get the hell out of here."[681]

Connors' prank sums up the film's indifferent reception. It came and went as it did for its lead actor, taking up time and treated without respect, lost in a sea of many minor efforts.[682] Dunlap, who remembered Ordung as "a strange person," thought the title better than the movie.[683] Brown lamented that Ordung was "really a very sweet, caring person. He was easily hurt over his work. I think he was ready to take out the samurai sword on some people." The remainder of Ordung's career might have been no worse if he had gone banzai. *Hell in the Heavens* was confirmed in a September *Reporter* as "the next film for Valor Pictures," but came to nothing.[684] Ordung brought a $300,000 lawsuit against Columbia Pictures "and six John Does" in the fall of 1954 in relation to the Rita Hayworth movie *Affair in Trinidad* (1952). As *Variety* reported, "Ordung declares *Trinidad* contains portion of his own story, *Gibraltar,* which he submitted to Columbia in 1951."[685] Ordung told Johnny Legend, "They stole it, and then my attorney sold me out. We were suing Columbia for $300,000 and the day before they settled the case he sold me out. I found that out eleven years later."

Ordung's name continued to pop up here and there in the trade press. *Daily Variety* reported in 1955 that he signed with agent Milt Rosner and sold a script called *White Fury*; in 1956 he was buying a share of a Sunset Strip nightclub and was hired to make a documentary by the Civil Air Patrol.[686] But in terms of completed feature film credits, his career became increasingly sparse. After having sold *Combat Squad* (1953) to Broder, contributing to Cohen's competently dull *Target Earth* (1954), and filming his own *Walk the Dark Street,* he had one more writing credit in the following years. According to producer Richard Gordon:

> It originated as a screenplay called *Satellite of Blood,* that had been written on speculation by a writer in Hollywood, Wyott Ordung . . . who was among those writers that were doing pictures for people like American International, and so on. [My brother] Alex sent me the screenplay, because it was something that AIP decided not to do, and I liked it very much and so we decided to use it as the basis for a film about space travel . . . we thought it would be a very timely subject.[687]

The resulting film was another medium-low-budget, non-embarrassing but unexceptional effort released in 1959 as *First Man into Space.* ("Not his autobiography," the Medveds noted.[688]) Along the way, he went uncredited on *The Phantom from 10,000 Leagues* but remembered working in its cast and crew, and recalled liking director Dan Milner less than his brother Jack (who "saved" *Monster from the Ocean Floor* by editing its mangled sound elements into shape).[689] Along with Baker, there was much crew crossover between *Phantom* and *Walk the Dark Street,* as well as some of Zimbalist's films, and the rest of Ordung's credits showed a pattern of taking small jobs for friends and acquaintances. When Broder produced a pair of cheap science fiction flicks in the mid-sixties, Ordung was involved officially and otherwise. In 1966 he script-doctored on *Women of the Prehistoric Planet* and was a credited assistant director on *The Navy vs. the Night Monsters.*

Recalling the *Navy* experience ruefully to Weaver, director Michael A. Hoey remembered Broder as a cheapskate, a control freak, and an incompetent. As for his first AD, "Wyott was a screwball, and I had a lot of problems with him. Wyott was Jack Broder's man, and was always on the phone telling him what I was doing wrong. I have no great respect for Wyott Ordung."[690] Hoey clarified his friction with Ordung for me: "I know that he really wanted to be a director and perhaps this caused some jealousy on his part, but at any rate I never felt that he was supportive of my efforts during the making of the film."[691] As star Anthony Eisley recounted to Weaver, Broder at one point watched dailies and expressed disgust at the poor quality of a fight scene.[692] It was a terrible fight, Broder believed, because he could not hear punches when they landed. In spite of working decades in the industry, Broder was so ignorant about filmmaking that he did not know that punch sounds are dubbed in. This tied in with his micromanaging of Hoey in absurd ways, such as his order to tear down a set that later had to be expensively rebuilt.

Ordung was soon involved in an even cheaper production, a bottom-level horror film directed by an associate from the same circle as he and Brown, Oliver Drake. With decades of experience writing and directing in Poverty Row, Drake recounted in his autobiography a project that began in a short-lived venture for filming in Las Vegas.[693] Drake's film ended up property of a lab with its own financial problems, thereby leaving it unreleased; barely anyone saw it until it briefly surfaced in the VHS home video boom of the eighties. *The Mummy and the Curse of the Jackals* (1969) might be the worst thing that Ordung ever got involved in, though it provides a generous helping of accidental humor and one of John Carradine's many bill-paying performances.[694] Eisley again starred, this time as an Egyptologist devoted to a supernaturally revived princess. He also transforms into a "jackal man," fights with her jealous and overweight mummy suitor, and (in a scene straight out of exploitation film) shows the princess how to put on a bra. As assistant director, Ordung may have been the one to capture the amused reactions of passersby to the mummy and the jackal man walking down the Las Vegas strip. And giving credit where it is due, when the movie abruptly crashes to a halt with the princess dying, the decomposition effects are genuinely disgusting.

Ordung's final credit was another favor, this time for Brown. *A Whale of a Tale* (1977) was an independent, inoffensive family film of the type that thrived in the seventies. With Hollywood coked out and in love with its new freedom to depict almost everything, indie kid-movies like *Benji* entered the market partially filled by corny Disney comedies. Brown's film (apparently filmed years before) told a typical animal story of a boy working at a water park and falling in love with the killer whale, while his single mother is drawn to the park director. William Shatner, in a needy decade between *Star Trek* TV and *Star Trek* movies, starred as the director; veterans Richard Arlen and Andy Devine also appeared. The cheap but competent film was a decent finale for Ordung, at least preferable to the job that preceded it.

But it remains regrettable that Ordung had to bow out at all, and that surviving hints of his other projects only point to them never getting off the ground. *Daily Variety* announced in March 1960 that Ordung would co-script *The Fiend,* "story of robbery and rape," for Paul Kramer Productions, a film that was apparently unmade.[695] Then in May 1960, the *Reporter* noted that he had started an acting workshop with "40 young thespians" who would be presenting a play for prospective reps after a month of intensive study.[696] And in March 1962, *Variety* reported that "Ordung sold two originals, *Beyond Valor* and *Night of the Dark Moon,* to Yearling Productions, deal calling for him to produce and direct former for Cavalcade Pictures release."[697] Neither film was made, nor did Ordung end up with the executive producer credit he was announced to have on a 1968 release from Gemini-American Productions, *Hell's Outcasts.*[698] (This movie was probably Robert F. Slatzer's *The Hellcats,* released that spring, produced by Gemini-American without Ordung.) He was added in October 1973 to the crew of *Tweet's Ladies of Pasadena,* a long developing and never completed indie project from oddball character actor Timothy Carey,[699] and had two more un-filmed scripts announced in *Daily Variety* during the mid-seventies, *Never Trust a Hungarian* and *Adventure in Bora, Bora.*[700]

Whether or not these glimmers of career activity did him much good, Ordung was at least still using his talents. They were undeniable, and he packed an astonishing amount of excellence into *Walk the Dark Street* while working with virtually nothing. But also representative of his life by this point was his making local news in 1975 as a "noted psychic" with his opinion that actress Pat Delaney was "reincarnated from the 1700s."[701] As Ackerman remembered:

> Well, he became very strange in the latter days of his life. One time, he was sitting with me in my living room and he pointed across the room and said, "Look, look, there's H.G. Wells. He's waving to you, Forry." And another time I believe he thought he was seeing Lon Chaney.[702]

Perhaps Ordung was lucky, given his personality and the cutthroat nature of the movie business, to make even one film as good as *Walk the Dark Street.* He was far, far better than anyone could have imagined on the basis of *Robot Monster.*

12

Lost Years, Lost Films

It was roughly when Wyott Ordung's *Walk the Dark Street* became double-bill fodder that traces of Phil Tucker become visible again. After his mid-fifties exploitation films, he would direct *The Cape Canaveral Monsters* in 1960, a last attempt in the genre that brought him closest to the mainstream. But some idea of what he was up to in the intervening years survived, beginning with a third collaboration with Lenny Bruce that for better or worse disappeared. According to the Albert Goldman biography, Bruce was scamming money out of a wealthy young woman, ostensibly to finance a TV pilot, when she demanded some documentation and to meet those involved. He cooked up a Western storyline about an orphaned pioneer boy raised by Indian braves and was increasingly excited about the show's prospects. Calling it *Fleetfoot,* Bruce enlisted Tucker as director and found a few professional actors (such as Mel Welles) and junkie jazz musician friends to round out the cast.[703] Also central to the production were recent acquaintances Frank Murphy (an industrial filmmaker who later designed titles for

Peter Gunn) and Bill Himes (president of an area chapter of the National Association of Broadcast Engineers and Technicians).

It may have been Tucker who suggested filming *Fleetfoot* at Bronson Canyon in Griffith Park, having filmed there before, but even so his involvement was probably not extensive:

> On the third day of shooting, Tucker and Lenny got into a quarrel so violent that the director walked off the scene and never again reappeared. The burden of the direction was now assumed by Frank Murphy, with Bill Himes and Lenny throwing in their suggestions.[704]

But with or without Tucker, *Fleetfoot* went nowhere. Although Bruce and company successfully completed the project, the end result could not be sold and to his frustration, a Western series with a similar premise appeared on television about a year later. Unaired, one copy of *Fleetfoot* supposedly remained in the possession of Himes. In the early sixties Bruce used production stills from the pilot in his self-published booklet *Stamp Help Out,* putting them in a new context as part of a satirical look at drug use. He also used a still of his mother Sally Marr, dancing the Charleston in *Dance Hall Racket,* for the same section.[705]

Apart from those stills, Bruce may have left no indication in his later, famous years of his work in bottom-end film, and most fans of the time had no idea his early films existed. In his autobiography *How to Talk Dirty and Influence People,* he summarizes his brief film career with *The Rocket Man,* and omits everything else but a hint of the uncompleted *The Leather Jacket* (1955) (reportedly attempted after *Fleetfoot* with no connection to Tucker). And in a 1960 interview in *The Realist* he was directly asked about his screenwriting career, replying "I've got one single credit—additional dialogue for *The Rocket Man* . . . ."[706] He did not remember, or chose not to remember, that he not only acted in *Dance Hall Racket* and *Dream Follies* but wrote them as well. For someone so publicly shameless, Bruce seemed strangely embarrassed by his film career.

From Tucker's perspective, *Fleetfoot* is unique for being his only work as a director in color film. According to Goldman, the production schedule was one week that may have been curtailed a day or two by union hassles.[707] Given that Tucker quit on day three, he could not have directed more than half the pilot. *Fleetfoot* also provides a counterpoint to Tucker's earlier career, when he made unsold TV pilots in his time with Gordon Avil. If Tucker was too stubborn about his ideas for *Fleetfoot*, backed up by experience, this may explain his falling out with Bruce. However, this blowup may not have been serious at all. Phil Tucker Jr. specifically remembers when his parents went out to see Bruce perform:

> I think they felt that he was really too good for the venues that he was performing in, they were just sort of biding their time until he hit the big time and somebody discovered his talent. They were friends. Contrary to any other reports you've heard, I can definitely tell you that they were pals.

A further piece of the Tucker puzzle was provided by Ed Wood biographer Rudolph Grey. Buried near the back of *Nightmare of Ecstasy* is this production note for *Plan 9 from Outer Space*: "Phil Tucker, director of *Robot Monster*, assisted Wood with the editing."[708] This startling item, long public knowledge but never commented on, places Tucker in the midst of Wood's most famous and enduring film, and paints a tantalizing image of them as the Steven Spielberg and George Lucas of bad fifties sci-fi, collaborating on the Worst Movie of All Time. Atypically for a book of many extended quotes from original sources, this statement is made by the author without attribution, but Grey told me he believes that it was Kathy Wood who gave him this information.[709] Since as she put it, the pair were "friendly enemies," they could have worked on the same project, though perhaps no closer than necessary. As Tucker Jr. noted, his father and Wood "were both ex-Marines and in the same business whether they liked each other or not, and I'm sure their paths crossed often enough to force them to maintain some civility or at least a 'working' relationship."[710]

Tucker seemingly gave himself an editor's apprenticeship by way of *Broadway Jungle* in 1955, and was a logical assistant editor on the 1956 production.[711] If Tucker had recently become an editor thanks to *Broadway Jungle*, then Wood might have actively wanted him involved for that expertise. With *Plan 9 from Outer Space* filming at Quality Studios, Tucker could also have moonlighted on the crew thanks to his history with Merle Connell and it seems that he did. According to Conrad Brooks, who acted in *Plan 9 from Outer Space* and specifically remembered not seeing Tucker earlier on the *Dance Hall Racket* set:

> I didn't know the man that well. I met him when we were doing *Plan 9*, and I actually just saw him there one time.

> I think he was doing a little production work there. . . . I just saw him one day, he could have been there [more].[712]

Tucker's presence is corroborated by an unexpected source. Playing one of the clueless alien invaders was Joanna Lee, a successful TV writer in decades to come, but at this point a struggling actress. In her autobiography she recalls the making of *Plan 9 from Outer Space* with a cringe. She felt that the experience was so beneath her that for many years she lived in denial of it.[713] (Grey told me that she not only refused to contribute to his Wood biography, but threatened legal action if her name was mentioned.[714]) Believing she had arrived at another address, she walked in disbelief down an alley to "an abandoned

WADE WILLIAMS DIST.

A *Plan 9 from Outer Space* still that reveals a small glimpse behind the scenes.

garage," with "a few grungy guys as crew," and soon formed an impression that most of those involved in the production were "freaks." Lee's account was perhaps unduly colored by her disgust. She paints Wood as a rude, snarling exploitation man with contempt for filmmaking who, among his unsavory qualities, was a "drug addict." While Wood was eventually an alcoholic and died from it, there is no evidence that he used such drugs as cocaine or heroin, his naïve love of his own films is well documented, and people generally found him charming.

But Lee connected a positive memory to the *Plan 9 from Outer Space* experience and, if one can believe she was more accurate when not embarrassed, her memoir contains an indirect reference to Tucker. One night after filming, "Phil, an assistant director" asked her to join him and "a friend" to get a bite to eat at "Canter's on Fairfax," and the friend was Lenny Bruce. Having recently seen him perform, she recognized him (and he recognized her, she says), and they were soon chatting in depth: "With Phil growing quietly furious in the background, we talked exclusively to each other." When Bruce suggested that they could all get together with a prostitute pal of his that he thought she "could be friends" with, he was angered by her disgust. Then "[b]oth Phil and Lenny laughed" at her "square" attitude and, having reconciled, she and Bruce made plans for a date while Phil was in the restroom. Lee states that they were never very serious, although she babysat his daughter Kitty when he feared that his estranged wife would take her.

While there are many Phils, few could have been working on *Plan 9 from Outer Space* and also be friends with Bruce. There are in fact no Phils or Phillips credited among the cast and crew, meaning that the identity of Bruce's friend must be drawn from an even smaller pool of uncredited assistants on the low-rent production. In all likelihood, "Phil" was Phil Tucker. This corroborates both his involvement in filming *Plan 9 from Outer Space* and his son's memory of his friendship with Bruce. Although production dates of such films are dimly recorded, *Fleetfoot* was likely made no later than 1955, and *Plan 9 from Outer Space* no earlier than late 1956. Whatever the nature of their dustup, it did not seem to last long. It is also worth a thought that Lee, sickened by the Quality environment, was willing to have dinner with Tucker. Her story focuses on Bruce, but the background details single Tucker out as not a "freak" like the others. Whatever he was doing at this time, he clearly had his typical energy and charisma, and was visibly not a loser. And Tucker Jr. finds the scenario very believable, noting, "I got a strong hunch that it was my dad when the piece mentioned him suggesting that they all get a bite to eat at Canter's on Fairfax. That would have been very much in character."[715]

Beyond *Fleetfoot,* there is one more lost Tucker film. It has no connection to Bruce and has not captured imaginations the way that *Space Jockey* did after it appeared in *The Golden Turkey Awards.* In the same book, the Medveds gave the film its only write-up:

> Tucker's third major film was his self-proclaimed "Masterpiece" and "greatest achievement," the drag-strip saga *Pachuco* (1956). This violent, incoherent effort told the story of two Mexican-American tough guys making their way in their adopted homeland. It received its world

> premiere at a drive-in theater in west Texas, where the audience found itself so deeply stirred by Tucker's film that a major riot ensued. The spectators robbed the candy counter and box office, as well as literally tearing down the screen, before *Pachuco* had even run its course. Not surprisingly, the film failed to achieve a broad national distribution after this controversial debut.[716]

One major, if inconclusive, addition to the *Pachuco* story is a pair of photographs that appeared in the *Los Angeles Examiner* in August 1957. Available online at the USC Digital Library, two pictures show Tucker in yet another suicide publicity stunt. In one he is seated on an examination table, looking exhausted as a uniformed policeman stands by. In the other, he is dramatically shot through a car's open passenger side door, clutching cans of film and apparently half-conscious, a 35 millimeter film box on the seat reading "PACHUCO."[717] (These photos clearly relate to what Conrad Brooks and Wyott Ordung remembered about Tucker's suicide stunts, as quoted in Chapter 9.) But *Pachuco* almost never shows up in references and there has rarely been even a discussion of it on the Internet; there is little hint of its existence beyond the above paragraph and archived photos.

Tucker's original comments on the film are therefore a revelation. Describing it in immense detail, and contradicting *The Golden Turkey Awards* on some points, the volume of Tucker's extensive memories of *Pachuco* meet or exceed his comments on *Robot Monster.* Two-thirds of the way through the interview, Tucker made his brief, previously quoted statement about editing and trying to sell *Dance Hall Racket.* The interview continued:

> *So after Dream Follies, what came next?*
>
> Probably *Pachuco. . . . Pachuco* was the first real picture I ever made. And when I say that, I mean in the sense that it was a real picture made in a real way for real markets, that told a story I wanted to tell. The usual shortage of money just didn't affect me this time. We would sleep in the studio at night, the same studio that I did *Dream Follies* and *Dance Hall Racket.* We would sneak in there at night and work from around 10:00 at night 'til about 4:30, 5:00 o'clock in the morning. If all the time had been like ten-hour days, we probably spent ten, twelve days on the picture, which was remarkable for me at that time. It was a very violent picture, it was a very realistic and true picture, and it told a little story.

However good *Pachuco* really was, it was not by-the-numbers burlesque junk, and Tucker remembered it with pride. As his repetition of the word "real" emphasizes, this movie was notches above his others, "a story [he] wanted to tell." Tucker was not financially strained either because of backing or, far more likely, because he was pulling the movie off on next to nothing. The paradox of how he made his best movie on no resources is unraveled by the fact that he worked late at night when no one was around. The location was Quality Studios and Tucker's familiarity with Connell and his back-alley soundstage may have literally given him the keys to using it in the off hours, with or without Connell's knowledge. Whatever the movie was like, it was violent and Tucker therefore believed it had box office potential.

> I subsequently got the picture in halfway decent shape; I edited myself. I took it to distributors, and some liked it, some didn't like it; nobody would really [release it]. Then a guy named Bill Hackel, who has since died, saw it. Bill produced most of Republic's cheap pictures. He was executive producer of all their "Bs." Bill loved it. He thought it would really do well.

The Bill Hackel that Tucker refers to was A.W. Hackel, who formed the independent company Supreme Pictures in 1934. Born in Austria in 1882, he was (according to Guy Woodward Finney's 1929 book *The Great Los Angeles Bubble*) one of many (including Louis B. Mayer) involved in the Julian Petroleum oil stock scam that collapsed in 1927.[718] Hackel was also there when Poverty Row kingpin Republic Pictures formed out of the 1935 union of Consolidated Film Laboratories and other small companies, including his own. His Supreme Pictures remained separate from the Republic conglomeration, but acted as distributor to many of the action-filled B Westerns he ground out with his stars, Bob Steele and Johnny Mack Brown. William C. Thompson shot a couple of Hackel's horse operas, 32 of which featured the steely-eyed Steele, and 16 with the athletic Brown. (Brown, first a football star, was an MGM lead in Hollywood, and starred in King Vidor's *Billy the Kid* [1930], shot by Tucker's mentor, Gordon Avil.)

According to Don Miller, ". . . the budgets were lower than before [in Steele's career], and the pictures were ground out two or three at a time . . .. they were conventional Westerns, made for and played in lesser theaters."[719] Miller allows that Hackel's

A.W. Hackel's Westerns featured stars Johnny Mack Brown and Bob Steele.

quality may have increased after he "signed a deal with Republic for the 1936-37 season," but still writes that Hackel's Steele Westerns "suffered in comparison" to Republic's own material. Republic dropped Hackel "at the end of the 1937-38 season," but he continued producing into the 1940s. *Am I Guilty?* (1940) was a state's-rights production aimed at black audiences, while most of his subsequent work as producer was done at Monogram. At least four of those productions, mostly crime thrillers, were directed by William Beaudine. Hackel's last credit is for co-producing the Nazi invasion melodrama *Strange Holiday* (1945) with Claude Rains, which was one of Arch Oboler's first movies as a director.[720] Hackel then appears retired from film production until his death in October 1959, and he may have never been very hands-on. According to Sam Sherman:

> Of the line producers who actually made films, many only received credit as production manager or supervisor, while many received no credit, so the production company head could claim the producer's credit for himself. The real producer of the 1935-36 Bob Steele series for A.W. "Bill" Hackel's Supreme Pictures was actually Sam Katzman, although you would never know it from the screen credits.[721]

Katzman would go on to become one of Hollywood's most prolific and profitable low-budget producers on his own, so this uncredited early work was good training.

Tucker's wording is ambiguous about when he met Hackel, but they could have easily known each other for years. Hackel's Bob Steele Westerns were at first directed by Steele's father, Robert N. Bradbury, but then by Sam Newfield.[722] His brother with an un-Americanized name, Sigmund Neufeld, would found PRC and keep Sam busy directing; *Robot Monster*'s director of photography, Jack Greenhalgh, was a PRC regular.

> So [Hackel] put up the money for me to make a trip to Texas—Amarillo—and do a test there. We had a three-day weekend; a Friday, a Saturday, and a Sunday. We had two days of promotion. In those days, you still couldn't use television; we used radio, we used newspapers. I think we spent about five or six hundred bucks for those two days, and a trailer that had been at the drive-in.

Tucker knew the state's-rights distribution system well and, from his years of making cheap Westerns, Hackel was just as familiar.. Why Amarillo was specifically chosen is unknown, but at the same time not a mystery. A Texas audience's reaction would be more representative of the film's long-term reception than a viewing closer to Hollywood and, as established in Chapter 9, Tucker's earlier films had played in Texas. They even seem to have kept on playing the Lone Star State up to that point, to judge by a March 1960 *Llano News* ad for *Bagdad After Midnight.*[723] Fifties Amarillo also had many theaters, including at least four drive-ins and some that catered to Spanish-speaking audiences. The city was also used to premiere actor Robert Clarke's own attempt at low-budget filmmaking, *The Hideous Sun Demon,* in August 1958. Clarke had no local prospects for his film but found that he could premiere it at an Amarillo drive-in, thanks to help from his brother who worked in sales at a local TV station. (Theater owner Blue Doyle had at least three Amarillo drive-ins.) Clarke prepared his own advertising materials, flew in with co-star Nan Peterson, and did a radio interview to promote the movie.[724] Depending on when *Pachuco* was made, Clarke's choice of the city could have been related to Tucker's own Amarillo movie premiere.

> Well, opening night they were turning away cars, oh, probably an hour before the picture opened. The next night, the cars weren't letting them[selves] be turned away, the cars were driving in anyhow. Two people were killed. It was a predominately Chicano crowd, and they just wrecked the theater totally; not from disapproval,

WADE WILLIAMS DIST.

Robert Clarke's *The Hideous Sun Demon* premiered in Amarillo, Texas in 1958.

> but from approval. They just loved the picture. The screen was never touched. But they ran, and just ripped up everything, and wrote all over the walls, "Viva la Pachuco!"

With his penchant for hyperbole, Tucker was probably leg-pulling on the detail that there were two deaths at the film's debut. But lest it seem that Tucker was remembering through a stereotypical filter and making the audience a bunch of "crazy Mexicans," the fact is that his movie focused on a very specific group that was likely well-represented in the audience:

> "Pachuco" was the term used for Mexican-American gangsters; kids. They were kid gangs; in the old days in the Valley, for instance. But it was a big thing all over the country, actually. People didn't realize that. I knew it; other people didn't know it.

Pachucos, with a distinctive style of zoot suits, long hair, wide-brimmed hats, and their own dialect, were publicly visible in the forties and fifties, particularly to anyone who lived in the southwest. Their style died out as part of the mass cultural shift away from sophisticated dress and swing jazz toward blue jeans and rock-n-roll, and seems foppish compared to the grittier gang aesthetic that followed. A recent guide to the argot of the drug trade gives the following definitions of "pachuco": "well dressed; well-to-do gangster; marihuana user; mamma's boy."[725] But in 1962, columnist Robert C. Ruark recommended that authorities dole out humiliation to juvenile delinquents, particularly that pachucos get a head-shaving as a blow to their "terraced pompadours and elaborately contrived duck-tailed grease jobs on the neck hair."[726] In a 1943 *Long Beach Independent* editorial, Ray Miller noted that the garishly tailored zoot suit was for pachucos a "symbol of social nonconformity," and that they were far removed from other wearers of the same garb:

> It is true that there are some Negro "zoot suiters" but they are not organized into gangs such as the "pachucos." . . . . The typical Caucasian "zoot suiter" is still in another category—that of a moron with exhibitionistic tendencies.[727]

Pachuco or not, Los Angeles had a youth gang problem. In a late 1953 series, the *Los Angeles Times* reported that "5,000 L.A. Hoodlums Belong to Violence-Dealing Gangs," with some members as young as nine.[728] At around the same time, *The Mirror* reported on the death of a middle-aged businessman, beaten up by three young men after he came to the aid of two Marines being attacked by the trio.[729] And Tucker was right that pachuco activity was "all over the country." The June 1954 death of an airman at Chanute Air Force Base in western Illinois, initially believed an accident, was subsequently found to be connected with an admitted pachuco airman (one among fifty of what the AP report termed the "terrorist pachuco society").[730]

In their era, pachucos were a regular media topic, at least so far back as the infamous Zoot Suit Riots in 1943 L.A., where sailors and Marines clashed with local Hispanic youths. Tucker joined the Marine Corps a year-and-a-half later, and easily could have heard first-hand accounts of the riots from others. (According to Goldman, Bruce's mother was briefly married to a pachuco.[731]) Reports from area papers were later decried as rabble-rousing, yellow journalism, with a tendency to make military personnel completely heroic. The *Long Beach Independent* carried the headline "Pachuco Gangs Tangle in New Street Brawls with Navy; Cry 'Death to Cops,'" and described them as "bent on revenge and with murder in their hearts."[732] But a June 21 *Time* article from the opposite angle also lacked any subtlety. An entire coast away from the riots, *Time* pontificated that the military men were a "*Panzer* division."[733] A 1944 story by a young Ray Bradbury in *New Detective Magazine* walked a middle road, narrated by a young Hispanic man solving his brother's

IN DARKEST L.A.

A late 1953 editorial cartoon, dramatizing Los Angeles youth crime.

murder and discovering a Nazi spy, while also trying to avoid getting beat up in the Riots.[734] "I'm no *pachucho*!" he exclaims at one point, the word spelled by Bradbury with a second h.

By making a movie about pachucos and titling it *Pachuco,* Tucker was courting some degree of trouble. With pachuco activity all over and particularly strong in the southwest, it should have been scientifically predictable that something bad could happen when the movie premiered in Amarillo. Even if the theater remained unscathed, there was so much antipathy toward pachucos that Tucker might have found himself over a barrel with city leaders and law enforcement. Although reports of the disaster do not seem to have survived, there is nothing unbelievable about Tucker's description, since Amarillo had as much of a pachuco problem as anywhere else. A May 1957 newspaper story described a group of barely adolescent Hispanic boys "being investigated by city juvenile officers this morning for possible connection with the California-style 'pachuco' gang," a group "confirmed" in the city earlier.[735] The report also noted the arrest of more boys for a violent crime, their moniker of the "Wolf Pack," and their pachuco tattoos.

According to Rogelio Agrasánchez Jr.'s study *Mexican Movies in the United States*, the pachuco crowd affected the movie-going experience just as Tucker remembered. The southwestern Mexican-American movie audience of the fifties was working class and family-oriented. Along with a mixture of Hollywood product, theaters that catered to this demographic showed many Spanish-language Mexican productions, typically programming a heavy proportion of escapist comedies, melodramas, and musicals. So far as this audience was concerned, the pachucos were undesirables at best. Agrasánchez provides this account of a checker for the Clasa-Mohme chain reporting on two theaters in Rio Hondo, Texas:

> The Rio is owned by Mr. Flores . . . He never lets the "pachuco" element run in and out of the theater like they do at the Rex. . . . Mr. Ruenes at the Rex encourages the tough young Mexicans to run in and out of the theater dating up girls, and doesn't care what noise or

> commotion they make. Almost no families go to the Rex. It is only mostly Braceros [migrant workers] and the tough "pachuco" element and the bad girls.[736]

Likewise, a Houston theater manager wrote to a regional Clasa-Mohme representative:

> Another thing you referred to was the "Pachucos." You know, the only time I let them in the theater is when I play Tin Tan, and I wish I didn't have them then [as] they go to the "Azteca" and have their fights there.[737]

Tin Tan was the stage name of Germán Valdés, a Mexican comic actor and singer whose screen persona was a buffoonish pachuco, complete with zoot suit.[738] The attitude of the mainstream Mexican film audience toward pachucos is illustrated by the fact that the one famous cinematic pachuco was a lovable good-for-nothing. This acknowledged the delinquency of real pachucos while rendering it unthreatening. The same attitude can be seen in a 1959 newspaper entertainment write-up from San Antonio, describing the Latino population's affection for Spanish-language vaudeville, with mention of a pachuco-centered routine that "brings down the house."[739] This attitude was seen even better in Mexico a month after the Zoot Suit Riots. According to a report that appeared in the July 9, 1943, *San Mateo Times*, residents of Mexico City viewed a wax mannequin in pachuco garb, and expressed their consensus: "'Countrymen or not,' was the general opinion, 'anybody who would wear an outfit like that ought to be beaten up.'"[740] By September, pachuco-mocking stage comedy was a hit in Mexico, *Variety* noting a

Tin Tan (Germán Valdés)

pair of "shows, burlesquing the Los Angeles zoot suiters" entitled *Pachuco Authentics* and *Pachuco Revue* that were "touring the provinces."[741] And by December, Mexico City nightclub owners were dealing with a rash of fake pesos, "dubbed 'Pachucos' by local newspapers," according to *Variety*.[742]

The formula of exploitation film, Tucker's cinematic cradle, was to make movies about subjects that Hollywood could not or would not touch. Given the notable absence of pachuco themes from juvenile delinquent films of the time, Tucker had astutely noticed a phenomenon that was in the public consciousness but un-reflected in mass culture. In late November

1951, King Brothers purchased a script entitled *Pachuco* and had Kurt Neumann signed to direct almost immediately, but the project was re-titled *The Ring* by early December.[743] (An intelligent, lower budget boxing drama about a young Latino, *The Ring* contained only a few fleeting references to pachuco culture or delinquency when it was released in 1952.) With the above reports indicating that pachuco moviegoers were unruly under normal conditions, and that they showed up to see themselves reflected by the silly Tin Tan, it is no surprise that "they just wrecked the theater totally; not from disapproval, but from approval."

Tucker continued:

> Sunday night, we were open. They had the state police out, and the city police, and everybody else. And that was it. I thought that was good. Money-wise, the opening night, they broke any record they'd ever had. Saturday night, nobody knows whatever happened to the box-office. The theater claimed they were robbed. I know at the first break, I saw the cashier take off with a whole sack of money, so I don't think they were robbed. I do know that their insurance didn't even begin to pay for the cost of [inaudible]. But me, I thought that was good. I thought, "Well, if we open in theaters and anybody particularly reacts that strong to the picture, obviously, it's a good picture." And it really was, I must say.

There is even less reason to doubt Tucker here, as the creative accounting practices of more than a few exhibitors are well-documented. According to Tom Weaver, reluctant teen actor Arch Hall Jr.'s father struggled to keep his Fairway Films afloat in the face of crooked distributors.[744] After a Fairway picture cleaned up over a weekend at a drive-in, the resulting payment could be in the range of $12.50, and the checks would sometimes bounce. As Hall Jr. remembered, his father was eventually forced out of business by years of loss. In this kind of situation, Tucker again faced the obstacle of a more powerful partner having control over money that should have come his way. But he continued to be unfailingly optimistic about the movie's prospects:

> So I came back all in a fizz. I had to drive back and my car petered out on me up around Needles [California]; I hitch-hiked the rest of the way and cramped my hand. I got back here, and Bill said, "Shit, man, you're fucked. There's no way you'll ever get even with it." He tried re-cutting, so he had [someone who] was head cutter for the B division of Republic, and he fucked around with it. I never did see it after that.

Hackel was apparently taken aback by the controversy, but for his part Tucker was only encouraged to keep on exploiting the film. If it continued playing across various territories, with perhaps his becoming a pariah in the public eye, it would have still gotten him to his goal.

> I don't know, to this day, whatever happened to it. I hear different stories. I hear people claim that I had a [deal] and he had given me twenty thousand dollars.

> But I signed a lot of papers; I have no idea what they were. I trusted the man totally. I know that he did give me money; he paid my lunches almost every day for a couple of months. [Inaudible.] He was very sick. He died right in the middle of all of the hassle about it. His widow claimed she knew nothing about it. Again, I didn't have the money to go to the attorneys and all that shit.

And as Tucker describes this aspect of the story, it parallels his experience with Al Zimbalist in the aftermath of *Robot Monster*. Tucker must have repeatedly believed in his enthusiasm that he could trust his partners, would not be swindled, and could surmount any problem. This belief extended to others as well:

> There were a couple of people who never got paid, particularly cameramen. A couple of others, they had money. They pursued it and nothing happened. Hunter Murchison, who was a cameraman—a *fantastic* cameraman—later, he and I were very good friends so, obviously, he probably didn't think that I had gotten any money and he hadn't gotten paid.

But no credits exist for any Hunter Murchison; "fantastic cameraman" that he no doubt was, he must have worked in industrial, animation, or educational films. And for the sake of Tucker's career in retrospect, the shame is just that *Pachuco* seems lost. Outside of the interview there is no evidence of the film, no news reports of the drive-in riot, and apparently no prints sitting around with Hackel's descendants or anywhere else. There are a couple of near misses from the same era that could almost fit the bill of being *Pachuco* by another name, but they do not quite fit the puzzle.

First, a case could be made that Tucker's *Broadway Jungle* was the same film as *Pachuco*. It featured two Hispanic gangsters, one of which ("Georgie Boy") was young enough to be a pachuco (his suit is wide in the lapels, if not quite zoot-worthy). And *Broadway Jungle* looks cheap enough to have been filmed in the off hours on little money, although some of it was clearly shot outdoors in broad daylight. Given that exploitation was all sizzle and no steak (to paraphrase some famous carnie wisdom), *Broadway Jungle* could have had the *Pachuco* title slapped on easily enough. With mass excitement in the pachuco audience over the title, the film would have been irrelevant as the craziness ensued.

But Hackel's involvement makes this theory problematic. First, one has to believe that the amateurish *Broadway Jungle* excited him enough to have Tucker on his payroll and spend more money having him debut it in Texas. Second and far more difficult to resolve is the date of Hackel's death. According to the *Hollywood Reporter*, Hackel died on October 21, 1959,[745] suggesting that the great Texas drive-in riot was perhaps not much earlier. Many months could have elapsed between that event and Hackel's death; perhaps he had played around with it for quite a while, but it is improbable that he had an interest in it back when Tucker was photographed with *Pachuco* film cans in 1957 Los Angeles. It is therefore unlikely that *Pachuco* could have been the 1955 *Broadway Jungle*.

Another possibility comes from Amarillo at the right moment in time. Producer John "Bushland"—who, in his Hollywood day job, edited *Cat-Women of the Moon* as John Bushelman—was reportedly in January 1959 planning to film *Switchblade*, a JD drug melodrama, in Amarillo.[746] But the production, including former Hollywood star Robert Hutton along with Carol Ohmart, was shortly in hot water. February news stories reported that the production ground to a halt due to some across-the-border filming, initially approved on the condition that the film was a documentary. The film was seized on the fear that it could be "derogatory to Mexico."[747] Gold Air Shows Inc. chief Fred Ready implored the Texas and U.S. governments to intervene[748] before finally, later the same month, the movie was returned and the situation ascribed to a "language mixup."[749] The film never appeared as *Switchblade*, but by October 1960 was playing as *Wild Youth*.[750]

It is tempting to wonder if Tucker's unreliable memory played a part here, and if he could have had some involvement in *Switchblade*. A youth crime film with Mexican overtones, filmed in 1959 Amarillo, seems just coincidental enough to raise associations with *Pachuco*. Most of the crew were lower-budget people and had Tucker-like credits ahead of them, editing and post-production in sixties and seventies television. But while the projects are similar, and Tucker likely knew about *Switchblade*, there is no reason to think he had direct involvement. His memories of *Pachuco* are so specific that it is hard to assign the same degree of confusion to them that surrounds his mid-fifties exploitation projects, and there is the unavoidable fact that *Pachuco* was already at least a title on a film box in 1957. *Switchblade* was shot on location, not at 2:00 A.M. in a ratty Santa Monica Boulevard studio, and along with Hutton and Ohmart had a cast of working actors. In direct contrast, it is impossible to say who appeared in *Pachuco*.[751]

But most damning of all for this theory is the fact that Hackel had no involvement in *Switchblade*. His name is never mentioned in any reports, nor is it listed in the reported credits of the finished film (and neither is Tucker's). Hackel's October 1959 death had no bearing on the film's distribution as it was, according to the *Reporter*, picked up in May by Sam Nathanson and Al Wieder, and Nathanson was in June trying to sell it in New York.[752] If *Switchblade* had any connection to Tucker's film, perhaps one film inspired the decision to premiere the other in Amarillo. Considering everything, it is hard to escape the conclusion that *Pachuco* came about more or less as Tucker remembered, and that the film is lost.

So after Pachuco . . . ?
Then I went into the theater business. I opened up a theater in Fairbanks. A main street type of theater, and the sheriff pulled me in on it.

Why did . . . ?
He said he didn't think we should have that kind of thing in Fairbanks. I took off and came back.

I'm presuming you must have been the only main street theater in Fairbanks.
Right. It's still open today and it's still playing those low-budget strip pictures.

But on this point Tucker is harder to believe. The burlesque craze was in its decline. It was still possible for him to launch such a venture somewhere, but Fairbanks was not ideal. Advertisements from the early fifties era of *Space Jockey* promised similar entertainment, such as a May 1951 *Fairbanks Daily News-Miner* ad for the Talk of the Town nightclub.[753] Appearing in her "3rd Big Week" was Lotus Wing, "China's Most Uncovered Girl." Burlesque was not shocking in Fairbanks during its heyday and, if Tucker did get "pulled in" by the law, it could have had more to do with his earlier adventure in the local movie business. A 1960 *News-Miner* story reported "State Police Crackdown on B-Girls in Bars Here," noting that two bars with liquor licenses "in the name of Sam Leacock" (producer of *Space Jockey*) had been raided.[754] With that in mind, Tucker might have been on the wrong side of "the B-girl law passed last spring" or just been on the wrong side of influential citizens. But even here, the implosion of *Pachuco* becomes an unavoidable difficulty, and this is because of Tucker's next project:

> *So what eventually led up to the making of [The] Cape Canaveral Monsters? Any other pictures before that?*
>
> Uh . . . well . . . let's go off the record a minute on this and come back.

13

Monsters

After leaving some unrecorded comments, Phil Tucker discussed the budget of *Robot Monster,* and his additional thoughts on his most famous film completed the interview. Harry Medved briefly summarized Tucker's thoughts in his transcript (partially quoted in Chapter 9), and this summary is evidence that Tucker mixed up the chronology of some of his life's experiences. As he admitted, his diabetes sometimes got the better of his memory:

> At this point, Mr. Tucker asked us to turn off the tape recorder. He told us roughly that, in order to earn a living, he had been washing dishes at this period of time. He met the mother of nightclub comic Lenny Bruce, who later introduced him to her son. Bruce and Tucker became as close to each other as two brothers. Oftentimes, when Tucker became tired of washing dishes, he would stage, along with Bruce, a mock suicide. Tucker would take a few sleeping pills, but not enough to be harmful.

> He would then go to a hotel, and lie down in his bed. Then Bruce would make an anonymous phone call to the newspapers and report an attempted suicide. Reporters would rush over to Tucker's hotel room, and he would then be taken to the Veteran's Administration Hospital. (He was a veteran of World War II.)
>
> Mr. Tucker dismissed these suicide attempts as mere gimmicks in order to procure free room and board. Tucker became friends with the psychiatrists at the hospital, and they soon decided to help him out with his financial troubles. As a favor, four of the psychiatrists at the Veterans' Administration decided to put up the money for him to direct another film, which was entitled [*The*] *Cape Canaveral Monsters.* Phil Tucker was released in 1960, and he was able to work in Hollywood once more. His film, [*The*] *Cape Canaveral Monsters,* however, was put in the vault for a year and was not released until 1961.[755]

As previously explained, Tucker probably met Bruce in the fall of 1953, and could have met him no later than the spring of 1954. But Tucker sometimes remembered details correctly while confusing their order. The summary explicitly describes Tucker's suicide hoaxes in the plural—they came along "oftentimes" in reaction to boredom and inertia. As his 1955 Fairbanks attempt establishes, Tucker was not sincerely suicidal when he got press in 1953 for the *Robot Monster* attempt. And by his own recollections his final film as director was connected to a fourth suicide scam (and there may have been even more than the four documented here). That Tucker remembered *The Cape Canaveral Monsters* with a sense of embarrassment does not mean that this suicide attempt was any more sincere. He simply connected that aspect of his life with *The Cape Canaveral Monsters* in mind, and neglected to link it with *Robot Monster.* His time-warping remembrance of Bruce in connection with *Canaveral* proves that he could not always keep the order of events straight ("diabetes affects your memory"). Phil Tucker Jr. remembered that "later in life I know he looked back and realized how foolish it was to do those things."[756] (Regarding the unrecorded gap, Medved told me that he "vaguely remember[ed] Tucker saying that he was depressed and wanted attention . . . ."[757])

Tucker also made a mistake by not linking *The Cape Canaveral Monsters* to the *Pachuco* incident, as the October 1959 death of producer Bill Hackel establishes that little time elapsed between the projects. The situation was parallel to the fall 1952 news reports of Tucker's Lucky Luciano film and the production of *Robot Monster* in the early months of 1953. *The Cape Canaveral Monsters* was dated "MCMLX" for 1960 in its credits, and according to one source was filmed in a very chilly December.[758] As the summary notes, the film was unreleased until 1961 after a year "in the vault." Putting these details together, *Canaveral* was filmed within two months of Hackel's death and followed hard upon the *Pachuco* situation, likely even dovetailing with it.

The Cape Canaveral Monsters was a comeback for Tucker but has never been given the attention that *Robot Monster* has, which is both fitting and a shame. *Canaveral* is not a great or even good

Phil Tucker directing *The Cape Canaveral Monsters.*

film and on its own merits did not deserve much publicity, but it is Tucker's finest work as a director. While never as impressive as Wyott Ordung's *Walk the Dark Street,* it has a sophistication and smoothness absent in his earlier movies. The film's relative excellence further refutes the great misconception that Tucker made bad movies in mad scientist fashion, filled with strange enthusiasm and unaware that a gorilla wearing a diving helmet makes a ludicrous monster. *The Cape Canaveral Monsters* was greater than anything he directed before and, as with Ordung, there is a discouraging sense that Tucker could have done better and better work if he had continued to struggle. *Canaveral* has unfortunately seldom been recognized for the step up that it is, and this is because it is a return to alien invaders, making it dismissible as a less kooky variation on *Robot Monster*. But the similarities between *Robot Monster* and *Canaveral* are a source of contrast as much as comparison, and they make clear the improvements in the latter film. What has been more limiting to the film's recognition is that it seems to have had literally no theatrical release, its small reputation stemming from years of late-night TV broadcasts that brought it to curious and devoted monster fans.

The Cape Canaveral Monsters begins with rapidly contracting and expanding flashes of light against darkness, accompanied by the hypnotic repetition of electronic pitches on the soundtrack and a disembodied female voice. These alien light-beings settle into pinholes as the film dissolves to a beach setting, before possessing a middle-aged couple and causing them to kill themselves in an auto wreck. The ragged corpses now possessed and reanimated by the lights, the female alien Nadja (Katherine Victor) reminds the male alien Hauron (Jason Johnson) to grab his newly owned but severed left arm from the car as the sequence ends. Rocket test stock footage follows and then the credits, which play over a control room where young scientists Tom (Scott Peters) and Sally (Linda Connell), her Teutonic uncle (Billy M. Greene), and some scientists and military men puzzle over the repeated failure of rocket tests.

From there the aliens bicker and make up like a married couple as they continue to disrupt tests, kidnap human specimens to dismember or send back to their home world (accessible via a mysterious, smoke-spewing chest full of bubbly liquid), and communicate with the voice of a patronizing off-world commander. Meanwhile Tom, frustrated at not being taken seriously by his superiors, detects unexplainable radio signals and soon discovers the aliens' hideout. After various misadventures and with the help of Sally, her uncle, a crazy old local, the police, and the military, Tom utilizes some outrageous pseudoscience to destroy the invaders. But in a strangely downbeat stinger ending, the aliens reappear, causing another car wreck and killing Sally. The lights contract and expand all over a black screen again, ending the film as it began.

This summary shows that Tucker had bookended his directing career with a film that on multiple levels harkened back to his debut of less than a decade before. *The Cape Canaveral Monsters* features alien invaders with conflicted emotions and an unsympathetic leader, a pair of young scientists who fall in love, a protective German scientist patriarch with a thick accent, stock footage, Bronson Canyon, war surplus equipment, an economic method of showing the monsters, bubbles, pseudoscientific dialogue, disrobed female captives, crunching electric sound effects, and an ambiguous ending that undermines triumph at the last moment. It closely echoes many elements of *Robot Monster* but everything was done better the second time around, and impressively so under conditions that were not much better than when Tucker made his earlier films.[759]

As Bill Warren notes, the plot of *The Cape Canaveral Monsters* is similar to Ed Wood's *Plan 9 from Outer Space.*[760] Both feature aliens invading by resurrecting corpses, and heroes who believe in aliens but are held back by superiors. But Tucker seems to have borrowed from a number of science fiction films of the previous decade. A guard dog pulling off the man-monster's arm was probably borrowed from Howard Hawks' *The Thing from Another World* (1951), while *Invisible Invaders* (1959) was recently in theaters and also featured reanimated corpses under the control of aliens.[761] But voracious reader that he was, Tucker could have had another contemporary source in mind. Ian Fleming's *Doctor No,* published in 1958, was the sixth James Bond novel that a few years later became the premiere chapter of the Bond film series. It is set in Jamaica, where the title villain sabotages Western rocket tests for the Russian group SMERSH. As he explains to the hero, "Then, suddenly, our pulses go out to the rocket, its brain is confused, it goes mad, it plunges into the sea, it destroys itself, it roars off at a tangent. Another test has failed."[762] With one of the aliens having the Russian name Nadja, it is even likelier that Tucker was inspired by the Fleming novel.

For his work that most closely resembled *Robot Monster,* Tucker assembled his best cast since that film. Playing Tom was Scott Peters (born Peter Sikorski), a Canadian actor with sporadic, often low-budget credits and a background in radio. Third-billed in the unusual Mickey Spillane adaptation *The Girl Hunters* (1963), in which Spillane himself plays his detective Mike Hammer, Peters at around the same time interviewed Spillane for the Canadian Broadcasting Corporation. Also in keeping with his Canadian roots, Peters was in Saskatchewan in 1965 to receive the microphone he had used when winning a talent show over two decades before, *Variety* noting that he was at the time "producing amateur variety shows" in the area.[763] Along with bit parts in major Hollywood productions like *The FBI Story* (1959) and *Marooned* (1969), and a recurring role in the 1974 series *Get Christie Love!,* Peters racked up an impressive number of appearances in bad monster films. Before bringing this side of his career to its culmination with *The Madmen of Mandoras* (1963) (also re-edited as *They Saved Hitler's Brain*), Peters appeared in two Bert I. Gordon efforts, *The Amazing Colossal Man* (1957) and *Attack of the Puppet People* (1958). Resembling an anxious Kurt Russell, he is a likable male lead despite being perpetually sweaty and hard-breathing much of the time. While lacking George Nader's wonderful cockiness, he is just right for a younger and less confident genius scientist. According to Tom Weaver, his *Puppet People* co-star Ken Miller remembered him as "a big 'blowhard' type of guy, really nice guy . . .."[764]

Not improbably, *The Cape Canaveral Monsters* was the second time that Peters appeared in the same film with Jason Johnson, who played the arm-challenged alien Hauron. Johnson and Peters both previously appeared in *Invasion of the Saucer Men* (1957), while Johnson's lengthy career would include a vast number of TV roles and a significant bit in Robert Wise's *The Andromeda Strain* (1971). Playing a (non-reanimated) corpse at the center of a scientific debate, one can pretend that he was cast thanks to his previous experience in *The Cape Canaveral Monsters.* Working in New York live television in his early

The main cast of *The Cape Canaveral Monsters* (*left to right*): Katherine Victor, Linda Connell, Scott Peters, and Jason Johnson.

years, he wrote and appeared in *The Catholic Hour*, a religious education program.[765] He also did some writing for *Gunsmoke*, wrote and appeared in an obscure sex crime melodrama called *Strange Compulsion* (1964), and showed up in three *Twilight Zone* episodes. Playing Sally to Peters' Tom was Linda Connell, the daughter of Merle Connell, who once again performed cinematography duties for Tucker. Though she displays occasional signs of amateurishness in her only film credit, the elfin Connell is generally expressive, believable, and has a warm chemistry with Peters.

The one other main cast member was also the only one to have been interviewed in detail about the project. Katherine Victor, imperious and a little over the top as Nadja, spoke to actor and part-time monster fan Barry Brown for an interview that ultimately appeared in Calvin Thomas Beck's 1978 anthology *Scream Queens.* Also interviewed in later years separately by Paul Parla and Weaver, Victor's collected memories provide a clearer window into the troubled production than what remains of Tucker's account. Previously landing few roles and making a living through modeling and odd jobs, she was contacted (specifically in 1959, according to Brown) about the project by Greene, already cast, and soon met with Tucker and joined a production that seemed to be going in the right direction.[766] She recalled that the generous budget ("around $150,000"[767]) was put up by "a group of dentists or doctors"[768]—corroborating Tucker's account—and was originally sufficient for color filming and a two-week schedule. But with the budget slashed "almost in half" soon before filming, color became black-and-white and compromises were made across the board.[769] The production actually ran out of money before it was finished, and at that point she became her own makeup artist. According to Weaver, Victor remembered:

> We shot the interiors at a small independent studio on Western Avenue in Hollywood. The cave scenes were shot in Bronson Canyon and the beach scenes at Malibu. I remember it was December and it was freezing![770]

Since John D.F. Black remembered Quality Studios as "located near Western Avenue on Santa Monica," and given that Connell photographed the film, Victor's comments mean that *The Cape Canaveral Monsters* interiors could have easily been shot there. However, a *Variety* story stated that it was "reportedly made at Telepix Studios in close to ten days . . .."[771]

But Victor remembered the experience as very pleasant and considered it her best film, despite the unattractive costume and scar makeup that the part required.[772] After a small debut role in the unbelievable *Mesa of Lost Women* (along with George Barrows, Jackie Coogan, and Ed Wood's then-girlfriend Dolores Fuller), Victor's largest role was in Jerry Warren's *Teenage Zombies* (1957) (where she plays her villainess very much like Nadja), and she unfortunately followed *The Cape Canaveral Monsters* with several more Warren credits. As fellow Warren regular Bruno VeSota remembered, "I swear, he is the only person I ever met in Hollywood who set out to make a bad picture on purpose."[773] It is debatable if Warren's full-length originals were better or worse than his re-edits of foreign imports, but his attitude remained consistent, as when Victor repeatedly asked him if they could try to make a good film for once. According to Weaver, Warren told her, "Why? People aren't interested in anything good, they don't know and they don't care. Just give them garbage!"[774] (Even Germán "Tin Tan" Valdés, Mexican cinema's clown prince of pachuco, was not safe from Warren when *La Casa del Terror* [1960] was edited into—no kidding—*Face of the Screaming Werewolf* [1964].) Victor attributed her mediocre career to association with such a low-rent director, and as a promotional ad she placed in the April 11, 1960, *Hollywood Reporter* shows, she was sincerely trying in those days.[775] And in a fleeting contrast to Warren, Victor

Katherine Victor's career did not remain stalled for a lack of trying.

recalled that Tucker "did the best he could under the circumstances" and praised his competence, enthusiasm, easygoing kindness, and willingness to let her play up her character: "But I think that in spite of everything Phil was very creative; it's just too bad that he didn't get the opportunity to do more, because he was good."[776]

Along the way Victor brought valuable production details to light. According to Brown's interview it was Richard Greer, producer and editor, who "arranged for healthy financing through the investments of a group of doctors,"[777] which complicates Tucker's claim that the doctors invested out of sympathy. Did Tucker have nothing to do with the financing, or was Greer's involvement a cover story to avoid embarrassing appearances? What is certain is that executive producer Lionel Dichter practiced medicine for decades[778] and Harriet Dichter, silently appearing first after the credits as a scientist, was his wife. Whoever pulled out of the financing at the last minute, it was not Dr. Dichter. And according to Victor, Tucker tried unsuccessfully to sell *The Cape Canaveral Monsters* to Universal Pictures[779] and one "year went by before the actors received their salaries."[780] Tucker even borrowed half of her paycheck from her after she had finally received it; as she sympathetically noted, "The poor guy, he was really flat broke."[781]

The California Division of Labor Law Enforcement may have been less sympathetic at the time, *Variety* reporting on April 5, 1961 that it had "filed $20,818 judgment in Superior Court against Cape Canaveral Monsters Inc. and C.C.M. Prod. Inc. for services performed by eleven Screen Actors Guilds [sic] members who appeared in film without permission of Guild."[782] The story itemized amounts owed to Johnson, Peters, Victor and other cast members, and that "money is owed performers more than a year." Both defendants cited "have no money and Sterling World Distributors,[783] handling pic, has not yet turned any cash for distribution to producers or Phil Tucker, prexy." On July 3, 1961, *Daily Variety* noted that the corporate defendants had made a "confession of judgment" against themselves and for the labor division "in amount of $4,570" to be paid to three actors.[784] (The three were Chuck Howard, Linda Connell, and—bizarrely—cameraman Merle Connell.)

One other important detail in the finished film is the presence of actor Lyle Felice as a policeman. Playing what could easily have been a Timothy Farrell role, Felice had a debonair appearance and smooth voice that stand out in the cast, especially because he has somehow been confused with director Al Adamson. While Felice worked with Adamson, he was a Los Angeles hairdresser according to Sam Sherman, Adamson's longtime producer. Along with noting that Felice was "a really good actor" with a "good speaking voice," Sherman made this clarification: "Some people have claimed that [Lyle Felice] was

Merle Connell and Katherine Victor on *The Cape Canaveral Monsters* set.

a name for Al Adamson . . . that's not true . . . Al Adamson and Lyle Felice are not the same person."[785]

Despite the film's deficiencies, it is surprising that it went unreleased. Its low-budget problems are no worse than those of many other films, and it could have easily fit American International or Crown International's line-up. If *The Brain Eaters, The Beast of Yucca Flats* and *Monster a Go-Go* could play, then there is no reason that *The Cape Canaveral Monsters* should not also have graced drive-ins and second-run theaters. But while it had no theatrical release, it frequently played as a late-late movie in local TV markets as early as 1963,[786] and copyright records assign it to CCM Productions, Inc. ("employer for hire") and Republic Pictures as of March 1, 1960.[787] But Republic is not listed on screen, only CCM Productions, and the film must have been rapidly assembled after it was filmed in a chilly December 1959 and then rejected by Universal. It is possible that March 1, 1960 simply refers to the copyright of the film, and there was a much longer period of selling the film before Republic picked it up and presumably got some television money for it. According to Kevin Heffernan, *The Cape Canaveral Monsters* was one of four in a "Chiller-Science Fiction Package" of movies for TV syndication in "early 1964."[788]

Tucker likely tried several others before settling on Republic, as the once powerful Poverty Row giant had steadily declined into insignificance in the late fifties. Almost as importantly, Republic never had any reputation for science fiction or horror films. That *The Cape Canaveral Monsters* was dumped on television is explained by the 1959 sale of Republic's library to National Telefilm Associates. As years went by, it went with the rest of Republic's catalog to become the property of Artisan Entertainment and then Lionsgate. Never given any legitimate VHS or DVD release and long available only in poor TV recordings, *The Cape Canaveral Monsters* finally became viewable in good quality for a time in 2010 through Netflix streaming, its first official home video release.[789] But that initial sale to Republic might have been related to *Pachuco*. Hackel had deep roots in Republic, and it was a Republic editor who Tucker claimed had tinkered with his controversial film. With the production of *The Cape Canaveral Monsters* beginning within two months of Hackel's death, there is an overwhelming circumstantial sense that it might have gone to Republic because of some connection to *Pachuco*, perhaps as a last resort or even to settle an obligation. Without Hackel's involvement in *Pachuco*, perhaps *Canaveral* could have gone to another distributor and played theatrically.

However the film was sold, it survives as testament to Tucker's heightened skill. Victor's high opinion of him is a world away from George Barrows' dismissal of him as "a nut," or Claudia Barrett's sense that he was inexperienced. Watching the film, Tucker's greater ingenuity is apparent right out of the gate. The shifting circles of light would have been a very cheap effect, but a labor-intensive one that only an editor and person of tactile talents would have conceived. While Bill Warren acknowledged that this effect was "not surrealistically ludicrous," like that of a robot-gorilla, he attributed it to "circles of unexposed areas of film."[790] This is half-right: Tucker was playing with film hands-on to get the effect, but it would have been with *over*exposed areas of film, as underexposure is dark and overexposure is bright. Tucker presumably already had the film developed normally, and then created the overexposed effect by selectively applying excess amounts of developing chemical in the needed areas. (Selective underexposure would be a much harder and perhaps impossible trick to pull off, as it would require a partial masking of areas of film before any of it was exposed.)

What is especially impressive about the effect is that Tucker was comfortable enough to vary the lights circles in multiple ways. Most obvious is the fact that they are shown contracting and expanding at the beginning, but they also move through the frame with a reasonably good sense of interacting with the filmed elements. They move with a straight and graceful motion in order to travel, they bob and weave when they attack, they become partial circles when entering or leaving a human body, and in one shot, one of them changes size and flies all over the screen before finally enlarging and filling it completely. More subtly, the small light circles at rest even have a pattern of their own, as they noticeably twinkle like stars at night (although with twenty-four frames of film for each second of screen time, this effect could have resulted from slight, unintended variations from frame to frame).

According to Warren, Tucker had at some point made a print of the film on which he hand-tinted the light circles.[791] This was probably a partial compensation for the fact that it had to be shot black-and-white, and perhaps a logical continuation of the process he had in mind from the beginning. He would have had to color the overexposed circles even if the film was shot in color, and it is a shame that someone decided to not add color circles to the black-and-white film, if a logical choice to restrict release prints to cheaper black-and-white film stock. Says Warren, "All I remember is that the alien lights weren't red or yellow—they were either blue or green, but I don't remember which." The color question is answered by one character when Hauron attacks: "Nothing but a little ol' green ball!" So it is at least clear that Hauron appears green in his non-corporeal form, though perhaps Nadja appeared as a contrasting blue. Warren further clarified that "evidently Tucker himself hand-colored a 35mm print . . . what I saw was a VHS tape video-chained from that print. Where the VHS is, I have no idea—I think it belonged to my late friend, Scot Holton."[792]

Tucker's use of this hand-tinting technique likely went back to his apprenticeship with old pros like Gordon Avil and Norman Dawn. Many silent films were selectively hand-tinted for effect; for example, the climax of *The Great Train Robbery* (1903).

Additional signs of Tucker's greater filmmaking powers pile on through *The Cape Canaveral Monsters.* The very shots and editing that open the film have a grace and smoothness never found in the choked, awkward esthetic of *Robot Monster.* A car travels down the highway by a dissolve from a beach scene—a perfectly commonplace edit—that feels surprising here simply because it so competent and without ragged edges. Tucker then effectively creates a no-budget car wreck by jostling the camera with ever-greater intensity from an inside-the-car perspective. Cutting to a still reverse angle of actors covered in stage blood through a cracked windshield, sound effects complete the illusion. This is not an extraordinarily daring cinematic car wreck, but it is noteworthy because it is done so believably without really showing anything. Such a seamless sequence was unknown in Tucker's earlier films, and now one of his films is awful not in poor execution but in its intended effect of horrifying the viewer. The driver's dismembered arm completes the scene, achieved by a view of a hidden, third actor's arm hanging over the back seat car window. Tucker had learned better and better how to create good effects with no money, and the scene is only undermined by a tin ear for dialogue that continued to plague him. Grabbing the arm, the now human-form Nadja says, "Hurry, Hauron. Your arm. I'll take it and sew it back on at the laboratory." But while *Robot Monster* had absurd robot-gorilla soliloquies, at least *The Cape Canaveral Monsters* split much of its inane dialogue between an alien couple, humanizing it somewhat and disguising its shortcomings. And the fact that the characters speak in an often stilted, pretentious, and odd manner further suggests that it was Tucker after all who wrote the bizarre Ro-Man soliloquies added to *Robot Monster* in post-production.

The film continues right into yet more impressive work from Tucker. An intelligently assembled stock footage montage shows a variety of perspectives; moving in progressively closer, machines alternate with people, military with scientists, and we see an impressive low angle view of a rocket. A pin is pulled from a device, and the film cuts straight into a control room set, the camera pulling back as the setting "CAPE CANAVERAL" types across the screen in a Courier sort of typewriter font.

Two words—"THE MONSTERS"—in a smeared, chaotic, finger-painting style zoom onto the typed letters to form the film's title. Tucker had progressed from a random typeface credit mixture (*Dance Hall Racket*) to mixing up typefaces on purpose and to dynamic effect. As the film proper begins, stock footage integrates beautifully with brief shots of the control crew looking upwards before the rocket spins out of control, represented by the point of view of jerky motion over a still photo of the Earth. Like the car wreck, this sequence is not innovative filmmaking but an estimable improvement on the crudeness of Tucker's early work, it now part of his skill set to match brief shots of various perspectives into a smooth viewing pattern. The work that he did learning editing from the time of *Broadway Jungle* and *Plan 9 from Outer Space* was paying off and, even with Greer credited as editor, Tucker's concept of creating aliens in post-production shows that he was well involved in forming the final shape of the film.

If there is any aspect of *The Cape Canaveral Monsters* that works less well than *Robot Monster,* it is its music. Guenther Kauer's brooding, modernist score lacks a distinct theme like Elmer Bernstein's frequently repeated one for *Robot Monster,* and at times veers into overdramatic musical stabs and an interlude of dorky comic music. But despite being selected by author Donald C. Willis as a "candidate for worst musical score" among monster films,[793] its frequent dissonant passages can be genuinely unsettling, and is at times better scary alien music than the action onscreen deserves. Kauer's simple but effective figure for the disembodied aliens—repeated, electronic quarter notes at the same pitch—has an un-nerving relentlessness and, even better, it is repeated in other settings. Played by woodwinds and clean-toned electric guitar in scenes when Hauron and Nadja assume human form, it is a subtle and astute bit of scoring for a movie of this kind, like Tucker's better dialogue—minimalist but effective. But Kauer was a composer of serious ability, as his memorable and dynamic music for *The Astounding She-Monster* (recycled repeatedly in *The Beast of Yucca Flats*) demonstrates. According to director Ronnie Ashcroft, he even went to the trouble of having it recorded by an orchestra in his native Germany.[794]

But by, in a sense, remaking *Robot Monster*, Tucker did most things better the second time. Beyond a creative way of cheaply showing alien invaders, the aliens have a lair with a smooth craft nestled within cave walls—by implication a spacecraft that landed and burrowed into the side of a hill (shades of 1953's *It Came from Outer Space*). The aliens also have an impressive array of equipment, with walls full of switches and dials and an imposing circular dish with prongs of electric current rising up behind. Along the way are scratchy electrical noises that seem identical to those in *Robot Monster*, but with better visual accompaniment than Ro-Man's paltry plywood-and-duct-tape viewscreen. Their communicator switches on with a sound like that of Ro-Man's, and a mysterious circular pattern swirls within the view disc, its disembodied voice criticizing their Earthling abductions with a patronizing drone: "You must be more careful with the electroconvulsive shock, and the freezing." In low-budget film, to be abstract is to be sophisticated. Just as there is paradoxically more terror on screen when it is invisible and kept in shadow, there is more eeriness and sense of unknown when an alien is not something recognizable. While a gorilla wearing a diving helmet has a certain shock value in addition to its silliness, there is something far more alien in *The Cape Canaveral Monsters*'s strange rotating disk station, imperiously close to the ceiling and emitting an unsympathetic voice of judgment.

Best of all is the chest filled with a bubbling mixture that seems related to off-world travel to their home (within the same solar system, says Hauron). With the 3-D craze a distant memory of half a decade ago, Tucker did not need a bubble machine spewing soap spheres everywhere, but he chose to repeat the visual motif of bubbles (further reinforced by the floating alien light circles) with a new alien invasion referred to by their leader as "Earth Expedition Number Two." Could Ro-Man, "Extension XJ-2," have been the first "Earth Expedition," or is "Number Two" a self-mocking, bathroom reference by Tucker to the quality of the film? Given the out-of-body abilities of these new aliens, there are endless meta possibilities that could connect Tucker's two space monster films; perhaps these newer aliens once had some reason to possess gorillas and attach diving helmets to them. The continued, mysterious motif of bubbles—unexplained, but presumably there for some purpose like the black slabs in Stanley Kubrick's *2001: A Space Odyssey*—suggests that Ro-Man, Hauron, and Nadja all follow "The Plan."

On top of the similarities that link *The Cape Canaveral Monsters* with *Robot Monster*, Tucker's later film contains many interesting thematic elements. Dovetailing with much of his earlier work, *The Cape Canaveral Monsters* revisits the deformity motif that first appeared in *Robot Monster*; it continued through his exploitation films and reaches its logical extreme here. While Tucker's earlier films dealt with an alien gorilla whose head was replaced by a mechanical one, a bleeding ear, a dog with diamonds glued to its ear, a severed tongue, and a pair of mutes, *The Cape Canaveral Monsters* involves the possessed dead and battered bodies of two car-wreck victims, and the further deformity of an arm that will not stay attached. In a weirdly hilarious sequence, Hauron sneaks around the base at night only to have his reattached arm ripped off in the maw of a German shepherd, while an armed guard fires nine rounds at him. The MP soon brings the severed arm of Hauron into the control room, and the comically cigar-worrying General Hollister puzzles, "It's impossible for a dog to pull a man's arm off this way. It just can't be done." The rocket crew staring in bewilderment at the arm, it rests over a chair and table as the camera pans down to show blood dripping steadily on the floor.

This bizarre arm business keeps haunting the aliens as Nadja needles Hauron over his lack of an arm, and later tries to entice him to take a break as she caresses a long tool in her hands. Hauron explodes, stating that he wants to be left alone to get his work done, but later smoothly informs her that work can wait and that they need "some rest." This is after he has gotten his work done by destroying another rocket test with a bazooka-like weapon. "Not bad for a one-armed man," he puffs himself up to her, and the Freudian implications of all this are too obvious to be worth discussing. There is more kinky stuff on the part of the aliens when they abduct Bob and Shirley, picnic friends of Tom and Sally. "We need more Earthlings for our experiments, especially females," their remotely voiced commander informs them (Ro-Man would have understood) and they proceed to undress the comatose Shirley, wrapping her in some sort of blanket. "Hurry with that metallic cloth," Hauron instructs. "She's unconscious now, but Earthlings are strange." The exploitation roots of Tucker and Connell show through as Shirley's bra is unbuttoned, the blouse-ripping motif from *Robot Monster, Dance Hall Racket,* and *Broadway Jungle* continuing here.

While Shirley is nonsensically propped against a wall and a plexiglass door covers her as part of an experiment, Bob gruesomely sacrifices an arm to replace Hauron's. As Nadja leans over to begin cutting on him the camera moves to his sleeping face and uncomfortably lingers, the air inflating and deflating within a pump in the background. His chin also removed to be given to Hauron—because Nadja found it more attractive—Bob

dies and the aliens stand conveniently in front of his remains as they discuss, Hauron all the while rubbing his new arm. Alien invaders, it seems to be Tucker's viewpoint, would be no more enlightened or humane than Earthlings. "His chin, to replace yours," so Nadja had said, and Hauron then rationalizes that with a better chin he could move around that much more easily in the human world (never mind Nadja's scars, or the blood-stained clothing they both inhabit); he clearly wants to be more attractive to her. And so Tucker again made a film about characters not good enough for their jobs. In *Robot Monster* it was the invader's infatuation with an intended victim that did him in, but in *The Cape Canaveral Monsters* the aliens cannot get along with each other in a love/hate dynamic that is their Achilles' heel. As with *Dance Hall Racket* and *Broadway Jungle,* both *Monster*(*s*) feature characters who have a job but who do not have what it takes.

In a vast contrast, Tom and Sally are a likable couple and as competent as can be. Tom is in fact better than anyone else; "his school records show that he is virtually a *maat-i-maat-i-kal geen-yus,*" according to Sally' German uncle, although Tom later bluffs the aliens that "[t]here are plenty of guys my age who are a lot smarter." His interest in alien forces of course allows him to crack the mystery of why rocket tests keep going up in flames, just as only ten-year-old boys can understand Godzilla. But Tom unfortunately shows his greatest prowess right as the film goes off the rails and never recovers. Nearly two-thirds of the way through the movie, Tom and Sally are abducted by Hauron and Nadja, but this confrontation of the two couples does not bring the film to a great resolution. Immobilized on their way to the aliens' lair, they are caught in a stasis field (one of three times that Tucker used the effect of the film going to a freeze frame, with a moving element superimposed over that still image—another excellent economy technique) and then hung against a lab wall, held in the confines of another beam but looking like they hang on invisible meat hooks.

Hauron questions and exchanges information with Tom, expressing bemusement that human beings dream in their sleep, while Tom is amazed that the aliens can breathe Earth's atmosphere. (They do not explain that they breathe the atmosphere because they have taken over human bodies, nor do Tom and Sally seem to notice the scarred and bloody condition of the aliens.) Most of this is not too illogical until Hauron speaks of an element in their bubble tank that would "correspond" to hydrogen and, unfortunately, it becomes clear this difference is not merely a matter of names. "Same atomic weight?" asks Tom. "Much higher," replies Hauron. Mechanical as Tucker was, he ignored some basic science when writing *The Cape Canaveral Monsters,* as hydrogen presumably has the same atomic weight on Earth or anywhere else. Tom soon escapes as the aliens are busy tormenting Sally with their treatment (very well portrayed with an advancing close-up on Tom's agonized face while Sally can be heard screaming off camera), his success possible because the stasis field is powered by "drozanon," identical to the radium in his watch dial. (The relative atomic weights of drozanon and radium are unfortunately never discussed.)

Breaking into a closed real estate office, Tom phones the police and is soon at the mercy of the kooky, gun-wielding proprietor, Elmer Wesson, in a scene reminiscent of *Invasion of the*

Saucer Men. At this point, the film's absurdities pile up and it falls hard. Between his ridiculous nightshirt and his unendurable voice, Wesson is perhaps the most irritating comic relief character in cinema history. With the police soon on the scene, everyone looks for the cave, while Hauron skulks around the outskirts and tries an out-of-body attack on the search party. Giving himself up to get back to Sally, Tom engages in more bizarre banter, including his pig Latin assurance to Sally that he is giving the aliens fake information: "Ixnay! Oney-phay ope-day!" The invading search party gets frozen as Hauron and Nadja escape (their light circles dissolving gradually into the tank, another nice touch by Tucker), but they are soon revived (one military guy remains humorously frozen in the background). Tom the genius soon comes up with a brilliant plan to defeat the aliens. After using litmus paper to verify the presence of hydrogen (with a much higher atomic weight)—even though litmus paper is designed merely to show if a substance is acidic or basic—they will add table salt (sodium chloride) and wallet inserts (polyethylene) to the hydrogen to cause a giant explosion. While hydrogen is highly flammable, there is nothing very reactive about the other two substances, and the explosion could have been more profitably achieved with hydrogen alone. But Tom, Sally, her uncle, Wesson, the cops, and the military are so overdramatically enthusiastic about the idea that one feels a little sorry for the actors, and of course the ploy works.

But scientifically absurd as this all is, it works no worse than most things in the realm of bad monster films. It at least brings the heroes to a satisfying resolution of their problems, particularly after Tom and Sally declare their love for one another,

her uncle now respecting him and the police expressing their gratitude. But it is soon after, with another crash and Sally horrifically screaming to her death offscreen, that the film becomes unacceptable on its own terms. The aspect of *The Cape Canaveral Monsters* that disappoints anyone who watches it is the fact that the heroes more than earn their happy ending, but have it utterly dashed at the end. Why Tucker wanted the film to end this way is an enormous puzzle. As someone struggling to make it in Hollywood, it is strange that he did not think the movie needed a happy ending. If it had ended on a triumphant note, it would have had far more audience appeal and perhaps that could have made the difference in selling it. Warren notes, "The it's-not-over-yet mood at the end of *Them!* is rare,"[795] and yet Tucker used this rare ending on both of his monster films.

But while the downbeat ending makes no sense it is not completely inexplicable, for such endings are another unifying thread in Tucker's films. It would be a mistake to write them off as simply unhappy, for their similarity is far more specific. Tucker's films end not so much in tragedy as *futility*. Achievement is always undermined in a Tucker ending: *Robot Monster* concludes with a series of Ro-Men lumbering into the camera, just after reassurance that the film's apocalyptic drama was only a dream. The crooks of *Dance Hall Racket* receive their comeuppance not long before the film's narrator informs us that the dance hall is back in crooked business under new owners, and the film closes with the very same shot of dancing that opened it. *Broadway Jungle*'s low-rent director narrowly escapes an attempt on his life, learns nothing, and promptly resumes his sleazy ways. And *The Cape Canaveral Monsters* builds to a triumphant defeat of alien invaders, only to have it destroyed at the last second with the sudden death of the hero's girl. One may question if Tucker's lost films actually continue the pattern, but the evidence suggests no reason to believe otherwise. The heroes of *Space Jockey* "don't make it back," and it is unlikely that the violent protagonists of *Pachuco* could have come to a good end. Even if one tries to factor in the phoned-in direction of his burlesque films, their static nature is merely the spreading of a futile ending across an hour of film (and *Dream Follies* ends with its nerdy hero winning a fortune that is immediately confiscated by the tax man). Was Tucker, then, more gloomy than he sometimes appeared, or was this pattern in a group of films he made quickly and cheaply the evidence of something that he did not fully realize?

What can be stated with certainty is that *The Cape Canaveral Monsters* essentially closes the era of Tucker as struggling director. One archival copy has survived of an "unsold pilot"[796] he directed, *The Peter Lorre Playhouse* (1961), but little account survives of the circumstances that led he and writer John Trayne to collaborate with Lorre, who was down-and-out and taking all kinds of jobs. (Lorre, who died in 1964, could have been the Bela Lugosi to Tucker's Ed Wood if they had continued collaborating.) According to Lorre biographer Stephen D. Youngkin, at the time Lorre often fared better on TV than in the movies where he was no longer star material. Regarding Tucker's series, Youngkin explained, "On May 25, 1961, Lorre signed with Moffett Enterprises Inc. to host and possibly appear in *Peter Lorre Playhouse* . . . Tucker created the series format, but Trayne took credit for introducing the actor, whom he sat behind a desk, back to the camera, wearing a bowler hat and facing a giant spider web." But the series, "scheduled to resume in August," never continued beyond the pilot after Paramount declined to pick it up.[797] The show's format was presumably inspired by the current vogue for anthology series such as *The Twilight Zone, Alfred Hitchcock Presents,* or more specifically *Thriller,* the series that Boris Karloff hosted from its 1960 debut.

There may have been more forgotten and lost projects scattered through the early sixties, but there was less and less reason for there to be any. The Lorre pilot showed that Tucker was by 1961 still working in many of the same patterns that had defined him for years. As he remembered his pre-*Robot Monster* days, "I made about twenty-five or thirty pilots for television. . . . I was never in TV; I just made pilots." With *The Cape Canaveral Monsters* the parallel bookend to *Robot Monster, The Peter Lorre Playhouse* was the parallel bookend to the outermost edges of Tucker's decade of struggle to make it, reflecting back to his apprenticeship days with Gordon Avil and TV as "movies at home."

Further proving how little Tucker distinguished movies from television, he had at least one successful TV credit from the same timeframe. *Lock-Up* was a half-hour, syndicated crime/legal show, produced by Ziv Television, that debuted in September 1959. Macdonald Carey portrayed real-life lawyer Herbert L. Maris in stories described as based on his experiences, with the wonderfully gruff John Doucette as his cantankerous friend in the police department. In effect, the series was a poor man's *Perry Mason* (which debuted in 1957), but was nonetheless good in its own right. Tucker had co-story credit on one episode titled *The Drop,* about a young man with a checkered past framed for drug possession while trying to elope with his girlfriend. The episode contains no obvious Tucker motifs, but it illustrates the fact that he was heading closer and closer toward the mainstream.

And by the mid-sixties, Tucker had finally broken through. At that point he was regularly working in editing and post-production, often on the numerous TV documentaries of David L. Wolper. Tucker Jr. concurs that this era "was really the beginning of the mainstream stuff."

> I think he had all the personality traits to be a good producer, maybe not a good director. But he gave it a shot and he did produce a few films. In the long run, I think he probably preferred the stability of getting into the mainstream jobs rather than just going as an independent. It's a lot of work, and you really have to go out there and hustle and sell yourself. Who wants to do that forever?

14

The Mainstream

In 1972, Phil Tucker edited a documentary about the making of an Academy Award-nominated short. It only took him a decade from the cursed making of *The Cape Canaveral Monsters* and an unsuccessful TV pilot with Peter Lorre to get to that point. By the mid-sixties, he had moved into the work for which he was always best suited, editing and post-production. Tucker's credits after *The Cape Canaveral Monsters* are devoid of writing and directing credits, painting him as a steady worker who gave up on the creative side of filmmaking and settled into comfortable employment. But Tucker had been trying to sell out to Hollywood from the beginning, just wanting to work in the film industry, and his slightly cracked films as a director were his attempt to create his own opportunities from the ground up. He had always been supporting himself with jobs of some kind, but he could now make a living mostly doing what he loved. And his ambitious, independent side would continue to assert itself on occasions that did not require him to write or direct.

Tucker finally succeeded in part because he had obtained marketable job skills, while there was also an increased demand for editors on the lower tiers of the industry. The low-budget world had been steadily changing around him, and the marginal meal ticket of exploitation film was dying out. Burlesque was losing its edge by the turn of the decade, eclipsed by a new form of smut that blatantly sold nudity. *Time* and *The New York Times* both printed June 1961 features on the cheaply made, lowbrow comedies known later as nudie-cuties. Russ Meyer famously pioneered the trend with *The Immoral Mr. Teas* (1959) but one of the other early examples, *Not Tonight Henry* (1960), was directed by Merle Connell, as enterprising as when he switched from peek show machines to burlesque films a decade earlier. Connell told the *Times* his concern of imitators going too far and creating a backlash but that, for the time being, "Public opinion is not against this type of picture."[798] After the early sixties, dirty cinema moved from quasi-innocent material to complete obscenity in about a decade, and accompanying that change was a shift in distribution. Ever since the 1957 *Roth v. United States* Supreme Court decision, there was less of any clear sense of what was legally obscene. With the cultural brakes increasingly off and little remaining off-limits, smut was evolving from mom-and-pop exploitation outfits, sideshow carnie barkers, and mail order dirty photo rackets into an increasingly large, professionalized business.[799]

But the end of the classic exploitation film did not leave Tucker in much of a lurch, for there was a surge of demand for documentary product for television, creating editing jobs perfect for a journeyman like himself. In 1957, David L. Wolper was a fledgling salesman of television content who purchased Soviet space mission footage, assembling it into a TV documentary titled *The Race for Space* in its 1959 debut. Encountering massive network TV resistance, Wolper eventually sold the documentary to individual stations with massive success. Encouraged further, he produced many more, making them more palatable to the networks with an emphasis on entertainment.[800] Wolper significantly ramped up his staff, as the *Hollywood Reporter* noted in August 1960,[801] and Tucker was swept up in the ongoing tsunami, credited for editing four 1960s Wolper productions, including two *National Geographic Specials.* These jobs are emblematic of Tucker's successful career after the years of struggle from *Monster* to *Monsters,* and those who remembered him often did so in these terms. Phil Tucker Jr. confirmed that his father did "many more films than appear on IMDb" and "worked on documentaries for a time, I don't think he cared for it much but it was steady work." Specifically, Tucker Jr. remembered his father working on a large number of non-fiction movies ("one of them was something to do with bears"), and his father's references to such makers of underwater films as Jacques Cousteau as "fish peddlers."[802] As Tucker Jr. recalled, Tucker belonged to both "IATSE and American Cinema Editors (ACE)," the first confirming Tucker's status as a Hollywood working stiff and the second that he was a man of ability.[803] Trustin Howard remembered seeing him in the years after *Robot Monster* "at Four Star, where he became a very respected editor,"[804] and Conrad Brooks recalled:

> . . . I got to meet him years later, he was working for CBS Studios—that was called Television City, on La Brea and

> Beverly Boulevard. He was working over there, doing something to do with film work. See, I met him in a bar and we talked. We really talked, and I got to know him within an hour.[805]

Tucker's editing skills were likely already honed during his exploitation years in the fifties, and the end of his efforts as a director at the turn of that decade may not have been a failure at all. For while *Pachuco* and *The Cape Canaveral Monsters* were barely released and are obscure to this day, their connections to Republic Pictures might have finally gotten Tucker in the door of mainstream Hollywood. Republic was partially formed out of a film lab when it originated in 1935, which gave it an advantage in churning out low-budget material. According to Richard Maurice Hurst, "Consolidated Film Laboratories ranked as the best sound laboratory in Hollywood and, together with Radio Corporation of America sound recordings, gave the Republic films a polish that other independent productions lacked."[806] *Pachuco* producer A.W. Hackel was a Republic associate from decades before, and Tucker notably remembered the film's troubled postproduction in reference to Hackel's "friend [who] was head cutter for the B division of Republic" re-editing it afterwards. And *The Cape Canaveral Monsters,* produced soon after *Pachuco* and apparently never shown in theaters, was eventually sold to Republic. Its studio was bought by CBS and became Studio City[807]—a separate location from the network's Television City, where Brooks remembered seeing Tucker, but still part of the same organization. Circumstantially, it looks as if Tucker failed as an independent director while that experience directly allowed him to finally succeed as a studio editor.

Phil Tucker in the early seventies.

(Courtesy of Phil Tucker Jr. All rights reserved.)

Tucker Jr. remembered going with his father to work at times:

> As a young kid I was fascinated watching him operate the Moviola. To me, editing machines and projectors seemed like Rube Goldberg contraptions the way the film wound around so many sprockets. It was almost mesmerizing. When I had a question, he would always do his best to answer it in terms that I could understand.[808]

He also remembered his father as up at the crack of dawn and sometimes not back until very late (work "sort of came first for him"), moving with blinding intensity on jobs but also having fun, sometimes with such industry pals as *Bonanza* star Dan Blocker.

> He sort of lived in the moment. He had his favorite restaurants that would he hang out at, and he'd have his [usual table] and he loved to eat, which was kind of his undoing. He lived life to excess in a lot of ways. He was a chain-smoker, he overate; as you know he had diabetes, so he had a lot of health problems.

Tucker found time to be an inventor, his mechanical tinkering leading to his plans for a heat-based engine, or "surge turbine." Teaching himself welding and constructing a prototype, Tucker eventually had to abandon the project after the negative opinions of some engineers. He also never failed to be a provider—habitually labeling the life he loved as "feast or famine"—and took whatever odd jobs necessary to get through longer stretches between film assignments. Tucker Jr. warmly remembered his patient intelligence:

> I remember that he was driving me somewhere in his car—a big black Cadillac—when a question popped into my mind. I asked him what would happen if he were to put one foot on the brake, and one foot on the gas. Would the car move, or not move? Or, would it move at half-speed? Rather than brushing off my question, he

> indulged my curiosity. He paused for a moment, then said, "Let's find out." He put one foot firmly on the brake and placed the other on the gas. He also probably slipped the car into neutral without me noticing. The engine roared, but the car did not move. After this experiment was over, he began to explain that the default state for any equipment must always be the most restrictive state. This is a fundamental principle of engineering that I began to notice in practically everything, and I wouldn't have thought about it except that he took the time to answer my question.[809]

It was Tucker's mechanical, tactile facility that led to his most ambitious project of the 1970s. Pyramid Films, an educational outfit (maker of "films that they would show in the high school auditorium," as Tucker Jr. put it) had produced *Solo*, a 1972 short about mountaineer Mike Hoover. The movie presented an impressionistic journey up and down a mountain, edited from a mixture of sometimes nerve-wracking footage and covering different seasons along the way. (Al Reinert's acclaimed 1989 documentary *For All Mankind* would use the same approach, combining material from different NASA moon missions into one surreal voyage.) Along with an Oscar nomination, the impressive film reportedly won "the Atlanta International Film Festival's Silver Phoenix, Special Jury Award and Gold Medal; Crystal Vase Award of the USSR Council of Ministers Committee for Physical Culture and Sport; Edinburgh Film Festival Award; Golden Eagle from C.I.N.E.; and Bronze Medal from the New York International Film and TV Festival."[810]

More prosaically, Kate Nixon in *Mass Media* wrote that *Solo* "scared the hell out of me."[811] According to Tucker Jr.:

> One of the films that my dad had worked on was *Solo,* and what my dad had done is he went back and he created *Solo: Behind the Scenes,* where he took the unused footage and sort of cobbled together this other film that was the making of the first film. It didn't cost anything to do that because it had already been shot, it was just sitting there. So they were very happy with him about this because here was a whole new source of revenue that they didn't have to pay any money for, he just came up with it. He was in their good graces at that time, and so they were talking about maybe branching out from just doing pure documentaries and actually doing some features. They wanted to just try making a light feature, release it in a few theaters and maybe make some money off it and see how that would go and maybe they could branch out from there. So my dad convinced them that he would be able to make something really, really cheap and they decided to go for it.

Pyramid's owner Dave Adams shared producer credit with Tucker on the film that was shot over a summer of traveling with the Death Riders Motorcycle Thrill Show across the mid- and southwest. The original plan was to make a narrative film along the lines of *Easy Rider,* "sort of a coming-of-age kind of thing," with the antics of the daredevil cyclists in the background, but the project drifted back into documentary for reasons unclear.[812] Originally planning for a feature, the production achieved a feature-length documentary and at least a very cheap one with an exploitable angle on the seventies craze for motorcycle stunts. *The Albuquerque Tribune* reported in June 1974 that the Death Riders would appear in a parade, and film "several bull-riding sequences at an Albuquerque corral," parts that both appear in the finished film. The *Tribune* incorrectly cited Tucker as "president of Pyramid Films," but quoted him that the production was "pulling out all stops in a major effort to win the Academy Award . . .." Another *Tribune* report from a week later noted that the production had an "18-member crew."[813] This crew, according to Tucker Jr., lived in a fleet of yellow vans that can be seen throughout the film, taking them along with the riders in economical fashion.

Phil Tucker (*center*) on location for *Death Riders*.

(Courtesy of Phil Tucker Jr. All rights reserved.)

The final film, which dropped the eccentric working title *Star Spangled Bummer* in favor of *Death Riders,* is a frustrating effort. Good sequences dovetail with others that are pedestrian or even clunky, the quality of cinematography comes and goes, and the film sometimes finds an interesting focus on the motivations of the young daredevils onscreen, but not nearly enough to liven up the spaces between stunts. There is too much footage of the group just going about their business of traveling from one location to another, setting up, and killing time. One of the better parts of the duller footage is when the younger guys play a prank on Henry, their cantankerous, complaining roadie. The guys having cooked some wet dog food as a hamburger, he consumes a good part of it wondering why the group's dog angrily barks at him, only understanding as the others crack up. Less successful is an earlier, painfully unfunny sequence where the group performs for a nudist colony, complete with a panning shot over a row of hairy, lumpy rear-ends that must have scarred the mind of the unfortunate cyclist who had to jump over them. Then the film moves to one of its best parts, where the mother of owner Floyd Reed (and grandmother of one of the riders) talks of her misgivings and nerves.[814] These two sequences sum up almost everything that is best and worst about the film, which feels like what it probably was: the best movie that could be assembled from the limitations of the footage that was shot.

Later in the film the Death Riders encounter a group of bikers, and there is a brief possibility for some real tension. But the motorcyclists turn out to be a friendly bunch and, yet again, the gut-wrenching aspects of the daredevils' lives are turned into something placid. This incident is emblematic of where the film falls short; there is just too little conflict for a movie that mostly stands back from its subject and does not intellectually engage it. The stunts themselves are fortunately as fearsome as advertised, and are sometimes shot in spectacular fashion. Cinematographer Vilmos Zsigmond, not yet an Oscar winner but having already lensed *Deliverance,* worked on the project, somewhat in line with early jobs he took on Fairway International (Arch Hall) films. Some of the stunts are effectively captured in slow motion, and with occasionally startling perspectives; the best being a camera mounted on a bike and pointing downwards during a jump. Contrasting with other, rather pedestrian footage, these unique camera moments were probably the work of Zsigmond. I was able to very briefly chat with him, and he told me that he worked on the film for seven days, greatly liked Tucker for his generosity, and was impressed by his uncommon courtesy in calling him up and updating him on how the project ended.[815] Tucker Jr. remembered "having dinner at the Zsigmond household one evening, while he and my father talked about *Star Spangled Bummer.*"[816] In sum, "I always felt he was too good for a film of that caliber, just as Elmer Bernstein was too talented for *Robot Monster.* Being able to attract big-budget talent to a low-budget picture was one of my dad's best abilities."[817]

With all its flaws accounted, however, *Death Riders* should have still been entertaining enough for the demolition derby audience, and perhaps it was. In March 1976, *Variety* reported that Crown International had picked it up with worldwide rights, and was planning a domestic summer release.[818] By June,

(Stills courtesy of Phil Tucker Jr.)

Crown had sold it as part of a film package for distribution in the Philippines, and by December 1978 was including it in a group of forty movies intended for TV sales.[819] The potential for making money with *Death Riders* was there, but Pyramid was at a disadvantage. An educational film producer and not a commercial movie distributor, Pyramid did not have an array of cheaply acquired, low cost product to sell, only its one little movie. They could have four-walled the film in rural venues, although this might have been too much work for too little reward. What seems to have discouraged Pyramid from distributing it was an unfortunate test screening that Tucker Jr. vividly remembered:

> They had a premiere in Westchester,[820] and they showed the film for the first time. I don't know where they got the audience from. I remember that the reaction was very negative. People in the audience were basically laughing out loud, and making comments and stuff like that. I think that kind of put the final nail in the coffin. After the film was over, my dad was there with a tape recorder trying to get people's exit comments after they'd seen the film ("What did you think of it," and that sort of thing). And then something interesting happened on the way home. He claims that there was some kind of technical glitch and he accidentally had erased everything on the tape. My dad was a pretty technical guy, I don't think that that would have happened accidentally, if you catch my drift.

Death Riders is not a laughable film and, despite flaws, has much going for it. This extremely negative reaction, therefore, was probably for reasons beyond simple quality, for some factor that made the audience completely unreceptive. The reason was probably cultural, by way of geography. If this Los Angeles audience was young and self-consciously hip, then they could have easily responded with derision to this very Midwestern and rural movie. The film's stars, some speaking thoughtfully on camera and others not, remain as down-home as their humble audience, who appear to live lives of family, work, and fleeting, simple pleasures. *Death Riders* may have just been too redneck for seventies L.A., a film for Eagles fans previewed in front of a Steely Dan audience. The original title, *Star Spangled Bummer*, summarizes how the film captures the Silent Majority's easy incorporation of counterculture fashion into its own lifestyle (witness the long hair everywhere onscreen). Tucker Jr. remembered that the film was conceived partially in line with the popularity of *Easy Rider*, which reinforces the point. *Easy Rider* was made by Hollywood hippies with characters who become victims of square America, while *Death Riders* shows real-life square Americans who were also, after a fashion, hippies.

The film should have been previewed elsewhere, perhaps in Amarillo where Tucker once had a lively experience with *Pachuco*. Tucker Jr. also remembered that the film's country-rock soundtrack was expected to be a success in its own right, and most of the tunes are melodic and catchy. In particular the song "Live for Now," performed by T.G. Sheppard, is repeated throughout and seems even more of a theme song than another one actually titled "Death Rider." "If you're afraid to chase your dream to the highest hill / How will you learn who you really are if you're just standing still?" sings Sheppard, the song playing after Floyd Reed's son Danny succeeds again at the incredibly dangerous human bomb act. Tucker Jr. believed that the song was a good encapsulation of his father's philosophy: "You have to take your chances, and otherwise you'll never know what you can accomplish if you don't." Even Tucker's editing here is a reminder of chances he took in his life. Stars, rectangles, and other transition shapes are used to go from one scene to another, much like the editing of *Broadway Jungle,* the film that Tucker may have used as an apprenticeship. Since *Death Riders* cost next to nothing, Tucker lost no momentum and kept at his career.

Amongst the inadequate surviving credits that have appeared on the Internet or in books, it is certain that Tucker had editing jobs on such shows as *Wonder Woman, The Next Step Beyond* (a follow-up to *One Step Beyond*), and Filmation's *Jason of Star Command.* (Universal's *Battlestar Galactica* had a few episodes with light-globe weapons, similar to the floating blobs from *The Cape Canaveral Monsters.* Tucker had no credits on the show, but it is tempting to wonder if he suggested the idea for this effect to others credited on the post-production.) But Tucker's skills got him into feature film work as well; he was post-production supervisor on two Dino De Laurentiis productions, the *King Kong* remake (1976) and *Orca* (1977):

> Him and Dino were pretty tight, he was kind of like Dino's right hand man in a sense. He was very proud of the work that he did on *King Kong*; he brought home all

> the posters and that kind of stuff. He was really proud of that, and I think in a sense he'd kind of put the stigma of all those others films behind him at that point, and he'd really become a formidable editor in his own right.

Joe Dante, Hollywood director and Monster Kid, knew Tucker during this phase of his career, meeting "Phil when he was a post production supervisor working for Dino De Laurentiis." Dante remembered:

> He was a genial, even garrulous guy who was happy to talk about his movies, especially the one he did with Lenny Bruce, *Dance Hall Racket.* Dunno where the print came from but he organized a screening of this one in a dailies room at CFI which was attended by many of us from the New World trailer department. Like his other work it was threadbare but offbeat. Phil confirmed the details of the sad story about how depressed he was to be treated so poorly during the limited theatrical release of *Robot Monster,* but he seemed to have come to terms with its place in Bad Movie History. I told him how the movie affected me as a kid (I thought it surreal and scarifyingly bleak, especially in its total destruction of the family unit) and he seemed pleased. Lost touch with him afterward, as is normal for Hollywood, but would see his name on movies occasionally.[821]

Tucker continued to edit and do other work into the early eighties, such as the theatrical movie *Charlie Chan and the Curse of the Dragon Queen* (1981), a comedy with Peter Ustinov, and the TV movie *The Seal* (1981), an action drama starring Ron Ely, evidence that for Tucker TV was still "simply movies at home."[822] But he still harbored greater ambitions that were evidenced by his unrealized project *Hollywood Fever*. Tucker Jr. remembered it as "an adult comedy, somewhat risqué without being over-the-top," noting, "I think his description went something like 'boy meets girl, boy loses girl, boy follows girl to Hollywood to win her back . . ..'" This project "represented the start of a new direction for him, the writing was actually good, the jokes were funny, he was doing what he loved again (producing) and things were generally looking up. Tragically, his health began to fall apart, so the most likely conclusion is that it was never finished."[823] Tucker had to manage increasing difficulty from the physical complications of diabetes. He simply decided to not curtail his unhealthy excesses because he enjoyed them too much. According to Tucker Jr., "He made the argument that I think a lot of smokers make, that he could give it up if he wanted to, but he simply chose not to because it gave him so much pleasure. So that's what he told himself anyway." Tucker passed away on December 1, 1985.[824] As his son remembered, he was at least somewhat philosophical about his life's choices:

> But I remember him saying once that his life had been so rich, that he had accomplished so much that if he were to die tomorrow, he wouldn't have any regrets. So I guess on balance it wasn't a bad way to live, for him. He seemed to be at peace with it.

15

Monster Reborn

In the subsequent years of Phil Tucker's successful career as part of the Hollywood mainstream, *Robot Monster* and its fellow cheap creature epics were largely dormant, while prowling sporadically. Attacking late night TV audiences for years, the film swirled ever more in the collective unconscious, the robot-gorilla stalking the dreams of those who once saw it at four in the morning on local TV. This late-night exposure would eventually saturate pop culture and produce a response, apparent in an explosion of interest in the genre from the late 1970s to the middle 1990s. Going far beyond appearances of *Robot Monster* and similar films in music videos (such as "You Might Think" by the Cars) comedy programs (such as *The Canned Film Festival*), the 1982 *Robot Monster: Special Edition* on MTV with Bob Burns assuming the mantle of Ro-Man, and a classic monster group cameo in Joe Dante's *Looney Tunes: Back in Action* (2003),[825] there arose a bad movie cult, which reached its apogee with *Mystery Science Theater 3000*. But the cult first came to

Bob Burns on the *Robot Monster: Special Edition* set with actress Keri Nichols.

prominence with the appearance of two books, *The Fifty Worst Films of All Time* (1978) and *The Golden Turkey Awards* (1980).

The first book was written from a joking proposal. Yale graduate Michael Medved had a literary agent and was suggesting a number of book projects, centered on such serious concepts as a history of White House staffers. Sardonically tossed in was a proposed book on terrible movies that was unexpectedly picked up by one publisher. With his youngest brother Harry and in-law Randy Dreyfuss, he completed *The Fifty Worst Films of All Time,* which went into at least three printings and led to an inevitable sequel, *The Golden Turkey Awards.*[826] (There were also two further, less famous bad movie books by the Medveds.) While many films and filmmakers were spotlighted in these books (and many of them were A-list, mainstream Hollywood productions), the work of Ed Wood and Phil Tucker stood out from the background in stark contrast. Wood's *Plan 9 from Outer Space* was famously the top vote-getter by fans of the first book for the title of Worst Film of All Time, almost incredibly defeating a large number of big-budget 1970s bombs. These all-time worst honors handed out in the second book, Wood was also selected as Worst Director of All Time, with a lengthy profile filled with original interview quotations, highlights of some of the weirder moments from Wood films, and details on Wood's unconventional lifestyle. Tucker was profiled as a contender for Worst Director, including a vaguely dated account of his suicide attempt, along with William Beaudine and Herschell Gordon Lewis. More importantly, *Robot Monster* was awarded Most Ridiculous Monster in Screen History, nominated for Worst Credit Line of All Time, and had already been selected as one of the unfortunate *Fifty Worst Films of All Time,* a book in which Wood was never even mentioned.

Behind the two books' references to Tucker was an interview that Harry Medved conducted in a 1976 visit to Tucker's home and preserved in a forty-five-minute recording. Phil

Tucker Jr. characterized his father's voice as "resonant," but not at the time of the interview.[827] Diabetes was already taking its toll on his health and, for anyone who knew Tucker well, the difference was clear.

> That was really limiting for him, he couldn't work because he had terrible pain in his legs, and that was sort of like the brave last days. In fact when that interview was conducted . . . you could really tell he was struggling in that. He didn't sound like himself at all when I heard it.

The opening minutes of the interview recording provide a view into Tucker's life at the time, with the ambient sounds of paper or wrapper crinkling, the clatter of silverware and plates, and a sound like a knife picking at butter in a dish. Voices soft and somewhat buried in hiss, Medved tells Tucker, "First of all . . . I am writing this book. Unfortunately your film is"—the sentence trailing off in something like "on the list." A little later, Tucker breaks to get "my teeth in," and walks away with more casual conversation on his unspecified domestic difficulties:

> *What do you mean, not letting you go home every day?*
> Well it's for the last two months.
>
> *Oh, I see.*
> I'm still not quite used to having all the things handy.

With a few more starts and stops along the way, the rest of the interview is mostly audible and continuous. Medved showed Tucker some promotional material for the film, which caused

Tucker to search for his glasses. "I'm sorry," said Medved, as Tucker expressed, "I never have anything where I want it," one of Tucker's occasional signs of exasperation. Medved noted, "The book should be out this January. We have some great stills."[828] Looking the one-sheet over, Tucker made an amused "Hmmm." Continuing along with little incident in the steady tick-tock of the tape recorder's internal sound, window traffic noise, and the scraping of a knife on toast, remain as much insight as Tucker left behind on his early career, and the films he directed in those days. Sparsely quoted in *The Fifty Worst Films of All Time* and *The Golden Turkey Awards*, the interview left as many intriguing questions as it answered, but is no less precious for that reason.

Whether through causation or simple correlation, the two books initiated the bad movie cult. The craze came about not so much because audiences suddenly found movies like *Robot Monster* ridiculous—they seem to have always felt that way—but for a reason less commonly realized. The very trend in American culture that had for two decades encouraged film criticism, art house cinema, college film classes, and the imported European notion of directors as auteurs, brought about the craze for enjoying terrible films. Without an incentive to take movies seriously enough to think and write about them in large numbers, no one would have taken bad movies seriously enough to laugh at them full time.

The trend was also not simply an ironic, hipster stance toward the earnest, square seriousness of earlier pop culture. The bad movie movement seemed to enjoy the badness of very recent films, and Hollywood blockbusters were as often attacked

SYNOPSIS

Grand Prize Winner "GOLDEN TURKEY AWARD - 1986"
One of the Greatest All Time "Cult" Motion Pictures Directed by Phil Tucker

starring **GEORGE NADER - CLAUDIA BARRETT**

Inhabitants of a distant planet, peopled by a race of mechanical monsters called Ro-Men are disturbed by the tremendous strides being made on Earth in the research fields of atomic development and space travel.

Anticipating the emergence of Earth as an important rival and a potential aggressor in the world of Space, the Supreme Ro-Man assigns one of his subjects to the destruction of the terrestial sphere.

He succeeds, but as far as they know only six people remain. These include a famous scientist; his assistant, Roy; his wife; his daughter, Alice, a famous researcher in her own right; and two children, Johnny, seven, and Carla, six.

Ro-Man has established headquarters in their vicinity in an effort to ferret them out. A sonic barrier, devised by Alice, seems to protect them. It is ultimately discovered however that an antibiotic serum, developed by the professor, has actually protected them not only against bodily ills but against the supersonic death ray which Ro-Man has used for destructive purpose.

Able to make contact with Ro-Man on a televiewer screen, the group seeks an explanation of why this terrible destruction has been wreaked on Earth. However, the invader from outer space, acting on instructions, offers no quarter and demands unconditional surrender in return for a painless death.

The first inkling the survivors have that they are impervious to the monster's weapons occurs when Johnny, the seven year old boy, sneaks away to face the monster. Inadvertantly, he blabs the secret of the protecting serum.

The survivors have, in the meantime, learned of the existance of an Earth space station which has survived the attack of the Ro-Men. Possessed with the unquenchable optimism which marks man's progress on Earth, they attempt to lead a normal life in the face of their peril.

As they prepare to meet him, the Supreme Ro-Man threatens to destroy his ambassador of death. Having become infected with human emotions, he is no longer useful.

A full scale attack is launched. The Robot Monster is destroyed by his master. A cataclysmic upheaval takes place on Earth as the result of a ray offensive aimed by the Ro-Men. Mountains are levelled, rivers dried up. Prehistoric monsters engage in deadly combat, Earth begins to return to its pre-evolutionary state.

AVAILABLE IN 3D OR FLAT

ORIGINAL MUSIC SCORE BY ELMER BERNSTEIN

8831 SUNSET BOULEVARD
WEST HOLLYWOOD, CALIFORNIA 90069
(213) 652-8100, TELEX FOR USA: 910-490-1139
ANS. BK. MEDALLION LSA
REGISTERED CABLE ADDRESS: "MEDALPIX"
FAX (213) 659-8512

WADE WILLIAMS DIST.

(*Above*) **Medallion Films promotional text for *Robot Monster*.**

(*Facing, above*) **Medallion Films promotional images based on vintage *Robot Monster* material** (*lobby card below*).

Starring George Nader and Claudia Barrett

"ROBOT MONSTER"

Photographed in
Tru-Stereo Process

Executive Producer
AL ZIMBALIST

Released thru
Medallion Pictures, Ltd. - Hollywood

BOTH IMAGES ABOVE - WADE WILLIAMS DIST.

by the Medved books as were hopeless no-budget items from decades before. When the essential and groundbreaking anthology *Kings of the Bs* appeared in 1975, documenting low-budget cinema in great detail, the editors stated, "The purpose here is not to argue that *The Amazing Colossal Man* (1957) is a better movie than *Citizen Kane* (1941). The purpose is simply to assert the existence of Bert Gordon's film."[829] But in taking conventionally terrible films seriously enough to ponder them, not everyone laughed. According to Jack Stevenson's *Land of a Thousand Balconies,* it was "fourteen years of wandering in the wilderness" in which a member of New York City's No Wave music scene struggled to document the life of Ed Wood.[830] Published in 1992, Rudolph Grey's *Nightmare of Ecstasy* was the opposite of *The Golden Turkey Awards'* approach to Wood, treating him as a misunderstood, outsider artist. Grey found a haunting sense of poetry in Wood's exceptionally odd cinema, and was irritated by the mainstream's scoffing at Wood's films and eccentricities. It was no mystery to what books, writers, and fans he referred to in this passage:

> Wood was the target of still more ridicule soon after his death. The jackals of bourgeois sensibility moved in. With an offensive smugness and condescension towards his movies and novels, they had a field day of derision over the revelation of his transvestitism.[831]

Grey also briefly brought Tucker into the discussion. Along with a tidbit about Tucker helping Wood edit *Plan 9 from Outer Space,* he noted:

> The climate of sensationalism that followed Wood's death proved to be yet another obstacle. Former associates, such as the late Phil Tucker, director of *Robot Monster*, refused to discuss the past; others flatly denied ever knowing Ed Wood—or came down with a sudden case of amnesia.[832]

Grey was kind enough to clarify this experience for me:

> That was my impression, in my one and only short phone call to Phil Tucker . . .that he was burned, no longer trusted writers. It's too bad, as I genuinely admired *Robot Monster*, but [regarding] Ed Wood, he said that was all in the past, no longer wanted to talk about it, and he was sorry he wasted my time. I even wrote a follow-up letter, to no avail . . . But the ridicule he was subjected to in the Medved book had done the damage . . ..[833]

Bill Warren also notably rebuked the Medveds in the first edition of *Keep Watching the Skies!*, calling *The Fifty Worst Films of All Time* "naive and contemptible" and labeling the Medved brothers "reprehensible," with "a repulsively arrogant attitude."[834] But by the time of the revised 2010 edition, Warren and Harry Medved were friends, and Warren allowed, "Harry has since reformed, is a good writer on film subjects, and has a fondness for *Plan 9* and Ed Wood."[835] The Medveds themselves displayed some of this mixed emotion about their film writing, noting in their later two books that they experienced "a special affection for the films assembled here," while stating elsewhere that "If, in our desire to cover every base, we have inadvertently omitted any major group as a target for our sophomoric abuse, then allow us to apologize in advance."[836]

The truth is that, whatever the authors' intention, the Worst of All Time hook was simply the perfect way to interest the mass public in unconventional films. A book on the weirdest movies of all time would be of limited interest, but everyone could relate to the experience of enduring a bad movie. Grey's intensively researched book took over a decade from inception to publication, missing the mass trend and also so focused on one filmmaker as to be of cult interest. If the Medveds had truly wanted nothing more than to heap abuse on their subjects, then they would have named Herschell Gordon Lewis—not Wood—the Worst Director of All Time. Of all those nominated for the dubious honor, Lewis' work stands out not so much as incompetent but repulsive, and the Medveds castigated him for saturating the fringe with blood and gore. While this is indeed the reason for his inclusion in the list, a mindset of contempt would have handed the award to him hands-down. But the Medveds chose a more benign figure whose recurring quirks formed a recognizable body of work. William Beaudine left behind a filmography of mostly average quality and Tucker's films as director were few. From a perspective of enjoying bad movies, no one besides Wood could have been declared Worst Director of All Time in *The Golden Turkey Awards.* As the Medveds ended their entry on *Plan 9 from Outer Space,* and ended the book proper, an anonymous Wood associate was quoted that, regarding Wood's making of his most famous film, "I can tell you one thing for sure: he loved every minute of it."[837] Printed below a grin-inducing photo of Tor Johnson menacing Mona McKinnon, it is difficult to believe that the Medveds wished Wood nothing but contempt.

Was Tucker put out by how he had been treated? Tucker Jr. believes that Grey's viewpoint is true to some degree. The negativity that had enveloped Wood and others was no incentive to revisit a time in his life that he mostly viewed as a formative experience. But Tucker Jr. also notes that his father was "more or less indifferent to" the sneers of the bad movie cult, having achieved his goal of becoming a Hollywood pro. Tucker's health was also deteriorating further from the time of the interview, and was another reason he declined further discussion of his early years. Others written up in bad film books or later mocked on television's *Mystery Science Theater 3000* have expressed a similar ambivalence about their past work. Interviewed by Tom Weaver, Arch Hall Jr. thought it "unfortunate" that some in the media might get mean in laughing at him or his father's movies, "But . . . I don't care. They can think anything they want to. They were not back there then—most of them probably weren't even *born.*"[838] Hall's *Eegah* co-star Richard Kiel likewise told Weaver, "I don't make any bones about it, I'm a three-time loser on *Mystery Science Theater,* I think I hold the record . . .. Hey, people can laugh at *Eegah,* it doesn't bother *me,* 'cause I went on to do [bigger, better] things."[839]

Tucker went as far as he could with *Robot Monster,* and then kept his nose to the grindstone the rest of his life. The melancholy of "what might have been" was not something that he would often let others catch him indulging in. And to understand just how gifted, industrious, and fortunate Tucker was,

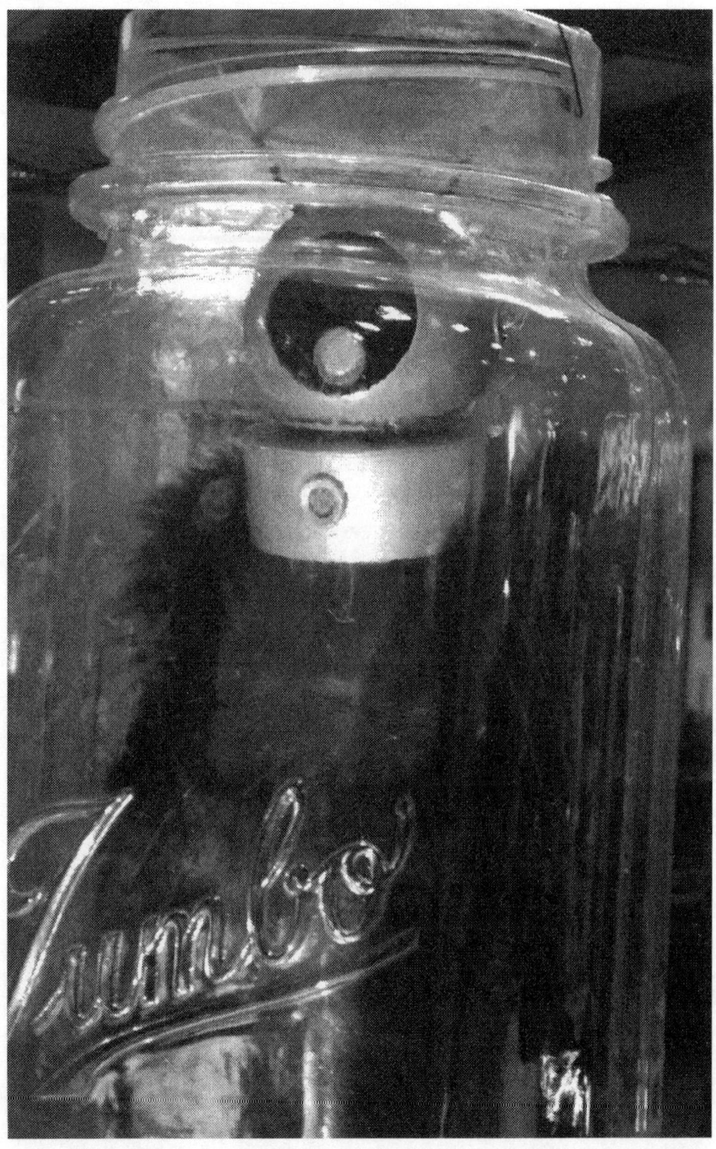

Ro-Man contained for the time being in Joe Dante's 2003 comedy *Looney Tunes: Back in Action.*

it only takes a comparison with some of his contemporaries. Without quite hitting Wood's downward slide, some got close enough, such as Titus Moede. A likable, goofy presence in movies of Ray Dennis Steckler and Coleman Francis, Moede had some mainstream parts in the same late fifties-early sixties timeframe, before pouring himself into four no-budget years of making his 1967 docudrama *The Last American Hobo.* The film exploring the dwindling hobo lifestyle, Moede "four-walled it around the country" but could never rise above breaking even.[840] Moede cursed "the Guggenheims and the Fords. I tried to get funding but I couldn't. Yet they fund ridiculous stuff like the sex life of the bumblebee or something like that."[841] Giving up on artistic ambition or attempting to crack the mainstream, he became a full-time pornographer for the rest of his life, sometimes working for the same employer as Wood.[842] Steckler also largely gave up on his fun, weird style of the sixties and thereafter made hardcore films. Francis avoided the sad, twilight world of smut by dying prematurely after years of destitution and excess drinking, his body found mysteriously in a station wagon in a parking lot in 1973.[843]

It seems that Wood was too proud, stubborn, or trapped to change his course and try flipping hamburgers. According to his colleague Dennis Rodriguez, the smut book racket was a low-paying "saturated market" by the late seventies, and Wood "was stuck in it, in a sense. He was a transvestite, he wasn't going to put on a straight costume to land a job . . .."[844] But for those willing to serve in Heaven rather than stubbornly trying to rule in Hell, there was hope to get by in the movie business. Sometimes maligned as a schlock director, William Beaudine shot hundreds of movies and TV episodes from the early silent years through the late sixties. A sensitive, intelligent, but very efficient director, he was chosen by Mary Pickford to film her 1926 comeback, *Sparrows.* When for unclear reasons he fell from the Hollywood elite in the thirties, he charged ahead as a director for hire on Poverty Row, exploitation, and TV projects, and was later dubbed "One Shot" by the Medveds for his speedy ways. (According to legend, he exclaimed on the set of a cheap Western in 1938, "You mean someone out there is actually waiting to see *this?*"[845]) But according to a biography by his granddaughter Wendy L. Marshall, Beaudine kept a positive attitude about life, and seldom expressed irritation with his place. Then an editor, Edward Dmytryk recalled a lunch at Paramount in 1932 when Beaudine grumbled in disgust after meeting one of the studio's star directors. "If I were given as much money and had as much time to shoot scenes as he does, I'd be a 'great' director too," he muttered.[846] But more representative of his life, and his focus as a devoted and loving father and husband, was this statement: "Every spare minute that I have is in study or play with my youngsters. I know just how Cordelia, the Roman matron, felt when she called her children to her in the presence of her rich and haughty gem-bedecked friend and said: 'These are my jewels.'"[847] It was with a similar sense of appreciation that Tucker remembered the path his life had taken, despite its hardships. As Phil Tucker Jr. remembered his father's summing up, "His life had been so rich, that he had accomplished so much that if he were to die tomorrow, he wouldn't have any regrets."

And perhaps Tucker would have appreciated just how much further *Robot Monster* and the films of Ed Wood continued to

Apparently unaware that her character's name is not Alice, Ro-Man hoists Jenna Elfman aloft in *Looney Tunes: Back in Action.*

flow through popular culture. *Mystery Science Theater 3000* was the logical culmination of the bad movie movement when it appeared in 1988, creator Joel Hodgson noting, "*The* [*Golden*] *Turkey Awards* was so influential on the creation of *Mystery Science Theater* [*3000*], it kind of helped me get to this idea of, "Oh, that's this unified body of bad movies out there, we can use these to make a show out of.'"[848] *Mystery Science Theater 3000* featured *Robot Monster* early on, and showed many such movies until it ended in 1999. The movement had dwindled into a cult by the time the show debuted, but the award-winning program kept it alive with its own rabid cult following, still collecting the show's constantly forthcoming DVD box sets. And director Tim Burton's highly fictionalized 1994 biographical film *Ed Wood* has likewise found a following after an indifferent time in a few theaters, along with winning one Oscar. The same charge of meanness leveled at the Medveds can be applied in spades to *Mystery Science Theater 3000*, and even to the Burton film, where Wood and others are treated semi-affectionately.

But however one appreciates the weirdness of a film like *Robot Monster*, and respects the effort of those who made it, it is really impossible to write about a robot-gorilla movie without a hint of a smile. The intrinsic absurdity of the material is what it is. And assuming one truly loves bad movies as something more dear than a punching bag, there is only one major point where anyone will go wrong in analyzing them. In *Kings of the Bs*, Flynn and McCarthy warn of "the fallacy of intention: judging a work on the basis of the (apparent) intentions of its maker(s), and not on the intrinsic merits of the work itself."[849] And as this book has shown, Tucker intended things with *Robot Monster* that he could not pull off while allowing other things that he never planned while, all along, it was his fateful bit of no-budget ingeniousness that gave the movie a robot-gorilla. And for all the wondering of what *Robot Monster* could have been if made successfully, it is no matter. A good bad movie is better than a bad good movie.

Phil Tucker had only wanted to work in show business, and he succeeded. But, in one of life's many ironies, he also succeeded in creating a film that is—in a certain light—above-average, unusual, interesting, and destined to be remembered. And he did it by not sitting around and waiting for permission. In a time of experts, when every activity is professionalized to the point of absurdity, it is good to remember G.K. Chesterton's observation that "if a thing is worth doing, it is worth doing badly." In other words, it is better to be an amateur creator than a professional critic. And whatever flaws *Robot Monster* undoubtedly has, it was the product of hard work, ingenuity, and creativity. It is a unique film, and one that will endure and entertain for ages to come. It is the work of many cast and crew, and absolutely the work of Phil Tucker.

All filmmakers should be so lucky.

Notes

Except where noted otherwise, all quotations from Phil Tucker throughout the book are from his 1976 interview with Harry Medved, conducted in Tucker's Los Angeles apartment. Likewise, many quotations from Phil Tucker Jr. are from our July 18, 2009, telephone conversation and noted when otherwise.

[1] G.K. Chesterton, *What's Wrong with the World* (Dover, 1910, 2007), p. 192.

[2] Harry and Michael Medved, *The Golden Turkey Awards* (Perigee Books, 1980), p. 175.

[3] Stephen King, *On Writing: A Memoir of the Craft* (Scribner, 2000), pp. 34-35.

[4] Stephen King, *Stephen King's Danse Macabre* (Berkley Books, 1983), p. 202.

[5] One of the strangest reactions to *Robot Monster* is probably a sonnet I wrote while sitting in a Renaissance literature class, early 1990s:

> O, to exist by the hu-man's fair way
> And navigate graphs of form complex;
> To live by such myst'ry from day to day,
> Ne'er more by programmed conflicts to be hexed.
>
> If I could loose these chains of logic's steel,
> My soul's hint could find its consummation.
> That base, wretched coils could forever feel
> This which I have known by mere intimation.
>
> 'Tis destiny most horrible I face,
> To have poet's soul but condition grave;
> I dread my lack of will to this erase
> That my true Ro-Man's honor I may save.
>
> But to postulate long for Earth-Girl's charms
> Is to waste away waving furry arms.

Renaissance poets wrote sonnets in a variety of forms; Ro-Man's sonnet is in the Shakespearean form of three quatrains ended with a couplet.

[6] Michael Barnum, "Gregory Moffett: *Robot Monster* Moppet," *Classic Images*, no. 413, November 2009.

[7] Harry Medved's interview with George Barrows, 1981 or 1982.

[8] Tom Weaver, *It Came from Weaver Five: Interviews with 20 Zany, Glib, and Earnest Moviemakers in the SF and Horror Traditions of the Forties, Fifties, and Sixties* (McFarland, 1996), pp. 366-367. Michael Medved, *Right Turns: Unconventional Lessons from a Controversial Life* (Crown Forum, 2004), p. 273.

[9] *Flying Saucers Over Hollywood: The "Plan 9" Companion* can be found on Image Entertainment's *Plan 9 from Outer Space* DVD.

[10] E-mail from Phil Tucker Jr., April 28, 2009.

[11] G.K. Chesterton, *George Bernard Shaw* (Hill and Wang, 1956), p. 73.

[12] E-mail from Harry Medved, March 19, 2013.

[13] Author interview with Trustin Howard, March 23, 2011.

[14] Rudolph Grey, "Umberto Scali Lives!!! The Timothy Farrell Interview," *Psychotronic*, no. 14, Winter 1992-1993, p. 24. (Complete article is pp. 22-27.) I am not sure if Scalli should be spelled with two Ls or one, as Grey has it. The makers of these films may not have been sure about it either.

[15] E-mail from Phil Tucker Jr., November 14, 2007.

[16] E-mails from Phil Tucker Jr., November 14, 2007; January 26, 2010. It should also be mentioned that there were at least two other Phil Tuckers working in the media at the same time as the subject of this book. There was an East Coast radio newsman named Phil Tucker whose name pops up during the 1960s (for example: *Variety*, April 3, 1963, p. 109). There was also a Chicago standup comedian named Phil Tucker who shows up fairly often during the 1950s. This comedian worked on the blue end of the comedy spectrum, as *Variety* reported on his March 1961 installation as "permanent headliner" at a Chicago club, "thereby erasing the longtime sophisticated tone of the room." The "blue material specialist" had lost a St. Louis job in the previous decade, "chased because of his unchaste material." (*Variety*, March 15, 1961, p. 59.)

[17] Phil Tucker family genealogical information and enlistment records obtained through Ancestry.com. Special thanks to Judith A. Runestad.

[18] E-mail from Phil Tucker Jr., June 26, 2008: "I knew he was an orphan, but I didn't know anything about his siblings. It would be interesting to know what became of them. They probably had enough sense to stay in Kansas."

[19] Bonnie Stepenoff, *The Dead End Kids of St. Louis: Homeless Boys and the People Who Tried to Save Them* (University of Missouri Press, 2010), p. 29. According to Stepenoff, the home was founded in 1889 by "the Christian Church" (now the Disciples of Christ). Stepenoff lists it as "the Christian Orphan Home," as does a genealogical website (http://genealogyinstlouis.accessgenealogy.com/greenwood.htm).

[20] E-mail from Phil Tucker Jr., September 8, 2015.

[21] Augustus Wilfrid Dellquest, *These Names of Ours: A Book of Surnames* (Thomas Y. Crowell Company, 1938), p. 276. J.R. Dolan, *English Ancestral Names: The*

Evolution of the Surname from Medieval Occupations (Clarkson N. Potter, 1972), p. 129.

[22] Dellquest, p. 158.

[23] Mrs. Tommie J. Crispino, *The Centennial Story of Parsons, Kansas* (Centennial Parsons, 1971), pp. 18-24, 28, 44 & 48.

[24] Carl Sifakis, *The Encyclopedia of American Crime*, second edition, vol. 1 (Facts On File, 2001), pp. 79-80.

[25] Duane Gilbert Meyer, *The Heritage of Missouri*, 3rd edition (River City Publishers, 1982), pp. 623-624.

[26] Stepenoff, p. 5.

[27] *The Salina Journal*, April 28, 1958, p. 11.

[28] *The Hutchinson News*, August 23, 1959, p. 3.

[29] *The Hutchinson News*, August 17, 1958, p. 26.

[30] I contacted St. Louis radio historian Frank Absher (http://www.stlradio.com) about Tucker's presence at KMOX, but he could not find any record of his time there. According to Absher, "Program producers were seldom publicized outside of credits at the end of a program." (E-mails from Absher, November 16 & 19, 2007.)

[31] Interview with Howard.

[32] According to Jerry Warren's ex-wife Bri Murphy, his slapdash movies were made with crews of a dozen people, which might dip down to around eight. Tom Weaver, *Monsters, Mutants and Heavenly Creatures: Confessions of 14 Classic Sci-Fi Horrormeisters!* (Midnight Marquee Press, 1996), p. 139.

[33] Joe Bob Briggs, *Profoundly Disturbing: Shocking Movies That Changed History!* (Universe, 2003), p. 8.

[34] Mark Thomas McGee, *Fast and Furious: The Story of American International Pictures* (McFarland, 1984), p. 1.

[35] Formation of Republic: Richard Maurice Hurst, *Republic Studios: Between Poverty Row and the Majors* (Scarecrow Press, 1979), pp. 1-2. Emphasis on entertainment and values: pp. 9-10. Prestige films: p. 6. For a good history of Republic, see pp. 1-34.

[36] According to William K. Everson, Republic films were highly polished and professional, Monograms were mind-numbing and PRCs, while dirt cheap, were sometimes at least unusual and creative. (Wheeler Dixon, *Producers Releasing Corporation: A Comprehensive Filmography and History* [McFarland, 1986], pp. 1-7.)

[37] Charles Flynn and Todd McCarthy, "The Economic Imperative: Why Was the B Movie Necessary?," Flynn and McCarthy, *Kings of the Bs: Working Within the Hollywood System: An Anthology of Film History and Criticism* (E. P. Dutton, 1975), pp. 13-43.

[38] Kevin Heffernan, *Ghouls, Gimmicks, and Gold: Horror Films and the American Movie Business, 1953-1968* (Duke University Press, 2004), p. 5.

[39] Packy Smith and Ed Hulse, *Don Miller's Hollywood Corral: A Comprehensive B-Western Roundup* (Riverwood Press, 1993), p. 4.

[40] *Mason City Globe-Gazette*, January 27, 1951, p. 16. The Iowa Kaufman is confirmed as the same as the Hollywood Kaufman in the July 14, 1960 *Globe-Gazette*, p. 11.

[41] Brian Lowry, "TV Scribe Kaufman Epitomized Another Era," *Variety*, December 4, 2001 (http://www.variety.com/article/VR1117856743?refCatId=9).

[42] *The Salina Journal*, August 23, 1951, p. 22.

[43] *Long Beach Press-Telegram*, September 12, 1951, p. A-23.

[44] *San Mateo Times*, October 13, 1952, p. 17; November 22, 1952, p. 1.

[45] *Daily Variety*, March 11, 1952, p. 8. The weekly edition of *Variety* also reported the same news on March 19, 1952 (p. 25).

[46] *Daily Variety*, April 16, 1952, p. 10.

[47] *Daily Variety*, August 21, 1952, p. 11; August 25, 1952, p. 9; *Variety*, August 27, 1952, p. 24.

[48] *Variety*, December 26, 1951, p. 26.

[49] Nancy Dowd and David Shepard, *King Vidor* (Scarecrow Press, 1988), pp. 96, 113.

[50] *The Times Recorder* (Zanesville, Ohio), "Kroger Section," March 14, 1933. The Kroger chain was the namesake of Kroger (Howard) Babb, whose *Mom and Dad* (1945) (directed by William Beaudine) was probably the most successful and long-running exploitation film of all time.

[51] *Greeley Tribune*, November 8, 1961, p. 4.

[52] *Reno Evening Gazette*, March 27, 1957, p. 20.

[53] Spencer Moon, *Reel Black Talk: A Sourcebook of 50 American Filmmakers* (Greenwood Press, 1997), p. 88.

[54] Brenda Scott Royce, *Hogan's Heroes: Behind the Scenes at Stalag 13* (Renaissance Books, 1998), p. 36.

[55] Gerry Dooley, *The Zorro Television Companion: A Critical Appreciation* (McFarland, 2005), p. 229.

[56] Flynn, p. 22-23.

[57] Weaver, *It Came from Weaver Five*, pp. 365-366.

[58] Flynn, pp. 348-351. Lewis' formula is less true today, as digital methods of filming and editing have made it possible to make movies with much less money.

[59] Eric Schaefer, *Bold! Daring! Shocking! True! A History of Exploitation Films, 1919-1959* (Duke University Press, 1999), pp. 2-6. The term "exploitation" was also used in the trade papers with the second, innocuous meaning of getting maximum value out of movies and TV shows. For example, the phrase "local stations have successfully whipped up exploitation excitement" appeared in

The Billboard in reference to TV programming, but not to any suggestive content (July 8, 1957, p. 8).

[60] Schaefer, p. 41.

[61] Schaefer, pp. 69-72. "Square-up" also had the secondary meaning of a nude reel hastily thrown on at the end of a movie, if the audience was becoming hostile over an exploitation film not living up to the hype.

[62] Schaefer, pp. 73-74.

[63] *Boxoffice*, April 4, 1953, p. 49.

[64] Schaefer, pp. 44-46 & 48-49.

[65] Schaefer, pp. 49-53.

[66] Fred Olen Ray, *The New Poverty Row* (McFarland, 1991), p. xi.

[67] Weaver, *Monsters, Mutants and Heavenly Creatures*, p. 133.

[68] Ray, p. 11.

[69] Robert S. Birchard, "Edward D. Wood Jr.—Some Notes on a Subject for Further Research," *Film History*, vol. 7, Winter 1995, pp. 450-455. Victor Adamson is most famous as the father of the even more notoriously cheap Al Adamson.

[70] Smith, p. 411. For an intricate discussion of independent distribution in the old days, see Brian Albright's interview with Sam Sherman in *Wild Beyond Belief!: Interviews With Exploitation Filmmakers of the 1960s and 1970s* (McFarland, 2008), pp. 188-192.

[71] Jim Thompson, *Nothing More Than Murder* (Vintage, 1949, 1991), pp. 6-14, 117. By "ten-frame shot," Thompson must have meant a ten-second shot, as ten film frames would amount to less than a half-second of screen time.

[72] DVD audio commentary for *Horror of the Blood Monsters* (1970), (Image Entertainment, 2002).

[73] *The Hollywood Reporter*, January 23, 1953, p. 10.

[74] *The Hollywood Reporter*, September 15, 1954, p. 4.

[75] Schaefer, pp. 391-392.

[76] Rudolph Grey, *Nightmare of Ecstasy* (Feral House, 1994), p. 42.

[77] *The Delta Democrat-Times*, February 19, 1953, p. 12 or 13. This was a widely printed United Press story; it appears as a clipping from a different newspaper in Grey's book (p. 222).

[78] Weaver, *It Came from Weaver Five*, p. 141.

[79] Ed Wood quote on Weiss is from Wood's later writings, quoted by Grey in *Nightmare of Ecstasy*, p. 198.

[80] Author interview with Conrad Brooks, August 3, 2009.

[81] Grey, "Umberto Scali Lives," p. 22.

[82] Grey, *Nightmare of Ecstasy*, p. 42.

[83] Interview with Brooks.

[84] Grey, "Umberto Scali Lives," pp. 22-23.

[85] Grey, *Nightmare of Ecstasy*, p. 83.

[86] Schaefer, p. 306, 308-309. Going by the audio of Harry Medved's interview with Phil Tucker, Connell's name was pronounced "cuh-NELL," rather than the typical "CON-uhl."

[87] *The Billboard*, January 8, 1944, p. 67.

[88] *The Billboard*, January 8, 1944, p. 46. Connell was once president of a 16 millimeter cinematography group, stepping down to become secretary-treasurer in 1949 (*Daily Variety*, September 18, 1947, p. 2).

[89] *The Billboard*, February 15, 1947, p. 120. Connell is listed as a partner with Nathan Robin, along with David Robin as personnel.

[90] Schaefer, p. 306.

[91] *The Billboard*, February 26, 1944, pp. 73-74.

[92] Schaefer, p. 306.

[93] *The Billboard*, March 12, 1955, p. 55.

[94] *Daily Variety*, July 23, 1940, p. 5.

[95] *Film Daily Year Book of Motion Pictures*, 1941, p. 557.

[96] The 1940 census notes that both Merle (as William M.) and Jean Connell were employed in "motion picture production," with Merle specifically employed as a "motion picture laboratory mgr.," but Jean specifically employed as a "waitress." James was so far their only child (daughter Linda, who would act in Tucker's *The Cape Canaveral Monsters*, would be born in 1942). According to the census, the Connell household also housed two teenage relatives, brother-in-law Eugene R. Johnson and niece Virginia Glaefke. Nineteen-year-old Eugene was also working in the "motion picture laboratory" trade as a "motion picture lab. technician." (Ancestry.com's listing for this census record transcribed "William M. Connell" as "Williamk G. Connell," but the accurate name can be seen on the scanned record image.) According to *Daily Variety*, Jean Connell worked "for years at the Metro commissary" (July 14, 1942, p. 5). *Variety*'s weekly edition also noted on July 22, 1942 that Merle was now "president of Modern Movies" (p. 46).

[97] Petroff's background as a ballet dancer and presenter is referenced in multiple newspaper sources. See: *The Fort Wayne Journal-Gazette*, March 23, 1919, section 4, p. 6; *The Modesto Evening News*, August 4, 1922, p. 10; *The Port Arthur News Editorial Page*, June 8, 1932, p. 4. This last one quotes Walter Winchell in his "On Broadway" column lamenting that Petroff was not given billing credit for shows he staged, a clue that restlessness with ballet may have driven him to other opportunities.

[98] *The Davenport Democrat and Leader*, May 19, 1925, p. 16.

[99] *The Ogden Standard-Examiner*, October 9, 1934, p. 7.

[100] *The San Mateo Times and Daily News Leader*, May 18, 1934, p. 10.

[101] Samuel Fuller, et al, *A Third Face: My Tale of Writing, Fighting and Filmmaking* (Knopf, 2002), pp. 85-86.

[102] Connell and Boris Petroff's *The Daughter of Mademoiselle from Armentieres* exists in a print at USC, Berkeley. There is also a copy with the last word misspelled and from another distributor, kept at UCLA.

[103] *The Billboard*, January 8, 1944, p. 67.

[104] *Independent Press-Telegram*, March 28, 1954, p. A-12.

[105] *The Bennington Evening Banner*, October 5, 1956, p. 8.

[106] David Hale, "Producer Sees Filmdom Ruin in Huge Star Salaries," *The Fresno Bee*, August 14, 1963, pp. 1-D, 3-D.

[107] Tom Weaver, *Science Fiction Confidential: Interviews with 23 Monster Stars and Filmmakers* (McFarland, 2002), pp. 15-18.

[108] Eric Levin, "An Eyeful Interview with Makeup Man Harry Thomas," *Filmfax*, no. 21, July 1990, p. 40. (Complete article is pp. 36-43, 88.)

[109] Tom Weaver, *John Carradine: The Films* (McFarland, 1999), pp. 233-234.

[110] Smith, p. 151. *The Irish Gringo* was in circulation as late as 1946 in Beckley, West Virginia (*Beckley Post-Herald*, November 1, 1946, p. 2). Fans of incompetent Westerns should also see *Trouble at Melody Mesa* (1949), shot by William Thompson and directed by Merle Connell. This film features an unappealing hero, a leading lady whose acting can be politely described as inexperienced, horrible attempts at comedy, and a completely incomprehensible ending. Best of all is the "intimidating" villain who spends much of his time in a drunken stupor.

[111] *Daily Variety*, June 16, 1953, p. 4.

[112] Thanks to Tom Weaver for information on what was in pre-production in 1952.

[113] *Daily Variety*, September 4, 1952, p. 1. Wyott Ordung could have been the writer of, as well as a cast member in, *Fabulous Murphys* and other Tucker pilots. Ordung later remembered having acted for Tucker before they began work on *Robot Monster*, and Tucker had to have known of his writing abilities somehow. The title *Fabulous Murphys* suggests *The Fighting Sullivans*, the wartime film biography of five Iowa brothers who fought and died in the war, and military themes were a favorite of Ordung's.

[114] *Daily Variety*, September 9, 1952, pp. 1, 6. The weekly edition of *Variety* reported the same story on September 10, with some wording variations in the Tucker quotes (p. 21). The same issue noted in the "Vidpix Chatter" column that the Screen Writers Guild was considering putting Tucker on the unfair list (p. 22), whereas *Daily Variety* already noted it as being done.

[115] *Daily Variety*, September 16, 1952, p. 6. Tucker may have only paid lip service to cooperating with the Guild. *Variety* reported in July and October 1953 that he and the Lea-Tuck company were still on the unfair list (July 22, 1953,

pp. 4, 17; October 21, 1953, pp. 7, 16).

[116] *Daily Variety*, October 15, 1952, pp. 1, 4.

[117] *Daily Variety*, October 21, 1952, p. 3. *Variety*'s weekly edition reported the story in abbreviated form on October 22, p. 1.

[118] *Daily Variety*, October 23, 1952, p. 4.

[119] *Daily Variety*, February 24, 1955, p. 7. Hilton directed a fair number of projects, mostly on a lower tier than his work as editor, including *Cat-Women of the Moon*, in some ways a companion film to *Robot Monster*. Listed as producer is Garrett King, who had no credits. (There is a much younger Garrett King listed on the IMDb.)

[120] Gordon Avil was listed as "Gordon Abel" in the October 23 report which, as will be discussed, was not the only time this mistake was made.

[121] *Variety*, October 29, 1952, p. 4.

[122] *Albuquerque Journal*, October 26, 1952, p. 27.

[123] *The Post-Standard*, October 30, 1952, p. 12.

[124] *Panama City News*, November 3, 1952, p. 4.

[125] Orson Welles and Peter Bogdanovich, *This is Orson Welles* (HarperCollins, 1992), pp. 311-312.

[126] Don Parson, *Making a Better World: Public Housing, the Red Scare, and the Direction of Modern Los Angeles* (University of Minnesota Press, 2005), pp. 167-168.

[127] *Los Angeles Times*, June 4, 1978, quoted in Neil J. Sullivan's *The Dodgers Move West* (Oxford University Press, 1987), p. 179.

[128] Medved interview with Barrows.

[129] *Fitchburg Sentinel*, August 31, 1946, p. 10. Thomas Ordung's Gold Star was awarded on Sunday, September 1, one of "90 Leominster [Massachusetts] boys who made the supreme sacrifice in World War II." All were awarded the Gold Star.

[130] *Los Angeles Times*, April 6, 1942, p. 4.

[131] Dwight R. Messimer, *Pawns of War: The Loss of the USS Langley and the USS Pecos* (Naval Institute Press, 1983), pp. 2-7, 18-20.

[132] Wyott Ordung family genealogical information and enlistment records obtained through Ancestry.com. Special thanks to Judith A. Runestad.

[133] *Daily Variety*, March 11, 1953, p. 2.

[134] *Syracuse Herald-American*, July 11, 1954, p. 21.

[135] William A. Emerson, *Leominster, Massachusetts, Historical and Picturesque* (The Lithotype Publishing Co., 1888), p. 222.

[136] *Fitchburg Sentinel*, August 31, 1946, p. 10.

[137] Author interview with Ewing Miles "Lucky" Brown, May 16, 2008.

[138] Ordung's unproduced script *The Yangtze Pirates* was registered for copyright by Leon Chooluck, production manager on many films. The record lists it as a "a five-part TV mini-series" (copyright record PAu-1-978-639).

[139] Johnny Legend, "The World According to Wyott," *Fangoria*, no. 38, 1984, pp. 60-61. (Complete article is pp. 58-61, 64.)

[140] Ordung as "a screwball": Michael Hoey quoted by Tom Weaver, *I Was a Monster Movie Maker: Conversations with 22 SF and Horror Filmmakers* (McFarland, 2001), p. 107. Ordung as "a strange person": Paul Dunlap quoted in e-mail from David Schecter, August 5, 2009. Ordung as "truly one of the most unusual characters in Hollywood": Mark Thomas McGee, *Beyond Ballyhoo: Motion Picture Promotion and Gimmicks* (McFarland, 1989), p. 81.

[141] Johnny Legend's interview states that Ordung had the interview already going with himself when Legend showed up. Legend specifically confirmed this point to Weaver (see DVD supplements for *Creepy Creature Double Feature, Vol. 1* [VCI Entertainment, 2013]). Ordung was also interviewed by Mark Thomas McGee and Ray Zone; they published some of his comments in their books.

[142] Don Graham, *No Name on the Bullet: A Biography of Audie Murphy* (Viking, 1989), pp. 138-9.

[143] Legend, p. 58.

[144] Interview with Brown.

[145] *Indiana Evening Gazette*, August 16, 1951.

[146] Ray Zone, *3-D Revolution: The History of Modern Stereoscopic Cinema* (University Press of Kentucky, 2012), pp. 57-58.

[147] Legend, p. 61. In Zone's quote from Ordung, Tucker "didn't even have a title" but suggested, "Let's call it *Googie-Eyes*" (Zone, p. 59).

[148] Interview with Howard.

[149] In 1953, Hans Conried starred in Arch Oboler's *The Twonky*, a strange comedy about a man's struggle with a hostile television. While the film can be seen as expressing its era's anxiety over rapid technological progress, it did not light up the box office.

[150] *The Hollywood Reporter*, March 26, 1952, p. 4.

[151] *The Hollywood Reporter*, September 25, 1952, p. 6.

[152] Sam Weller, *The Bradbury Chronicles: The Life of Ray Bradbury* (Harper, 2005), pp. 104-105.

[153] E-mail from Bill Warren, March 11, 2008.

[154] Robert Silverberg, *The Collected Stories of Robert Silverberg, Volume One: To Be Continued* (Subterranean Press, 2006), pp. 9-10.

[155] Frank Gruber, *The Pulp Jungle* (Sherbourne Press, 1967), p. 23.

[156] E-mail from Joseph McBride, July 23, 2015.

[157] *Variety*, July 13, 1992, p. 55. The Writers Guild of America, West has so far not listed any restored credits for Rinaldo: http://www.wga.org/content/default.aspx?id=1958.

[158] *The Hollywood Reporter*, January 29, 1953, p. 7.

[159] *The Hollywood Reporter*, January 30, 1953, p. 10.

[160] *The Hollywood Reporter*, February 18, 1953, p. 4.

[161] *The Hollywood Reporter*, March 4, 1953, p. 6.

[162] Ancestry.com.

[163] Zimbalist's employment at Film Classics is confirmed by a reference on the Internet Movie Database's IMDb Pro.

[164] Gabe Essoe, *Tarzan of the Movies: A Pictorial History of More Than Fifty Years of Edgar Rice Burroughs' Legendary Hero* (Citadel Press, 1968), p. 151.

[165] Harry and Michael Medved, *Son of Golden Turkey Awards* (Villard Books, 1986), p. 215.

[166] *Star-News*, February 2, 1961, p. 17.

[167] *The Hollywood Reporter*, July 6, 1960, p. 9.

[168] *The Hollywood Reporter*, October 9, 1959, p. 1.

[169] *Variety*, April 16, 1930, p. 11.

[170] *Variety*, November 7, 1933, p. 61; May 8, 1934, p. 61.

[171] *Variety*, January 1, 1936, p. 68; February 12, 1941, p. 11.

[172] *Variety*, April 2, 1941, p. 12.

[173] *Variety*, October 15, 1941, p. 15; December 30, 1942, p. 4.

[174] *Variety*, January 27, 1943, p. 14.

[175] *Variety*, February 3, 1943, p. 16; August 9, 1944, p. 9; September 6, 1944, p. 26.

[176] *Variety*, September 24, 1947, pp. 5-18.

[177] *The Hollywood Reporter*, August 27, 1952, p. 2.

[178] *The Hollywood Reporter*, September 12, 1952, p. 1.

[179] *The Hollywood Reporter*, October 9, 1952, p. 1.

[180] *The Hollywood Reporter*, October 14, 1952, p. 2.

[181] *The Hollywood Reporter*, January 13, 1953, p. 1. This news was also reported in *Daily Variety* on the same day, p. 8.

[182] *The Hollywood Reporter*, February 27, 1953, p. 2.

[183] *The Hollywood Reporter*, March 18, 1953, p. 6.

[184] Zone, p. 59.

[185] *The Hollywood Reporter,* March 10, 1953, p 1. Cousin of Tyron Power, Crane Wilbur had a fascinating career from silent film acting to later screenwriting, as well as directing the 1934 exploitation film *Tomorrow's Children.* This movie was an anomaly for being anti-progressivist, since it was about the plight of the forcibly sterilized (this practice, employed against supposed "defectives," was a progressive cause).

[186] *The Hollywood Reporter,* November 21, 1952, pp. 1, 5.

[187] *Harrison's Reports,* January 3, 1953, pp. 1, 4.

[188] Sidney Pink, *So You Want to Make Movies: My Life as an Independent Film Producer* (Pineapple Press, 1989), pp. 30-49. Tucker could be viewed as a less successful version of Pink; both were independent filmmakers, worked in burlesque, had a forward-looking view of TV, made 3-D films, and had the need to do things in their own ways.

[189] *The Hollywood Reporter,* December 30, 1952, pp. 1, 14.

[190] Hal Morgan and Dan Symmes, *Amazing 3-D* (Little, Brown and Company, 1982). This thorough, reader-friendly book is a very well illustrated introduction to 3-D's origins and classic era; many anaglyph 3-D images are included.

[191] Author interview with Jeff Joseph, October 2, 2007.

[192] Morgan and Symmes, pp. 92-95.

[193] However, according to 3-D pioneer Lenny Lipton, "*Robot Monster,* and I am not making this up, is the first movie in history to show one movie in one eye and another movie in the other. . . . If you closed one eye you saw hurricanes and if you closed the other eye you saw building[s] crumbling, or some such." (https://lennylipton.wordpress.com/2008/03/25/robot-monster-makes-history-with-overlooked-effect/)

[194] Ray Bradbury and Donn Albright, *It Came from Outer Space* (Gauntlet Press, 2004), p. 323.

[195] Barnum, "Gregory Moffett: *Robot Monster* Moppet."

[196] *Daily Variety,* May 2, 1950, pp. 1, 5. Greenhalgh's military assignment is mentioned in *Daily Variety,* December 14, 1942, p. 6.

[197] Tom Weaver, *Poverty Row Horrors! Monogram, PRC, and Republic Horror Films of the Forties* (McFarland, 1993), p. 101.

[198] Smith, p. 97.

[199] *Daily Variety,* January 26, 1953, pp. 1, 2.

[200] *Daily Variety,* February 2, 1953, p. 11.

[201] *The Hollywood Reporter,* February 18, 1953, p. 1.

[202] *Pacific Stars and Stripes,* March 12, 1953, p. 10.

[203] *Harrison's Reports,* February 28, 1953, p. 33.

[204] *Daily Variety,* January 28, 1953, p. 4.

[205] *Motion Picture Herald,* February 7, 1953, p. 13.

[206] *Boxoffice,* March 28, 1953, p. 18.

[207] *The Hollywood Reporter,* June 29, 1953, p. 3.

[208] *The Hollywood Reporter,* March 23, 1953, p. 43.

[209] *Harrison's Reports,* May 30, 1953, p. 87.

[210] *Daily Variety,* March 19, 1953, pp. 1, 3, 9.

[211] *The Hollywood Reporter,* March 19, 1953, p. 1.

[212] *Harrison's Reports,* May 30, 1953, pp. 85, 88.

[213] Mark Thomas McGee, *Beyond Ballyhoo,* p. 81. It was a challenge indentifying "Gordon Abel." Harry Medved gave me his interview transcript in late 2006, and Tucker's mentions of Gordon Avil were transcribed as "Gordon Haywood." By early 2008 it occurred to me that the two Gordons were probably the same man, and I searched the Internet for cameramen named Gordon. "Gordon Avil" closely fit the vowel sounds of the two names, and his filmography looked right (including Westerns, TV episodes, industrial films, a couple burlesque movies, and another Al Zimbalist production). Later that year I noticed that Avil was listed prominently in the *Robot Monster* credits, although his credit was missing from the Internet Movie Database's *Robot Monster* listing. In early 2009 Harry found and sent me his original interview audio, and the sometimes faint quality of the recording explained Avil's name being written down as Haywood. (Ray Zone also transcribed "Avil" as "Abel," suggesting that Ordung consistently misremembered the name whenever he was interviewed.)

[214] Legend, p. 61.

[215] Zone, p. 59.

[216] *Daily Variety* reported Warner Brothers giving Barrett first movie role on August 17, 1949 (p. 8), in a project titled *After Nightfall,* released in 1950 as *The Great Jewel Robber.* It was, however, not her first part for Warner.

[217] *Daily Variety,* August 15, 1951, p. 2. Dagmar was the stage name of Virginia Ruth Egnor, a star of early TV for whom a car bumper and anti-aircraft tank were named.

[218] Michael G. Fitzgerald and Boyd Magers, *Ladies of the Western: Interviews with Fifty-One More Actresses From the Silent Era to the Television Westerns of the 1950s and 1960s* (McFarland, 2002), pp. 14-19. Paul Parla and Charles P. Mitchell, *Screen Sirens Scream! Interviews with 20 Actresses from Science Fiction, Horror, Film Noir, and Mystery Movies, 1930s to 1960s* (McFarland, 2000), pp. 13-17.

[219] *The Hollywood Reporter,* June 18, 1952, p. 8.

[220] Medved interview with Barrows.

[221] Parla, p. 18.

[222] Letter from Claudia Barrett to Wade Williams, August 9, 1990.

[223] *The Hollywood Reporter,* December 26, 1952, p. 2.

[224] *Daily Variety*, May 11, 1953, p. 15.

[225] *The Hollywood Reporter*, February 6, 1952, p. 2.

[226] *The Hollywood Reporter*, April 18, 1952, p. 4.

[227] *The Hollywood Reporter*, August 4, 1952, p. 6.

[228] *The Hollywood Reporter*, October 13, 1952, p. 7.

[229] *The Hollywood Reporter*, December 30, 1952, p. 15.

[230] *The Hollywood Reporter*, November 4, 1960, p. 11.

[231] *The Hollywood Reporter*, January 14, 1959, pp. 1, 10.

[232] *The Hollywood Reporter*, November 13, 1959, p. 4.

[233] *Who's Who in Hollywood, 1900-1976* (Arlington House, 1976), p. 319. A 1953 story noted, "Ursula [Thiess] hasn't been dating George Nader. He hasn't seen her for months—and certainly not at a seaside spot where they're supposed to be hanging out." *The Mirror* (Los Angeles), December 30, 1953, p. 30.

[234] Howard Johns, "What Ever Happened to George Nader?", *Filmfax*, no. 68, August/September 1998, pp. 102-108.

[235] *Best Sellers*, vol. 38, no. 5, August 1978, p. 150.

[236] *Isaac Asimov's Science Fiction Magazine*, vol. 3, no. 9, September 1979, pp. 19-20.

[237] DeMille only made multiple versions of one other film—*The Ten Commandments* (1923, 1956)—but *The Squaw Man* holds his record for most versions filmed.

[238] *The Hollywood Reporter*, March 9, 1953, p. 4.

[239] Gene Ringgold and DeWitt Bodeen, *The Films of Cecil B. DeMille* (Citadel Press, 1969), p. 24. Royle's quote is part of something apparently longer from *The Moving Picture World*, February 21, 1914.

[240] *Variety*, September 3, 1924, p. 49.

[241] *Variety*, October 20, 1926, p. 90.

[242] Larry Swindell, *Spencer Tracy: A Biography* (World Pub. Co., 1969), pp. 44-45, 49-50, 206.

[243] *Red Channels* (American Business Consultants, 1950), pp. 126-127. The publisher described itself as "Publishers of *Counterattack*, the newsletter of facts to combat communism" (title page).

[244] Selena Royle Papers, located at the University of Wyoming's American Heritage Center. Thanks to Shannon Bowen.

[245] I do not know the outcome of this lawsuit.

[246] *Daily Variety*, July 8, 1952. Clipping from the Selena Royle Papers.

[247] *Boxoffice*, July 26, 1952, p. 37. Clipping from the Selena Royle Papers.

[248] Selena Royle Papers.

[249] *Daily Variety,* December 23, 1952. Clipping from the Selena Royle Papers.

[250] Selena Royle Papers.

[251] Reviews are clippings from the Selena Royle Papers, as follows: *Los Angeles Herald & Express,* date unknown, p. B-6; *Los Angeles Times,* August 12, 1953, page unknown; *Los Angeles Examiner,* August 13, Section 11, p. 6; *Variety* (may or may not be *Daily* edition), August 13, page unknown; *Los Angeles Daily News,* August 14, p. 24. One day before her first *Variety* open letter, the *Hollywood Reporter* noted that Royle was "signed" for the lead in *Black Chiffon* at the Laguna Playhouse; director Demetrios Vilan would also direct *September's Morn.* (*The Hollywood Reporter,* July 7, 1952, p. 8.)

[252] *Charleston Daily Mail,* March 7, 1954, p. 41.

[253] E-mail from Phil Tucker Jr., April 28, 2009.

[254] *Pacific Stars and Stripes,* March 12, 1953, p. 10.

[255] Edward Dmytryk, *Odd Man Out: A Memoir of the Hollywood Ten* (Southern Illinois University Press, 1996).

[256] Dmytryk, p. 96. See also Tom Weaver, *Science Fiction and Fantasy Film Flashbacks: Conversations with 24 Actors, Writers, Producers and Directors from the Golden Age* (McFarland, 1998), p. 114.

[257] Dmytryk, pp. 91-92, pp. 179-181.

[258] According to his obituary, John Mylong was born in Austria (*Variety,* September 17, 1975, pp. 86-87).

[259] Patrick McGilligan, *Alfred Hitchcock: A Life in Darkness and Light* (Regan Books, 2003), pp. 135-137.

[260] Harry Medved with Randy Dreyfuss, *The Fifty Worst Films of All Time* (Popular Library, 1978), p. 195.

[261] Dean Chambers, "*Robot Monster*: An Affectionate Recollection," from the column "Cinepan, Shlock [sic] in the Cinema" pp. 34-35. This is a clipping provided by Harry Medved; source uncertain, but may be *Midnight Marquee.*

[262] Barnum, "Gregory Moffett: *Robot Monster* Moppet."

[263] Bob Burns and Tom Weaver, "George Barrows, Gorilla Guy!" *Monsters from the Vault,* vol. 12, no. 23, 2007, pp. 46-52. (Thanks to Tom Weaver for providing this article.) Burns, et al, *It Came from Bob's Basement: Exploring the Science Fiction and Monster Movie Archive of Bob Burns* (Chronicle Books, 2000), pp. 82-88. Some details are from Medved's interview with Barrows. For a detailed account of Charlie Gemora, see Burns and Weaver's *Monster Kid Memories: Behind-the-Scenes, First-Hand Encounters with the Men Who Made the Classic Movie Monsters!* (Dinoship, Inc, 2005), pp. 81-93. Barrows left some great anecdotes in his Medved interview, including these that follow.

Working with Errol Flynn:

> [Raoul Walsh] was a tough guy; a very, very rough guy. Flynn had to throw a punch at me in a picture called *Silver River* (1948), and he has to throw a punch at me that's supposed to knock me off the chair. (That is, knock me back away from the bar.) And the first time he did it, Raoul

> Walsh says, "Now I want it to look like a real punch, huh? Flynn, don't give me any of these phony punches." So Errol said "Fine." So he threw the punch and he hit me. Right on the chin. Down I went. It didn't knock me out; I got right up but everything was sparkling.
>
> So Errol was a little gassed about this time of the day, he was drunk. He went up and grabbed me, says, "George, chum, I'm sorry." "Okay, Errol. Don't hit me again. Miss me."
>
> So Walsh came up and he says, "Goddamn it, what did you get up for?" "I don't know. It was instinctive, because he really hit me. If he would have missed me, but I didn't know what I was doing, I got up, you know—" And he says [to Flynn], "Goddamn it, don't hit him, what the hell's the matter with you, frosted again or something? But make it close."
>
> So this time Flynn hits me *that* far, it looked so phony it took four takes before he finally made it so it looked good. He was afraid he was going to hit me again. So I said, "Jesus, Flynn, hit me then. I'd rather do [that] than sit here all day long doing this."

Doubling George Sanders in *The Black Swan* (1942):

> [Impersonating Sanders] "I don't care for this sort of thing. Georgie, take the sword. I will stand *en garde. Cut* to Mr. Barrows." I didn't give a shit, because I worked! The minute we started a sequence, if it was a six-, eight-, ten-week sequence, I was in it. He'd call for me. "I refuse to do anything physical. I'd rather do something lying down, sleeping with a drink in my hand and a cigarette." He was beautiful.

264 Weaver, *It Came from Weaver Five,* p. 16.

265 Parla, p. 19.

266 *The Vidette-Messenger,* November 15, 1962.

267 *New Castle News,* July 7, 1967, p. 7.

268 http://www.sos.ca.gov/archives/oral-history/pdf/mosk.pdf.

269 http://www.oac.cdlib.org/findaid/ark:/13030/ft2f59n6c7. Ed Mosk, "attorney and American Civil Liberties Union member," once debated against the death penalty. *Van Nuys News,* April 29, 1973, p. 24-A-Central.

270 Selena Royle Papers.

271 Dmytryk, pp. 183-184.

272 Hurst, p. 6.

273 Mark Thomas McGee, *Faster and Furiouser: The Revised and Fattened Fable of American International Pictures* (McFarland, 1996), p. 13. See also McGee's earlier 1984 edition of the book (*Fast and Furious*), p. 6. *The Outlaw Marshal* was in the "Pictures Now Shooting" list in the *Reporter* on June 20, 1952, p. 11; it was eventually released as *The Lawless Rider.*

274 In light of its budget, it is amazing that Tucker's *Robot Monster* ended up being unusual, entertaining, and a weird classic of its kind. According to ex-wife Bri Murphy, Jerry Warren was making his threadbare fifties monster movies

for around $15,000 each but, while they were cheap enough to be profitable, they were mostly painfully dull. (For Warren budget information, see Weaver's *Monsters, Mutants and Heavenly Creatures,* pp. 133-137.) Zimbalist claimed in a *New York Times* profile on the widescreen and 3-D movie industry trends that he "spent an additional $4,510.54 to obtain that three-dimensional look" for *Robot Monster,* and listed itemized amounts of where it all went. (*The New York Times,* May 10, 1953, p. X5.)

[275] Thanks to Tom Weaver for this observation. Urban legend had it that Ed Wood "borrowed" the octopus prop for his *Bride of the Monster* (1955) from Republic when the studio was closed, although Alex Gordon told Weaver that, in reality, Wood simply rented it. This means that Republic's robot suit was probably more desirable than its octopus prop and therefore more expensive. (And Tucker's *Robot Monster* budget may have been lower than Wood's *Bride of the Monster* budget.) Republic was still using its robot shortly before *Robot Monster* was made, as the serial *Zombies of the Stratosphere* opened in July 1952.

[276] Bill Warren, *Keep Watching the Skies! American Science Fiction Movies of the Fifties, The 21st Century Edition* (McFarland, 2010), p. 10.

[277] Mark F. Berry, *The Dinosaur Filmography* (McFarland, 2002), p. 347.

[278] Phil Tucker Jr. recalled a poignant impression about his father and the gorilla suit from watching the film: "He was about 6'5" tall with a stocky build. He could easily have put on the gorilla suit and played the part of Ro-Man. Although I have no hard proof, there are certain scenes where it really looks like him walking inside the suit." (E-mail from Phil Tucker Jr., January 26, 2010.)

[279] Many thanks to Bill Littman, by way of Tom Weaver, for providing a copy of the script.

[280] *The Hollywood Reporter,* March 25, 1953, p. 2. The headline read, "'Robot Monster' 3D Film Brought in for $50,000." The piece calls *Robot Monster* "Tucker's debut as a director."

[281] Packy Smith and Ed Hulse, *Don Miller's Hollywood Corral: A Comprehensive B-Western Roundup* (Riverwood Press, 1993), p. 446.

[282] Harry Medved with Bruce Akiyama, *Hollywood Escapes: The Moviegoer's Guide to Exploring Southern California's Great Outdoors* (St. Martin's Griffin, 2006), pp. 234-236.

[283] *Daily Variety,* March 16, 1953, p. 4.

[284] "Larry Blamire Geeks Out! *Robot Monster,*" *Mystery Science Theater 3000: Volume XIX* (Shout! Factory, 2010).

[285] It is worth noting here that the marching, repeating Ro-Man at the end of the film wears the Guidance helmet, which has some logic.

[286] Parla, pp. 18-19.

[287] Barnum, "Gregory Moffett: *Robot Monster* Moppet."

[288] E-mail from Gregory Moffett, December 18, 2011.

[289] *Daily Variety,* March 20, 1953, pp. 3, 15.

[290] From reading the script schedule, Phil Tucker Jr. commented: "I love that they all met at the Formosa Grill in the morning prior to shooting, that place captures the very essence of old Hollywood. It's one of those joints with the movie stars' pictures up on the wall, a-la the Brown Derby. I can only speculate as to where they went after the Martini Shot, could be any number of places. It's great to think of these guys sitting around some lounge in the 50s, fully believing they had a hit on their hands." (E-mail from Phil Tucker Jr., June 26, 2008.)

[291] *Harrison's Reports*, March 21, 1953, p. 45.

[292] *The Hollywood Reporter*, March 23, 1953, pp. 1, 3, 41.

[293] *The Hollywood Reporter*, March 27, 1953, p. 2.

[294] *Motion Picture Herald*, April 4, 1953, p. 26.

[295] *The Hollywood Reporter*, April 24, 1953, p. 15.

[296] *Daily Variety*, April 24, 1953, p. 3.

[297] *The Hollywood Reporter*, April 28, 1953, p. 4.

[298] *The Hollywood Reporter*, May 14, 1953, p. 9.

[299] Thanks to Ned Comstock at the USC Cinematic Arts Library for access to the *Robot Monster* score. There was some doubling up written in; for example cello and bass at one point have the note "col TBN," meaning "double the trombone part." The percussion parts include passages for bass drum, glockenspiel, vibraphone, tam-tam, and xylophone. Some brass passages are muted. Comstock indicated that Bernstein had a flute passage played on the ondes Martenot. Another early electronic instrument, Bernstein was fond of it throughout his career and kept using it in later scores such as *Ghostbusters*. There has been no soundtrack album or rerecording of the *Robot Monster* score; however, the main theme was reused in Edgar G. Ulmer's *Daughter of Dr. Jekyll* (1957). The Image Entertainment DVD of the Ulmer film contained an isolated music/sound effects track, which is the closest thing to a *Robot Monster* soundtrack yet available. Bernstein's score was also reused in the *Alfred Hitchcock Presents* series. (Thanks to Tom Weaver for noticing those score recycles.)

[300] Zone, p. 59.

[301] Warren, p. 703.

[302] http://www.elmerbernstein.com/bio/scrapbook/waldenschool.html.

[303] http://www.guardian.co.uk/film/2002/oct/06/guardianinterviewsatbfi-southbank1.

[304] In 1946, *Variety* reviewed a live theater production by the Peoples Radio Foundation at New York City's Barbizon-Plaza Hotel, with music by Bernstein. Intended "to convince the FCC that PRF deserves a [radio] license," the series of three plays was well-produced in all respects, with the exception of "the running continuity which was intended to be critical of commercial radio" by way of a "network vee-pee" character. It seems that the show descended in these parts into humorless, self-important agitprop as the character was

"so obviously a straw man set up for the purpose of being knocked down that he was pathetic rather than the 'menace' the originators intended him to be" (*Variety*, December 18, 1946, pp. 38, 48). Whatever political groups Bernstein might have joined at one time, composing for productions like this one could have tainted him as communist.

[305] *The Hollywood Reporter*, June 27, 1952, p. 4.

[306] *Daily Variety*, June 23, 1953, p. 6.

[307] Elise Christenson, "From the Gray List to the A List," *Newsweek*, March 10, 2003, p. 12.

[308] Spencer, Kristopher, *Film and Television Scores, 1950-1979: A Critical Survey by Genre* (McFarland, 2008), p. 171. Nick Joy's interview is from a 2002 issue of *Music From the Movies*; the full interview can be found at www.musicfromthe-movies.com.

[309] E-mail from Harry Medved, February 24, 2009.

[310] E-mail from Phil Tucker Jr., September 8, 2015.

[311] *The Hollywood Reporter*, April 28, 1953, p. 4.

[312] *Variety*, April 29, 1953, p. 26.

[313] *The Hollywood Reporter*, May 13, 1953, p. 4.

[314] *The Hollywood Reporter*, May 14, 1953, p. 9.

[315] *The Hollywood Reporter*, May 20, 1953, p. 3.

[316] Hurst, p. 6.

[317] Berry, pp. 295, 299, 300.

[318] Berry thinks that *Untamed Women* is worthy of the kind of attention that *Robot Monster* has received, and humorously notes that the female costumes are "like something Betty Rubble might have worn on her wedding night." He also mentions the film's pressbook, which encouraged lady wrestling matches for promoting the film (pp. 395, 397). (George Weiss' *Racket Girls* was released the previous year.) *Harrison's Reports* on August 16, 1952, also criticized the film for being "in questionable taste because of the obvious double-meaning of some of the dialogue" (p. 130).

[319] Berry, p. 234.

[320] The British Film Institute's *Monthly Film Bulletin* (1954, p. 180) reviewed *Robot Monster*, claiming that it included "a sequence of prehistoric monsters previously seen in *King Kong*. The film was originally made in 3-D, but is now shown 'flat.'" Tucker was therefore not the only one who could not keep *King Kong* straight in relation to other dinosaur movies.

[321] Warren, pp. 413, 777, 875.

[322] Robert and Dennis Skotak, "Special Effects Designed and Created by: Jack Rabin & Irving Block," *Fantascene*, no. 2, p. 10.

[323] Skotak, pp. 10-23.

[324] Tom Weaver, *A Sci-Fi Swarm and Horror Horde: Interviews with 62 Filmmakers* (McFarland, 2010), p. 137.

[325] Thomas A. DeLong, *Radio Stars: An Illustrated Biographical Dictionary of 953 Performers, 1920 Through 1960* (McFarland, 1996), p. 43. Alan R. Havig, *Fred Allen's Radio Comedy* (Temple University Press, 1990), pp. 70, 72, 73. Roger C. Paulson, *Archives of the Airwaves, Volume 1* (BearManor Media, 2005), p. 177. For details of Brown's versatility, see Havig.

[326] Gerald Nachman, *Raised on Radio* (Pantheon Books, 1998), p. 247.

[327] *Daily Variety*, February 19, 1953, p. 4.

[328] *Red Channels*, p. 30. Brown's list is about half the length of Royle's.

[329] *Tri-City Herald*, May 19, 1957, p. 21. According to an obituary, Brown was "one of the founders of AFTRA," the American Federation of Television and Radio Artists (*Daily Variety*, May 20, 1957, p. 11).

[330] Morgan, p. 107. Initial development of 3-D comics: pp. 107-109.

[331] Barnum, "Gregory Moffett: *Robot Monster* Moppet."

[332] Morgan, p. 130.

[333] I figured out the identities of all of the comic books in December 2008 with the aid of the Grand Comics Database (www.comics.org).

[334] *Daily Variety*, May 25, 1953, p. 2.

[335] *The Hollywood Reporter*, June 11, 1953, p. 3; *Daily Variety*, June 11, 1953, p. 3. Both reviews shared the page with reviews of *Murder Without Tears*, an Allied Artists mystery directed by William Beaudine, who was later lambasted alongside Tucker in *The Golden Turkey Awards*.

[336] *The Hollywood Reporter*, June 12, 1953, p. 8.

[337] *Daily Variety*, June 12, 1953, p. 4.

[338] *Daily Variety*, June 18, 1953, p. 3.

[339] *Boxoffice*, June 20, 1953, p. 51.

[340] *Hollywood Citizen-News*, June 22, 1953, p. 12.

[341] *Hollywood Citizen-News*, June 23, 1953, p. 13.

[342] *Hollywood Citizen-News*, June 24, 1953, p. 10.

[343] Interview with Joseph.

[344] Morgan, pp. 76-77. Both the Nat King Cole and Slick Slavin shorts are available on the *3-D Rarities* Blu-Ray disc from Flicker Alley.

[345] *Hollywood Citizen-News*, June 25, 1953, p. 17.

[346] *The Hollywood Reporter*, June 29, 1953, p. 5.

[347] *Harrison's Reports*, July 11, 1953, p. 111.

[348] *The Hollywood Reporter*, July 28, 1953, p. 3. The news was also reported in

Motion Picture Herald, August 1, p. 29.

[349] Smith, p. 268.

[350] *The Hollywood Reporter,* April 2, 1952, p. 3.

[351] *The Hollywood Reporter,* August 22, 1952, p. 11.

[352] Warren, pp. 573, 718, 336.

[353] Schaefer, pp. 60-61.

[354] Flynn, p. 18.

[355] *The Fresno Bee,* April 21, 1929, p. 1.

[356] Heffernan, p. 123. According to a footnote, this information is from "Film Shortage? Indie Distribs Say, 'Look to Us,'" *Variety,* September 5, 1962, p. 3. Astor filed for bankruptcy in February 1963 (p. 133). Savini died on April 29, 1956 (*Daily Variety,* May 1, 1956, p. 4).

[357] *The Hollywood Reporter,* September 15, 1954, p. 6.

[358] Oliver Drake, *Written, Produced and Directed: The Autobiography of Oliver Drake* (Outlaw Press, 1990), p. 92-93.

[359] *The Hollywood Reporter,* November 5, 1953, p. 4.

[360] *The Hollywood Reporter,* April 26, 1954, p. 4.

[361] *The Hollywood Reporter,* February 18, 1952, p. 10.

[362] *Variety,* April 30, 1953, p. 16; *The Hollywood Reporter,* May 1, 1953, p. 7. Astor also once had a music publishing branch (*Daily Variety,* November 18, 1947, p. 3).

[363] *The Hollywood Reporter,* May 8, 1953, p. 4.

[364] *Motion Picture Herald,* February 14, 1953, p. 46.

[365] *The Hollywood Reporter,* March 13, 1953, p. 4; *Variety,* March 23, 1953, p. 5. Boris Petroff also had a slight connection to Astor. His 1936 production *Hats Off* was released by Grand National Pictures, a short-lived production company, the library of which was acquired by Astor.

[366] Many thanks to Harry Medved for providing a photocopy of the press book.

[367] Legend, p. 61.

[368] Ro-Man's viewscreen from the front appears to be the same as the family's viewscreen—wing nuts are not visible unless from the side of Ro-Man's viewer.

[369] Weaver, *Science Fiction and Fantasy Film Flashbacks,* p. 165.

[370] Burns and Weaver, "George Barrows, Gorilla Guy!", pp. 46-52.

[371] Weaver, *Poverty Row Horrors!,* p. 79.

[372] John Beifuss, "All Roads Lead to Ro-Man (and Olive Branch): *Robot Monster* Reunion!," June 4, 2008, http://blogs.commercialappeal.com/the_bloodshot_

eye/2008/06/robot-monster-reunion.html.

[373] Parla, p. 18. Both in this interview, and in her comments to Beifuss, Barrett stated that the film was made without any intention of "dream sequences." Since the script spells out the dream structure of the story, she may have been referring to the non-sensical dinosaur footage that was not indicated in the script.

[374] *Variety*, July 1, 1953, p. 8.

[375] Medved interview with Barrows.

[376] Letter from Wade Williams, November 17, 2007.

[377] Parla, p. 19.

[378] John Beifuss, "All Roads Lead to Ro-Man (and Olive Branch)."

[379] E-mail from Tom Weaver, September 9, 2015.

[380] Ronnie, Tucker's friend, could have been Ronnie Ashcroft, editor who frequently worked with Ed Wood and others in the film fringe of the time.

[381] Vera Hruba Ralston was the wife of Republic president Herbert Yates, who cast her in the studio's biggest and most expensive productions, despite public indifference to her.

[382] Tucker's memory is both impressive and spotty here. He clearly understood low budgets extremely well for remembering that Republic had multiple levels. However, his wording makes it seem like the cheap Republic films were made for $100,000-$250,000 instead of $20,000-$30,000. He might have been thinking of the Ralston films and mixing their budgets with cheaper Republic films when quoting those numbers.

[383] *The Hollywood Reporter*, May 26, 1953, p. 2.

[384] *The Hollywood Reporter*, June 24, 1953, pp. 1, 4.

[385] For an example of alternating color tinting, see *Nero, or The Fall of Rome* (1909).

[386] *Daily Variety*, June 25, 1953, p. 4.

[387] Warren, p. 145.

[388] Medved, *The Golden Turkey Awards* (Perigee Books, 1980), p. 176.

[389] *Fairbanks Daily News-Miner*, July 6, 1953, p. 1.

[390] Tucker may have been encouraged to get out of Hollywood by the Screen Writers Guild. *Variety* reported on July 22, 1953 that he and his Lea-Tuck company were still on the Guild's unfair list (pp. 4, 17). According to *Variety* on October 21, Tucker and Lea-Tuck were still on the list (pp. 7, 16).

[391] Interview with Howard.

[392] Wade Williams, "The Life and Times of Mikel Conrad, the Boy from Columbus Who Brought the First Flying Saucer to Hollywood," *Filmfax*, no. 8, October-November 1987, p. 26. (Complete article is pp. 24-29, 48-51.)

[393] *Variety,* March 14, 1919, p. 50.

[394] *Variety,* July 27, 1927, p. 13.

[395] *Variety,* January 4, 1928, p. 13.

[396] Shirley, Graham and Brian Adams, *Australian Cinema: The First Eighty Years* (Angus & Robertson Publishers and Currency Press, 1983), pp. 20 90-94, 110-111. Australia's government considered suppressing export of *For the Term of His Natural Life* for making the nation look bad to other countries. (*The Lincoln Sunday Star,* November 28, 1926, page B-Four.) Dawn actually started a lawsuit in 1922 to prevent others from using matte paintings, based on a 1918 patent. (*Oakland Tribune,* Amusement Section, August 20, 1922, p. 1.)

[397] William C. Thompson was credited for some of the new camerawork on *Arctic Fury.* Another minor connection to Alaska is *Red Snow* (1952), an anticommunist thriller that Petroff directed with no work credited to Dawn. Petroff bragged it up in the press, noting that as a Russian he was uniquely positioned to make the movie about Bering Strait espionage and Eskimo soldiers. Petroff claimed that "100,000 feet of film" were shot in Alaska, while the *Reporter* noted "a lot of stock footage dragging out the film . . . ." (*Independent Press-Telegram,* February 25, 1951, p. 4; *The Hollywood Reporter,* June 20, 1952, p. 4.)

[398] Berry, p. 387.

[399] Michael G. Fitzgerald and Boyd Magers, *Ladies of the Western: Interviews with Fifty-One More Actresses From the Silent Era to the Television Westerns of the 1950s and 1960s* (McFarland, 2002), p. 228.

[400] *Iowa City Citizen,* November 1, 1919, p. 5.

[401] *The Decatur Review,* October 12, 1919, p. 16.

[402] *The Washington Post,* June 5, 1921, p. 2. Said Dawn, "Sunlight glinting on a turquoise sea is just as exhilarating as Mendelsohn's [sic] 'Spring Song.'" Another source praised the movie's visuals "as a magnificent scenic record of the grandeur of the Arctic circle." (*The Atlanta Constitution,* June 24, 1921, p. 10.)

[403] *Fairbanks Daily News-Miner,* August 14, 1963, p. 6. Reported in the "40 Years Ago Today" section.

[404] The following additional *News-Miner* reports each appeared in a retrospective section of items from 30 or 40 years previous: October 16, 1963, p. 6; October 25, 1963, p. 4; January 10, 1964, p. 4; April 15, 1964, p. 4; November 13, 1964, p. 4; editorial pages of October 1, 1973, July 3, 1974, and July 29, 1974.

[405] *Fairbanks Daily News-Miner,* May 4, 1929, p. 6. Printed in the "Five Years Ago Today" section. Another such section noted that in 1924, Dawn and his wife and baby were sailing to Fairbanks on a steamship (May 14, 1929, p. 3).

[406] *Appleton Post-Crescent,* May 14, 1937, p. 27.

[407] *Fairbanks Daily News-Miner,* July 11, 1953, p. 5.

[408] *Fairbanks Daily News-Miner,* July 25, 1953, p. 3.

[409] *Fairbanks Daily News-Miner,* August 5, 1953, p. 3.

[410] According to *Harpoon*'s entry at www.tcm.com, the film opens with a statement that it was shot entirely in Alaska. (It would not be surprising, however, if some forgotten earlier film was an all-Alaska production.)

[411] *Fairbanks Daily News-Miner*, April 28, 1951, p. 3; June 16, 1951, p. 3; November 6, 1952, p. 6; September 8, 1953, p. 1; October 5, 1953, p. 3; April 5, 1954, p. 1; October 10, 1953, p. 3.

[412] *The Fresno Bee*, October 12, 1945, p. 13.

[413] *Fairbanks Daily News-Miner*, April 6, 1953, p. 5; August 8, 1953, p. 6.

[414] *Fairbanks Daily News-Miner*, September 24, 1959, pp. 1, 3; October 20, 1959, p. 8; March 7, 1960, p. 3.

[415] *Honolulu Star-Bulletin*, June 6, 2003, obituaries, http://archives.starbulletin.com/2003/06/06/news/obits.html.

[416] *Fairbanks Daily News-Miner*, July 24, 1951, p. 6; January 13, 1953, p. 1; December 18, 1953, p. 1; October 30, 1956, p. 1; May 17, 1958, p. 1; June 8, 1960, p. 1.

[417] *Fairbanks Daily News-Miner*, July 5, 1960, p. 8; April 25, 1961, p.14; May 8, 1961, p. 13.

[418] http://www.usc.edu/libraries/collections/elmer_bernstein.

[419] http://www.filmthreat.com/features/1199.

[420] The "Space Jockey" radio show premiered in the *Long Beach Press-Telegram* radio schedule on January 19, 1953, p. B-7. It subsequently appeared in these issues: January 22, p. C-4; January 23, p. 27; January 26, p. 15; January 29, p. 24; January 30, p. B-7; February 3, p. A-6; February 10, p. B-12; February 13, p. B-6; February 16, p. B-8; February 17, p. A-6; February 19, p. 24; February 20, p. 23.

[421] Williams, "The Life and Times of Mikel Conrad," p. 49.

[422] Warren, pp. 10-11.

[423] Robert A. Heinlein and Jack Seaman, *Project Moonbase and Others* (Subterreanean Press, 2008), pp. 171-228.

[424] Warren, p. 126.

[425] http://www.solarguard.com/tctvopen.htm.

[426] http://www.solarguard.com/tchome.htm.

[427] The earliest use of the term "space jockey" I could find is from "Horrors of Space Travel Under Study at Randolph," *San Antonio Express*, September 12, 1951, p. 6.

[428] *Oakland Tribune*, January 18, 1953, "Magazine Features," p. 1.

[429] *Kokomo Tribune*, February 6, 1959, p. 4.

[430] *Parade*, April 26, 1959, p. 18.

[431] *The Abilene Reporter-News*, September 25, 1951, p. 2-A.

[432] *Independent Press-Telegram,* December 5, 1954, p. E-7.

[433] McGee (1996), p. 21.

[434] *The Mirror* (Los Angeles), December 15, 1953, pp. 1, 3, 52. Wyott Ordung and Ray Zone deserve posthumous recognition for drawing attention to this story. Until this book was very close to finished, I could find no reference to Tucker's suicide attempt any closer to the event than the story printed in the *Los Angeles Times* on December 16, 1953. In his interview with Zone, Ordung remembered Tucker getting on the cover of *The Mirror* with his stunt. From there I was fortunately able to find the original account of Tucker's suicide attempt from the publication that received his suicide letter. According to posts on the forum at Geneaology.com, Detective Arnold Hubka was an LAPD sergeant. Pictures of him investigating the 1952 death of a woman named Marjorie Page appear in USC's online Digital Library. Hubka also worked the infamous 1947 murder of Elizabeth Short ("The Black Dahlia"), a May 1950 United Press story noting that he and another detective had narrowly missed apprehending a suspect in Houston, Texas (*Eugene Register-Guard,* May 10, 1950, p. 6A).

[435] *Los Angeles Times,* December 16, 1953, Part I, p. 18. The *Times* report quoted Tucker, "When I was refused a job—even as an usher, I finally realized that my future in the film industry was bleak." *The Mirror* rendered this phrase in Tucker's letter "as even an usher," while quoting earlier in the article "even as an usher" like the *Times* did. The *Times* version seems to be the source of this statement as quoted in *The Fifty Worst Films of All Time.* Also, the *Mirror* story described a "packet of sleeping powders," while the *Times* referred to "a box of sleeping tablets" that accompanied the issue of *Fantastic Tales* at Tucker's bedside.

[436] Bill Warren, *Keep Watching the Skies! American Science Fiction Movies of the Fifties,* original edition, Volume 1, (McFarland, 1982), p. 147.

[437] E-mail from Phil Tucker Jr., May 7, 2008.

[438] E-mail from Phil Tucker Jr., April 11, 2008.

[439] As of March 9, 2013, this urban legend was still maintained in the trivia sections of these websites' *Robot Monster* entries: http://www.bmoviecentral.com/bmc/reviews/113-robot-monster-1953-62-minutes.html, http://www.tcm.com/tcmdb/title/556625/Robot-Monster/trivia.html.

[440] Interview with Brooks.

[441] *Los Angeles Times,* December 16, 1953, Part I, pp. 1, 16, 32.

[442] E-mail from Phil Tucker Jr., October 17, 2008.

[443] Zone, p. 59.

[444] *The Mirror* (Los Angeles), January 8, 1954, p. 3.

[445] I cannot keep track of—and do not particularly care—which of the *After Midnight* series is supposed to have the word "midnight" spelled as "midnite."

To keep it simple, I have just spelled it correctly across the board.

[446] Grey, "Umberto Scali Lives," p. 24.

[447] E-mails from Grey, September 22 and October 4, 2007.

[448] Grey, *Nightmare of Ecstasy*, p. 43.

[449] *The Brownsville Herald*, April 27, 1937, p. 2.

[450] *The Corpus Christi Times*, May 14, 1937, section B, p. 1. De Zita kept pulling this stunt as recently as 1948: *The Long Beach Independent*, May 16, 1948, p. 14. He was driving three-wheeled as recently as 1950, but with no mention of the blindfold: *Daily Independent-Journal*: June 30, 1950, p. 4. In what is probably just a weird coincidence, a creepy human head model is visible in *The Unearthly* that bears a striking resemblance to De Zita.

[451] October 2, 1936, p. 3.

[452] Albert Goldman with Lawrence Schiller, *Ladies and Gentlemen—LENNY BRUCE!!* (Random House, 1974), p. 124.

[453] Goldman, pp. 122-124.

[454] Harry Medved, typed transcript of Phil Tucker interview. Related to the subject of dishwashing, Bob Burns stated, "I had heard a story that after [*Robot Monster*] flopped that he ended up working as a box boy at a grocery store but I never could confirm that." (E-mail from Tom Weaver, September 9, 2015.)

[455] Goldman, p. 130.

[456] Goldman, pp. 128-129

[457] *The Hollywood Reporter*, April 28, 1954, p. 3.

[458] *The Hollywood Reporter*, November 3, 1953, p. 3.

[459] Goldman, p. 129.

[460] Goldman, pp. 130-131.

[461] Parla, p. 18.

[462] Goldman, p. 131.

[463] Schaefer, pp. 76-95.

[464] The *Dance Hall Racket* cold print appears on the Alpha Video DVD, minus the time-warp edits from the version that has floated around elsewhere. A complete print of the film appears as a bonus feature on an Image Entertainment/Something Weird burlesque DVD of *Dreamland Capers* paired with Tucker's *Dream Follies.* The complete print lacks the time-warps and adds a few short scenes missing from the cold print, making the film a more linear experience. This version also has complete opening credits that state "Copyright MCMLV Screen Classics Productions." This copyright statement is missing from the cold print, which is perhaps why some sources have listed the film as a 1953 release.

[465] Grey, "Umberto Scali Lives," p. 23.

[466] Schaefer, pp. 57-58.

[467] Schaefer, p. 54.

[468] Grey, "Umberto Scali Lives," p. 22.

[469] Goldman, p. 131.

[470] Warren (2010), p. 703.

[471] Internet Movie Database (http://www.imdb.com) entry for *Dance Hall Racket*; comment by madsagittarian, posted October 2, 2002.

[472] Grey, *Nightmare of Ecstasy*, p. 46.

[473] Goldman, p. 131.

[474] Grey, "Umberto Scali Lives," p. 24.

[475] Weaver, *Monsters, Mutants and Heavenly Creatures*, p. 139.

[476] Grey, "Umberto Scali Lives," p. 22.

[477] Schaefer, p. 94.

[478] Interview with Brooks.

[479] Grey, "Umberto Scali Lives," p. 22.

[480] William Karl Thomas, *Lenny Bruce: The Making of a Prophet* (Archon Books, 1989), p. 34.

[481] Schaefer, pp. 49-53.

[482] *San Antonio Light*, August 30, 1955, p. 31.

[483] *The Waco News-Tribune*, December 6, 1955, p. 14.

[484] *The Ada Evening News*, April 4, 1956, p. 2.

[485] *Burlington Daily Times-News*, September 22, 1956, p. 3.

[486] Goldman, pp. 132-133.

[487] Warren, p. 145.

[488] Schaefer, 307-308.

[489] *Variety*, March 26, 1952, pp. 1, 61.

[490] Schaefer, p. 309. Sam Sherman made the same point about B Westerns in an essay in *Don Miller's Hollywood Corral* (p. 318).

[491] Schaefer, p. 350. There was even going to be a *New York After Midnight* from George Weiss and Walter Bibo, according to *Variety* (August 14, 1957, p. 4).

[492] Schaefer, pp. 55-56.

[493] *Daily Variety*, August 26, 1953, p. 8.

[494] *The Hollywood Reporter*, November 3, 1952, p. 5.

[495] Schaefer, pp. 82-83.

[496] *The Hollywood Reporter*, December 31, 1954, p. 3.

[497] *Daily Variety,* January 9, 1953, p. 2; January 13, 1953, p. 2.

[498] *Daily Variety,* January 14, 1953, p. 11.

[499] *Daily Variety,* May 13, 1953, p. 4. Other *Daily Variety* references to Christine Jorgensen's career: December 10, 1952, p. 2; April 24, 1953, p. 2; May 22, 1953, p. 1.

[500] *Daily Variety,* August 7, 1953, p. 9.

[501] *The Hollywood Reporter,* July 24, 1959, p. 1.

[502] *Variety,* May 8, 1957, p. 4; June 19, 1957, p. 20. Meanwhile, *Bagdad After Midnight* had been rated as "a very mild burlesque" by a San Francisco policeman who was also unimpressed by *The Main Street Girl,* but who "got a warrant" against the theater owner for showing the allegedly racier *Back to Nature* (*Variety,* December 14, 1955, p. 25). The title *Paris After Midnight* had a longstanding history of troublemaking. With probably no relation to the 1951 burlesque film, runners of a 1929 stage revue with the same title were faced with "charges of running an indecent show" that forced it out of Los Angeles and into Long Beach (*Variety,* June 5, 1929, p. 60).

[503] *The Billboard,* July 31, 1954, p. 51.

[504] Wald's family donated hundreds of reels of film to Washington University in St. Louis. Two of his children were interviewed on his career: https://wufilmarchive.wordpress.com/category/harry-wald-collection/.

[505] *Broadway Jungle* has shown up online here and there, and is available from Something Weird Video. Readers who are unfamiliar with Something Weird should be advised that a noticeable percentage of their material is "adult," and their website does not disguise that fact. Some of their titles have also been distributed through Image Entertainment on DVD and show up on Amazon.

[506] Wood's way of charming money out of backers and then losing it is referenced in multiple sources. See Weaver's interviews with Gregory Walcott (*It Came from Weaver Five,* pp. 328-332 & 335) and Anthony Cardoza (*Science Fiction Confidential,* pp. 37-38).

[507] Grey, *Nightmare of Ecstasy,* pp. 92-93.

[508] Turkish baths were also a major Hollywood trend at the time. "Hollywood's glamour queens are flocking to Terry Hunt's bathing parlor," noted the *Long Beach Independent,* (September 4, 1953, p. 13-A). This report also claims that Jack Broder's *Battles of Chief Pontiac* featured a Turkish bath sequence.

[509] *Variety* printed a reference to a Jack Housch on August 10, 1927 (p. 58), a Chicago stage singer with a "strong, likeable lyric tenor voice that clicked with the ticket buyers."

[510] Weaver, *A Sci-Fi Swarm and Horror Horde,* pp. 178-179 & 183.

[511] *Broadway Bound: A Guide to Shows That Died Aborning* (Scarecrow Press, 1983), pp. 406-408.

[512] *The New York Times,* October 14, 1959, p. 45.

[513] Thank to Tom Weaver for pointing out that this joke is from Laurel and Hardy's *Babes in Toyland* (1934).

[514] *Fairbanks Daily News-Miner,* May 11, 1955, p. 8.

[515] *Fairbanks Daily News-Miner,* May 14, 1955, p. 10.

[516] *The Hollywood Reporter,* March 6, 1953, p. 3.

[517] *Harrison's Reports,* October 31, 1953, p. 174.

[518] *The Hollywood Reporter,* March 31, 1953, p. 3.

[519] *The Hollywood Reporter,* May 5, 1953, p. 3.

[520] *The Hollywood Reporter,* June 22, 1953, p. 2.

[521] *The Hollywood Reporter,* July 6, 1953, p. 2.

[522] *The Hollywood Reporter,* July 7, 1953, p. 7.

[523] *The Hollywood Reporter,* April 15, 1953, p. 2.

[524] *The Hollywood Reporter,* June 2, 1953, p. 3.

[525] *The Hollywood Reporter,* June 23, 1953, p. 3.

[526] *The Hollywood Reporter,* July 1, 1953, p. 4.

[527] *The Hollywood Reporter,* July 17, 1953, p. 2.

[528] *The Hollywood Reporter,* August 7, 1953, p. 11.

[529] *The Hollywood Reporter,* August 17, 1953, p. 6.

[530] *The Hollywood Reporter,* September 4, 1953, p. 4.

[531] *Variety,* September 2, 1953, p. 61.

[532] *The Hollywood Reporter,* September 21, 1953, p. 8.

[533] *The Hollywood Reporter,* September 28, 1953, p. 2.

[534] Skotak, pp. 11, 13.

[535] *The Hollywood Reporter,* September 30, 1953, p. 8.

[536] *The Hollywood Reporter,* October 2, 1953, p. 16.

[537] *The Hollywood Reporter,* October 6, 1953, p. 3.

[538] *The Hollywood Reporter,* October 9, p. 11; October 16, p. 11.

[539] *The Hollywood Reporter,* October 15, 1953, p. 11.

[540] *The Hollywood Reporter,* October 19, 1953, p. 4.

[541] *The Hollywood Reporter,* October 28, 1953, p. 2.

[542] *The Hollywood Reporter,* November 13, 1953, p. 10.

[543] *The Hollywood Reporter,* November 24, 1953, p. 4.

[544] *The Hollywood Reporter,* December 3, 1953, p. 7.

[545] *The Hollywood Reporter*, December 8, 1953, p. 3.

[546] *The Hollywood Reporter*, December 9, 1953, p. 7.

[547] Warren, pp. 148-152.

[548] *Daily Variety*, June 8, 1953, p. 4.

[549] *The Hollywood Reporter*, August 18, 1953, p. 7.

[550] It should also be noted that in 1954, Roland Reed produced *Rocky Jones, Space Ranger*, a syndicated juvenile space adventure show, similar in concept to the earlier *Tom Corbett, Space Cadet.*

[551] *The Hollywood Reporter*, March 27, 1953, p. 8.

[552] *Daily Variety*, May 27, 1953, p. 3.

[553] *Variety* claimed that Zimbalist and Rabin "signed Bill Phipps for three pictures, *Baby Face Nelson, Miss Robin Hood* and *Pirate Women*, with the possibility of a fourth, *Robinson Crusoe on Venus*" (November 11, 1953, p. 26). As Phipps confirmed to Tom Weaver, he only worked once with Zimbalist and much of what appeared about actors in the trade press was fiction (e-mail from Weaver, September 5, 2014).

[554] The giant spider puppet was made by Wah Chang. (Skotak, p. 13.)

[555] Tom Weaver, *Attack of the Monster Movie Makers: Interviews with 20 Genre Giants* (McFarland, 1994), pp. 256-257.

[556] Weaver, *Monsters, Mutants and Heavenly Creatures*, p. 217.

[557] Rabin said that he utilized sets from *The Adventures of Marco Polo* (1938), paintings by Irving Block, and many Chesley Bonestell moonscapes. (Skotak, p. 13.)

[558] Weaver, *Monsters, Mutants and Heavenly Creatures*, p. 218; Weaver, *Attack of the Monster Movie Makers*, p. 256.

[559] Skotak, p. 13.

[560] Weaver, *Monsters, Mutants and Heavenly Creatures*, p. 219.

[561] *The Hollywood Reporter*, June 23, 1953, p. 3.

[562] *The Hollywood Reporter*, December 21, 1953, p. 3.

[563] *The Hollywood Reporter*, January 8, 1954, p. 1.

[564] *Variety*, January 13, 1954. It was a decade before the beloved cult film *Robinson Crusoe on Mars* appeared, and it presumably had no connection to this Zimbalist project.

[565] *The Hollywood Reporter*, January 29, 1954, p. 8.

[566] *The Hollywood Reporter*, February 11, 1954, p. 11.

[567] *The Hollywood Reporter*, March 11, 1954, p. 3.

[568] *The Hollywood Reporter*, March 24, 1954, p. 7.

[569] *The Hollywood Reporter*, June 7, 1954, p. 7.

[570] *The Hollywood Reporter*, July 7, 1954, p. 11.

[571] Skotak, p. 11.

[572] *The Hollywood Reporter*, September 14, 1954, p. 3.

[573] *The Hollywood Reporter*, September 15, 1954, p. 4.

[574] *The Hollywood Reporter*, December 7, 1954, p. 3.

[575] *The Hollywood Reporter*, December 16, 1954, p. 3.

[576] Tom Weaver believes that *Serpent Island* was never released theatrically and debuted on TV. Like other Zimbalist titles, it was sold to Medallion Television.

[577] E-mail from Bert I. Gordon, March 23, 2011.

[578] Warren, p. 483.

[579] Berry, p. 179. Berry provides many observations from animal trainer Ralph Helfer on how he used lizards and other creatures to create the dinosaur effects (pp. 181-183).

[580] Berry, p. 347.

[581] *Daily Variety*, December 24, 1954, p. 30; June 25, 1957, p. 8.

[582] Don Siegel, *A Siegel Film: An Autobiography* (Faber & Faber, 1993), pp. 198-206.

[583] Mickey Rooney, *Life is Too Short* (Villard Books, 1991), p. 255.

[584] *Corpus Christi Times*, September 19, 1957, p. 12-B.

[585] Phil Hardy, editor, *The Overlook Film Encyclopedia: The Gangster Film* (The Overlook Press, 1998), p. 177.

[586] Rabin might not have been involved a year later. In January 1958, Zimbalist sought in court "to seek recovery of $96,000 and rescind a deal under which Karl S. Price and Jack Rabin acquired an interest in *Baby Face Nelson*." While Zimbalist had agreed to a settlement in August, he claimed it was only because of being "under pressure" at the time (*Daily Variety*, January 10, 1958, p. 7).

[587] Skotak, p. 15.

[588] Warren, p. 587

[589] Randy Palmer, *Paul Blaisdell, Monster Maker: A Biography of the B Movie Makeup and Special Effects Artist* (McFarland, 1997), pp. 134-136.

[590] *Variety* printed an August 13, 1958 profile of Zimbalist's involvement with MGM (p. 16). By November 2, 1960, he had "recently left [his] Metro producer berth" and was in with Columbia (p. 3). Edgar Rice Burroughs Inc. sued MGM and Loew's Inc. for $1,500,000 because of "radically changing the

original *Tarzan* characterizations in *Tarzan, the Ape Man*" (*Variety*, December 14, 1960, p. 11).

[591] Essoe, *Tarzan of the Movies*, pp. 151 & 154.

[592] David Fury, *Kings of the Jungle: An Illustrated Reference to "Tarzan" on Screen and Television* (McFarland, 2001), pp. 175 & 177.

[593] Weaver, *Science Fiction Confidential* (McFarland, 2002), pp. 211 & 213.

[594] *The Hollywood Reporter*, October 28, 1960, p. 3.

[595] *The Hollywood Reporter*, December 19, 1960, p. 2.

[596] Tom Weaver, *Interviews with B Science Fiction and Horror Movie Makers: Writers, Producers, Directors, Actors, Moguls, and Makeup* (McFarland, 1988), pp. 62-63. In Ray Bradbury's novel *Let's All Kill Constance*, set in 1960, a Hollywood director grouses about his current project, "A Jules Verne novel in the public domain, free and clear, with a dumb-cluck fly-by-night producer who says nothing and steals much . . .." (p. 144). This almost has to be a reference to Zimbalist and *Valley of the Dragons.* The movie is available on a fun and economical 2015 two-disc DVD set from Mill Creek, *Vintage Sci-Fi 6 Movie Collection.*

[597] Palmer, p. 135.

[598] Berry, p. 407. *Variety* reported on February 15, 1961 that Columbia and Zimbalist were promoting the movie with "10 50-foot replicas of monsters used in [the movie] to go on tour of both the U.S. and England" (p. 4).

[599] According to director Richard E. Cunha, *Missile to the Moon* "was Astor's idea." (Weaver, *Interviews with B Science Fiction and Horror Movie Makers*, p. 116.) And Warren notes, "It's odd how often the same phrase regarding this film recurs: however bad *Cat-Women of the Moon* may have been, this one ***is*** far worse." (Emphasis original; Warren, p. 576.)

[600] Mariette Hartley and Anne Commire, *Breaking the Silence* (G.P. Putnam's Sons, 1990), p. 153.

[601] *Variety*, June 10, 1964, p. 4.

[602] *Taffy and the Jungle Hunter* was also released in 1965 and filmed just before *Young Dillinger.*

[603] *Syracuse Herald-Journal*, October 16, 1965, p. 2.

[604] *Variety*, August 19, 1964, p. 3.

[605] *Daily Variety*, November 20, 1964, pp. 1, 4.

[606] *Daily Variety*, November 24, 1964, pp. 1, 19.

[607] *Variety*, December 12, 1956, p. 47; January 18, 1961, p. 17; April 5, 1961, p. 30. The January 18 report also noted that Zimbalist was moving into music publishing.

[608] *The Daily Review*, August 1, 1957, p 24. In early 1961, *Variety* reported that Zimbalist was largely unconcerned about an estimated rise in rates for IATSE

labor. He preferred the "'craftsman-like' label" to describe his modest budgets and praised the talents of local workers: "The greatest craftsmen in the world are right here in Hollywood." It was in the area of script that Zimbalist could cut corners and save money, as *Variety* noted, "Zimbalist leans toward properties or personalities whose life stories are in public domain. . . . If scripts farmed out, Zimbalist tallies cost as prohibitive and beyond his ken." (*Variety*, February 8, 1961, pp. 3, 60.) Given the "craftsman-like" nature of Zimbalist's productions, this was probably not mere ballyhoo and sheds further doubt on reports of his buying story rights for anything (even if his affection for Hollywood labor is dubious in light of his conflict the same year with IATSE).

609 *The San Mateo Times*, January 18, 1965, p. 23. According to *Variety* on January 18, 1961, *Christie O'Hara* (different spelling) was "a semi-musical being aimed as a special" for television (p. 17).

610 *Variety*, August 4, 1965, p. 3.

611 *The Daily Gleaner*, August 9, 1969, p. 7.

612 *The Cedar Rapids Gazette*, August 8, 1969, p. 14.

613 *The Bridgeport Post*, February 7, 1962, p. 32; March 12, 1962, p. 10. *Variety* devoted a lot of ink to Luciano's passing and its effect on Hollywood. For example, *Variety* reported on January 31, "No sooner had the news flashed that Charles (Lucky) Luciano died in Italy when indie producer Al Zimbalist registered title *Lucky Luciano*" (p. 1). By February 7, there was a "flood" of titles registered (pp. 2, 66).

614 *Milwaukee Sentinel*, October 10, 1959, p. 6, part 1. This column appeared with slightly different details in *The Cedar Rapids Gazette*, October 12, 1959, p. 21.

615 *Variety*, August 20, 1969, p. 6.

616 *Variety*, October 10, 1962, p. 6.

617 *Variety*, September 24, 1969, p. 7.

618 Jack Vance published his novel in the December 1952 issue of *Space Stories*, and Harry Harrison's novel was published in 1962.

619 http://www.tcm.com/tcmdb/title/556625/Robot-Monster/notes.html.

620 Zone, p. 59.

621 Legend, pp. 58-61, 64. Except where indicated otherwise, all Wyott Ordung quotes in Chapter 11 are from this interview.

622 DVD audio commentary for *First Man Into Space* (The Criterion Collection, 2007).

623 *Daily Variety*, October 17, 1947, p. 10.

624 *Daily Variety*, November 3, 1947, p. 9. Both John Brown and Selena Royle signed the ad.

[625] *Daily Variety*, August 28, 1951, p. 8; October 15, 1951, p. 22. The episode "Dick Tracy and BB-Eyes" is a great opportunity to see Ordung act. He gets to portray a variety of emotions, has a lot of dialogue and stage business, and appears in close-up.

[626] *Daily Variety*, January 23, 1952, p. 12; February 19, 1952, p. 14; March 11, 1952, p. 10; *Variety*, August 6, 1952, p. 22. Ordung appeared in two *Dangerous Assignment* episodes, "The Blood-Stained Feather Story" and "The Death in the Morgue Story." They are widely available on the Internet, as is his *Dick Tracy* episode.

[627] *The Hollywood Reporter*, February 16, 1953, p. 7.

[628] *Daily Variety*, May 7, 1953, p. 7; *The Hollywood Reporter*, June 5, 1953, p. 2.

[629] *The Hollywood Reporter*, July 13, 1953, p. 3.

[630] *The Hollywood Reporter*, July 29, 1953, p. 5.

[631] *The Hollywood Reporter*, August 12, 1953, p. 10.

[632] Interview with Brown.

[633] *Variety*, May 4, 1938, p. 49.

[634] *Variety*, October 9, 1940, p. 15.

[635] *The Hollywood Reporter*, March 5, 1952, p. 10.

[636] *The Hollywood Reporter*, March 10, 1952, p. 1.

[637] *The Hollywood Reporter*, April 24, 1952, p. 5.

[638] *The Hollywood Reporter*, May 13, 1952, p. 10.

[639] Weaver, *A Sci-Fi Swarm and Horror Horde*, pp. 93-94 & 96-97.

[640] *The Charleston Gazette*, June 11, 1952, p. 21.

[641] *The Hollywood Reporter*, May 20, 1952, p. 1, 4.

[642] *The Hollywood Reporter*, August 21, 1953, p. 1, 4.

[643] *The Hollywood Reporter*, November 20, 1953, p. 11; November 23, 1953, p. 11.

[644] Weaver, *Attack of the Monster Movie Makers*, pp. 57-58.

[645] The origin story of AIP has been told in multiple sources, including McGee's *Faster and Furiouser* (1996), pp. 9-10.

[646] McGee (1996), p. 12.

[647] According to *The Hollywood Reporter*, Cohen left Broder's employment "effective Nov. 14" (November 7, 1952, p. 2).

[648] *The Hollywood Reporter*, October 6, 1953, p. 4.

[649] *The Hollywood Reporter*, October 16, 1953, p. 11.

[650] Corman told interviewer Tom Weaver that he himself was responsible

for the half-accurate nature of the *Reporter*'s entries. Because he wanted to avoid attention from union reps while making his ultra-cheap monster film, Corman intentionally garbled some details he gave to the *Reporter*. For the interview and a very interesting trivia track by Weaver, see VCI Entertainment's 2013 DVD *Creepy Creature Double Feature, Vol. 1,* including both *Monster from the Ocean Floor* and Bert I. Gordon's *Serpent Island.*

[651] McGee (1996), p. 16. According to McGee's earlier version of the book (*Fast and Furious* [1984], p.10), Corman knew Broder before Ordung and brought them together because Broder wanted "a war script."

[652] Roger Corman with Jim Jerome, *How I Made a Hundred Movies in Hollywood and Never Lost a Dime* (Random House, 1990), pp. 18-21. In the course of researching this book, I sent letters and e-mails to more than one individual who never replied. But after sending a letter to Corman, I very soon got an e-mail from his assistant that he had nothing to tell me, but wished me well.

[653] McGee (1996), p. 17.

[654] Ordung claimed that he financed most of *Monster from the Ocean Floor* in Legend's *Fangoria* interview. McGee puts Ordung's and Corman's contrasting claims together in *Faster and Furiouser* (1996), pp. 15-16.

[655] *The Hollywood Reporter,* November 2, 1953, p. 7.

[656] McGee (1996), p. 17.

[657] McGee, *Fast and Furious* (1984), p. 9.

[658] DVD supplements for *Creepy Creature Double Feature, Vol. 1* (VCI Entertainment, 2013).

[659] Corman, p. 20.

[660] McGee (1996), pp. 15-16, 20.

[661] McGee (1996), p. 20.

[662] *The Hollywood Reporter,* February 9, 1954, p. 6.

[663] *The Hollywood Reporter,* May 11, 1954, p. 3. According to *Daily Variety,* Valor Pictures was initiated in March (March 16, 1954, p. 8).

[664] *Daily Variety,* June 2, 1954, p. 9; *Variety,* June 9, 1954, p. 18.

[665] *The Hollywood Reporter,* June 30, 1954, p. 9.

[666] *Cumberland Sunday Times,* July 11, 1954, p. 20.

[667] *Daily Variety,* June 24, 1954, p. 4.

[668] *The Hollywood Reporter,* July 7, 1954, p. 3.

[669] *The Hollywood Reporter,* August 10, 1954, p. 2. A *Gusher* screenplay had been sold for independent production two years previously (*Daily Variety,* June 13, 1952, p. 11).

[670] *The Hollywood Reporter,* August 17, 1954, p. 6.

[671] *Variety* reviewed the play *Webster's Widow* on February 18, 1953 (p. 56), which included Brown and Ross in the cast of eight listed performers. Not

impressed, the reviewer noted that "only Joyce Widoff, as the gal, and Wyott Ordung, as a jockey, ever manage to be even credible."

[672] *Daily Variety*, June 18, 1954, p. 3.

[673] *The Hollywood Reporter*, September 14, 1954, p. 3.

[674] Author interview with Forrest J Ackerman, April 12, 2008.

[675] Adding more to the confusion is the fact that there was a 1950 *Studio One* drama called *Walk the Dark Streets* (plural, not singular), based on the 1949 novel by William Krasner.

[676] *Daily Variety*, February 21, 1956, p. 2.

[677] *The Sun* (Flagstaff, Arizona), April 8, 1959, p. 2.

[678] *The Anniston Star*, August 16, 1960, p. 2.

[679] Eddie Kafafian was a *Variety* staffer from around the time of *Walk the Dark Street* who went into public relations (*Daily Variety*, March 8, 1961, p. 57). He was also a decorated veteran who lost his war medals in a fire (April 17, 1972, p. 2); his ability to speak Armenian came in handy on at least one occasion at *Variety* (August 31, 1983, p. 3).

[680] Tom Weaver, *Wild Wild Westerners: A Roundup of Interviews with Western Movie and TV Veterans* (BearManor Media, 2012), p. 194.

[681] Interview with Brown.

[682] Alpha Video released *Walk the Dark Street* on DVD-R in 2013. The picture quality is very poor, similar to a copy of the film currently on YouTube, and the disc is authored to go right into a fifteen-minute trailer reel when the movie ends. Most of these trailers are for movies directed by Ted V. Mikels, and some are definitely "red band" previews (R-rated).

[683] E-mail from David Schecter, friend of Paul Dunlap, August 5, 2009.

[684] *The Hollywood Reporter*, September 15, 1954, p. 4. Someone in *Daily Variety* described *Hell in the Heavens* as "a crazy, mixed-up title" (September 17, 1954, p. 4).

[685] *Variety*, October 6, 1954, p. 13.

[686] *Daily Variety*, June 24, 1955, p. 5; September 27, 1955, p. 6; May 11, 1956, p. 2; September 21, 1956, p. 5.

[687] DVD audio commentary for *First Man Into Space*, (The Criterion Collection, 2007). *Daily Variety* reported the sale of *Satellite of Blood* to Richard Gordon on January 17, 1958 (p. 6).

[688] Medved, *Son of Golden Turkey Awards*, p. 211.

[689] *Daily Variety* announced that Jack Milner was sound editor for Valor Pictures on July 14, 1954 (p. 25).

[690] Weaver, *I Was a Monster Movie Maker*, p. 107. Weaver's entire interview with Michael A. Hoey covers the troubled production of *The Navy vs. the Night Monsters* in great detail (pp. 96-111). See also Hoey's autobiography *Elvis, Sherlock & Me: How I Survived Growing Up in Hollywood* (BearManor Media, 2007), pp. 191-200. In both sources, Hoey mentions that Roger Corman had a stake in the production; this fact could have contributed to Ordung's attitude.

[691] E-mail from Michael A. Hoey, April 26, 2008.

[692] Weaver, *Interviews with B Science Fiction and Horror Movie Makers*, pp. 133-134.

[693] Drake, p. 134.

[694] Some sources list the title as *The Mummy and the Curse of the Jackal*, altering the plural *Jackals*. This is accurate in relation to the story, but the word is nonetheless spelled plural onscreen. The singular spelling seems to derive from the movie's one official home video release on VHS from Academy Home Entertainment, where it is spelled in singular form on the cover. (Did someone notice that there was only one jackal in the movie and fix the title on purpose for this release?)

[695] *Daily Variety*, March 31, 1960, p. 6.

[696] *The Hollywood Reporter*, May 4, 1960, p. 5. On the same page is the note that "Chuck Connors returns Sunday with his rodeo troupe from week's Winnipeg Arena booking, a sellout with an added performance."

[697] *Variety*, March 28, 1962, p. 4.

[698] *Daily Variety*, April 4, 1968, p. 2.

[699] *Daily Variety*, October 26, 1973, p. 8. *Tweet's Ladies of Pasadena* had appeared without Ordung as far back as the June 23, 1972 *Daily Variety*.

[700] *Daily Variety*, June 28, 1974, p. 9; January 15, 1976, p. 34

[701] *Van Nuys News*, November 9, 1975, p. East-3-A.

[702] Interview with Ackerman.

[703] Goldman, pp. 142-145.

[704] Goldman, p. 144.

[705] Lenny Bruce's *Stamp Help Out* was republished in its entirety in the posthumous compilation *The Unpublished Lenny Bruce* (Running Press, 1984), pp. 46-85. *Fleetfoot* photos appear on pp. 64, 66, & 74. Sally Marr appears in a *Dance Hall Racket* still on p. 77.

[706] *The Unpublished Lenny Bruce*, p. 41. According to *Daily Variety*, Bruce completed a script entitled "The Grinder" for Alfred Hitchcock, presumably for the *Alfred Hitchcock Presents* TV show (January 17, 1957, p. 2).

[707] Goldman, p. 144.

[708] Grey, *Nightmare of Ecstasy*, p. 203.

[709] E-mail from Rudolph Grey, September 22, 2007.

[710] E-mail from Phil Tucker Jr., November 20, 2007.

[711] The digitization of old newspapers has revealed that *Plan 9 from Outer Space* was released earlier than the commonly accepted date of 1959, and was almost immediately shown on television. It played as a second feature with *Torpedo Run* in 1958 according to *The Coshocton, Ohio, Tribune* (November 28, 1958, p. 10) and appeared on California TV in spring 1960 (*Oakland Tribune,* May 1960 [Sunday issue, date uncertain], p. B-13.)

[712] Interview with Brooks.

[713] Joanna Lee, *A Difficult Woman in Hollywood* (Vantage Press, 1999), pp. 27-33. A big thanks to Rudolph Grey for bringing this book to my attention.

[714] E-mail from Rudolph Grey, December 1, 2007.

[715] E-mail from Phil Tucker Jr., March 7, 2008.

[716] Medved, *The Golden Turkey Awards,* p. 176.

[717] http://digitallibrary.usc.edu/cdm/compoundobject/collection/p15799coll44/id/74734/rec/5. I pursued including these photos in this book, but it would have meant licensing them for a specific number of copies. As I wanted the book to be an unlimited edition, I decided it was better to do without them.

[718] The beginning of Supreme Pictures is outlined in Michael R. Pitts' *Poverty Row Studios, 1929-1940: An Illustrated History of 53 Independent Film Companies, With a Filmography For Each* (McFarland, 1997), pp. 378-379. This book also contains a Supreme Pictures filmography, pp. 379-392. The Julian Petroleum scandal is documented in Guy Woodward Finney's *The Great Los Angeles Bubble: A Present-Day Story of Colossal Financial Jugglery and of Penalties Paid* (Forbes, 1929). Hackel is mentioned multiple times in Chapter Six (pp. 81-100) and also near the end (p. 191).

[719] Smith, pp. 45-46.

[720] *Strange Holiday* had its origins in an Arch Oboler radio play that was in 1942 adapted as a short war propaganda film with the sponsorship of General Motors. This short was eventually acquired and expanded by Oboler, Hackel, and Elite Pictures.

[721] Smith, p. 315.

[722] Smith, p. 46.

[723] *The Llano News,* March 3, 1960, p. 6.

[724] Gary D. Rhodes, "A Drive-In Horror by Default, or, The Premiere of *The Hideous Sun Demon,*" from Rhodes (editor), *Horror at the Drive-In: Essays in Popular Americana* (McFarland, 2003), pp. 53-66.

[725] Heinrich Costas, *The Hidden Language of Narcoterrorism: A Spanish-English Dictionary with a Quechua Glossary, Volume I* (The Edwin Mellen Press, 2006), p. 355.

[726] *El Paso Herald-Post,* October 5, 1962, section B, p. 2.

[727] *Long Beach Independent,* June 11, 1943, p. 14.

[728] *Los Angeles Times,* December 16, 1953, p. 2; December 17, 1953, p. 2. The December 16 report shared the page with a note that "the last of four officers" involved in the 1951 "Bloody Christmas" incident had been sentenced.

[729] *The Mirror* (Los Angeles), December 7, 1953, p. 2.

[730] *Portsmouth Herald,* August 25, 1954, p. 1.

[731] Goldman, p. 70.

[732] *Long Beach Independent,* June 8, 1943, pp. 1, 8.

[733] *Time,* June 21, 1943, pp. 18-19.

[734] Ray Bradbury, "The Long Night," *A Memory of Murder* (Dell, 1984), pp. 67-82. Mystery writer Ross MacDonald included an unthreatening pachuco interlude in the first Lew Archer novel, *The Moving Target* (Knopf, 1949), p. 140. Archer narrates a stop at "an overgrown cigar store" with a crowd of "Mexican boys with grease-slicked duck-tail haircuts [who] were swarming in and out of the store, drawn two ways by the pinball machines in the back and the girls on the street." While up to no good, the boys give Archer directions and then "bowed and smiled and nodded as if I had done them a favor."

[735] *The Amarillo Globe-Times,* May 15, 1957, p. 29.

[736] Rogelio Agrasánchez Jr., *Mexican Movies in the United States* (McFarland, 2006), p. 148.

[737] Agrasánchez, p. 17.

[738] Agrasánchez mentions Tin Tan on pp. 9, 17, 20, 78-79, & 144. *Daily Variety* reported on November 29, 1944 (p. 9) that he had signed a film contract, which must have been near the beginning of his movie career.

[739] *The San Antonio Light,* March 4, 1959, p. 27.

[740] *San Mateo Times,* July 9, 1943, p. 2.

[741] *Variety,* September 8, 1943, p. 3.

[742] *Variety,* December 15, 1943, p. 18.

[743] *Daily Variety,* November 26, 1951, p. 11; November 27, 1951, p. 10; December 5, 1951, p. 11. Notable in the cast of *The Ring* are Rita Moreno, and Lalo Rios as the main character with Victor Millan in a supporting role. Both Rios and Millan had parts in Orson Welles' legendary film noir *Touch of Evil* (1958).

[744] Tom Weaver, *Earth vs. the Sci-Fi Filmmakers: 20 Interviews* (McFarland, 2005), pp. 203-206.

[745] *The Hollywood Reporter,* October 23, 1959, p. 8.

[746] As Roger Corman did when producing *The Sea Demon* (*Monster from the Ocean Floor*), John Bushelman might have deliberately distorted his name to the press to avoid union problems.

[747] *El Paso Herald-Post,* February 12, 1959, p. 11. See also *The Hollywood Reporter,* February 18, p. 1.

[748] *El Paso Herald-Post,* February 16, 1959, p. 26.

[749] *El Paso Herald-Post,* February 21, 1959, p. 18. *Pachuco* could also show an influence from Norman Dawn, who in 1920 made a feature "on both sides of the Rio Grande." (*The Brownsville Sunday Herald,* March 7, 1920, p. 5.)

[750] The Charleston Gazette, October 18, 1960, p. 16.

[751] Tucker made a fleeting remark in the Medved interview that may have referred to the *Pachuco* cast, but the context is uncertain: "They were all real pachucos." It is worth noting that *Switchblade* has no pachuco characters, although the Mexican border plays a part in the story and there are some scenes set in Mexico.

[752] *The Hollywood Reporter,* May 18, 1959, p. 3; June 18, 1959, p. 3.

[753] *Fairbanks Daily News-Miner,* May 12, 1951, p. 3.

[754] *Fairbanks Daily News-Miner,* May 23, 1960, p. 7.

[755] Harry Medved, typed transcript of Phil Tucker interview.

[756] E-mail from Phil Tucker Jr., October 17, 2008.

[757] E-mail from Harry Medved, March 7, 2008.

[758] Tom Weaver, *Science Fiction Stars and Horror Heroes: Interviews With Actors, Directors, Producers and Writers of the 1940s-1960s* (McFarland, 1991), p. 392.

[759] *Robot Monster* and *The Cape Canaveral Monsters* relate closely not only to each other, but to 1954's *Killers from Space.* Directed by W. Lee Wilder (brother of Billy), the film apparently had no connection to Tucker. Similar to *Robot Monster,* the alien leader looks ridiculous, talks to a human in condescending tones about its invasion, uses a view-screen, hides in a cave, decorates with electrical equipment, talks about "platforms in space," and uses an army of giant animal-monsters to conquer the earth (while at least in this movie it is explained). Similar to *The Cape Canaveral Monsters,* the aliens have a machine in the cave by which they teleport away, they operate on a human and mutilate him, smoke wafts around as they do so, and the human is a prisoner who tries to stop their invasion.

[760] Warren, pp. 143.

[761] Thanks to Tom Weaver for pointing out the *Invisible Invaders* connection, as well as some similarities (discussed later in the chapter) to *It Came from Outer Space* and *Invasion of the Saucer Men.*

[762] *A James Bond Omnibus, Volume 1* (MJF Books, 1996), pp. 194-195.

[763] *Variety,* April 7, 1965, p. 17.

[764] Weaver, *Science Fiction and Fantasy Film Flashbacks,* p. 232.

765 *Variety,* January 14, 1953, p. 27; November 30, 1977, p. 78.

766 Katherine Victor interview by Barry Brown, from Calvin Thomas Beck, *Scream Queens: Heroines of the Horrors* (Macmillan, 1978), p. 236.

767 Paul and Donna Parla, "The Batwoman from Cape Canaveral: An Interview with Katherine Victor," *Filmfax*, no. 58, October 1996, p. 43. (Complete article is pp. 40-43, 129.)

768 Weaver, *Science Fiction Stars and Horror Heroes*, p. 391.

769 Brown, p. 236.

770 Weaver, *Science Fiction Stars and Horror Heroes*, p. 392.

771 *Variety,* April 5, 1961, p. 56.

772 Weaver, *Science Fiction Stars and Horror Heroes*, pp. 391-393; Parla, "The Batwoman from Cape Canaveral," p. 43.

773 Barry Brown, "It's VeSota!", *Magick Theatre*, 1987. (Reference from Fred Olen Ray's *The New Poverty Row*, p. 16.) In Brown's interview, Bruno VeSota remembered with disgust how he and Katherine Victor once sat outdoors recording random dialogue into Jerry Warren's single, cheap recorder for future use. VeSota said, "If I ever see that mike again, I'll break it over Jerry Warren's head."

774 Weaver, *Science Fiction Stars and Horror Heroes*, p. 396.

775 *The Hollywood Reporter*, April 11, 1960, p. 10.

776 Weaver, *Science Fiction Stars and Horror Heroes*, pp. 391-392.

777 Brown interview with Victor, p. 236.

778 For example, a 1971 newspaper story mentions him as a psychiatrist. *Nevada State Journal,* January 15, 1971, p. 2.

779 Parla, "The Batwoman from Cape Canaveral," p. 43.

780 Brown interview with Victor, p. 236.

781 Weaver, *Science Fiction Stars and Horror Heroes*, p. 393.

782 *Variety,* April 5, 1961, p. 56.

783 Sterling World Distributors was an exceptionally obscure and short-lived company, apparently releasing only five movies from 1958 to 1961. Three of the five were imports, two Mexican and one Indian.

784 *Daily Variety,* July 3, 1961, p. 3.

785 DVD audio commentaries for *Psycho-a-Go-Go* (Troma, 2004) and *Blood of Ghastly Horror* (Troma, 2001).

786 *The Modesto Bee,* July 21, 1963, p. G-4.

787 Copyright information from http://www.copyright.gov/records. The "CCM" in "CCM Productions" must of course stand for [*The*] *Cape Canaveral Monsters.*

788 Heffernan, p. 229.

789 It has since disappeared from Netflix, but as of this writing is available through Amazon Instant Video.

790 Warren, pp. 143-144.

791 Warren, p. 144.

792 E-mails from Warren, March 11, 2008.

793 Donald C. Willis, *Horror and Science Fiction Films: A Checklist* (Scarecrow Press, 1972), p. 72.

794 Weaver, "*The Astounding She-Monster*: Featuring an Interview with 50's Director Ron Ashcroft," *Fantastic Films*, no. 43, January 1985, pp. 46, 52. (Complete article is pp. 45-46, 52.) Guenther Kauer, often credited as Gene Kauer, frequently contributed to low-budget cinema. According to the *ASCAP Biographical Dictionary*, fourth edition, he was born in Germany and did all kinds of music jobs ("radio & nightclubs") in America along with composing classical works (ASCAP, 1980, p. 262).

795 Warren, p.18.

796 From firstsearch.oclc.org.

797 Stephen D. Youngkin, *The Lost One: A Life of Peter Lorre* (University Press of Kentucky, 2005), pp. 382, 387. The UCLA Film & Television Archive appears to own the only copy of Tucker's pilot for *The Peter Lorre Playhouse.*

798 *The New York Times*, June 15, 1961, p. 51. Hank Henry, star of *Not Tonight Henry*, was a mainstream actor and comedian of the era. *The Hollywood Reporter* printed this boxed notice on December 30, 1960 (p. 4): "Formost Films presents for Academy Award consideration Hank Henry in *Not Tonight Henry*." This was probably a prank by his Rat Pack pals. On January 13, 1960, the *Reporter* (p. 5) quoted Roger Corman, expressing concern over Hollywood's exploitation of America's "decay of moral standards," noting that the industry "should give up pandering to the public with the morbid, illicit and perverted." In the 1970s, Corman did not shy away from producing some R-rated films, a melodrama like *Big Bad Mama* including some nudity for the grindhouse and drive-in audiences. Corman's real motivation for his indignant reaction to Hollywood in 1960 may be revealed by this sentence: "The public will condone only so much before it becomes nauseated."

799 And according to Joe Bob Briggs, "The Mafia had had a direct interest in making [porn films] at least since 1965, but it was not much more than a penny-ante sideline until 1971. That's when Reuben Sturman, working under the protection of the Gambino family, imported the first peepshow machines from Copenhagen and installed them in murky theaters around Times Square" (Briggs, p. 138).

800 David L. Wolper with David Fisher, *Producer: A Memoir* (Scribner, 2003), pp. 29-53.

801 *The Hollywood Reporter*, August 17, 1960, p. 6.

802 E-mail from Phil Tucker Jr., September 8, 2015.

[803] E-mail from Phil Tucker Jr., May 6, 2008.

[804] Interview with Howard.

[805] Interview with Brooks.

[806] Hurst, p. 8.

[807] Hurst, p. 28.

[808] E-mail from Phil Tucker Jr., November 16, 2007.

[809] E-mail from Phil Tucker Jr., November 16, 2007.

[810] *Pasadena Star-News,* November 6, 1974, p. D-12.

[811] *Mass Media* (Boston, Massachusetts), October 26, 1977, p. 19.

[812] A likely influence on *Death Riders* was the Four Star Productions syndicated series *Thrill Seekers.* Hosted by Chuck Connors, the program showcased dangerous stunts including those involving motorcycles; both Tucker and director Jim Wilson were involved. *Variety* noted on June 18, 1975 (p. 4) that a Shelby, North Carolina outfit, Eo Corporation, had "started principal photography on *Death Driver—The True Story of Rex Randolph*" with the involvement of the Death Riders crew and Earl Owensby starring. Owensby ran Eo, and produced and starred in many southern indie films for decades. *Death Driver* was released in 1977 and appears to have no connection to the *Death Riders* movie beyond the cyclists themselves, but it is worth noting that this movie was a narrative, fiction film, as *Death Riders* was originally intended to be.

[813] *The Albuquerque Tribune,* June 11, 1974, p. A-2; June 18, 1974, p. A-6.

[814] Tucker scripted her lines, indicating that he realized that the movie needed more conflict where it could be added. (E-mail from Phil Tucker Jr., September 9, 2015.)

[815] Brief telephone chat with Vilmos Zsigmond, February 27, 2008.

[816] E-mail from Phil Tucker Jr., November 16, 2007.

[817] E-mail from Phil Tucker Jr., March 3, 2008.

[818] *Variety,* March 31, 1976, p. 4.

[819] *Variety,* June 30, 1976, p. 31; December 27, 1978, p. 5.

[820] Westchester is a neighborhood in western Los Angeles.

[821] Joe Dante quote courtesy of Tom Weaver. (E-mail from Weaver, November 15, 2015.)

[822] According to *Daily Variety,* Tucker edited *The Seal* (November 27, 1981, p. 6).

[823] E-mails from Phil Tucker Jr., August 7 & 12, 2015.

[824] Ancestry.com. Tucker's death date is listed as December 1, 1985 in both the

"California Death Index" and "U.S. Veterans Gravesites."

[825] Tom Weaver wrote a very fun account of visiting the amazingly detailed "Area 52" set from the *Looney Tunes* movie with Dante, Bob Burns, Kevin McCarthy, and a slew of enthusiastic cast and crewmembers (*Starlog*, December 2003, pp. 32-38).

[826] Michael Medved's autobiography contains biographic details and background of the bad movie books; see *Right Turns*, pp. 233-236, 258-263, 270-275. Randy Dreyfuss is better known as actor Randy Lowell.

[827] E-mail from Tucker Jr., February 25, 2008.

[828] *The Fifty Worst Films of All Time* was reviewed in *Pacific Stars and Stripes* on September 7, 1978 (p. 17), indicating that it appeared around mid-year.

[829] Flynn, p. 7.

[830] Jack Stevenson, *Land of a Thousand Balconies: Discoveries and Confessions of a B-Movie Archaeologist* (Critical Vision, 2003), p. 54.

[831] Grey, *Nightmare of Ecstasy*, p. 10.

[832] Grey, *Nightmare of Ecstasy*, p. 7.

[833] E-mail from Grey, September 22, 2007.

[834] Warren (1982), p. 145; Warren *Keep Watching the Skies! American Science Fiction Movies of the Fifties*, original edition, Volume 2, (McFarland, 1986), p. 412.

[835] Warren (2010), p. 662.

[836] Harry and Michael Medved, *The Hollywood Hall of Shame* (Perigee Books, 1984), pp. 7, 15, 16; *Son of Golden Turkey Awards*, pp. xiii-xv.

[837] Medved, *The Golden Turkey Awards*, p. 208.

[838] Weaver, *Earth vs. the Sci-Fi Filmmakers*, p. 184.

[839] Tom Weaver, *Eye on Science Fiction: 20 Interviews with Classic SF and Horror Filmmakers* (McFarland, 2003), p. 213.

[840] Michael Copner, "Titus Moody: The *Only* Ed Wood of the '90s," *Cult Movies*, no. 17, 1996, p. 51. (Complete article is pp. 50-51.)

[841] Rudolph Grey, "Titus Moody: Those Who Are Dedicated are Indestructible," *Psychotronic*, no. 12, Spring 1992, p. 57. (Complete article is pp. 54-60.) Coincidentally or not, there was a character on Fred Allen's radio program named "Titus Moody"; both interviews spell his name like that of the radio character, instead of "Moede." Grey does not clear up his origins, but quotes him that he "was born in Chicago" (p. 54). Grey's interview also seems to be the source of a rumor that James Woods appeared in Ray Dennis Steckler's 1964 *The Incredibly Strange Creatures Who Stopped Living and Became Mixed-Up Zombies* (p. 55). According to Moede, "James Woods I got into that one, it was his first part, as an extra."

[842] Copner, p. 51.

[843] Weaver, *Science Fiction Confidential*, p. 45.

[844] Grey, *Nightmare of Ecstasy*, p. 141.

[845] Flynn, p. 6. Leonard Maltin recounted another version of this story in his introduction to the 1987 edition of Don Miller's *B Movies* (p. xiv): "You'd think someone was *waiting* for this!"

[846] Wendy L. Marshall, *William Beaudine: From Silents to Television* (Scarecrow Press, 2004), p. 152.

[847] Marshall, p. 43.

[848] "Citizen Wood: Making the Bride, Unmaking the Legend," *Mystery Science Theater 3000: Volume XIX* (Shout! Factory, 2010).

[849] Flynn, p. 4.

Appendix A: George Barrows Gallery

The following images reveal George Barrows' workshop and costume in detail, and show him working in a variety of contexts. Special thanks to Bob Burns and Tom Weaver.

Gorilla man

IT'S A LIVING

George Barrows makes a fine gorilla, but first he had to learn to keep his mouth shut

by A. L. SIMON

For two hundred and fifty dollars a day, George Barrows will turn into a gorilla. Owner of the most fantastic gorilla suit in the country, George naturally lives in Hollywood. Tarzan movies are his favorites; he appeared first as a gorilla in one of them over thirteen years ago and has been at his odd profession ever since.

Barrow's latest gorilla suit simulates a five-hundred-pound animal; every digit on both hands and feet moves, as well as eyes, nostrils and lips. It is so realistic no animals can work with him when he wears the costume. Even the tamest lion would try to tear it apart. Once, dangling in mid-air on a rope over a group of elephants, he started a stampede.

Before designing his costume, Barrows spent seven years visiting zoos, talking to curators, sketching apes and reading literature on the life of this mammoth animal. Then he drew plans, specifications and details and made his own outfit. The job required months to sew each tuft of hair in place. Costing more than three thousand dollars, the suit is molded of sponge rubber, with yak hair imported from Tibet. It also has an intricate system of levers to operate the fingers of the hands. The completed costume weighs seventy-five pounds. Temperature in the suit becomes so unbearable that George can remain in it only about twenty minutes at a time. At the end of some working days, he has lost as much as twelve pounds.

An assistant has to help him into the suit. He begins with the body of the suit, followed by the arms, legs and finally the head. At first, the gorilla's head wasn't vicious enough, so George rigged up a few rough-looking teeth and put a strap arrangement under his chin which enables the ape man to snarl at will. The sneer makes George very happy. For the movies, he mostly just looks ferocious or swings on a vine. Occasionally, he has to carry a lightly clad girl in his arms. Because of the flexible jaw arrangement on his gorilla, Barrows has an added attraction available to directors at no extra charge: he eats bananas.

Once, when times were a little tough in the gorilla business, George got himself a job with a local circus romping inside a cage in the wild animal section. Everything went well until he peered at the startled spectators one night and noticed a former girl friend. George forgot the cage and circus, waved casually and said, "Hi, Mabel!" That was the end of his job.

A George Barrows press clipping, source unknown.

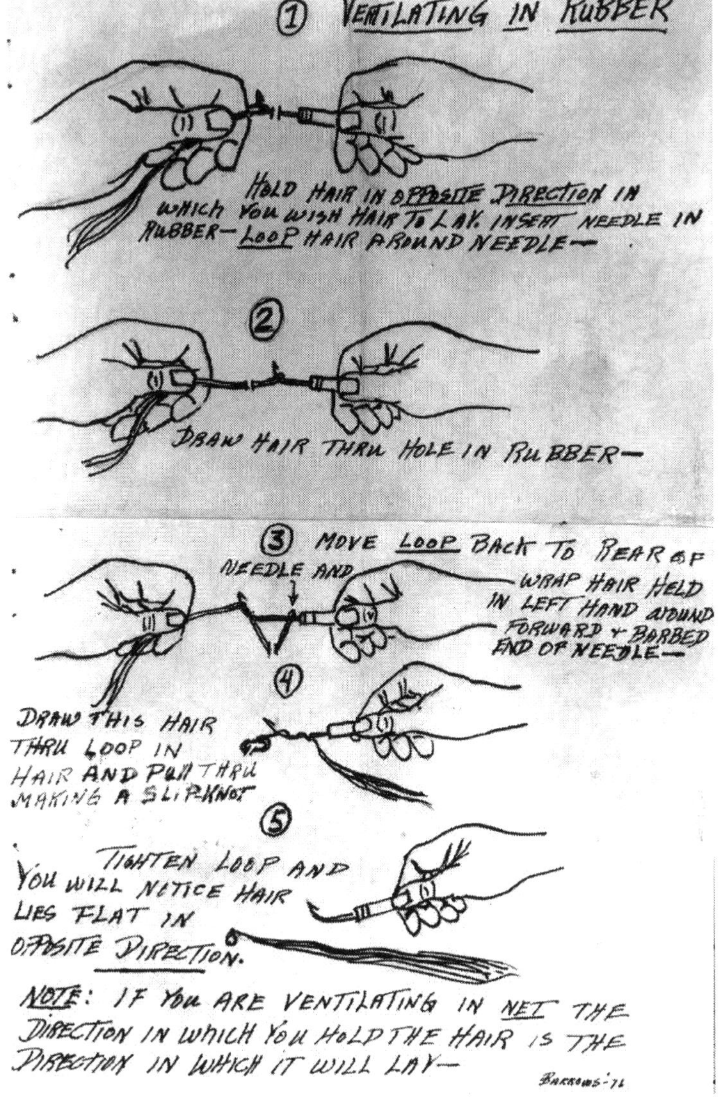
① VENTILATING IN RUBBER
HOLD HAIR IN OPPOSITE DIRECTION IN WHICH YOU WISH HAIR TO LAY. INSERT NEEDLE IN RUBBER—LOOP HAIR AROUND NEEDLE—
②
DRAW HAIR THRU HOLE IN RUBBER—
③ MOVE LOOP BACK TO REAR OF NEEDLE AND WRAP HAIR HELD IN LEFT HAND AROUND FORWARD + BARBED END OF NEEDLE—
④
DRAW THIS HAIR THRU LOOP IN HAIR AND PULL THRU MAKING A SLIP-KNOT
⑤
TIGHTEN LOOP AND YOU WILL NOTICE HAIR LIES FLAT IN OPPOSITE DIRECTION.
NOTE: IF YOU ARE VENTILATING IN NET THE DIRECTION IN WHICH YOU HOLD THE HAIR IS THE DIRECTION IN WHICH IT WILL LAY—
BARROWS-'76

HAND SAW

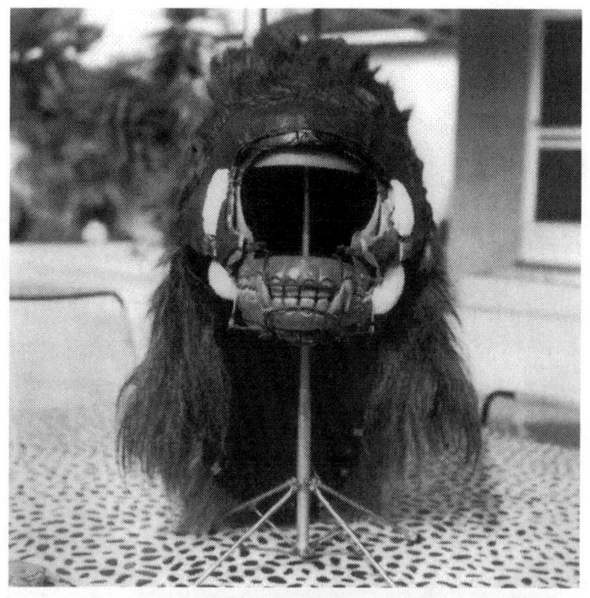

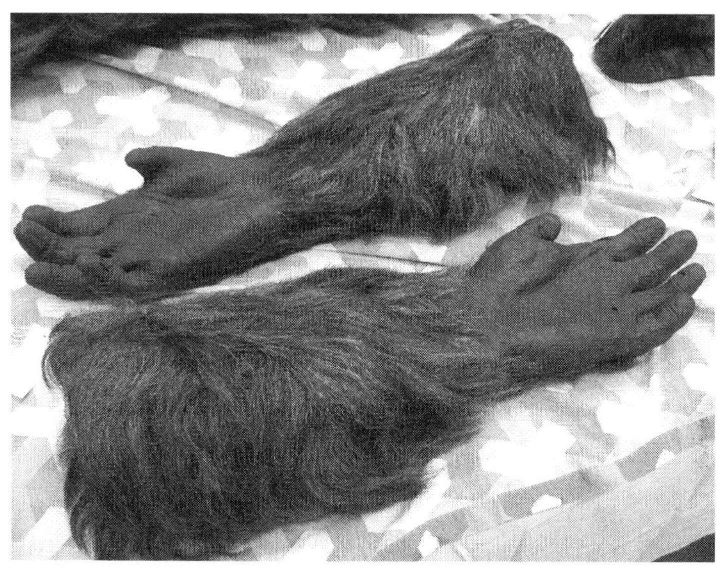

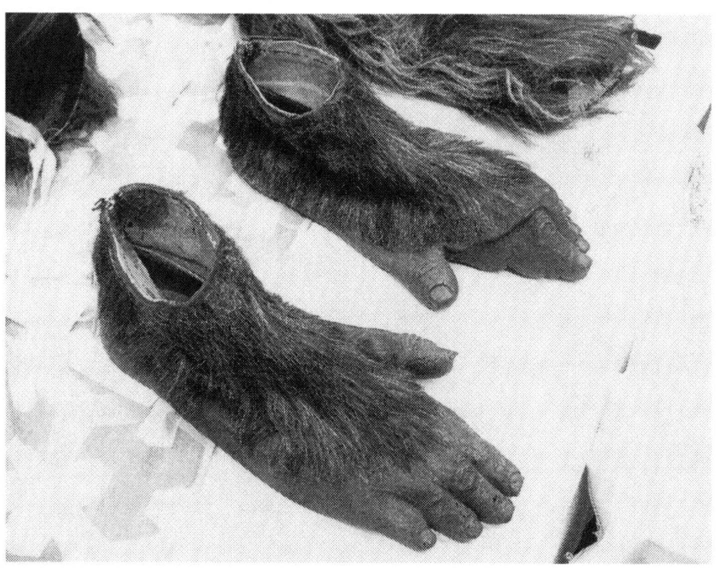

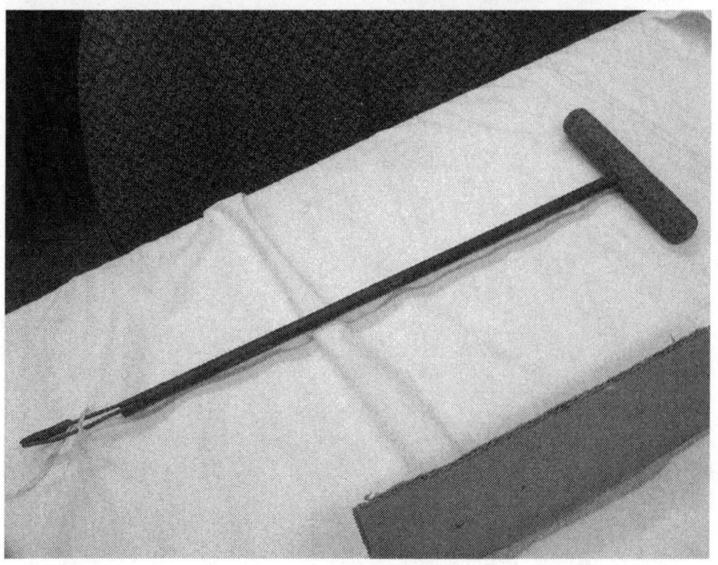

(*This page and next three pages*) ***Gorilla at Large***

P4-2

(*Above*) ***The Black Swan***

(*Below*) **An obscure shot with Andy Devine, possibly taken from the *Adventures of Wild Bill Hickok* series.**

(*Above*) ***The Beverly Hillbillies***

(*Below*) ***Black Zoo***

The Addams Family

(*Above*) ***The Lucy Show***

(*Below*) ***The Man from U.N.C.L.E.***

(*Above*) ***The Black Shield of Falworth***

(*Below*) ***Adventures of Don Juan***

Adventures of Don Juan

Appendix B: Robot Monster Script

Reproduced by permission of Wade Williams. Thanks to Tom Weaver for making the script available. Special thanks to Bill Littman for providing his copy of the script.

WADE WILLIAMS DIST.

L = Cam - Left
R = " Right
C = " Center

A = 25 - lens
B = 50 - "
C = 2 - "
D = 4 - "

L C R

THREE DIMENSION, INC. PRESENTS

"R O B O T M O N S T E R"

Screenplay by
Wyatt Ordung

Executive Producer
Al Zimbalist

Direction-Production
Phil Tucker

A THREE DIMENSION, INC. PRODUCTION

WADE WILLIAMS DIST.

"ROBOT MONSTER" 1.

FADE IN:

1 EXT. WOODS - DAY - MED. SHOT - SPACE HELMET APPEARING FROM BEHIND BUSHES

It is the traditional plexiglass kind with antennae on top of it. At first CAMERA sees only the top part. On SOUND TRACK we hear a persistent "Beeeep-booooop" sound.

The wearer scuttles behind bushes a moment, then appears in open. He is JOHNNY, a seven year old, completely outfitted in Spaceman's costume. He has a Spaceman's gun. He is making the "beep-boop" sounds orally.

Johnny sees something offscene, raises his gun and fires, imitating the "sssss" effect of a ray gun.

2 MED. CLOSE SHOT - CARLA

Johnny's younger sister. She is sitting on a rock holding a doll.

CARLA
(looking off
toward Johnny;
patiently)
Am I dead?

Johnny enters to her.

JOHNNY
You're disintegrated.

CARLA
Good. Can we play house now?
You promised.

JOHNNY
Not yet. These woods are
full of Spacemen. It's
either them or us. Come on.

He leads the way, 'beeping' and 'booping'. She follows reluctantly.

2

2

3 MED. SHOT - CAVE SECTION OF WOODS

CAMERA PANS JOHNNY AND CARLA to entrance of cave. They start to go by when Johnny hears a "chipping" sound from inside cave. He indicates for Carla to follow him. They sneak into cave.

4 INT. CAVE ENTRANCE - DAY

as Johnny and Carla enter. They look off curiously.

5 MED. SHOT - PROFESSOR AND ROY

The Professor is sitting on a stool examining a rock. Roy is chipping away at a picture on the wall. They do not see Johnny and Carla enter to them. Johnny raises his gun.

JOHNNY
Spacemen -- you must die!

PROFESSOR
(to Roy; vaguely)
Did you say something?

ROY
(indicating
Johnny)
He said we must die.

PROFESSOR
(to Johnny)
Well, if you insist. But wouldn't it be nicer if we could live at peace with each other?

JOHNNY
(sheathing gun)
Okay. I'll be from a friendly planet.

CARLA
Does that mean we can play house now?

JOHNNY
No. I'm friendly but I still have to find out what they're doing here.

(CONTINUED)

5 (CONTINUED)

PROFESSOR
We're archeologists, son: people who try to find out what Man was like way back before he could read or write, when the only way he could pass on what he knew was through pictures like this one here.

He points to picture. Kids look up.

6 CLOSE SHOT - PICTURE

SEEN clearly for first time. It is of an ape-like creature. The face is missing.

ROY'S VOICE
Did you kids know this was in here?

7 MED SHOT - GROUP

Kids shake their heads.

CARLA
My mother told us to stay away or we could get hurt.

JOHNNY
(indicating picture)
Is that what would hurt us?

PROFESSOR
If it was alive it could. But this picture was painted almost a million years ago.

ROY
Our job is to chip it carefully out and take it to a museum so people can study it.

JOHNNY
Gee. Are you scientists?

ROY
That's even better than being cowboys, huh?

(CONTINUED)

4.
4

7 (CONTINUED)

JOHNNY
You bet.

CARLA
(indicating
picture)
Was he a Spaceman Robot?

PROFESSOR
So far as we know, there
weren't Spacemen in those
days.

CARLA
(bored glance
at Johnny)
I wish I'd been born then.

JOHNNY
But what *was* he?

ROY
The Missing Link perhaps. If
we knew what his head looked
like we could judge better.

JOHNNY
(big shot)
He looks like some of the
people I saw last time I was
on Pluto.

Professor and Roy exchange amused glances.

PROFESSOR
What's your name, son?

JOHNNY'S MOTHER'S VOICE
(from outside
cave)
JOH - NNY!

They look toward sound of voice.

ROY
Sounds like you strayed a
little out of your orbit,
Johnny.

5.
5

8 EXT. WOODS - CAVE SECTION - MED. LONG SHOT - JOHNNY'S MOTHER AND HIS SISTER ALICE

Alice is a pretty, intelligent looking girl. She carries a box of Kleenex. Both look faintly annoyed.

ALICE
(calling)
Carla?

JOHNNY'S VOICE
(disgusted)
Here we are. In the cave.

They start toward cave.

9 MED. SHOT - FRONT OF CAVE

Johnny and Carla come out with Roy and Professor.

JOHNNY
(looking off)
It's my mother and sister.
(to Roy; scornfully)
I bet _you'd_ like her.

ROY
(eyeing Alice)
No doubt.

Mother and Alice enter to them.

MARTHA
(Johnny's Mother)
That wasn't fair, Johnny.

ALICE
You kids promised if we took you on this picnic you'd take a rest after lunch. And off you scoot.

CARLA
I didn't want to go. I wanted to play house.

JOHNNY
And I'm too old for naps. Besides these men are _real_ scientists. I want to watch awhile.

(CONTINUED)

9 (CONTINUED)

ALICE
(sarcastic)
I'm sure they'd love that.
(to Roy)
I hope he hasn't given you any trouble.

She wipes her nose with Kleenex.

ROY
Not at all.
(to Johnny)
But Johnny, at the camp I used to go to we had to take an hour's rest after lunch, right up until we were fourteen.

JOHNNY
You did? Well...Will you be here when I get back?

PROFESSOR
If we are, you're welcome to join us.
(to Martha)
Goodbye. Nice children you have.

MARTHA
Thank you.

Professor and Roy return into cave. Johnny looks after them.

ALICE
Come on, come on. Stop stalling.

10 CLOSER SHOT ON FAMILY GROUP

JOHNNY
If Dad was still alive I bet _he'd_ let me stay.

MOTHER
I don't think he would, John.

JOHNNY
Say, are we ever gonna have a new father around our house?

(CONTINUED)

10 (CONTINUED)

MOTHER
I don't know dear. Would you like that?

JOHNNY
If we do, I hope he's a big scientist, making rocket ships, things like that.

ALICE
(sniffing;
taking another
piece of Kleenex)
If he finds a cure for the common cold he'll be the biggest man of all.

JOHNNY
Really?

ALICE
Oh come on!

Reluctantly Johnny and Carla follow them.

WIPE TO:

11 MED. SHOT - JOHNNY AND CARLA TAKING REST

Picnic lunch on blanket in b.g. Carla is asleep. Johnny appears to be napping. But he opens one eye, sees himself unobserved, carefully gets up and sneaks away.

12 MED. SHOT - WOODS - NEW ANGLE

Johnny makes a dash for it, looking back. He doesn't see the gully ahead of him. He falls into it.

13 INT. CAVE

It is deserted now. We hear Johnny running toward it. He enters, looks disappointed men are gone. Then he studies picture. He grabs a piece of rock to climb closer. The rock comes loose. Another piece of rock hits him on the head. He falls.

8.

14 CLOSE SHOT - JOHNNY ON GROUND

On sound track we hear the Vibrator noise associated with loss of consciousness. Johnny lies still. CAMERA MOVES IN, BLURRING, AS NOISE INCREASES.

BRIEF FADE:

FADE IN:

15 EXT. WOODS - NIGHT - MED. SHOT - ENTRANCE TO CAVE

There is a light inside the cave. CAMERA STARTS TO MOVE IN.

LAP DISSOLVE TO:

16 INT. CAVE - CLOSE SHOT - JOHNNY

He is painting a picture on the wall. He is dressed now just in shorts. He works feverishly. His space-gun is on the floor.

17 CLOSE SHOT - PICTURE

Johnny is filling in the face -- and it is the face of a Spaceman -- that is to say, the heavy features of the ape-man are there, but covered by the plexiglass hood and the antennae.

18 CLOSE SHOT - JOHNNY

Suddenly he listens. Faintly we hear a "beep-boop" sound. It comes from the rear of the cave. Johnny backs toward entrance, fearful. Too late he remembers the space-gun, does not dare return for it. CAMERA PANS HIM TO ENTRANCE OF CAVE where he hides behind a rock and peers back in.

19 INT. CAVE

with space-gun in med. foreground. The SOUND GETS LOUDER.

THEN RO-MAN APPEARS. He is just like the drawing on the wall and we can see what parts of him Johnny has failed to paint in -- particularly an adding machine type gadget inside the plexiglass helmet that has wires connected into Ro-Man's ears.

(CONTINUED)

9.

19 (CONTINUED)

Ro-Man looks at the space-gun, then at the painting. His "calculator" begins to work and we hear the faint click and clunk of bolts falling into place. Then Ro-Man turns toward entrance to cave and raises his hands. From his long fingers come sparks accompanied by a droning, static sound.

20 CLOSE SHOT - JOHNNY AS HE RUNS AWAY.

21 EXT. FAMILY "CAMP" SITE - NIGHT - MED. LONG SHOT

We see the wire barricade, behind it the ruins of the house. CAMERA MOVES IN SLOWLY.

The Professor comes to the wire barricade, peers out, troubled. He hears the sound of Johnny's approaching footsteps. He tenses.

22 MED. SHOT - BARRICADE

3/19/52 Blue denim shorts tan T shirt & tennis shoes blue striped socks

Johnny comes running up to it.

JOHNNY
(breathless)
Pop!

The Professor reaches through wires and clamps his hand over Johnny's mouth. He pantomimes vigorously for him to come inside the barricade without speaking. Johnny nods, indicating he understands. As he climbs through wires, Professor calls back toward ruins.

PROFESSOR
It's all right, Martha. He's home.

JOHNNY
Pop -- what do you think --

But he is interrupted by his Mother's entrance, followed by Alice.

MARTHA
I've a good mind to give you a thrashing. Didn't we tell you? Didn't we? Never, never, <u>never</u> to go outside these wires without our permission?

(CONTINUED)

10.

22 (CONTINUED)

She starts to shake him.

JOHNNY
But Mom -- Pop --

PROFESSOR
(restraining
Martha gently)
Now Martha. Anger won't stop the boy from doing it again. He must be made to understand _why_.

JOHNNY
But will you listen to me? Will you?

PROFESSOR
No, Johnny, you listen to me first. After that you can tell us all about it.

Johnny tightens his lips in exasperation but he listens.

PROFESSOR
You know the terrible things that have happened since this "Ro-Man" landed on Earth. The only reason we are still alive is that his directional beams are bent around this house by these syntochron wires. He cannot hear us. He cannot see us. But one word spoken _outside_ this barrier could bring him down on us. _Do_ you understand that, Johnny?

JOHNNY
But I _saw_ him.

ALICE
Saw who?

JOHNNY
Ro-Man! He's in the cave at the end of the ravine.

MARTHA
(weakly)
He's found us out.

(CONTINUED)

11.

22 (CONTINUED)

ALICE
Not yet or we'd be dead by now.
(to Johnny)
Are you <u>sure</u>?

JOHNNY
I was in the cave painting his picture the way we saw him on the Viewscreen. --

ALICE
Why were you doing that, Johnny?

JOHNNY
So in case he <u>did</u> wipe out the human race there'd be some record of how it happened...

Alice and Professor exchange glances.

PROFESSOR
Go on.

JOHNNY
I heard him coming. Ducked out just in time. Then he moved in.

ALICE
Into the cave?

JOHNNY
Looked to me like he was making it his headquarters.

23 CLOSE SHOT - PROFESSOR

thinking hard.

PROFESSOR
But why here? So close? Hasn't he anything better to do?

24 MED. GROUP

JOHNNY
Maybe we could kill him, huh, Pop?

24 (CONTINUED)

PROFESSOR
No, son. The armies of the entire world tried that and failed. We threw everything we had at him. He's impervious.

ALICE
Unless we can find his weak spot.

Professor heads back toward the ruins. Others follow.

25 MED. SHOT - RUINS

We see now more clearly how the family is living: mostly in the open, a few rude leantos; dishes on a broken table; a few open cans in evidence. Carla sleeps on a pallet. Her mother covers her. Then the family comes and sits wearily at the table. Behind them is the Viewer Screen and associated gadgets.

JOHNNY
(licking lips)
Could I have just a <u>little</u> water, Mom?

Martha sighs, nods, pours him a scant half inch into a glass. Johnny sips it eagerly but carefully. The Professor pounds the table in frustration.

PROFESSOR
But why here?

ALICE
Perhaps we're the last people on earth, Dad. He senses our presence. He keeps calculating closer and closer.

PROFESSOR
I can't believe that. Surely there were other scientific minds capable of rigging a foil to prevent detection. If we can only hang on long enough to figure some way of communicating with each other...

(CONTINUED)

25 (CONTINUED)

ALICE
Do you think we still have a garrison on the space platform? Ro-Man hasn't destroyed that yet.

PROFESSOR
We can hope so. If someone could only get through to them --
(hopelessly)
Ah but why should they succeed where so many failed?

MARTHA
(patting his arm)
Don't _you_ talk like that, dear.

Suddenly the Viewer Screen starts to buzz. They jump up.

26 CLOSER SHOT - VIEWER SCREEN

They gather around it.

PROFESSOR
This may be it -- someone's gotten through!

After a brief flicker, the horrid face of Ro-Man appears on Viewer Screen. Behind him we see the wall of the cave and many scientific gadgets.

RO-MAN
Humans! Listen to me. I have calculated your tele-screen wave lengths, so if you have a set you must be watching....

27 REVERSE - THE FAMILY GROUP

Martha shudders. Alice watches in horror. The Professor puts his arm around Martha. Johnny watches wide-eyed.

(CONTINUED)

14.

27 (CONTINUED)

RO-MAN'S VOICE
Humans, there are only five of you left in the whole world. I do not know why the catatomic ray has not killed you too, nor why I cannot do more than estimate your general position...

28 INT. CAVE - MED. SHOT - RO-MAN BEFORE VIEWER SCREEN

RO-MAN
...But in time I will calculate this problem as I do all others. There is no escape from me. However, I have much work to do, preparing this planet for my people. Give me your terms of surrender. It is your last chance.

He presses the receiving button for the Viewscreen. Pin points of light appear on the screen.

29 MED. SHOT - FAMILY GROUP

All look to Professor for his reaction.

MARTHA
Perhaps we should talk to him. See if it isn't possible to arrange a truce - make peace.

PROFESSOR
(shaking head)
He'd be able to plot our position immediately.
(to screen)
No thank you, Ro-Man. If you want us, calculate us.

30 INT. CAVE - MED. SHOT - RO-MAN

He flicks off button in annoyance.

(CONTINUED)

30 (CONTINUED)

RO-MAN
Do you really think you can
outwit me? Watch, then,
while I show you something
of what I have done to the
rest of the world...

He starts fiddling with dials.

31 FULL SCREEN SHOT - VIEWSCREEN

We see Ro-Man's face fade out and a SERIES OF STOCK SHOTS FADE IN.

32 STOCK SHOTS

showing horrible destruction. OVER THIS RO-MAN'S VOICE NARRATES.

33 REACTION SHOT OF GROUP

34 CLOSE - VIEWSCREEN

As disaster shots end, Ro-Man's face comes onto screen again.

RO-MAN
Humans, you have seen my power.
Now I will tell you _my_ terms:
immediate surrender, and you
will die a painless death; resist me and you will suffer
infinite torture infinitely
prolonged.

35 REVERSE - FAMILY GROUP

PROFESSOR
(calmly)
Stand firm.

RO-MAN'S VOICE
(angrily)
All right. I have warned you.

We hear the Viewscreen disconnect. Family returns to table.

(CONTINUED)

16.

35 (CONTINUED)

PROFESSOR
Just the five of us...Incred-
ible.
(soberly)
And it means that Roy is gone
too.

JOHNNY
I'll bet Alice is happy --
the way they used to fight.

ALICE
Don't say that Johnny. Roy
was a great scientist.

PROFESSOR
I could never have developed
the serum without him.

ALICE
The trouble was he wouldn't
admit I was good in my own
field.

MARTHA
(patting her
arm)
Anyone who could fix that Viewscreen after what the Blast did
to it is better than good.

Suddenly Alice bursts out crying.

PROFESSOR
Easy, easy.

ALICE
(through her
tears)
I'm sorry. It seems silly,
after all the terrible things
that have happened, to go to
pieces over one miserable,
egotistical, impossible guy,
but...Oh Roy!

She leaves the table and throws herself on a pallet in
b.g. The others look at each other glumly.

WIPE TO:

17.

36 INT. WOODS - NIGHT

Roy comes sneaking along.

37 MED. SHOT - CAVE

Roy almost passes mouth of cave before he hears the BUZZ SOUND INSIDE. He shrinks against side of cave. The sound gets louder. Ro-Man comes out.

38 CLOSE UP - ROY

He reacts in horror.

39 CLOSE UP - RO-MAN

He senses something. The calculators click. Then his hand goes to his head. He shakes it, returns to cave.

40 MED. CLOSE - ROY

He watches Ro-Man go. Then his face breaks into a triumphant smile and he hurries on.

41 INT. BARRICADED AREA

The family are asleep. Suddenly the Professor rears up. We hear faintly the sound of scrambling footsteps. Alice also wakes up. Footsteps get closer. The Professor reaches under his pallet and takes out a gun. Alice crosses to him.

ALICE
If atom guns couldn't stop him --

PROFESSOR
It's not for him. It's for us.

42 MED. CLOSE SHOT - WIRE BARRICADE

Roy comes up to it, slips through.

ROY
(gayly)
Hey there -- anybody home?

V

18.

43 MED. SHOT - GROUP

All wake up. Alice and Professor rush to Roy as he comes forward.

AD LIBS
Roy!
He made it!
Roy's here!

CARLA
(sleepily)
What of it: He always hangs around.

She goes back to sleep. The others gather around Roy.

ROY
Of course I made it. Do you know who's in the cave at the end of the ravine?

ALL
Ro-Man.

Roy's face falls.

ROY
I was as close to him as I am to you.

JOHNNY
So was I.

ROY
But he didn't know I was there! Do you know why?

ALICE
Maybe you weren't worth noticing.

ROY
(throwing up hands)
Now I know I'm in the right house.

PROFESSOR
Yes. And just a few moments ago she was crying because you were dead.

(CONTINUED)

43 (CONTINUED)

ALICE
(lamely)
Well...

ROY
You didn't have to waste tears
on me, sweetie. I bear a
charmed life.

PROFESSOR
(nodding)
Ro-Man spoke to us on the Viewscreen. He claimed we were the
last five people on earth. Now
you manage to get past him too.
Why? Is he lying? <u>Are</u> there
any other people?

ROY
Two more. Jason and McCloud.

ALICE
At the lab? But why them?
That doesn't make sense.

ROY
Doesn't it? The Professor
here gives his entire life to
the development of an anti-
biotic serum that will cure all
disease -- even the common cold.
Thanks to his wise choice of
assistants, he achieves his
goal.

ALICE
"In spite of," not "thanks to."

ROY
(giving her
a mock bow)
So upon whom does he experiment
with his first injections?
(ticking them
off on his
finger)
Himself, his family, myself and
Jason and McCloud. Result:
the great anti-biotic is also
the immunizer to Ro-Man's death
ray.

(CONTINUED)

43 (CONTINUED)

PROFESSOR
So that's it. I thought it
was the barricade.

ROY
Alice's Folly? Well, let's
admit it does prevent Ro-Man
from finding and blowing us
up....

ALICE
Which is nothing...

ROY
But against the sweep of the
death ray, it is powerless.
The serum! That's the thing.

PROFESSOR
Couldn't you find any more at
the lab?

ROY
Plenty. But I didn't bring
it.

He sits at the table and leans back, satisfied.

ALICE
It's a stage wait. We're
supposed to ask, "Why?"

ROY
Ask.

ALICE
(in bored tone)
Why.

ROY
(suddenly
energized)
Because we managed to get together enough fuel to take a
rocket ship to the space platform. There's enough serum
aboard to immunize the entire
garrison there. We'll give
Ro-Man the biggest surprise of
his life!

(CONTINUED)

21.

43 (CONTINUED)

ALICE
Does the garrison know you're coming?

ROY
How could we tell them without letting Ro-Man know too?

ALICE
But they know what's going on down here. They'll figure it's Ro-Man and blast the ship right out of the sky.

MARTHA
She's right, Roy.

ROY
(troubled)
I don't know what else we could do. Jason and McCloud are taking off in two days. On foot it would take me longer than that to get back there.

ALICE
Big genius.

ROY
All right! What do you suggest?

ALICE
We'll have to get word to the space platform, that's all, and rewire the circuits on the Viewscreen so we can broadcast without Ro-Man picking it up.

PROFESSOR
In theory it's possible. But such a complicated job in two days?

ALICE
I can try at least. And if I had a decent assistant who could take orders instead of trying to be the boss...

(CONTINUED)

22.

43 (CONTINUED)

ROY
I'm bossy?

PROFESSOR
Children, please. The fate of civilization may be at stake.

ROY
(sobered)
Sorry, Prof.
(to Alice)
Okay, Boss. Where do I begin?

DISSOLVE TO:

44 CLOSE SHOT - ALICE AT WORK ON INNER WORKS OF VIEWSCREENER - DAY

It should look like a brain operation in progress. Highly specialized tools to hold highly specialized tools. Alice is chief surgeon; Roy her assistant. He has a two days' growth of beard; Alice looks pale and drawn. She is breathing heavily as she makes a minute, delicate adjustment. Suddenly she pulls her hands away. They are trembling visibly.

ALICE
(half hysterical)
I can't control my hands any more.

ROY
Let's rest a little.

ALICE
But we can't.

45 MED. SHOT - ROY AND ALICE

The Professor and Johnny join them.

PROFESSOR
Roy is right, Alice. It is time you got some sleep.

JOHNNY
Jiminy. Two days you been at it.

(CONTINUED)

45 (CONTINUED)

ALICE
Not that long! It can't be that long!

PROFESSOR
The rocket ship must have taken off at dawn. They are either there by now or...

He shrugs. Alice collapses dejectedly against Roy.

ALICE
Then I failed you. I'm sorry, Dad.

ROY
Failed! Do you realize that what you tried was impossible -- and yet you almost did it?

ALICE
But I didn't.

ROY
I'm so proud of you I could kiss you.

ALICE
(wearily)
Go ahead.

ROY
(suddenly feeling the weariness in himself)
I'm too tired to enjoy it.

ALICE
(dropping off to sleep)
Know just...how...you feel...

Suddenly the light and buzzer on the Viewscreen begin to operate. Roy and Alice snap awake.

PROFESSOR
Maybe they made it. This might be them.

They rush around to the Viewscreen.

46 CLOSE SHOT - VIEWSCREEN

The face of Ro-Man appears.

ROMAN
Humans...I thought I would tell you that I made a mistake. But my automatic calculator caught it. I have rechecked and found that there are six of you, not five.

47 REACTION - GROUP

Martha and Carla have joined them by now.

ALICE
Then he still doesn't know about Jason and McCloud!

48 CLOSE - VIEWER

RO-MAN
There were eight of you, of course. I found that out too. But the others were foolish enough to reveal their presence taking off in a rocket ship. The chances were 734.568 they would have been shot down by their own people, but Ro-Man does not take chances. I have destroyed them. And now, to prove to you once again my power, watch closely.

The scene changes to:

49 LONG SHOT - SPACE PLATFORM

50 REACTION SHOT

ROY
The space platform!

51 CLOSE SHOT - VIEWER

An object approaches it, explodes it. Then Ro-Man's face appears again.

RO-MAN
You see? There is no hope. If you contact me today I will still allow you the painless death.

FADE OUT:

FADE IN:

52 MED. SHOT - GROUP

Alice is half asleep standing up, her head on Roy's shoulder.

CARLA
(indicating screen)
Mommy, why doesn't he like people?

MARTHA
I don't know darling. Perhaps if we could talk to him...

Suddenly Alice crumbles. They pick her up and lay her on her pallet. Roy covers her tenderly. Martha takes the Professor aside.

53 TWO SHOT - MARTHA AND PROFESSOR

MARTHA
We can't go on much longer like this. The food is almost gone.

PROFESSOR
But what else can we do, Martha? Commit suicide? Give in to Ro-Man? Us, the last people on earth?

(CONTINUED)

53 (CONTINUED)

MARTHA
Talk to him, George. Make him see we won't harm him, that he can let us live. If Alice had finished the re-wiring of the Viewscreen you could have talked to the Platform without Ro-Man discovering our presence. Why couldn't you talk directly to him?

PROFESSOR
We could. Of course we could! And as soon as Alice has had her sleep, we will.

DISSOLVE TO:

54 INT. RO-MAN'S CAVE - DAY

He is puttering around with his logarhythm tables when the light and buzzer on his Viewscreen start up. Ro-Man chuckles and walks over to Viewer.

RO-MAN
So, Earthmen, you have decided to take the easy way after all.

55 CLOSE SHOT - VIEWER

The Professor's face is on it.

PROFESSOR
No, Ro-Man. We have fought you to a standstill and we can go on doing it as long as necessary.

56 CLOSE SHOT - RO-MAN

He starts calculating like mad. The tumblers roll, he writes rapidly.

(CONTINUED)

56 (CONTINUED)

PROFESSOR'S VOICE
If you are trying to calculate our position, you are wasting your time. We are not fools. ~~We only called you because we have solved the problem of high frequency dispersal. Given a little more time, we earth people would have known as much as your people -- and used our knowledge more wisely.~~

Ro-Man stops calculating.

RO-MAN
(angrily)
I'll get you yet! None shall escape me.

57 MED. SHOT - PROFESSOR

PROFESSOR
We humans do not intend to give up this earth of ours. What have you to fear from us, Ro-Man? Let me show you the six people you want to destroy...

The Professor's hands start turning a dial. CAMERA MOVES FROM HIM TO PICK UP MARTHA.

PROFESSOR
First my wife, Martha, my companion for twenty-three years. Is there anything to fear from such a woman?...

CAMERA MOVES TO PICK UP ALICE, CARLA AND JOHNNY.

PROFESSOR'S VOICE
Or my children, Alice, Carla and Johnny...

Alice looks dignified and poised. Carla gives a forced, hoping-to-please smile. But Johnny resolutely sticks out his tongue.

(CONTINUED)

57 (CONTINUED)

PROFESSOR'S VOICE
Is it in the ethical code of your people that children must be murdered?

58 CLOSE SHOT - RO-MAN

He looks at the screen more closely.

PROFESSOR'S VOICE
Or take my assistant, Roy, who has helped me with a serum that would have wiped out disease among my people...

RO-MAN
Let me see the girl again.

59 VIEWSCREEN

It comes back to Alice.

ALICE
We want peace, Ro-Man. But peace with honor.

RO-MAN'S VOICE
Come closer to the screen.

Alice moves closer.

60 CLOSE UP - ROMAN

RO-MAN
I will talk to the girl. She will be safe with me.

61 MED. SHOT - FAMILY GROUP BEFORE VIEWER

The Professor quickly readjusts viewer.

PROFESSOR
I am the head of this family unit, Ro-Man. You will have to talk with me.

(CONTINUED)

29.

61 (CONTINUED)

RO-MAN'S VOICE
That's not very smart, Human. The girl could accomplish more.

PROFESSOR
Name the place, Ro-Man, and I will be there, unarmed.

62 CLOSE SHOT - RO-MAN

RO-MAN
Let me see the girl.

63 MED. SHOT - FAMILY GROUP

Alice suddenly moves up beside her father.

ALICE
(determined)
Here I am, Ro-Man. Where shall we meet?

RO-MAN'S VOICE
Do you know the area of the two sewers?

PROFESSOR
I will not allow this.

RO-MAN
I will meet you there in an hour. But no tricks.

ALICE
I will be there.

PROFESSOR
You will not!

The screen fades out.

PROFESSOR
(to Alice)
Have you gone crazy?

ALICE
We've played every other card. Why not try this one?

(CONTINUED)

3●.

63 (CONTINUED)

MARTHA
But have you any idea of what might happen to you?

ALICE
If there's a chance that I can strike a better bargain than Father, I'm the one to go.

64 CLOSE SHOT - CARLA AND JOHNNY

CARLA
(to Johnny)
Is Alice gonna have a date with Ro-Man?

JOHNNY
How can you figure girls?

65 MED. SHOT - GROUP

PROFESSOR
Alice, this is madness. Roy, you speak to her.

ROY
I know I'm not in the family, Alice. But your Father is right.

ALICE
(sarcastic)
You mean there are some things that nice girls don't do?
(passionately)
Even if it means that Man's millions of years of struggle, up from the sea, the slime, the fight to breathe air, to stand erect, to think, to build, to conquer Nature -- even if all this is stopped cold by a doting father and a jealous suitor?

ROY
(calmly)
I just don't happen to believe that any human being should degrade himself in order to survive.

(CONTINUED)

31.

65 (CONTINUED)

ALICE
You'd rather have ust just go out of business? Is that it? Letter returned, no forwarding address. Can't you see you're being sentimental idiots who let your emotions run away with you?

PROFESSOR
(gently)
Perhaps that is the quality of being human, Alice -- the very thing that makes us different from Ro-Man, the thing we are trying to preserve.

ALICE
Very pretty talk. But I still intend to do something about it.

She starts off but Roy places himself in her way.

ALICE
Get out of my way.

ROY
You're not going.

ALICE
I said, "Get out of my way!"

She tries to push him aside. He grabs her and holds her. She struggles with him fiercely.

ROY
(grimly)
You're not going anywhere, kiddo. I'm holding on to you -- now and in the future.

ALICE
(weeping hysterically)
You fools, you fools!

But Roy holds on to her. And the Professor helps drag her over to her bed.

32.

66 CLOSE SHOT - JOHNNY

He watches the struggle thoughtfully. Then he backs toward the barricade, slips through and hurries away.

DISSOLVE TO:

67 EXT. DISASTER AREA - DAY - MED. CLOSE SHOT - TWO SEWERS

Hold on this shot until Johnny's legs come in.

68 WIDER ANGLE

Johnny stops and looks at the two sewers. CAMERA PANS as he looks around, taking in the layout. CAMERA goes to a flight of stairs that lead to the sky as the building is no longer there, then PANS back to that spot. Johnny walks up to the stairs and triggers it to let loose when he kicks the support from under it. He then sits down on a ledge.

69 SAME AREA BUT DIFFERENT PART - FULL LENGTH SHOT

Ro-Man comes around the corner of a destoyed building and moves toward CAMERA. CAMERA PANS WITH HIM as he misses CAMERA by a few feet and passes on. CAMERA PANS HIM TO steps. Johnny gets up slowly and faces him. Ro-Man stops.

RO-MAN
What are you doing here, boy?

JOHNNY
My sister isn't coming.

RO-MAN
So they sent you?

JOHNNY
I came by myself. I wanted to find out what you had against me.

RO-MAN
You are human. Your people were getting too smart. We could not wait until you were strong enough to attack us. We _had_ to attack you first.

(CONTINUED)

33.

69 (CONTINUED)

JOHNNY
I think you're just a big bully. Picking on people smaller than you are.

RO-MAN
Now I will kill you.

JOHNNY
(on qui vive)
You'd have to catch me first.

Ro-Man raises his hands. Electric sparks shoot from his finger tips. There is a weird humming sound. But Johnny stands his ground.

JOHNNY
You look like a pooped out pinwheel.

RO-MAN
So. The calcinator ray <u>really</u> cannot harm you. Your father must be a brilliant man.

JOHNNY
He's smart enough.

RO-MAN
Did I understand him to say that medicine is his special field?

JOHNNY
He's got a super serum that keeps people from ever getting sick.

RO-MAN
How do you know it works?

JOHNNY
Because he injected it into me and Carla and Alice and Roy -- everybody -- and we don't get sick even when we swallow capsules with real bad bugs in 'em.

(CONTINUED)

34.

69 (CONTINUED)

RO-MAN
And the two who took off on the rocket ship -- they also had this injection?

JOHNNY
Sure. They --

Then he realizes that he has been trapped. He claps his hand to his mouth.

RO-MAN
You have told me all I need to know, stupid boy. I will now calculate the spectrum dust in the calcinator to counter-attack this anti-biotic. But there is a much easier way of killing you.

He starts toward Johnny. Johnny prepares to trip trap at the top of the stairs. As Ro-Man gets to first step Johnny lets the trap fall and runs away. Ro-Man tries to sidestep the trap and as he does he trips on a bit of rubble and falls down as the trap misses him. He gets up burning with anger and climbs the steps. CAMERA sweeps the area but Johnny is nowhere to be seen.

70 CLOSE UP - RO-MAN

RO-MAN
(shaking fist)
I'll destroy you yet. I'll get you all.

71 FULL CLOSE - RO-MAN

He walks toward CAMERA.

FADE OUT:

FADE IN:

72 PROFESSOR'S VOICE
(calling)
Johnny! Johnny!

(CONTINUED)

35.

72 (CONTINUED)

The Professor's back moves away from CAMERA. He runs several steps, stops, looks around wildly. We see that we are inside the BARRICADE AREA.

CAMERA PANS PROFESSOR TO MARTHA.

PROFESSOR
Johnny's gone!

MARTHA
You don't think he'd --

PROFESSOR
That fool romantic kid would try anything. What a family I have.

CARLA
(hurt)
I didn't do anything.

PROFESSOR STORMS ACROSS AREA to where Alice sits, bound hand and foot. Roy is beside her, calmly reading a torn, partly burned book. Alice eyes her father with resentment. He kneels beside her and starts untying her bonds.

PROFESSOR
(quietly)
Johnny has left the barricade. He may have it in his head to meet Ro-Man. We have got to find him.

Roy quickly puts his book aside and helps untie Alice.

ROY
Sure Prof. Don't worry. Alice and I can find him.

ALICE
I'll go, of course. But don't either of you speak to me.

She hurries off. Roy follows her.

PROFESSOR
Be careful. Ro-Man will be stalking the woods too. If Johnny comes back, I'll set off a flare.

36.

73 MED. SHOT - JOHNNY IN WOODS

making his way home cautiously but rapidly.

74 MED. SHOT - ROY AND ALICE

searching. He pantomimes for her to take one direction. He goes in another.

75 MED. SHOT - JOHNNY

He stops as he hears noise of footsteps near him. He hides carefully. CAMERA PANS UP to Roy as he hurries by. After he passes, Johnny gets up and moves on again.

76 MED. SHOT - ALICE

She stops dead in her tracks, shrinks back against a tree.

On SOUND TRACK WE HEAR THE APPROACHING BUZZ-BUZZ OF Ro-Man.

Alice turns and runs. She comes smack into Roy. She pulls him behind a rock.

77 OVER-SHOULDER ALICE - MED. SHOT - RO-MAN

He goes through the woods, saying something to himself. As he passes the hideaways we hear it:

RO-MAN
(rolling it over his tongue with relish)
Al - ice...Al - ice...

78 CLOSE SHOT - ALICE AND ROY

She gives an involuntary shudder and hides her face on Roy's chest. He strokes her hair, but cannot resist grinning down at her. Alice looks up, catches the grin. Annoyed, she breaks away from him, hurries through woods.

37.

79 BARRICADE AREA

Johnny enters it, starts toward his father.

PROFESSOR
(relieved)
Johnny...Where did you go?

Suddenly Johnny rushes to his mother, buries his head in her lap and starts to cry.

MARTHA
There, there, darling. It's all right now. Tell us about it.

JOHNNY
(sobbing)
No it isn't Mom. I gave it all away. I didn't mean to, but I did.

PROFESSOR
Did what, son?

JOHNNY
I wanted to talk to Ro-Man. But he got out of me how we were protected from the death ray and, and now he's gonna do something about it.

The Professor looks serious, but he pats Johnny's shoulder.

PROFESSOR
That's all right, boy. You did your best. And Ro-Man won't find it so easy to counteract the serum. We still have a little time left.

MARTHA
I almost wish it were over.

CARLA
Well, when it is, can I go over to Janee's house to borrow her dolls?

PROFESSOR
(absently)
Yes, darling, of course.

He gets a flare gun and fires it.

38.

80 INT. WOODS - EDGE OF CLIFF

Alice and Roy are searching. There is a whistling sound overhead followed by a series of sharp pops. They look up, look at each other and sigh in relief,

81 EXT. CAVE - CLOSE SHOT - RO-MAN

He too is looking up. The calculator noise works briefly. Then Ro-Man shakes his head slightly and enters the cave.

82 TWO SHOT - ALICE AND ROY

She nods her head to indicate that they should head back. As she starts off he takes her hand. He indicates he would like to stay here awhile. For a moment she resists, then she allows herself to be drawn down beside him in the ground.

Roy opens his mouth to speak. Alice puts her fingers to her lips quickly; Roy remembers. He casts about for a way to get across what he wants to say.

He picks a pretty flower and pantomimes that it's really not so much. He throws it away. Then he points overhead and makes the outline of a full moon. He shrugs that he can take it or leave it. But -- and he points at Alice -- then he kisses his fingertips to indicate the ultimate in perfection.

Alice smiles. She pantomimes back. First she points to Roy's head, then indicates it's not such of a muchness. Next she points to his hands, and indicates they are not any good at all, at all. But lastly she points to his heart. She holds her hands wide apart to show how big it is, then she warms them at his breast to show how warm it is. Finally she circles thumb and forefinger in approval.

Roy puts his palm over his heart, then holds it out to her, indicating that it is hers.

Alice takes Roy's hand tenderly and holds it to her cheek. Suddenly Roy tightens his grip on her hand and pulls her toward him. They embrace fiercely, their lips meet in torrid passion. Then they fall forward onto the ground, still locked in each other's embrace.

FADE OUT:

39.

FADE IN:

83 EXT. BARRICADE AREA

Alice and Roy come slowly and dreamily into the camp site. Her head is on his shoulder. They approach the family group.

PROFESSOR
What kept you two? We've been worried.

MARTHA
(smiling softly)
Now really, Father. Isn't it obvious?

JOHNNY
Not to me.

CARLA
Have you been playing house?

ROY
(awkwardly)
Prof...Sir...This might not make much sense to you, but Alice and I would like to get married, and we were wondering if you would feel right about performing the ceremony.

PROFESSOR
Do you want me to?

ALICE
Oh yes.

PROFESSOR
(to Roy; kidding)
You're quite sure there's no one else, son?

ROY
I'll be the most faithful husband this world has ever known.

PROFESSOR
(clapping Roy on shoulder)
In that case, let's get to it.
(continued)

(CONTINUED)

83 (CONTINUED)

PROFESSOR (cont'd)
(in high spirits)
And I want you to know this is the biggest social event of the year. The whole darn community is going to turn out for my daughter's wedding, so I want it done right. Martha, scurry up a veil and a handkerchief to cry into. Carla, you're the flower girl. John, you be best man. Hop to it now.

Each one dashes about his business. Carla searches the compound for flowers. Johnny tries to make Roy look as presentable as possible. Martha digs up an old piece of cheesecloth and drapes it over the back of Alice's hair.

PROFESSOR
Everybody set?

CARLA
(agonized)
I can't find any flowers but these!

ALICE
That's all right dear. We'll pretend you have a basket of rose petals.

PROFESSOR
All right. Places.

He indicates to Roy and John to stand at his left hand. Martha takes her position to the right. Alice backs up a bit to make an entrance down the "aisle". She places Carla in front of her.

PROFESSOR
Good.

He starts to Dum De Dum the wedding march, beating the stately rhythm with his palms. Carla starts down the aisle, seriously throwing her pretend rose petals. Alice takes dignified half steps until she is beside Roy.

(CONTINUED)

83 (CONTINUED)

The Professor indicates for them to face him. He looks at them for a long moment, then speaks in a quiet, mellow voice.

PROFESSOR
(looking upward)
Dear Lord. You know that I'm not trained for this job. I guess you know I haven't even been too regular in my attendance at church. But I have tried to live by Your Laws: the Commandments, the Beatitudes, the Golden Rule. And I'd like you to look down now and give Your blessing to Alice and Roy who are about to enter into holy matrimony. Even in this darkest hour, Lord, we keep the Faith. In Your Grand Design it may be that there is no room for man's triumph over this particular evil that has beset us, but if, by chance, victory will be ours, give to Roy and Alice a long life, and a fertile one, that Men might sing Your praises, and do Your Work. But no matter how it ends, Lord, watch over them this night. Watch over us all. Amen.
(looking down at the couple; simply)
I pronounce you man and wife. Have you got a ring, Roy?

ROY
(flustered)
I - I didn't think of it.

JOHNNY
Oh brother.
(to Alice)
Are you gonna have to pick up after <u>him</u>.

Martha quickly slips her wedding ring off, hands it to Roy.

(CONTINUED)

42.

83 (CONTINUED)

MARTHA
(to Alice)
I wanted you to have it some day anyhow, dear.

Alice smiles warmly. Roy slips the ring on her finger.

ROY
With this ring I thee wed.

PROFESSOR
All it takes to seal it is a kiss.

Roy and Alice kiss tenderly. Then the others crowd around and ad lib congratulations.

JOHNNY
Where you going on your honey-moon -- Niagara Falls?

ROY
To tell the truth, ~~we thought we'd sneak~~ I Don't off to the gully. Ro-Man never comes around there.

PROFESSOR
[illegible]-- be careful. And back here first thing tomorrow. In case you've forgotten, there's a war on and now more than ever I don't intend we should be beaten.

ROY
Thanks for everything, Dad. Most of all for having raised Alice. You too, Mom.

He kisses Martha's cheek. Then he and Alice start to gather a few blankets and a pallet.

84 CLOSE TWO SHOT - CARLA AND JOHNNY

CARLA
She ought to have <u>some</u> flowers. It isn't right.

(CONTINUED)

43.

84 (CONTINUED)

JOHNNY
(carelessly)
So hop down to the meadow
and pick her some.

He leaves her. Carla considers this, then hurries off. CAMERA PANS TO ALICE AND ROY as they leave the barricade, amid ad lib farewells.

DISSOLVE TO:

85 EXT. WOODED AREA - DAY - TWO SHOT - ROY AND ALICE

They are walking away from the CAMERA up a small foot-hill.

CARLA
(behind Camera)
Roy...Alice...wait for me.

They turn to look behind them and see...

86 MED. LONG SHOT - CARLA - DOLLY

She runs toward the CAMERA and CAMERA PULLS BACK SLIGHTLY to let her meet with Roy and Alice directly in front of CAMERA. She jumps into Alice's arms and kisses her generously.

87 MED. CLOSE - ALICE

ALICE
Carla...What are you doing
here?

CARLA
I didn't get you any present.

Carla hands the flowers she has to Alice.

ALICE
Oh...You little rascal.

88 TWO SHOT - ALICE AND CARLA

ALICE
Thank you very much. You
run right on home now.

89 THREE SHOT - ALICE, CARLA AND ROY

ROY
Quick now, Carla.

90 FULL ANGLE - GROUP

CARLA
Aw...awright.

Carla turns away, waves goodbye and starts down the hill. Roy and Alice watch her.

91 TWO SHOT - ROY AND ALICE

ALICE
Do you think she'll be safe
or had we better go with her?

ROY
Ro-Man has never come around
this part yet.

They continue on their way.

92 EXT. SUNNY PATCH OF GRASS - DAY - MED. FULL ANGLE

Carla is going from spot to spot picking and smelling flowers. On SOUND TRACK we hear the approaching Buzz-Buzz of Ro-Man. Carla is too preoccupied humming a little song to notice.

93 MED. LONG SHOT - RO-MAN

His antennae move. He turns slightly and stares.

94 MED. CLOSE - CARLA

still picking flowers.

95 MED. CLOSE - RO-MAN

He starts toward her. He keeps coming until they are both in shot. Then Carla sees him. Her eyes widen.

CARLA
My daddy won't let you hurt
me. He said so.

(CONTINUED)

95 (CONTINUED)

RO-MAN
What are you doing here alone? Did they send out here to trick me?

CARLA
I picked some flowers for Alice and Roy. They just got married.

RO-MAN
(angry)
Married?

CARLA
I have to get back now.

RO-MAN
Wait. Give me those flowers.

CARLA
(hesitant)
If you want.

She holds them out.

96 MED. CLOSE - FLOWERS

All we can see is the hands of Carla handing the bouquet toward Ro-Man. Then we see Ro-Man's hands come out toward the flowers. At first it appears as though he is going to take them. Then his hands go on past and we hear Carla scream. Then Ro-Man pushes in until the CLOSE-UP is on him. (CAMERA MUST NOT MOVE DURING THIS SHOT.)

DISSOLVE TO:

97 CLIFF AREA - NIGHT

By moonlight, CAMERA PANS OFF SOME TREES to pick up Roy and Alice kissing.

ALICE
(as they break)
At this rate we'll never get there.

Roy pantomimes that she shouldn't be talking. Alice re-acts contritely. She takes his hand to lead him on. But he pulls her back. He pantomimes that he wants one more kiss. She comes to him. As they embrace...

46.

98 MED. CLOSE SHOT - RO-MAN

He parts some bushes and watches balefully. Then he starts to move forward.

99 CLOSE SHOT - ROY AND ALICE STILL KISSING

Slowly Ro-Man's hands come into scene. He grabs Alice. She screams.

100 MED. SHOT - GROUP

Ro-Man tries to pick Alice up. Too late Roy tries to slug him. His punch doesn't phase Ro-Man one whit. With a free hand Ro-Man shoves Roy in the face. Roy flies out of scene.

101 CLOSE SHOT - GROUND

Roy lands into scene with a thud. For a moment he is stunned. Then he shakes his head. He sees a boulder beside him. He picks it up. He rushes out of scene.

102 MED. CLOSE SHOT - RO-MAN AND ALICE

Ro-Man has Alice in his arms now. He is starting back down the trail. Roy comes into scene, lifts the boulder high and crashes it over Ro-Man's head. Ro-Man turns slowly around. He acts as if he hadn't even felt the blow. As Roy watches, stunned, Ro-Man takes him by the arm and drags him back toward the edge of the precipice. Roy struggles, but he is weak as a baby in the hands of the Monster.

103 MED. SHOT - EDGE OF CLIFF

Ro-Man, carrying the struggling Alice over his shoulder, drags Roy to the edge of the precipice and drops him over.

104 CLOSE SHOT - EDGE OF PRECIPICE

Roy manages to grab hold with his fingers and hang on.

105 CLOSE SHOT - RO-MAN - ALICE OVER HIS SHOULDER

He looks down at Roy.

47.

106 CLOSE SHOT - ROY HANGING ON FOR DEAR LIFE

Ro-Man's HEAVY foot comes into scene and crushes Roy's fingers. He loses his grip and falls. His agonized cry gets fainter as he falls.

107 CLOSE SHOT - RO-MAN AND ALICE

Ro-Man listens until the cry is broken by a heavy thud. Then he shifts Alice so he can hold her in both arms.

RO-MAN
Now you are mine.

108 CLOSE - ALICE

She stops struggling. Her eyes narrow.

ALICE
How is it you are so strong, Ro-Man? It seems impossible.

RO-MAN
We have atomic energizers that instantaneously repair any damaged part.

ALICE
Small enough to carry with you?

RO-MAN
No. At the cave. Come.

They start off.

109 MED. SHOT - GRASSY PLOT - NIGHT

Martha and Professor have found the limp body of Carla. Martha kneels beside it, weeping bitter tears.

PROFESSOR
Ssssh, Mother. He'll hear us.

MARTHA
(wailing)
I don't care. I don't care.

(CONTINUED)

109 (CONTINUED)

PROFESSOR
You _must_ care. We must not give up.

The Buzz-Buzz of Ro-Man is heard. The Professor quickly gathers Carla in his arms and hurries away. CAMERA PANS TO PICK UP RO-MAN as he hurries toward CAMERA, carrying Alice.

DISSOLVE TO:

110 EXT. BARRICADED CAMP SITE - NIGHT

The Professor, Martha and Johnny have just finished burying Carla.

JOHNNY
(choked)
I wish now I'd played house with her more often when she wanted to.

PROFESSOR
No regrets, Johnny. We enjoyed her while she was with us. Now - somehow - we must find a way to ~~get revenge.~~ TO LIVE

There is a sound of something dragging through the bushes. They freeze. It keeps coming closer. The Professor rushes for his ray gun. He holds it trained against Johnny's head, ready to fire if it should be the Ro-Man.

111 CLOSE SHOT - BARRICADE

Roy staggers into scene, bloodied and but barely conscious. He collapses just outside the barricade. The others rush into scene and pull him through.

PROFESSOR
Roy! Where's Alice?

ROY
(gasping)
Ro-Man's - cave -

He faints. The others look gravely at each other. Martha shudders.

(CONTINUED)

111 (CONTINUED)

PROFESSOR
And there's nothing we can do. Nothing!

JOHNNY
If one of us could lure him out for a moment, the other could maybe rush in and grab her.

PROFESSOR
Easier said than done.

JOHNNY
He'd come if he could be sure of killing us.

PROFESSOR
(intrigued)
Go ahead, Johnny....

JOHNNY
We call him on the Viewerscreen. Tell him we don't want to fight any more, he can get us in the ravine if he promises us that easy death. Then, if he hears me out there, crying and carrying on, he'll come after me. You slip in and grab Alice.

PROFESSOR
(reluctantly)
It might work.

MARTHA
It would work. But with me, not Johnny.

112 CLOSE UP - JOHNNY

JOHNNY
No, Mom. We're gonna win this fight. And when we do, Alice and Roy's children will start coming along and somebody will have to teach them.

(CONTINUED)

112 (CONTINUED)

MARTHA
Alice is smarter than I am dear.

JOHNNY
Maybe about some things. But can she plant rose bushes like you? Or make a feller feel better when he's feeling bad? Gosh there's a lot more to knowing than blueprints and formulas.

113 TWO SHOT - JOHNNY AND MARTHA

Martha takes him to her bosom and cries over him.

MARTHA
Johnny, Johnny...

JOHNNY
It's all right Mom. I'm only a sort of a caterpillar still. It don't matter so much if I get stepped on.

114 MED. CLOSE - PROFESSOR

He makes his decision.

PROFESSOR
The boy is right, Martha. There's no time to lose.

He rises with determination.

115 INT. CAVE - MED. SHOT - RO-MAN AND ALICE

She is about as undressed now as the law allows. She is backing away from Ro-Man who pursues her, breathing heavily with passion.

ALICE
(desperately)
But Ro-Man, you must try to understand us women. Before I can really love you, I must know all about you. And you haven't told me yet where the energizer is kept.

(CONTINUED)

51.

115 (CONTINUED)

RO-MAN
Tomorrow -- maybe. Now --

116 INT. CAVE

Ro-Man enters it, carrying Alice. He sets her down, she starts to escape. In the struggle her clothing is torn. At the last moment, as he has her cornered the Viewer-screen lights up and buzzes. Ro-Man pauses a moment, then lumbers over to it, holding Alice.

RO-MAN
(as he snaps switch)
What do you want?

117 CLOSE - VIEWER

The faces of Professor, Martha and Johnny appear.

PROFESSOR
Ro-Man! We can't stand this any longer. You promised us a painless death if we gave ourselves up. Come and get us.

118 CLOSE SHOT - RO-MAN

RO-MAN
(impatient)
All right. All right. To-morrow...

119 VIEWSCREEN

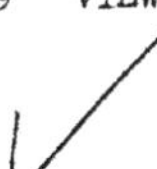

PROFESSOR
Now! Hurry. We will meet you halfway -- in the ravine.

120 CLOSE - RO-MAN

He looks puzzled a moment. Then:

(CONTINUED)

52.

120 (CONTINUED)

RO-MAN
(yelling into
Viewscreen)
All right. In the ravine.
But hurry.

He snaps off switch, takes Alice over to the wall and chains her there. Then he exits. He tosses keys on a table.

121 MED. SHOT - PROFESSOR AND JOHNNY AND MARTHA

The first two hurry through the barricade. Martha watches them go, her face lined with grief.

122 MED. SHOT - RO-MAN HURRYING UP RAVINE

123 INT. CAVE

as Alice struggles to free herself - without success.

124 MED. SHOT - RO-MAN

RO-MAN
Humans! Where are you?

125 MED. SHOT - JOHNNY COMING TO OPEN SPOT

He stops.

JOHNNY
(calling)
Here we are. ~~Hold my hand,
Mom, Hold my hand, Pop.~~
Here we are!

126 PAN SHOT - RO-MAN

He hurries toward voice. CAMERA HOLDS ON BUSH. RO-MAN EXITS FROM SCENE, PROFESSOR COMES FROM BEHIND BUSH, HURRIES TOWARD CAVE.

127 CLOSE SHOT - JOHNNY

He peers into the darkness. Then his eyes widen.

53.

128 REVERSE - RO-MAN COMING TOWARD HIM

129 INT. CAVE

Professor rushes in.

ALICE
The keys - on the table.

Professor grabs them, frees her.

PROFESSOR
Run.

ALICE
No. Help me.

She starts wrecking the joint. Professor joins in.

130 RO-MAN COMING TOWARD JOHNNY

He is quite close now. He raises his arm to strike his blow.

131 CLOSE - JOHNNY

He shuts his eyes and lowers his head ready for the kill.

132 INT. CAVE

Professor and Alice are tugging at a heavy, black metal object, wired to the sides of a cabinet. This is the energizer. Suddenly it comes loose. Both go out of scene. Tongues of flame lick toward the CAMERA.

133 MED. SHOT - JOHNNY AND RO-MAN

Johnny's back is to CAMERA. Ro-Man reaches him, is about to strike when the skyline behind him is lit up like summer heat lightning. We hear the sound of explosions. For a long moment Ro-Man freezes in his upraised arm position. Suddenly he topples forward on Johnny.

134 CLOSE SHOT - JOHNNY

He struggles to get out from under.

(CONTINUED)

54.

134 (CONTINUED)

ROY'S VOICE
Take it easy, kid. You're all right.

CAMERA RETREATS TO REVEAL JOHNNY IN INTERIOR OF CAVE WHERE HE FELL AND KNOCKED HIMSELF COLD. Roy holds him firmly while the Professor gives him a quick going over for possible broken bones.

ROY
We want to be sure you're going to get up with everything you fell down with.

PROFESSOR
He's okay.
(calling)
Hallo! We found him. In the cave.

Feet can be heard crashing through the underbrush.

ROY
You gave your mother quite a scare, son. It's almost night time and no Johnny.

Johnny looks at him hard.

JOHNNY
You're alive?

Then as Martha, Alice and Carla hurry up to them he stares at Carla.

JOHNNY
Her too? Boy, was that a dream! Or was it?

He looks toward the picture.

135 CLOSE SHOT - PAINTING - RO-MAN WITHOUT THE FACE

136 REVERSE - GROUP

JOHNNY
That's him, all right: the worst thing that ever happened to the world. But we licked him anyway. And we'd lick him if he came again.

(CONTINUED)

136 (CONTINUED)

ALICE
(to Roy)
Don't think he's like that
all the time -- because he
is.

MARTHA
(to Professor)
I really must try to repay
you for all the trouble
you've gone to. We live so
near here, won't you and
your assistant join us for
dinner?

ALICE
(to Roy)
Do.

ROY
Done.

JOHNNY
Yessir. We were the greatest
gang of people you ever saw.
(to Carla)
Even you.

CARLA
Will you play house with me
when we get home?

Johnny almost says yes.

JOHNNY
No. I got to keep an eye out
for Ro-Man.

They start to leave the cave.

ALICE
Really, Johnny, you overdo
that Spaceman act. There
simply aren't any such things.

They exit.

CAMERA PANS TO PICTURE ON WALL. ON SOUND TRACK WE HEAR
BUZZ-BUZZ SOUND.

(CONTINUED)

56.

136 (CONTINUED)

CAMERA PANS TO REAR OF CAVE. After a couple of seconds Ro-Man appears, rears into CAMERA AND PASSES IT BY.

HE IS FOLLOWED BY ANOTHER RO-MAN...AND ANOTHER...AND ANOTHER AS WE:

FADE OUT:

T H E E N D

3rd Dimension Prod.

Prod. ROBOT MONSTER

SHOOTING SCHEDULE
Shooting at 8 A.M.

EXECUTIVE PRODUCER - AL ZIMBALIST
PRODUCER-DIRECTOR - PHIL TUCKER

1st and 2nd DAY
Thurs.3/19-Fri.3/20.

Location at Chavez Ravine -- Effie and Bishop Road
Leave from parking lot Formosa Grill - Santa Monica and Formosa - 7:00 A.M.

- -

Ext. Family Camp Site — Night — 3 Pages
Sc. #21-22-23-24
Professor-Johnny-Martha-Alice (Tries to tell of Ro-Man)

Int. Barricaded Area — Night — 4-1/2
Sc. #41-42-43
Professor-Alice-Roy-Carla-Martha-Johnny (Roy arrives)

Int. Barricaded Area 1 line — Day — 3-3/4
Sc. #44-~~45~~-~~46~~-47-48-50-51A-52-53
Alice-Roy-Professor-Johnny-Ro-Man-Martha-Carla (Ro-Man appears on screen)

Int. Barricaded Area 1 line — Day — 4
Sc. #55-57-59-61-63-64-66
Professor-Martha-Alice-Carla-Johnny-Roy (Talk to Ro-Man over Screen)

Int. Barricaded Area none — Day — 1
Sc. #72
Professor-Martha-Carla-Roy-Alice (They miss Johnny)

Int. Barricaded Area — Day — 1
Sc. #79
Professor-Johnny-Martha-Carla (John tells of Ro-Man)

Ext. Barricaded Area — Day — 4
Sc. #83-84
Professor-Martha-Alice-Roy-Carla-Johnny (Marriage)

Ext. Barricaded Camp Site — Night — 2-1/2
Sc. #110-111-112-113-114 (Bury Carla)
Professor-Johnny-Martha-Roy (Roy tells of Fight)

Int. Barricaded Area (View Screen) — Day — 1/4
Sc. #117-119-121
Professor-Martha-Johnny (Talk to Ro-Man)

Ext. Patch of Grass — Day — 1-3/4
Sc. #92-93-94-95-96-109 (Ro-Man kills Carla)
Carla-Ro-Man-Professor-Martha (They find Carla)

1st & 2nd Days Continued 2.

Location / Scenes / Cast	Time / Notes	Pages
Ext. Cliff Area Sc. #97 thru 108 Alice-Roy-Ro-Man	Night (Ro-Man and Roy fight)	2
Ext. Wooded Area Sc. #85 thru 91 Roy-Alice-Carla	Day (Carla looks for flowers)	
Int. Woods Sc. #73-74-75-76-77-78-80-82 Johnny-Roy-Alice-Ro-Man	Day (Meet Ro-Man. Make Schmoo)	1-7/8
Int. Ruins and View Screen Sc. #25-26-27-29-31-32-33-34-35 Carla-Johnny-Martha-Professor-Alice	Night (Ro-Man appears on screen)	4
Ext. Disaster Area Sc. #67-68-69-70-71 Johnny-Ro-Man	Day (Johnny meets Ro-Man)	1-7/8

3rd Day Shooting Schedule - Saturday March 21st
Shooting at 8:00 A.M.

Location Bronson Canyon
Leave Parking Lot Formosa Grill - 7:00 A.M.

- -

Scene	Time	Pages
Ext. Woods Sc. #1-2 Carla-Johnny	Day (Opening Sequence)	1 Page
Ext. Woods and Cave Sc. #15 Camera Move Only	Night	1/8
Ext. Cave Sc. #81 Ro-Man	Day (Ro-Man enters cave)	1/8
Ext. Woods and Cave Sc. #36-37-38-39-40 Roy-Ro-Man	Night (Roy meets Ro-Man)	1/2
Ext. Woods and Cave Sc. #8-9-10-11-12 Alice-Johnny's Voice-Roy-Martha-Carla	Day (Johnny sneaks to cave)	2-3/4
Int. and Ext. Cave Entrance Sc. #3-4-5-6-7 Johnny-Carla-Professor-Roy-Martha O.S.	Day (See picture on wall)	3
Int. Cave Sc. #13-14-134A-135-136 Johnny-Martha-Alice-Professor-Roy-Carla	Day (Comes out of dream) (Johnny falls)	2-1/2
Int. Cave Sc. #16-17-18-19-20 Johnny in Shorts Ro-Man	Night (Johnny runs out of cave)	1
Int. Cave Sc. #28-30 Ro-Man	Night (Ro-Man talks to Family)	1/2
Int. Cave Sc. #115-116-118-120-123-129-132 Ro-Man-Alice-Professor	Night (Professor frees Alice) (Ro-Man enters with Alice)	1-1/2
Int. Ro-Man's Cave Sc. #54-56-58-60-62 Ro-Man	Day (Talks to Family)	3/4
Ext. Ravine Sc. #122-124-125-126-127-128-130-131-133-134 Ro-Man-Johnny-Professor-Roy	Night (Johnny fights Ro-Man)	1

Space Platform - Miniature
Sc. #49-51

WADE WILLIAMS DIST.

INDEX

ABOUT THE AUTHOR

Anders Runestad lives in the Midwest with his wife and family. *I Cannot, Yet I Must* is his first book, but more are on the way and are rumored to be thinner than the present one. He maintains the blog www.runestadwrites.com.

WADE WILLIAMS DIST.

Made in the USA
Middletown, DE
11 August 2024

58925886R00387